AF361633

Nature & Nature's God

Nature & Nature's God

A Philosophical and Scientific Defense of Aquinas's
Unmoved Mover Argument

Daniel Shields

The Catholic University of America Press

WASHINGTON, D.C.

Nihil obstat:
Rev. Msgr. James D. Watkins, Ph.D.
Censor deputatus

Imprimatur:
Very Rev. George E. Stuart, J.C.D.
Episcopal Vicar for Canonical Services
Archdiocese of Washington
August 8, 2022

The paper used in this publication meets the
minimum requirements of American National Standards
for Information Science—Permanence of Paper
for Printed Library Materials, ANSI Z39.48-1992.
∞

Cataloging-in-Publication Data is available
from the Library of Congress
ISBN: 978-0-8132-3667-4
eISBN: 978-0-8132-3668-1

To the memory of my father
who loved both truth and persons
and bore fruit that will last

May I be able to say
"My father, my father! The chariots
of Israel and its horsemen!"

Contents

Acknowledgments

I wish to thank all the people who helped to make this book possible. Michael Bolin, Andrew Seeley, Joe Zepeda, and Thomas McLaughlin read all or portions of the book in draft and provided very helpful comments, objections, and suggestions. Any errors in the book are, of course, my own. I would like also to thank Stephen Baldner and the anonymous referees of the manuscript. Their reviews, including their criticisms, helped me to improve the book immensely.

Many of the ideas in this book were discussed in my electives Aquinas and the Unmoved Mover and Medieval Proofs for God's Existence at the Pontifical College Josephinum, and the central argument was discussed in my yearly Philosophy of Nature class there. I wish to thank especially my students Fritz Schlueter, Cassian Harman, Aaron Alford, David England, Kevin Girardi, Joey Rolwing, and Peter Scheck.

This book would not have been possible without the excellent library of the Pontifical College Josephinum and the help of those who made that library what it is: Peter Veracka, Beverly Lane, and Michelle Brown.

I wish especially to thank my wife Rebecca and our children, without whose patience and encouragement I could not have succeeded at this work.

I also wish especially to thank my father, Larry Shields, who read the drafts of my chapters and spent many hours discussing the book with me and sharing my excitement. Without him as a teacher and father, I never would have been capable of writing this or any book. He passed away during the final preparations for its publication, and I regret not being able to place the book in his hands.

Finally, I wish above all to thank God for His grace and mercy. He is the beginning and the end of all things.

Abbreviations

The following abbreviations are used when referring to St. Thomas's works:

Comp.	*Compendium of Theology*
De Ente	*On Being and Essence*
G1	Aquinas' first motion proof for God's existence in *SCG* I, c. 13
G2	Aquinas' second motion proof for God's existence in *SCG* I, c. 13
In I, II, III De An.	*Commentary on Aristotle's* On the Soul, book I, II, or III
In I, II, etc. De Caelo	*Commentary on Aristotle's* On the Heavens, book I, II, etc.
In I, II De Gen.	*Commentary on Aristotle's* On Generation and Corruption, book I or II
In I, II, etc. Eth. Nic.	*Commentary on Aristotle's* Nicomachean Ethics, book I, II, etc.
In I, II, etc. Meta.	*Commentary on Aristotle's* Metaphysics, book I, II, etc.
In I, II, etc. Phys.	*Commentary on Aristotle's* Physics, book I, II, etc.
In I, II Post. Anal.	*Commentary on Aristotle's* Posterior Analytics, book I or II
In I, II, etc. Sent.	*Commentary on Peter Lombard's* Sentences, book I, II, etc.
In De Trin	*Commentary on Boethius'* On the Trinity
SCG	*Summa contra Gentiles*
ST	*Summa Theologiae*
QDA	Disputed Questions on the Soul (*De Anima*)
QDSC	Disputed Questions on Spiritual Creatures (*De Spiritualibus Creaturis*)
QDP	Disputed Questions on the Power of God (*De Potentia*)
QDV	Disputed Questions on the Truth (*De Veritate*)
Quod.	Quodlibetal Questions
Resp. 43 Artic.	Response to 43 Articles

Nature & Nature's God

Introduction

Thomas Aquinas's "Five Ways"[1] are certainly among the most famous of proofs for God's existence. They are often advanced in favor of God's existence and often criticized. Many have found them thoroughly convincing and many have found them thoroughly unconvincing.[2] Aquinas himself speaks of the "First Way," the proof from motion, as the "more manifest way."[3] In this proof Aquinas argues as follows: Everything that is in motion is moved by something else. If what is causing the motion is itself in motion, it too must be moved by something else. But there cannot be an infinite regress of such movers, and so there must be some first mover, which is not moved by anything else. "And this everyone understands to be God."

At first glance this seems to be the same type of cosmological argument that modern theists such as William Lane Craig offer.[4] One event

---

1. St. Thomas Aquinas, *ST*, I, q. 2, a. 3. I will generally quote from *Summa Theologiae*, trans. Fr. Laurence Shapcote, OP, ed. John Mortensen and Enrique Alarcón (Lander, WY.: The Aquinas Institute for the Study of Sacred Doctrine, 2012), although where noted I have emended the translation. This translation is a reprint of the Fathers of the English Dominican Province translation.

2. Edward Feser is one who found the First Way convincing; see Brian Besong and Jonathan Fuqua, eds., *Faith and Reason: Philosophers Explain Their Turn to Catholicism* (San Francisco: Ignatius Press, 2019), 40, fn. 13. Among those who criticize the Five Ways, see (especially) Anthony Kenny, *The Five Ways: St. Thomas Aquinas' Proofs of God's Existence* (New York: Schocken Books, 1969); Antony Flew, *God and Philosophy* (New York: Harcourt, Brace & World, 1966), 58–74, 85–98, 119–22; J. L. Mackie, *The Miracle of Theism: Arguments for and against the Existence of God* (Oxford: Clarendon Press, 1982), 87–92; and Graham Oppy, *Arguing about Gods* (New York: Cambridge, 2006), 98–107.

3. *ST* I, q. 2, a. 3, c.

4. William Lane Craig, *The Kalām Cosmological Argument* (New York: Barnes & Noble, 1979).

is caused by another event prior to it in time, but the process must have started somewhere, so it is argued. Time and the whole universe had to have a beginning, and this beginning had to have a cause. Hence there exists outside the whole physical universe some being powerful enough to bring it into existence and set it in motion.

So interpreted, Aquinas's argument would be very understandable and carry a certain amount of weight. I have a great deal of respect for Craig's argument, but my goal here is not to defend it. My interest in this book is in defending Aquinas's argument, which despite the apparent similarity cannot be the same sort as Craig's. For Aquinas insists that it is *impossible* to prove that the universe has a beginning.[5] That is a truth that Christians can be certain about only because God has revealed it to them. For this reason, it is commonly said that Aquinas's proof does not argue backward in time, but rather upward in the moment, proving that every motion requires a simultaneously acting mover, and that this mover must ultimately be God, either moving all things immediately by His power or mediately through certain secondary movers, as a hand might move a stone by means of a stick.[6]

I must confess that I, although a committed believer, found myself unable to see the cogency of Aquinas's First Way for quite a long time. For one thing, it seemed to rely on a premise that was contradicted by modern science, namely that everything that is in motion is currently moved by something else. Bodies moving inertially seem to violate this principle. Secondly, even granting the principle on which it is based, the argument still seemed lacking in many ways. Suppose, for instance, that each motion is caused by an unmoved, primary mover, that is, a mover that terminates the regress of causes *presently* responsible for the motion in question. Why does every motion have to be caused by the same un-moved mover? Why must there be only one primary mover? Why must it have divine attributes? Why could not humans, even animals and plants perhaps, initiate motion, thus constituting mundane primary movers?[7] And if the motion of one body is caused by another body, why is any fur-ther simultaneous mover necessary? A rock will not fall unless the earth pulls it, but why would any further mover be necessary besides the earth?

---

5. *ST* I, q. 46, a. 2.

6. See, for example, Edward Feser, *Aquinas: A Beginner's Guide* (Oxford: Oneworld, 2009), 69.

7. See Scott MacDonald, "Aquinas's Parasitic Cosmological Argument," *Medieval Philosophy and Theology* I, no. I (1991): 119–55, at 147.

If two asteroids collide in space, each changes the speed and direction of the other. Why would any further mover be necessary to explain the change? Finally and most importantly, if God stopped causing motion was everything in the universe supposed to freeze in its place?[8] Was this really the best that Aquinas could give as a rational argument for God's existence? How could he think that this was sufficient?

After many years, I have come to understand this argument in a way quite different than before, and I now believe that it is sound and convincing. My goal in this book is to show that Aquinas's argument, in a natural philosophical rather than metaphysical form, is cogent on its own, historical terms, and that it can be quite convincingly adapted to what modern science has brought to light about the physical world. My project will involve a thorough investigation of Aquinas's texts in their own medieval cosmological context, as well as an account of the development of physical theory, from the scientific revolution to the twenty-first century.

The First Way is deceptively short. It might seem that it could be treated adequately in a single class period, or a single scholarly article. When the argument's context is taken into consideration, however, it becomes obvious that Aquinas does not believe that coming to know the existence of a transcendent God is as easy as reading his 230 word First Way. The *Summa Theologiae* is a theology textbook,[9] and, at medieval universities at least, students would not take up the study of theology until they had completed a course of study in the arts, including a thorough philosophical education.[10] A lot of background knowledge is presupposed in the

8. As a believer I could imagine that such might be the case, but how was this argument supposed to convince a nonbeliever that things needed a mover to keep them going, despite the law of inertia? For the argument to work, the premise that things cannot keep going on their own has to be more certain and evident than the conclusion that God exists.

9. Admittedly he intends it to be a beginner's theology textbook, but still not a beginner's philosophy textbook. See *ST* I, prol.

10. Cf. Timothy B. Noone, "Scholasticism," in *A Companion to Philosophy in the Middle Ages*, ed. Jorge J. E. Gracia and Timothy B. Noone (Malden, MA: Blackwell Publishing, 2003) 55–64, at 58 and 60. Thomas wrote the first part of the *Summa*, containing the five ways, while teaching Dominican friars at Rome. These friars—not university students—would have been rather poor students, and a background in philosophy could not have been presupposed. (Cf. Jean-Pierre Torrell, OP, *The Person and His Work*, trans. Robert Royal, vol. 1 of *Saint Thomas Aquinas* [Washington, DC: The Catholic University of America Press, 1996], 142–46. Cf. also M. Michèle Mulcahey and Timothy B. Noone, "Religious Orders," in *A Companion to Philosophy in the Middle Ages*, 45–54, at 46–50). If the *Summa* were meant for them—and given its overall philosophical acumen it certainly cannot have been meant exclusively for them—there would have been even more reason for Thomas to give the Five Ways in a summary and less than fully adequate format, since the students would

First Way. Moreover, Aquinas himself states earlier in his *Summa Theologiae* that "even as regards those truths about God which human reason can investigate, it was necessary that man should be taught by a divine revelation, because the truth about God such as reason could discover would only be known by a few, and that after a long time, and with the admixture of many errors."[11] Certainly Aquinas would not, pages later, present a proof for God's existence that he regarded as so manifest that anyone could grasp it fully without prior preparation.[12]

To truly demonstrate the existence of the transcendent God, the First Way must be elaborated and supplemented. Indeed, when Aquinas presents corresponding proofs from motion in the *Summa contra Gentiles*,[13] he goes on for pages and pages (about 2,200 words). Furthermore, Aquinas's proof derives from books VII and VIII of Aristotle's *Physics*, where Aristotle gives a proof that is certainly quite complex and depends upon points that he has argued for in the previous books of the *Physics*. One must, then, draw upon a lot of different resources to make sense of Aquinas's argument, which is what I propose to do in this book.

I believe that, when read in the context of Aquinas's thought as a whole, the motion proofs are sound. But the First Way has been often misunderstood, even by those who defend it. In particular, those who defend the argument tend to insulate it as much as possible from Aquinas's physical theory. For they believe that if the argument *were* dependent on Aquinas's views about physics, it would have to be abandoned, since the scientific revolution definitively debunked Aristotelian physics.[14] The

---

not have been capable of following the full philosophical demonstrations. Thomas was an excellent teacher, and it seems likely that the arguments were meant to be both easy to follow for beginners—who could get enough out of them for the purposes of beginning the study of revealed theology—and hold up under stricter scrutiny, in which their demonstrative character could be developed by further distinctions and supporting arguments.

11. *ST* I, q. 1, a. 1, c. I have emended the translation.

12. Aquinas does not believe that the existence of God is self-evident (*ST* I, q. 2, a. 1), but he does believe that there is a sort of natural, vague knowledge of God's existence that most people arrive at, since the order in the world suggests that there is something or someone ordering it. (See *SCG* III, c. 38 and the prologue to Aquinas's commentary on John's Gospel. The text from *SCG* is discussed more fully in chapter 3 below, p. 111–113.)

13. *SCG* I, c. 13.

14. Feser, for example, says: "It has also sometimes been claimed (for example by Anthony Kenny) that Aquinas's proofs rest on outdated Aristotelian scientific theory, and thus are irrelevant in the present day. But as noted in chapter 2, Aristotle's metaphysics stands or falls independently of his physics, and as we shall see, while the Five Ways definitely presuppose certain Aristotelian metaphysical claims, there is never a point in any of the arguments where appeal need be made to now falsified theories in physics or any of the other sciences." *Aquinas*, 65.

argument could have no merit or weight in a contemporary context and certainly could not be persuasive. It would become of merely historical interest. Hence there has been a marked tendency to interpret the argument *metaphysically*, and not as an argument from *natural philosophy*. I believe this is a mistake, not only for historical, but also for sapiential reasons.

Aquinas places natural philosophy, the philosophical study of nature, between metaphysics and natural science, the latter of which he would have called *scientia media*, that is, applied math.[15] Natural philosophy serves as the bridge between sense-experience of the physical world and the necessarily abstract character of metaphysics. If natural philosophy is neglected, Thomistic metaphysics is in danger of devolving into rationalism, that is, the attempt to draw substantive conclusions merely from supposedly clear and distinct ideas. Thomists have the great merit of insisting that all human concepts derive from, but are not reducible to, sensory experience, but the danger still exists of treating concepts such as act and potency *as if* they were innate ideas anyways. The influential twentieth century Thomist Fr. Réginald Garrigou-Lagrange, for example, seems to have succumbed to this temptation.[16] The motion proof, understood as part of natural philosophy, serves as a way into metaphysics, and at the same time grounds metaphysics in our experience of the world.[17]

15. For the distinction and relationship between science, natural philosophy, and metaphysics, see James A. Weisheipl, OP, "Medieval Natural Philosophy and Modern Science," in *Nature and Motion in the Middle Ages*, ed. William C. Carroll, 261–76 (Washington, DC: The Catholic University of America Press, 1985). However, unlike Fr. Weisheipl, I am a proponent of a moderate form of scientific realism. Empirical science studies the natural world under the formality of measured quantity, but when successful grasps truths about reality itself, rather than merely saving the phenomena and providing predictive power. Furthermore, empirical science always proceeds on the basis of one or another implicit natural philosophy (this is the true significance of Kuhn's work on the place of paradigms in science), and at the same time its progress sheds light on, and sometimes requires renewed work in, natural philosophy (particularly when science uncovers anomalies). My stance in the philosophy of science is thus a kind of neo-Kuhnian realism.

16. See Fr. Réginald Garrigou-Lagrange, OP, *God: His Existence and His Nature*, 2 vols., trans. Dom Bede Rose, OSB (St. Louis: Herder, 1949).

17. This understanding is shared by Fr. Benedict Ashley, OP, *The Way toward Wisdom: An Interdisciplinary and Intercultural Introduction to Metaphysics* (Notre Dame: University of Notre Dame Press, 2006). Mark Johnson also shares a similar understanding: "Immateriality and the Domain of Thomistic Natural Philosophy," *The Modern Schoolman* 67, no. 4 (1990): 285–304. The primary opponent of the natural philosophical reading of Aquinas's motion proofs is John F. X. Knasas; see *Thomistic Existentialism and Cosmological Reasoning* (Washington, DC: The Catholic University of America Press, 2019), ch. 6. Knasas consistently fails to provide a plausible reading of a key text put forward by Johnson (*In De Trin.*, q. 5, a. 2, obj. 3 and ad 3.) The celestial spheres fall squarely within the consideration of natural philosophy, not at its boundary as nonnatural principles of natural motion, as Knasas would have it. Moreover, since *Physics* VIII explicitly proves the existence of a

But natural philosophy itself stands in need of modern science, and this for two reasons. The first is principled: natural philosophy depends on attentiveness to nature. Ordinary experience must retain its authority, but the hard sciences call attention to many important and undeniable experiential facts that would otherwise be out of view. The second reason is pragmatic: science is the only intellectual authority acknowledged by western culture. Philosophy is certainly not highly regarded in our culture (although I believe it in fact has a higher intrinsic certitude than the sciences). Philosophy will only gain significant traction if it engages seriously with hard science.

Since I hold that one cannot make sense of Aquinas's First Way of proving God's existence apart from its original context in Aquinas's physical theory, in this book I will dive into Aquinas's account of the motion of the elements, the influence of the "heavenly spheres," and so forth, rather than shying away from such matters. I believe that when one takes the context of Aquinas's physical theory seriously, an interesting argument emerges that is supported by modern science in surprising ways, even given the vast differences that exist between Thomistic and modern physics. I believe that the proof for an unmoved mover can make a greater impact if brought into engagement with modern science. But, paradoxically, this can only happen if its original setting in Aquinas's medieval physical theory is taken seriously. This book is part of a project of bringing together Thomism and modern science *via* a process of digging deeply into historical, Thomistic physical theory.

My strategy in the present book will be as follows: In the first part, comprising the first five chapters, I accomplish the historical task of

---

"wholly incorporeal" being and ends with God (*In VIII Phys.*, l. 21, n. 1141 and l. 23, n. 1172), Knasas is forced to read *Physics* VIII, implausibly, as belonging for Aquinas to the science of metaphysics. Aquinas himself, however, explicitly includes it within natural philosophy (see, e.g., *In III Phys.*, l. 1, n. 275, *In VII Phys.*, l. 1, n. 884; *In I Phys.*, l. 1, n. 1–4; l. 2, n. 12.) Knasas's own favored texts—which do clearly assign the understanding of immaterial beings to the science of metaphysics—do not count against the natural philosophy reading of Aquinas's motion proofs. Natural philosophy can only just reach the existence of at least one immaterial being, and it can know very little about it. A true understanding and developed *science* of God and angels belongs exclusively to metaphysics and goes far beyond anything found even in Aristotle's *Metaphysics*, as Aquinas indicates in *In III De An.*, l. 12, n. 785 (cited by Knasas, *Thomistic Existentialism*, 182–83.) In speaking of such a science, Aquinas seems to have in mind something like what is found in Proclus's *Elements of Theology*, or the *Book of Causes*. Furthermore, as I explain in this book, metaphysics has its own, alternative demonstrations for God's existence, and these have a more robust conclusion than the motion proofs, but are correspondingly less accessible and manifest. Examples are the Fourth Way in *ST* and the proof from the *De Ente*, which I favor highly.

clarifying the motion proof as Aquinas understood it, within the context of medieval physical theory. In the second part, comprising the last three chapters, I adapt the historical proof to the conclusions of modern science.

In the first part, I begin with the premises on which the proof is explicitly based. Aquinas himself states,[18] and many commentators agree,[19] that there are two key premises in the motion proof: that everything in motion is moved by another (*omne quod movetur ab alio movetur*)—which I will call the mover principle—and that an infinite regress of movers is not possible. Both of the premises are open to objection. The first premise is often rejected as irreconcilable with the basic principles of modern science, particularly with the first law of motion, the principle of inertia. But the mover principle was subject to criticism already in the Middle Ages, for example by Duns Scotus.[20] The second premise, namely the impossibility of an infinite regress, has been a subject of intense debate for a long time, and it still has its defenders and critics.[21]

I believe that both premises are true and can be defended and justified. This task will occupy the first two chapters of the present book. In the first chapter I will consider the meaning of the mover principle and two of the three sub-arguments Aquinas offers for it in the course of his motion-based proofs for God's existence.[22] I will advance a neglected

18. *SCG* I, c. 13, n. 84 [4].

19. See, for example, Christopher Shields and Robert Pasnau, *The Philosophy of Aquinas*, 2nd ed. (New York: Oxford University Press, 2016), 105 and 107 and William L. Rowe, *The Cosmological Argument* (Princeton: Princeton University Press, 1975), 13.

20. See Roy R. Effler, *John Duns Scotus and the Principle "Omne quod movetur ab alio movetur"* (St. Bonaventure, NY: Franciscan Institute, 1962).

21. Some arguments against infinite regress were already criticized in medieval times by William Ockham, but perhaps the most famous criticisms are found in the modern period in the writings of David Hume, *Dialogues concerning Natural Religion*, part IX and Immanuel Kant, *Critique of Pure Reason*, Transcendental Dialectic, The Antinomy of Pure Reason. Examples of contemporary critics are C. J. F. Williams, "Hic autem non est Procedere in Infinitum," *Mind*, New Series 69, no. 275 (1960): 403–5 and Paul Edwards, "Objections to Cosmological Arguments," in *Philosophy of Religion: A Guide and Anthology*, ed. Brian Davies, 202–12 (New York: Oxford University Press, 2000). Examples of contemporary defenders are Caleb Cohoe, "There Must Be a First: Why Thomas Aquinas Rejects Infinite, Essentially Ordered Causal Series," *British Journal for the History of Philosophy* 21, no. 5 (2013): 838–56 and Alexander R. Pruss, "The Hume-Edwards Principle and the Cosmological Argument," *International Journal for Philosophy of Religion* 43, no. 3 (1998): 149–65.

22. I leave out of consideration the first argument for the mover principle presented by Aquinas in *SCG* I.13, an argument based on Aristotle's reasoning in the opening passage of *Physics* VII.1. This is the most neglected of Aquinas's arguments because it is so difficult to understand and seems at first glance less promising. Fr. William Wallace, OP, however, was partial to it. See "Cosmological Arguments and Scientific Concepts," in *From a Realist Point of View: Essays on the Philosophy of Science*, 2nd ed. (Lanham, MD: University Press of America, 1983), 309–23.

interpretation of the mover principle, developing it and unpacking its role in the motion proof more fully than has ever been done.[23] Most scholars of Aquinas's thought, ever since the publication of Fr. Weisheipl's work,[24] believe that what Aquinas means is that "everything *being moved* must be moved by something else." But I will demonstrate that Aquinas means that "everything *in motion* is moved by something else." Furthermore, in rightly distinguishing Aquinas's First Way from the kalām cosmological argument—as advanced by William Lane Craig and others—scholars and teachers routinely assert that, according to Aquinas, the mover's moving and the mobile's being in motion are simultaneous in time. But I demonstrate that this is not universally and straightforwardly the case on Aquinas's view. So in some ways the old translation of Fr. Shapcote[25] turns out to be appropriate: "Whatever is in motion is *put in motion* by another." So understood, Aquinas's mover principle is consistent with Newtonian physics. I believe Aquinas's First Way to be cogent on the interpretation of the mover principle that I argue for, and only on that interpretation. Nor does Aquinas's argument collapse into an argument for a temporal beginning to the universe. Rather, it retains its Thomistic identity.

In the second chapter I will defend Aquinas's argument against an infinite regress. All defenders of Aquinas's argument rightly distinguish between essentially ordered and accidentally ordered causal series. The former cannot regress infinitely, Aquinas says, while the latter can. The motion proof establishes God's existence as the first cause in an essentially ordered series. I will use this distinction to respond to prominent objections

---

23. In 1974 Antonio Moreno, OP, proposed an interpretation of the mover principle similar to mine, although he does not explicitly distinguish his interpretation of the mover principle from Weisheipl's: "The Law of Inertia and the Principle *Quidquid Movetur ab Alio Movetur*," *The Thomist* 38, no. 2 (1974): 306–31, at 320–23. Michael Augros also presents an interpretation like mine, first in a little-known article entitled "Ten Objections to the *Prima Via*," *Peripatetikos* 6 (2007): 59–101, at 68–73, then in his book *Aquinas on Theology and God's Existence: The First Two Questions of the* Summa Theologiae *Newly Translated and Carefully Explained* (Neunkirchen-Seelscheid: Editiones Scholasticae, 2019), 267–75. The textual case I make in chapter 1 below and in my article on which it is based ("Everything in Motion is Put in Motion by Another: A Principle in Aquinas' First Way," *American Catholic Philosophical Quarterly* 92 [2018]: 535–61) is much more developed.

24. Fr. James A. Weisheipl, OP, *Nature and Motion in the Middle Ages*, ed. William E. Carroll (Washington, DC: The Catholic University of America Press, 1985). Nearly all the essays collected in this volume are in some way related to the mover principle, but see especially chapter IV, "The Principle *Omne quod Movetur ab Alio Movetur* in Medieval Physics," 75–97 and chapter V, "The Specter of *Motor Coniunctus* in Medieval Physics," 99–120. The essays reprinted in this volume date from the 1950s to the 1980s.

25. I.e., The Fathers of the English Dominican Province translation.

from Paul Edwards, Anthony Kenny, and others. Most importantly, the famous Hume-Edwards objection misses the mark, since Aquinas's argument against infinite essentially ordered series is not a composition type argument, as Edwards supposes. But I also consider a neglected but crucial additional Thomistic conclusion about causal series, namely that infinite accidentally ordered series would necessarily depend upon a separate, finite, essentially ordered causal series to sustain it. Here the Hume-Edwards objection is relevant, but I show how Thomistic philosophy defeats it.

But many interpreters of Aquinas utilize the three marks given by Duns Scotus to characterize essentially ordered series.[26] One of these marks is that in essentially ordered series the causes act simultaneously. I will show that Aquinas does not completely agree. For him, the prior and posterior causes in an essentially ordered series of movers can in certain cases exercise their causality successively, rather than simultaneously. This fact facilitates the integration of Aquinas's First Way with modern science.

In the third chapter I show how Aquinas can conclude to God's existence from these premises. I first consider and reject the conventional interpretation of the First Way, according to which the argument demonstrates that all motion continuously requires the simultaneous action of God as a conjoined mover. By presenting texts in which Aquinas discusses what will happen to the physical universe at the end of time, I show that Aquinas rejects the idea that the whole universe would instantly freeze in place without a mover. Aquinas holds, rather, that without a sustaining mover the universe would enter into a wind-down period as compounds dissolved into their elements and the elements moved to their natural places.[27] Once an equilibrium condition was reached, the universe would then remain forever motionless, barring God's renewed action.

I then present an alternative interpretation of the First Way. Once the premises have been defended, the argument is really quite simple, but its conclusion correspondingly modest. By itself the First Way is not

---

26. See, for example, William Rowe, *The Cosmological Argument*, 23–29 and Edward Feser, *Scholastic Metaphysics: A Contemporary Introduction* (Heusenstamm, Germany: Editiones Scholasticae, 2014), 148–150.

27. This thesis is one of the most original contributions of my book. The evidence for it is provided in chapter 3 below, p. 89–96. The wind-down motion flows spontaneously from the natures of elemental bodies, but God does, on a metaphysical level, cause such motion insofar as He is the continual cause of the dynamic act of being of these natures. But this metaphysical truth is not part of Aquinas's motion proof for God's existence; it is a more difficult conclusion to derive. For more on this, see chapter 3, fn. 1 below.

supposed to establish that there is only one unmoved mover, or that an unmoved mover need be anything more than a natural being. Yet it does establish that for any motion there must be something primarily responsible, something that possesses, either formally or eminently, the act toward which the motion tends. Aquinas says that anything fundamentally responsible for the order of things (and by extension, for any form of motion) can legitimately be called a god, even if it were a mere physical element. In fact, all motion is due fundamentally to the one transcendent God, but by itself the First Way does not establish this. The First Way only establishes the existence of god (to be precise, one or more gods) in a minimal sense.

But Aquinas does intend to prove a more robust conclusion, and so in chapter 4 I explain how Aquinas extends the argumentation to prove the existence of an immaterial, everlasting, immovable mover. Scott Mac-Donald, in his important and insightful article "Aquinas's Parasitic Cosmological Argument," also argues that the First Way is valid but incomplete, and that Aquinas intends to complete it with the Third Way, the argument from possible beings to a necessary being. I argue however, that Aquinas can and does complete the motion proof through consideration of motion, remaining squarely within the realm of natural philosophy.

There are three ways to extend the First Way that are in line with Aquinas's intentions. One is with the Third Way, as MacDonald suggests. Another is with, surprisingly, the Fifth Way, the argument from final causality in mobile beings. The other way of completing the proof is with a disjunctive move: either motion in the universe is sempiternal[28] or not. If not, then an immaterial God must exist to initiate motion in the universe; if motion is sempiternal, an immaterial God must exist to sustain the motion. This disjunctive path is explicitly taken in Aquinas's second motion proof in the *Summa contra Gentiles* (*SCG*). (Aquinas presents two proofs for an unmoved mover in that work. Following Norman Kretzmann, I will refer to the first and second motion proofs in *SCG* as G1 and G2 respectively.[29]) That proof, G2, itself completes the first motion proof in the same work. The latter, in turn, corresponds nearly perfectly with the

---

28. I will reserve the word "eternal" for the attribute of possessing the whole duration of one's being simultaneously—i.e., being completely outside of time—and use words like "sempiternal," "everlasting," etc., in a more general sense, which includes both the former condition and that of existing for an infinite amount of time, having an extended, flowing duration without beginning or end.

29. Norman Kretzmann, *The Metaphysics of Theism: Aquinas's Natural Theology in* Summa Contra Gentiles I (Oxford: Clarendon Press, 1997), 61.

First Way in the *Summa Theologiae*. In the fourth chapter I will elucidate how G2 establishes the existence of an immaterial, everlasting, immovable mover, thus completing the First Way.

That an immaterial mover is required to sustain motion in a beginningless universe is the converse of Aquinas's claim, presented in chapter 3, that without a sustaining mover the universe would come to rest within a finite time. If it were the case that the universe had already existed for an infinite time, it would have already come to rest by now, contrary to fact, unless an immaterial, immovable mover were sustaining it in motion. In Aquinas's eyes, the principal parts of the universe in fact continue in perfectly uniform motion, without winding down toward a state of equilibrium,[30] and this requires a super-mundane mover just as much as actually sempiternal motion would. Thus an immaterial mover is required both to sustain the universe's motion *and* to initiate it, although the later point is known only by faith. The motion proof thus allows one to conclude to the existence of one *or more* immaterial, everlasting, immovable movers.

In the fifth chapter I will take up Aquinas's Fifth Way as well as his account of life as self-motion. This will enable me to show how the Fifth Way in *ST* completes the First Way. The causal regularity displayed by efficient causes implies that they are directed to final causes. But, contrary to some interpretations, Aquinas has more in mind in his Fifth Way, namely, that nature displays what I call beneficial adaptation. It is because natural substances are coordinated with each other in such a way that they regularly conserve themselves, benefit each other, and reach a higher level of actualization than their own specific intrinsic principles can account for, that one can confidently conclude that nature is governed by an intelligent being.

Inanimate, natural efficient causes are determined to one effect and they tend unswervingly to their result without moderation, coming to rest in an extreme condition. In order to display beneficial adaptation, as the motion in the universe does, natural causes must be moderated and directed by an intelligent, self-determining being who can comprehend them all and coordinate them with one another. Since the world as

---

30. In Aquinas's day there was absolutely no empirical evidence that the universe was not in motion in perfectly uniform cycles. As far as any recorded observation indicated, the sun, moon, planets, stars, seasons, and generations of living beings had always been progressing in exactly the same way as they currently were. Evidence to the contrary did not emerge until the nineteenth century (advances in geology and paleontology) and the twentieth century (Edwin Hubble's discovery of galactic redshift, and Penzias's and Wilson's discovery of the microwave background radiation).

a whole displays a unity of order, there must be a single such intelligent mover governing the universe.

The living beings of our experience, unlike inanimate natural causes, do maintain orderly motion; they move themselves. They can do this by participating more or less remotely in intelligence, having a capacity to discriminate between helpful and harmful.[31] Yet the most basic tendencies, instincts, and inclinations of *physical* living beings are determined for them, and they cannot sustain motion *forever* on their own, since they are corruptible. Furthermore, their life depends on many environmental factors outside themselves; they too must be coordinated with each other by a higher being. The possibility of truly perpetual, ordered motion in the universe requires a single completely self-determining, non-natural living agent who can direct all things. Aquinas's two ways of completing the motion proof thus converge in an illuminating way, and allow him to demonstrate that a unique, living, intelligent, volitional, everlasting, immutable, and immaterial being exists as a cause of motion in the universe.

The results of my historical investigation are that Aquinas's argument is valid and convincing given Aquinas's physical theory. But my most important task is to show that the argument is still sound and convincing, given the progress of modern science. This I do in the second part of the book, comprising chapters 6, 7, and 8. My goal is not to use science to prove God's existence. That is a task that can only be achieved by philosophy. Rather, I wish to show that Aquinas's motion proof not only does not clash with modern science but is actually corroborated by it.

At first glance however, the principles of inertia and conservation of energy wreck Aquinas's argument, since motion can continue forever without any sustaining cause.[32] In chapter 6 I address these concerns, beginning with the principle of inertia. David Hume—armed with this principle—argues that the universe can remain in motion forever all by itself, and that in infinite time all possibilities will be actualized. One possibility is a tolerably self-sustaining configuration of matter, such as we see today in organisms and the solar system. Hence, in his view, in an infinite tract of time a self-maintaining, orderly motion will arise in the universe—once in a quadrillion years, say—and persist for a long but

---

31. The only organisms that are actually intelligent, of course, are human beings, but animals have perception and plants have nonconscious discriminatory capacities that enable them to grow their branches toward sunshine and roots toward water, for example. Thus animals and plants have something analogous to intelligence, participating remotely in it.

32. Kenny argues thus: *The Five Ways*, 28.

finite time. In total, the universe spends far more time in a disordered state than in an ordered one, but it still spends huge stretches of time in an ordered state. No immaterial mover, then, is required to explain the observed universe.

But as I show, Newton himself, far from undermining Aquinas's kind of motion proof, actually supports it and demonstrates its validity. Collisions are not perfectly elastic, he reasons, and so the quantity of motion in the universe is constantly on the decrease.[33] Furthermore, the motion in the universe slowly tends toward disorder. The solar system, for example, must eventually fly apart. According to Newton, perpetual orderly motion would require God's recurring influence.

In chapter 7 I turn to the nineteenth century development of thermodynamics. The first law of thermodynamics—the principle of the conservation of energy—was established by means of Joule's determination of the mechanical equivalent of heat, and it too seemed to threaten Aquinas's proof. For on this principle the quantity of motion lost in collisions is not actually destroyed. Rather, this quantity of motion is converted into heat, which is itself interpreted as just a form of microscopic motion. Heat can be used to do work, that is, converted back into useful macroscopic motion. It seems, then, that perpetual motion is guaranteed by the laws of physics, rather than being in need of a sustaining immaterial mover. Yet the *second* law of thermodynamics—the entropy principle—as formulated by Kelvin and Clausius in the nineteenth century, once again validates the motion proof. For it is never the case that all of the waste heat generated in a process can be converted back into macroscopic motion so as to do useful work. No machine can run at 100 percent efficiency. The *free* energy of any closed system is always on the decrease and the entropy or disorder is always on the increase. A perpetual motion machine cannot exist—at least, not without an infinite supply of free energy. The universe itself cannot be a perpetual motion machine, unless God continues to supply it with free energy. Indeed, twentieth century cosmology shows that the universe, if left to its own devices, must end in either a heat death or a giant black hole within a finite but huge amount

---

33. As I discuss in chapter 6, if quantity of motion is taken as a vector quantity, it is conserved in all collisions. This is what is known nowadays as the principle of the conservation of momentum. But if momentum is taken as an absolute quantity, it decreases in every collision. Newton understands the conservation of momentum in terms of a vector quantity, whereas Descartes had understood it in terms of an absolute quantity, and accordingly gave rules for colliding bodies that are wildly at odds with experience.

of time. Without God's act of moving, the universe inevitably winds down to a state of equilibrium, just as Aquinas says.

In the final chapter—chapter 8—I explore the connection between entropy, information, and life to corroborate Aquinas's view that the unmoved mover of the universe must be a living and intelligent being. A whole body of literature has developed around the "Maxwell's demon" thought experiment. Despite the "merely statistical" validity of the second law of thermodynamics, this literature elucidates how the use of random fluctuation phenomena to (locally) reduce entropy depends upon an ability to gather, store, and utilize information. This local reduction of entropy is compensated by the entropy generated by the physical agents that process the information.

Information processing *machines* wear out and break down over time. Indefinite maintenance of orderly motion is a property of life. Living information processors, unlike machines, self-organize through the process of embryogenesis and physiological development, heal themselves, and reproduce themselves *indefinitely*.[34] The connection between life and localized entropy reduction has been recognized by contemporary scientists, as illustrated for example in Erwin Schrödinger's classic, *What is Life?*[35] Life's ability to indefinitely maintain a localized low-entropy condition depends upon its ability to process information. Even plants and microbes, although not conscious or percipient, are sensitive[36] and can discriminate between light and dark, wet and dry, and so forth. This is how they maintain their own structure and orderly motion. Higher, percipient forms of life—animal and human—can organize their external environment, to varying degrees.

Yet as long as life is instantiated in a physical form, it remains subject to the laws of physics, including the second law of thermodynamics. Hence such living beings can reduce entropy locally, but not in the universe overall. Not even these life forms can remain in perpetual motion of themselves. They can only continue to live, reproduce, and maintain order so long as they are supplied with free energy by an external source,

34. If artificial productions could be made to do these things, then they would count as living beings in my eyes. I do not believe it is possible, in principle, for humans to construct such living beings artificially from nonliving sources. But my argument in this book does not depend upon this view.

35. Erwin Schrödinger, *What is Life? The Physical Aspect of the Living Cell, with Mind and Matter & Autobiographical Sketches* (Cambridge: Cambridge University Press, 1992). *What is Life?* was first published in 1944.

36. For Aquinas, "sensitive" always implies conscious awareness and perception. I am using "sensitive" here in a more modern sense that does not imply conscious awareness.

namely, the sun. Once the sun burns out, ordered, living motion will cease. If orderly motion is to be truly perpetual, there must be a living, intelligent being who is not bodily, and not Himself subject to the laws of physics, just as Aquinas's combined First and Fifth Ways had argued.

In the same chapter I give an overview of contemporary fine-tuning arguments so as to defend Aquinas's teleological argument for God's unity. Aquinas argues that the unity of order in the cosmos demonstrates the unity of its intelligent mover. This claim was easier to make in Aquinas's day, since in medieval cosmology the universe was a closed world, encased in a sphere concentric with the earth, and every star and planet had an effect on what happens here on earth. The modern image of the open universe makes it much harder to think of the universe as teleologically unified. Aren't we just an insignificant speck in a small corner of a vast universe? But Aquinas's argument is still in fact reasonable, for contemporary science has uncovered a number of well recognized "anthropic coincidences," ways in which the universe, in its fundamental aspects, is fine-tuned to make complex life forms possible. I consider scientific evidence that the universe's initial conditions and all its fundamental particles and forces converge to support life. The universe arguably *is* teleologically unified, even on scientific grounds, and thus indicates the unity of its intelligent mover.

The conclusion of this book is that the observed motion in the universe demonstrates the existence of an immaterial God. The interpretation of Aquinas's proof for an unmoved mover that I have given brings it surprisingly close to the more familiar and popular kalām type proofs, as proposed by William Lane Craig, Fr. Robert Spitzer, SJ[37] and others. But it is importantly different, and this difference gives it an advantage: the more common cosmological arguments require establishing that the universe had a beginning. On scientific grounds, it does seem likely that the universe has a beginning. But although science can strongly suggest this, it cannot demonstrate it. It is always possible that something else was going on before the big bang, even if we have no good evidence that anything was. *Perhaps* philosophy can demonstrate a beginning, but it is no easy task. *Aquinas's argument, however, does not depend on establishing*

---

37. Fr. Robert J. Spitzer, SJ, *New Proofs for the Existence of God: Contributions of Contemporary Physics and Philosophy* (Grand Rapids, MI: Eerdmans, 2010), ch. 1 and 5. Fr. Spitzer does not build his whole case for God's existence on kalām type argumentation but bolsters it with other arguments, including an argument from fine-tuning, an argument modeled on Aquinas's Second Way, and one based on the work of Fr. Bernard Lonergan, SJ.

that the universe had a beginning. The argument I have proposed reasons that *either* the orderly motion in the universe has a beginning and is initiated by a powerful, intelligent, living being, *or* orderly motion in the universe is perpetual and sustained by a powerful, intelligent, living being, or both.

One final point needs to be addressed to preclude any misunderstandings of my position. Fellow Thomists are likely to think that I am perverting Aquinas's conclusion, attempting to prove the existence of a deist God rather than the Christian God. But that is not at all the case. A deist God does not act within the universe He makes, nor exercise particular providence over each individual creature and event. Nothing in the motion proof as I interpret it suggests that God does not act within the universe that He either initiates, or sustains, or both initiates and sustains. Nothing in the proof as I interpret it excludes God's particular providence. Nothing in the proof as I interpret it excludes the possibility that God performs miracles within the world. As will be abundantly clear from my book, I believe that God does all these things, as well as conserves all creatures in being every moment, and even takes prior initiative with respect to each act of each creature. Yet *the motion proof* does not prove that God does these things. The proof does not prove that God has all the attributes that Christians assign to God, nor does it argue that He does not have these attributes. It also does not prove or argue that He has any attributes incompatible with the Christian concept of God. Just because a proof does not prove everything one believes is no reason to reject it when it proves some of the things one believes, and argues for nothing incompatible with what one believes. Aquinas's metaphysical proofs for God's existence have a more robust conclusion than his natural philosophical proofs, but they are correspondingly harder proofs, especially for those educated in conventional ways. Aquinas has presented us with many ways to God. We ought not to close any of the paths to Him.

As I hope my book demonstrates, proponents of Aquinas's First Way have nothing to fear from, and everything to gain by, serious engagement with modern natural science, and with Aquinas's own physical theory.

PART I

Aquinas's First Way in Its Historical Context

Chapter 1

The Mover Principle

In this first chapter, I will begin with an explanation of the Thomistic meaning of key terms having to do with motion. In the second, longest section I will take up Aquinas's inductive argument for the mover principle, as presented in G1 and Aquinas's commentary on Aristotle's *Physics* VIII.4. In this section I will engage with Fr. Weisheipl's extensive work on the mover principle as well as David Twetten's response to Weisheipl, showing how both misunderstand Aquinas's meaning. In the third section, I will allow *SCG*'s inductive second argument for the mover principle to shed light on the argument based on act and potency. This third argument in *SCG* is the only one given in the *Summa Theologiae*'s version of the proof, and the one that has received the most attention from Thomists. In this third section I will show that on my interpretation Aquinas's mover principle evades a criticism leveled against it by John Duns Scotus and some modern philosophers, while on the standard interpretation it does not.

THE MEANING OF THE TERMS

At the start, it will be helpful to see the mover principle in its context in Aquinas's First Way, which runs as follows:

> The first and more manifest way [to prove God's existence] is the one that is taken from motion (*motus*). For it is certain and evident to the senses that some things are in motion (*moveri*) in this world. Now whatever is in motion is moved by another. (*Omne autem quod movetur, ab alio movetur.*)

[Proof of mover principle:] For nothing can be in motion except insofar as it is in potency to that to which it is moved. A thing moves, however, insofar as it is in act. For to move is nothing else than to draw a thing out from potency to act. A thing cannot be reduced from potency into act, however, except through some being (*ens*) in act, as what is hot in act—for example fire—makes wood, which is hot in potency, to be hot in act, and through this moves and alters it. However, it is not possible that the same thing be at the same time in potency and act in reference to the same thing, but only in reference to diverse things. For what is hot in act cannot be at the same time hot in potency, but it is cold in potency at the same time. Therefore it is impossible that something be both mover and moved in reference to the same thing and in the same way, or that it move itself. It is necessary, therefore, that everything that is in motion is moved by another. (*Omne ergo quod movetur, oportet ab alio moveri.*)

If, therefore, that by which it is moved be in motion, it is necessary that it also is moved by another, and that by another. But this cannot proceed to infinity.

[Proof of the impossibility of such an infinite regress:] For in that way there would not be any first mover, and consequently neither any other mover, because secondary movers do not move [anything] except insofar as they are moved by a first mover, just as the stick does not move [anything] except insofar as it is moved by the hand.

Therefore it is necessary to arrive at some first mover which is moved by nothing (*primum movens, quod a nullo movetur*), and this all understand to be God.[1]

To understand this argument and the mover principle on which it is based, one must note that the term motion (*motus*) is not restricted to

---

1. *ST* I, q. 2, a. 3, c. Translation mine. For *ST* I use the Latin text from the Leonine edition (*Sancti Thomae de Aquino Opera omnia* [Rome: Typographia Polyglotta S. C. de Propaganda Fide, 1882–], Vol. 4, p. 31 = Leon. 4:31): "Prima autem et manifestior via est, quae sumitur ex parte motus. Certum est enim, et sensu constat, aliqua moveri in hoc mundo. Omne autem quod movetur, ab alio movetur. Nihil enim movetur, nisi secundum quod est in potentia ad illud ad quod movetur: movet autem aliquid secundum quod est actu. Movere enim nihil aliud est quam educere aliquid de potentia in actum: de potentia autem non potest aliquid reduci in actum, nisi per aliquod ens in actu: sicut calidum in actu, ut ignis, facit lignum, quod est calidum in potentia, esse actu calidum, et per hoc movet et alterat ipsum. Non autem est possibile ut idem sit simul in actu et potentia secundum idem, sed solum secundum diversa: quod enim est calidum in actu, non potest simul esse calidum in potentia, sed est simul frigidum in potentia. Impossibile est ergo quod, secundum idem et eodem modo, aliquid sit movens et motum, vel quod moveat seipsum. Omne ergo quod movetur, oportet ab alio moveri. Si ergo id a quo movetur, moveatur, oportet et ipsum ab alio moveri; et illud ab alio. Hic autem non est procedere in infinitum: quia sic non esset aliquod primum movens; et per consequens nec aliquod aliud movens, quia moventia secunda non movent nisi per hoc quod sunt mota a primo movente, sicut baculus non movet nisi per hoc quod est motus a manu. Ergo necesse est devenire ad aliquod primum movens, quod a nullo movetur: et hoc omnes intelligunt Deum."

change of place. In Aristotelian-Scholastic physical theory there are three forms of motion in the strict sense: locomotion, alteration, and growth or diminution (change of place, quality, and size respectively) plus an additional fourth kind of change, generation and corruption—that is, change of substance—which could sometimes be included under the term *motus* taken a little more broadly.[2] The examples Aquinas gives of motion in the argument are instances of locomotion and alteration. But in the context of the argument, substantial change is also included under the term motion, for, as John Wippel points out, Aquinas states in his commentary on book III of the *Physics* that Aristotle's definition of motion—the act of that which exists in potency insofar as it is in potency—applies to substantial change.[3] This definition is explicitly used in Aquinas's third argument for the mover principle in G1,[4] and it seems implicit in *ST*'s version of the proof of the mover principle, which corresponds closely to G1's third argument.[5]

Aquinas states the mover principle at the beginning of the argument as follows: *omne quod movetur, ab alio movetur*, everything in motion is moved by something else. This principle has its source in Aristotle's *Physics*, and it has been the subject of much debate, from Aquinas's day down to our own.[6] It is rendered in English in different ways in accordance with different interpretations of its meaning. The key verb is *movere* (an active infinitive; *moveri* is the passive infinitive form). Aquinas uses the active voice of the verb *movere* transitively, that is, to move in the sense of causing motion (in another). Here the verb is used in the passive voice: *movetur*.

2. *In V Phys.*, l. 2–3.

3. *In III Phys.*, l. 2, n. 286 [4]. Cf. also *In V Phys.*, l. 2, n. 649 [1].

4. *SCG* I, c. 13, n. 89 [9].

5. Cp. John Wippel, *The Metaphysical Thought of Thomas Aquinas: From Finite Being to Uncreated Being* (Washington, DC: The Catholic University of America Press, 2000), 445–46. But Wippel draws a different conclusion from the same evidence. He regards it as probable that in the first part of the argument motion is taken strictly, as excluding substantial change, and that in the later part of the argument—that concerned with infinite regress—substantial change is included. But Wippel has not given any reason to exclude it from the starting point of the argument.

6. Much of this debate in the generations immediately following Thomas's was motivated by concerns to safeguard the freedom of the will. Henry of Ghent for example, claims that self-motion is possessed by all things in varying degrees, but above all by the will: *Quodlibet* IX, q. 5. Godfrey of Fontaines defends an intellectualist account of the will by insisting on the principle that everything that is in motion is moved by something else. His adherence to the mover principle is absolute, and his interpretation of it is very strict: *Quodlibet* VI, q. 7. The interpretation of many modern Thomists actually shares as much in common with Godfrey's interpretation as it does with Thomas's. Duns Scotus argues against the mover principle in general and certainly shares the concern about the freedom of the will: see his *Questions on Aristotle's* Metaphysics, q. 14 and *Ordinatio* II, d. 2, p. 2, q. 6. For an example of a contemporary critique, see Anthony Kenny, *The Five Ways*, 12–23, 27–33.

Does this mean "is moved" or "is in motion," passive reception of motion or simply moving in the intransitive sense? (In the original Greek wording of this principle, the word form used can be interpreted in either the passive or the middle voice.[7]) Is Aquinas claiming that everything that is moved passively is moved *by something else*? In that case, is the principle more than a tautology?[8] That would endanger the argument, for one could end the regress of movers with a mover that was in motion but not itself moved by anything. Or is Aquinas making the stronger claim that everything *in motion* is passively being moved by something else? In that case, the argument could clearly move forward, but the premise seems false.

Contrary to the majority view, it is certainly best to translate *movetur* in the mover principle as "in motion" for one very simple reason: in the earlier version of the argument—G1 in *SCG*—Aquinas begins as follows, according to Pegis's translation: "Everything that is moved [should read: "in motion"] is moved by another. (*Omne quod movetur, ab alio movetur.*) That some things are in motion (*moveri*)—for example, the sun—is evident from sense. Therefore, it is moved (*movetur*) by something else that moves it."[9] *Now it is certainly not manifest to the senses that the sun is*

7. "Ἅπαν τὸ κινούμενον ὑπό τινος ἀνάγκη κινεῖσθαι." Aristotle, *Physics* VII.1, 241b34. I have used the Oxford Classical Text, ed. W. D. Ross (Oxford: Clarendon Press, 1973).

8. John Wippel, following Van Steenberghen and Weisheipl, interprets *movetur* passively and says that it is not a tautology because it denies that anything can be moved *by itself*. See *The Metaphysical Thought of Thomas Aquinas* (Washington, DC: The Catholic University of America Press, 2000), 444 and 414–415. Scott MacDonald also interprets it passively but makes the principle as strong as it would be otherwise by using Aquinas's definition of motion (*motus*) and a principle of sufficient reason to argue that everything in motion is being moved passively, and passively by something else. See "Aquinas's Parasitic Cosmological Argument," fn. 6 and 123–132. Timothy Pawl agrees with MacDonald and Wippel in preferring the passive translation ("The Five Ways," in *The Oxford Handbook of Aquinas*, ed. Brian Davies and Eleonore Stump, 115–31 [Oxford: Oxford University Press, 2012], 116–17.) Although James Weisheipl interprets the principle passively, he gives a sophisticated account of it sensitive to Aquinas's physical theory. His understanding will be engaged in this chapter below, section titled "Elemental Motion and First & Second Potency," p. 23–30. David Twetten, *contra* Weisheipl, thinks that the understanding of the principle as requiring a (current) mover for everything *in motion* is correct. See "Back to Nature in Aquinas," *Medieval Philosophy and Theology* 5, no. 2 (1996): 205–43 and, more succinctly, "Why Motion Requires a Cause: The Foundation for a Prime Mover in Aristotle and Aquinas," in *Philosophy and the God of Abraham: Essays in Memory of James A. Weisheipl, OP*, ed. Raymond James Long, 235–54 (Toronto: Pontifical Institute of Medieval Studies, 1991), at 238–39 and fn. 8. Thus Twetten and MacDonald agree that for Aquinas everything in motion is currently being moved by a distinct efficient cause currently in contact with it. (Twetten argues for what he calls a "metaphysical" reading of the First Way—as opposed to physical or existential—in "Clearing a 'Way' for Aquinas: How the Proof from Motion Concludes to God," *Proceedings of the American Catholic Philosophical Association* 70 [1996]: 259–78.)

9. *SCG* I, c. 13, n. 83 [3]. For the Latin text of the *Summa Contra Gentiles* I have used the Marietti edition: *Liber de Veritate Catholicae Fidei contra errores Infidelium seu Summa Contra Gentiles,*

passively being moved, but it certainly does appear to the senses that the sun is in motion. (Aquinas believed that the sun was really orbiting the earth. Classical physics says instead that the earth is moving around the sun, which only appears to orbit the earth. But according to the theory of relativity, it would depend on one's frame of reference.) Pegis, by translating the mover principle as he does in the quoted text, has Aquinas committing the fallacy of a syllogism in four terms. Hence it seems clear that Aquinas really means to say that everything *in motion* is being moved by something else. I will proceed with a strong *prima facie* presumption that the principle should be read this way, but in responding to objections and in analyzing Aquinas's arguments further supporting evidence will emerge.

From here on out, I will use the English "move" in a transitive sense only, "in motion" for the intransitive sense, and "is moved" for the passive sense, but I will translate *"movetur/moveri"* as either "in motion" or "is moved," depending on context. For the mover principle itself implies that every case of "in motion" is a case of "is moved," and vice versa.

THE INDUCTIVE ARGUMENT:
THE CONTEXT OF THOMISTIC PHYSICS

Before turning to the argument for the mover principle in the First Way (which parallels the third argument for it in G1), I will take up Aquinas's "inductive" argument, the second argument in G1. Some scholars pass over this argument as less promising and therefore less important to them.[10] I, on the other hand, believe that this argument provides the key for understanding the other arguments, precisely because it opens up Aquinas's physical theory.

Elemental Motion and First and Second Potency

The one who has given the most serious consideration to the inductive argument is certainly James Weisheipl, who has done the great service of laying bare Aquinas's understanding of the natural motion of the

---

ed. Ceslai Pera, OP, Peter Marc, OSB & Peter Caramello (Turin: Marietti, 1961). For the English text I have used *Summa Contra Gentiles, Book One: God,* trans. Anton C. Pegis, FRSsC (Notre Dame, IN: University of Notre Dame Press, 1975), although I have frequently emended the translation. The Marietti Latin text numbers the paragraphs consecutively throughout the work, but Pegis begins the paragraph numbering over again in each chapter, although he divides the paragraphs in mostly the same way as the Marietti text. I have provided paragraph numbers under both forms for ease of reference.

10. For example, Scott MacDonald, "Aquinas's Parasitic Cosmological Argument," 120.

elements, thereby disproving a common erroneous understanding of the mover principle as meaning that everything currently in motion is currently being moved by something currently in contact with it.[11] But in Weisheipl's view, the alternative, correct way to read the mover principle is with a passive subject: not everything in motion, but everything *being moved*, is being moved by something else currently in contact with it. My view is that neither way of reading the mover principle is correct. The principle states, rather, that everything *in motion* has an efficient cause of its motion, whether currently in contact with it and exerting force or not. Investigating the inductive argument in dialogue with Weisheipl and David Twetten (who has provided the most serious response to Weisheipl) will best allow me to clarify my understanding of the mover principle and avoid any misunderstanding.

The inductive argument is based on Aristotle's *Physics* VIII.4. Aquinas presents the argument as follows:

> In the second way, Aristotle proves the proposition [i.e. the mover principle] by induction. Whatever is moved by accident is not moved by itself, since it is moved upon the motion of another. So, too, as is evident, what is moved by violence is not moved by itself. Nor are those beings moved by themselves that are moved by their nature as being moved from within, such as the animals, which evidently are moved by the soul. Nor, again, is this true of those beings, such as heavy and light bodies, which are moved through nature. For such beings are moved by the generating cause and the cause removing impediments. Now, whatever is moved is moved through itself (*per se*) or by accident (*per accidens*). If it is moved through itself (*per se*), then it is moved either violently or by nature; if by nature, then either through itself (*ex se*), as the animal, or not through itself (*ex se*), as heavy and light bodies. Therefore, everything that is in motion is moved by another (*ab alio*).[12]

---

11. Texts contrary to this common interpretation can be found throughout Aquinas's writings, but see for example *QDP*, q. 5, a. 5, c.; *In III De Caelo*, l. 7, n. 593–594 [8–9]; and *ST* I, q. 105, a. 2, c. In *In I De Caelo* l. 18, n. 175 [1] Aquinas states that Aristotle says "that natural bodies are not borne upwards and downwards as moved by something exterior. He is to be understood as excluding an exterior mover that would move such bodies *per se* after they have been allotted their specific form. For light bodies are indeed moved up, and heavy bodies down, by the generator, insofar as it gives them the form from which such motion follows. [They are moved] by that which removes an impediment *per accidens* and not *per se*. (… dicens [Aristoteles] quod … corpora naturalia non feruntur sursum et deorsum neque sicut ab alio exteriori mota. Per quod quidem intelligendum est quod removet exteriorem motorem, qui per se huiusmodi corpora moveat postquam sunt formam specificam sortita. Moventur enim levia quidem sursum, gravia autem deorsum a generante quidem, inquantum dat eis formam quam consequitur talis motus; sed a removente prohibens, per accidens et non per se.)" Text from Marietti ed., translation mine.

12. *SCG* I, c. 13, n. 88 [8], translation modified.

This is rather confusing for an argument whose conclusion is supposed to be that everything in motion is moved by something else. It presupposes familiarity with a lot of background concepts. First of all, what is moved accidentally depends upon what is moved essentially. For example, cargo in a ship is in motion because the ship itself is in motion. Thoughts go from place to place because the person whose thoughts they are goes from place to place.[13] Certainly, then, what is moved accidentally is moved by something else. Secondly, what is moved "violently" or by force is moved by something else. This is obvious with regard to the initiation of violent motion: a rock only begins to move across a yard because someone throws it. However, once it leaves the hand, is there still a mover in contact with it and moving it? Aquinas and Aristotle would say yes: the hand of the thrower imparts to the air the power to continue to move the rock after it leaves the hand.[14] However, as Weisheipl demonstrates, Aquinas looks for a medium-as-mover in contact with the projectile not because the projectile is in motion, but rather because the motion is violent and not natural for the projectile.[15]

Aquinas is content to refer to animals as self-movers in the motion proofs in *SCG*, but contrary to what one might expect they do not constitute an exception to the principle that everything in motion is moved by another. For animals have heterogeneous parts, and one part—the soul—can move another part—the body—and one bodily part can move other bodily parts. The whole does not move the whole, nor does any part move itself.[16]

13. *In VIII Phys.*, l. 7, n. 1022 [2]; *In IV Phys.*, l. 5, n. 450 [6]; *In V Phys.*, l. 1, n. 639–40 [2–3].

14. Aquinas, *In VIII Phys.* l. 22; Aristotle, *Physics* VIII.10, 266b27–267a20. This view of projectile motion certainly does not represent either Aristotle's or Aquinas's finest work. As Weisheipl documents, however, once the impetus theory of projectile motion was developed (early fourteenth century), some Thomists had no problem incorporating it into Aquinas's physical theory. Impetus could be regarded as a quality temporarily imparted to the projectile body by the one throwing it, and motion would follow from that quality somewhat as from a second nature, just as downward motion followed from the heavy body's first nature. See Weisheipl, "Natural and Compulsory Movement," in *Nature and Motion in the Middle Ages*, 25–48, at 32–33 as well as "Galileo and the Principle of Inertia," in *Nature and Motion in the Middle Ages*, 49–73, at 68–69.

15. See "Natural and Compulsory Movement," 27–31 and "The Principle *Omne quod Movetur ab Alio Movetur*," 92–93. A clear text in Aquinas is the following (*In III De Caelo*, l. 7, n. 594 [9]): "For that which is undergoing motion naturally has a virtue imparted to it which is the principle of motion, *whence it is not necessary that it be moved by something else impelling it*, as is that which is undergoing motion by violence, since it has not been endowed with any virtue upon which such motion would follow. (Quia id quod naturaliter movetur, habet sibi inditam virtutem, quae est principium motus: unde non oportet quod ab alio impellente moveatur, sicut id quod per violentiam movetur, quia nullam virtutem inditam habet, ad quam sequatur talis motus.)" Emphasis added.

16. *SCG* I, c. 13, n. 85 [5], 88 [8], and 102–03 [22–23]; *In VIII Phys.*, l. 7, n. 1028 [8]; l. 10–11;

The most interesting of all cases is that of inanimate *natural* (as opposed to violent) motion. Aquinas held to the existence of four elements: earth, water, air, and fire—earth being the heaviest, water less heavy, air being light, and fire the lightest of all. As heavy or light each element would undergo motion to its proper place: earth at the bottom, water above earth, air above water, and fire at the top, all in concentric spheres. Motion downward is natural for earth, and it goes downward spontaneously whenever there is nothing holding it up so as to impede its downward motion. This phenomenon poses the greatest difficulty for the mover principle, for rocks (composed predominantly of the element earth) seem to go downward without anything moving them at all. (It can be hard for us to understand why this is a problem, as we have been taught from an early age that the planet Earth *pulls* the rock downward with the pull of gravity. But if one reflects on sense-experience, one will see that one has never observed the earth or anything else *pull* rocks down. All one observes is that as soon as they are let go, they proceed into motion without any apparent cause. Even Sir Isaac Newton, who established the scientific law of universal gravitation, stated that he could not determine what causes gravitational motion.[17])

According to a common interpretation, the mover principle would require that free-falling heavy bodies are being pushed downward by some mover in contact with them as they fall. As Weisheipl shows, however, Aquinas argues—against Averroes and others—that when heavy bodies are in their natural downward motion or light bodies in their natural upward motion, there is nothing that is currently in contact with them and actively exerting a motive force.[18] Downward motion just follows from what heavy bodies are, as heat from the nature of fire, or having angles equal to two rights from what triangles are. The nature of such bodies is

---

Weisheipl, "The Concept of Nature," in *Nature and Motion in the Middle Ages*, 1–23, at 18–21. When the soul moves the body, it is in turn moved by the body *accidentally*, because the body of which it is the form changes place. But this does not mean that the soul moves itself, for, strictly speaking, it cannot be in motion. Only corporeal, divisible things can be in motion. See *SCG* I, c. 13, n. 90 [10].

17. He professed only to describe gravitational motion with mathematical precision, not to give its cause: *Principia*, Definition 8; book I, section 11, proposition 69, scholium; book III, general scholium (trans. Andrew Motte, rev. Florian Cajori [Berkeley: University of California Press, 1934], vol. 1, 5–6, 192; vol. 2, 546–47.)

18. *In III De Caelo*, l. 7, n. 594 [9]: "For that which is undergoing motion naturally has a virtue imparted to it which is the principle of motion, *whence it is not necessary that it be moved by something else impelling it*. (Quia id quod naturaliter movetur, habet sibi inditam virtutem, quae est principium motus: unde non oportet quod ab alio impellente moveatur.)" Emphasis added. Cf. the whole discussion in n. 593–594 [8–9], in which Aquinas criticizes Averroes.

the formal cause, but not the efficient cause of their downward motion. Yet on Thomas's view such natural inanimate motion does have an efficient cause, namely whatever generated the body and made it heavy in the first place.[19] But the "generator" may in some cases no longer exist when the heavy body is falling (especially if its downward motion is impeded for a time by something holding it up; anything that removed such an impediment would be considered an accidental efficient cause of the ensuing natural motion.[20])

Weisheipl's work provides a full and accurate documentation of Aquinas's view on the issue of elemental motion, and I would direct interested readers to his excellent work.[21] But Weisheipl draws the wrong conclusion regarding the mover principle from Aquinas's account of natural inanimate motion. He holds that such motion is exempt from the mover principle, because it is not a case of "being moved" passively but only of "being in motion" intransitively. The mover principle, as he interprets it, states that everything that is being moved (*movetur* taken as passive) is being moved by *something else*.[22] However, Aquinas's commentary on Aristotle's original inductive argument for the mover principle in *Physics* VIII.4 will reveal both the grounds for Weisheipl's claim and evidence that Weisheipl is not thinking about the matter in quite the same way as Aquinas is.

As Aquinas explains there, Aristotle regards natural inanimate motion as presenting the greatest difficulty for the mover principle, because

---

19. The following text can also serve as an example of Aquinas's doctrine: "However in heavy and light bodies there is a formal principle of motion. (But a formal principle of this sort cannot be called the active potency to which this motion pertains. Rather it is understood as a passive potency. For heaviness in earth is not a principle for moving, but rather for being in motion.) For just as the other accidents are consequent upon substantial form, so also is place, and thus also 'to undergo motion to place.' However the natural form is not the mover. Rather the mover is that which generates and gives such and such a form upon which such a motion follows." (*In II Phys.*, l. 1, n. 144 [4], trans. Richard J. Blackwell, Richard J. Spath, and W. Edmund Thirlkel [South Bend, IN: Dumb Ox Books, 1995].) Translation emended. As Fr. Weisheipl shows, the text in parentheses is an interpolation, taken from Aquinas's *Commentary on the* Metaphysics (*In V Meta.*, l. 14, n. 955 [2]). See "The Concept of Nature," fn. 78. But it is printed in the Leonine and Marietti editions, and if considered carefully it does not affect the meaning of the text, so I have included it. For Aquinas "active potency" generally means "a principle for causing motion *in another*," (emphasis mine) as stated in the original context of the passage interpolated into the commentary on the *Physics*. Aquinas does not intend his "formal principle" to be an active potency in this sense. See also Twetten, "Back to Nature," 216–18.

20. See, e.g., *In VIII Phys.*, l. 8, n. 1035 [7].

21. See Weisheipl, *Nature and Motion in the Middle Ages,* esp. ch. 1, 2, 4, and 5.

22. Weisheipl, "The Principle *Omne quod movetur*," 75–79, 92, 95; "The Specter of *Motor Coniunctus*," 99–101, 107.

there is no apparent mover. Yet the difficulty is solved by distinguishing between two different sorts of potency, first potency and second potency. He gives the example of someone learning a science:

> A thing is reduced from first potency to second when something active is joined to its passivity. And then this passivity, through the presence of that which is active, comes to be in this kind of act, which up to this point was in potency. For example, the learner, through the act of the teacher, is reduced from potency to act, to which act is joined another potency. Thus, a thing existing in first potency comes to be in another potency. For one who has science but who is not contemplating it is in a certain way in potency to the act of science, but not in the same way as he was before he learned. Therefore he was reduced from first potency to act—to which act is joined a second potency—through some agent, namely, a teacher. *But when one possesses the habit of science, it is not necessary for him to be reduced to second act by some agent. Rather he does this immediately by his own contemplation unless something else prevents him*, for example, business, sickness, or his will.[23]

Aquinas's position, then, is that the reduction of first potency to first act/second potency requires contact with a mover. The reduction of second potency/first act to second act, however, is spontaneous and merely requires a suitable occasion, not contact with a mover. Someone who has learned his lesson well can think about and express what he now knows without any further help from his teacher. Aquinas proceeds to apply this analysis to the case of inanimate natural motion:

> Water, therefore, is first in potency to become light, and afterwards it becomes light in act [through changing substantially into air], and then it immediately possesses its operation, unless something prevents it. But the now existing light thing is compared to place as potency to act (for the act of a light thing, as such, is to be in some determined place, namely, up). But it is prevented from being up because it is in the contrary place, namely, down. For it cannot be in two places at once.... In one way, while it is still water, it is in potency to become light. In another way, when air has already been made from water, it is still in potency to the act of the light, which is to be up, *just as one who has the habit of science but is not contemplating it is still said to be in potency.* For it happens that what is light may be prevented from being up. But if that impediment is removed, it rises immediately so that it may be up.[24]

---

23. *In VIII Phys.* l. 8, n. 1031 [3], translation emended, emphasis added.
24. *In VIII Phys.*, l. 8, n. 1033, 1035 [5, 7], emphasis added.

Weisheipl concludes that the mover principle applies only to the reduction of first potency to first act, not the reduction of second potency to second act. Hence natural inanimate motion, as a case of second potency proceeding to second act, does not fall under the mover principle at all.[25] But this is not how Aquinas sees it. First of all, he refers constantly to heavy bodies going downward, and light bodies going upward, with the word *movetur*, which Weisheipl himself says should be translated as "being moved." Secondly, Aquinas does not himself draw the conclusion that natural inanimate motion does not fall under the mover principle. Rather, he sees it as another instance in which the principle is verified:

> Next where he says "If, then, the motion …", he arrives at the conclusion principally intended in this whole chapter. He says that if it is true that everything that is moved is moved according to nature or outside of nature and by violence, then it is clear that all things which are moved by violence are moved not only by some mover but by some other extrinsic mover. And further of things which are moved according to nature, some are moved by themselves [e.g., animals], in which it is clear that they are moved by something, not, indeed, extrinsic, but intrinsic, and some are moved (*moventur*) according to nature but not by themselves, as heavy and light things. These latter are also moved by something (*ab aliquo moventur*), as was shown (because either they are moved *per se* by the generator which makes them heavy and light, or they are moved *per accidens* by that which removes what impedes or prevents their natural motion). Therefore, it is clear that whatever is in motion (*omnia quae moventur*) is moved by some mover, either intrinsic or extrinsic, which he calls "being moved by another" (*ab alio moveri*.)[26]

So natural inanimate motion is also a case of *movetur*, and hence falls under the mover principle. Something other than the body experiencing natural motion is its mover. Aquinas identifies the mover as the "generator," whatever it was that gave the body in motion its nature, from which nature such motion necessarily flows. The mover is whatever was the agent of the substantial change that brought the body into existence

---

25. Weisheipl, "The Specter of *Motor Coniunctus*," 105–8; "The Principle *Omne quod movetur*," 78, 92. There is some ambiguity in Weisheipl's presentation however. Because he so often echoes the words of Aquinas, there are times at which he speaks as if a body currently in natural free fall is moved by its generator, which is no longer in contact with it (which is my view). But in his clearest formulations Weisheipl denies that the mover principle applies to such motion, because, as he holds, it is not a case of something *quod movetur*—something that is moved—being only a case of something in motion (*in motu*).

26. *In VIII Phys.*, l. 8, n. 1036 [8]. Translation emended. Emphasis added.

in the first place. The body's nature is the formal cause of the natural motion, and the generator is its efficient cause.

> Granted that the act of a light thing is to be up, nevertheless some ask why heavy and light things are moved to their proper places. The reason for this is that they have a natural aptitude for such places. For to be light is to have an aptitude for that which is up. And the nature of the heavy is to have an aptitude for that which is down. Hence, to ask why a heavy thing is moved downward is nothing other than to ask why it is heavy. The same thing which makes it heavy also makes it to be moved downward.[27]

The Issue of Simultaneity

Aquinas's position seems clear, but it leaves his reader with a puzzle. The generator is only in contact with the body generated at the moment of generation. Once it begins its natural motion, it loses contact with the generator. In some cases, if the natural motion has been impeded for quite some time and the body is then released, the generator may not even exist any longer. How, then, can it be the mover for such motion?

For this reason, David Twetten has criticized Weisheipl's account of natural motion. He points to the fact that Aquinas, following Aristotle, believes that the causality of astronomical bodies is involved in every substantial change occurring on this planet. The "generator," then, may refer to the sun or some planet or star, which remains in permanent contact-by-power (*virtute*) with every natural substance generated on this planet. As such, the astronomical generator is the mover exerting its causality in the natural downward motion of heavy bodies and natural upward motion of light bodies. It exerts its causality while, and as long as, the body is in motion. Hence, he argues, it is right to interpret the mover principle as stating that everything *in motion* is *currently* being moved by something else currently in contact with it.[28]

Twetten supports his claim with the following argument:

> For Aquinas, to say that a potency actualizes of itself is equivalent to saying that a potency acts. But two reasons can be found in Thomas why passive potency of itself cannot act. First, that which is in potency *as in potency* does not yet exist, but what does not exist cannot act. Second, nothing acts except insofar as it is in act. Hence, if potency acts, it must be in act. But nothing is

27. *In VIII Phys.*, l. 8, n. 1034 [6], translation modified.
28. Twetten, "Back to Nature," 237–41.

simultaneously both in potency and in act. It follows, therefore, that every passive potency as such requires something distinct from it in act in order that it be reduced into act.[29]

But this is clearly opposed to Aquinas's own way of speaking in his commentary on *Physics* VIII.4. What is in second potency is in first act. Therefore, second potency has the kind of existence required to act. It is simultaneously in potency and act: second potency, and first act. It acts insofar as it is first act.

But Twetten has a textual argument as well:

Without the heavens' constant causation present to every motion, no motion can occur. Not surprisingly, therefore, the heavens also cause all natural motion since they reduce nature as an active principle from potency to act by conserving the substantial form of natural bodies. At the same time, emphasizes Aquinas in an important text [*ST* I-II, q. 109, a. 1, c.], we must avoid the impression that the form alone of such bodies, once possessed, suffices for motion to occur. Instead, no matter how perfect that form is, it cannot proceed to its act, that is, it cannot be reduced from potency to act without being moved by the first corporeal mover, as well as by the absolutely first mover. Through the causality of the heavens and, ultimately, of the first cause, therefore, Aquinas finds the principle *OQM* [i.e., the mover principle] to be fulfilled: everything being moved, including everything being naturally moved, must here and now be moved by another.[30]

The text to which Twetten refers is indeed an important one:

In corporeal things we see that for movement there is required not merely the form which is the principle of the movement or action, but there is also required the motion of the first mover. Now the first mover in the order of corporeal things is the heavenly body. *Hence no matter how perfectly fire has heat, it would not bring about alteration, except by the motion of the heavenly body.*[31]

This text seems to say that a physical body cannot move or alter another physical body without itself being moved by an astronomical ("heavenly") body, as the ocean cannot carry driftwood ashore without being moved by the moon to high tide. But Aquinas's example of fire is a case of one body actively moving another (in the sense of altering it). I have found other texts in which Aquinas makes a similar point, but in none of them has he applied the idea to the case of one physical body

---

29. Twetten, "Back to Nature," 236.

30. Twetten, "Back to Nature," 241.

31. *ST* I-II, q. 109, a. 1, c. Emphasis added.

being in natural motion to its own proper place, size, or quality.[32] In fact, in texts I discuss below in chapter 3, Aquinas asserts that if the heavenly bodies ceased rotating terrestrial bodies would undergo a spontaneous process of dissolution and the elements undergo spontaneous motion to their natural places.[33] Despite Twetten's claims, the texts in which Aquinas explicitly discusses the natural motion of the elements must stand:

> [Aristotle says in *De Caelo* I.8] that natural bodies are not borne upwards and downwards as moved by something exterior. He is to be understood as excluding an exterior mover that would move such bodies *per se* after they have been allotted their specific form. For light bodies are indeed moved up, and heavy bodies down, by the generator, insofar as it gives them the form from which such motion follows. [They are moved] by that which removes an impediment *per accidens* and not *per se*.[34]
>
> For that which is undergoing motion naturally has a virtue imparted to it which is the principle of motion, *whence it is not necessary that it be moved by something else impelling it.*[35]

32. *QDP*, q. 5, a. 8 (in regard to this text it is helpful to recall the precise meaning of active potency—see above, fn. 19); *ST* I, q. 115, a. 3.

33. See below, chapter 3, section titled "Against the Conventional Interpretation: What Happens if God Does Not Move the Universe?" (p. 89–96.) The key texts are *QDP*, q. 5, a. 5–10 and *Responsio ad XLIII Articulis*, art. 20–24.

34. *In I De Caelo* l. 18, n. 175 [1]: "... Dicens [Aristoteles] quod ... corpora naturalia non feruntur sursum et deorsum neque sicut ab alio exteriori mota. Per quod quidem intelligendum est quod removet exteriorem motorem, qui per se huiusmodi corpora moveat postquam sunt formam specificam sortita. Moventur enim levia quidem sursum, gravia autem deorsum a generante quidem, inquantum dat eis formam quam consequitur talis motus; sed a removente prohibens, per accidens et non per se." Translation mine.

35. *In III De Caelo*, l. 7, n. 594 [9]: "Quia id quod naturaliter movetur, habet sibi inditam virtutem, quae est principium motus: unde non oportet quod ab alio impellente moveatur." Emphasis added. Cf. also *In VIII Phys.*, l. 8, n. 1035 [7]: "For example, if a sphere, that is, a ball, rebounds from a wall, it is moved by the wall *per accidens* and not *per se*. It is moved *per se* by the initial thrower. For the wall did not give it any impetus toward motion, but the thrower did. It is *per accidens* because, when the ball was impeded by the wall, it did not receive a second impetus. Rather, because of the same remaining impetus it rebounded with an opposite motion. And similarly, one who destroys a column does not give to the supported weight an impetus or inclination downward. For it has this from its first generator which gave to it the form which such an inclination follows. Therefore, the generator is the *per se* mover of heavy and light things. But that which removes an obstacle is a *per accidens* mover." The immediate, proper, *per se* mover of the rebounding ball is the particular person who threw it at the wall, not a heavenly body. So too, the immediate, proper, *per se* mover of the heavy body is the particular, terrestrial generator. In neither case is the immediate *per se* mover of the object in constant contact with it. The heavenly body, that is, the "universal generator," is the heavy body's remote mover, insofar as—on Aquinas's view—a terrestrial body can only generate another body in virtue of the sun's power. But even the heavenly body, as "universal generator" (a cause of becoming) rather than as conserver (a cause of being), acted only when the heavy body was generated, not while it was in the midst of its downward motion.

There need be no mover at all currently moving by contact for such motion to occur. The motion is a natural result of such bodies' forms.

But how can it make sense to say that the mover principle applies to such motion? How can the generator be the mover, if it is not in contact with the body when it is in motion? The answer, I believe, lies in Aquinas's understanding of efficient causality, which is different from the contemporary understanding. For him, efficient causality is not conceived on the model of a push or an impulse, but rather on the model of a *responsible agent*.[36] For something to happen a certain way, it must somehow be determined that it happen that way rather than some other way, or not at all. The efficient cause is that which determines something to happen; it is that which "makes" the determination.[37] The material cause is that which is determined, and the final cause is that to which it is determined. The formal cause is itself the determination/determinateness of being a certain way. In the case of a heavy body, it is determined to move downward. Its substantial form just is the determination to possess a certain essence and set of characteristics, among which is downward motion (which is entailed by the substantial form through the mediation of the quality of heaviness, which itself is entailed by the substantial form). What gave it the determination to move downward? What *determined* it to move downward? That which made it heavy, the generator. *It* is *responsible* for the natural motion, for it made the determination.[38]

That this is Aquinas's view is evidenced both by the texts quoted above and by his account of why the rock moving downward by nature is not a case of self-motion (in the sense that animals are self-movers.) He

36. Patterson Brown makes a similar point in "Infinite Causal Regression," *The Philosophical Review* 75, no. 4 (1966): 510–25, at 524–25, reprinted in *Aquinas: A Collection of Critical Essays*, ed. Anthony Kenny (Notre Dame, IN: University of Notre Dame Press, 1976).

37. This view of efficient causation helps to explain its intrinsic connection to final causality and is in evidence in *ST* I-II, q. 6, a. 1, which should be read with I-II, q. 1, a. 2.

38. Francisco Suárez, SJ (1548–1617), slightly misunderstands Aquinas on this point. He rightly recognizes that for Aquinas no external mover impels a heavy body downwards during free fall, and that the generator, after having lost contact with the heavy body, is still the efficient cause of its motion insofar as it is responsible for the downward motion, and the substantial form of the heavy body acts as its instrument. Nevertheless Suárez understands the "natural resulting" of downward motion from the form of a heavy body as a case of efficient causality. Thus the form of the heavy body is the proximate efficient cause of its downward motion, according to him. (*Metaphysical Disputations*, 18, s. 3, n. 3–14 and s. 7, n. 1–28. A translation by Alfred J. Freddoso is available: Suarez, *On Efficient Causality* [New Haven, CT: Yale University Press, 1994.]) Yet for Aquinas the form of the heavy body is a *formal* cause, not an efficient cause, of its downward motion. (Aquinas also calls it a "formal active principle," but never an "efficient principle.") For the substantial form does not make a determination, it *is* the determination to fall.

sees Aristotle as providing four arguments for this in *Physics* VIII.4. The first is that only living things move themselves, and inanimate bodies are not living. The second and third arguments go together. The second argues that if inanimate bodies in natural motion were moving themselves, they could stop themselves as well, whereas they never stop until they reach their proper place or are impeded by something external. Animals, by contrast, can change their minds and stop before they reach their goal. The third argument is the most helpful:

> It is irrational to say that things which move themselves are moved by themselves with respect to only one motion and not a plurality of motions. *For that which moves itself does not have its motion determined by another, but determines its own motion. Sometimes it determines for itself this motion, and sometimes another. Hence, that which moves itself has the power to determine for itself either this or that motion.* Therefore, if heavy and light things move themselves, it follows that if fire has the power to be moved upward, it also has the power to be moved downward. But we never see this happen except through an extrinsic cause. Therefore they do not move themselves.[39]

The generator must have been in contact with the body undergoing natural motion at some point, so as to provide it with the determination to move in a certain way. But it need not remain in contact with it to remain the determiner, the one responsible for such natural motion. It can move by means of a form or power it imparts to the body, which form or power serves as its instrument in moving the body. Aquinas states just this in *De Potentia*, q. 3, a. 11:

> An instrument is understood to be moved by a principal agent as long as it retains the power (*virtutem*) impressed by the principal agent. For this reason an arrow is moved by the projector as long as the force (*vis*) of the impulse of the projector remains. In this way also that which is generated is moved by the generator in regard to heavy and light things as long as it retains the form given to it by the generator. Whence also semen is understood to be moved by the soul of the generator as long as the power (*virtus*) impressed by the soul remains there, although it be physically divided. *It is necessary, however, for the mover and the moved to be together* (simul) *in regard to the beginning of motion, not, however, in regard to the whole motion*, as appears in projectiles.[40]

---

39. *In VIII Phys.*, l. 7, n. 1027 [7], emphasis added.

40. *QDP*, q. 3, a. 11, ad 5, as referenced by Weisheipl, "Natural and Compulsory Movement," 31, n. 30. Translation and emphasis mine. The Latin text is as follows: "Instrumentum intelligitur moveri a principali agente, quamdiu retinet virtutem a principali agente impressam; unde sagitta tamdiu movetur a proiciente, quamdiu manet vis impulsus proicientis. Sicut etiam generatum tamdiu

The comparison to animal reproduction is helpful. There is a delay between sexual intercourse and the conception of the embryo. In the period of that delay, the male parent could be elsewhere, or even die. Yet he would still be, together with the female parent, the cause of the child animal. Indeed, in Aquinas's (biologically mistaken) view of reproduction, the semen is at work inside the body of the female parent for quite a long time (in the order of months) before a new member of the species is generated.[41] Hence such a scenario of the death of the male parent before generation must certainly have been considered by Thomas. Nevertheless, the male parent is still the cause, in his view, of the child generated, because his semen is still at work.

So too, in the case of natural inanimate motion, the generator is still at work, because the substantial form it brought into being still remains in the body generated, even if the generating body has gone out of existence (as would be the case if one torch lit another and then were extinguished while the second burned on.) But there is a difference between this and the case of an animal generated through semen: the semen is a distinct being from the child generated, but the substantial form is an intrinsic principle of the heavy or light body. Hence the semen is an instrument in the manner of an efficient cause by determining the female matter (on Aquinas's view) to the form of a new animal. The substantial form of a heavy or light body, by contrast, is an instrument in the manner of a formal cause,[42] by being itself a determination to be in a certain natural place, and hence to movement toward that place when elsewhere.[43]

---

movetur a generante in gravibus et levibus quamdiu retinet formam sibi traditam a generante; unde et semen tamdiu intelligitur moveri ab anima generantis quamdiu remanet ibi virtus impressa ab anima, licet corporaliter sit divisum. Oportet autem movens et motum esse simul quantum ad motus principium, non tamen quantum ad totum motum, ut apparet in proiectis." (Latin text for *QDP* is from *Quaestiones Disputatae*, vol. II, ed. P. Bazzi, Mannes Calcaterra, Tito S. Centi, E. Odetto, and P. M. Pession, 10th ed. [Turin: Marietti, 1965].) In the case of projectiles such as arrows, since the motion is violent, there is a mover—the air—present throughout the whole motion, but it is a secondary mover, and *the archer remains the primary mover throughout the duration of the motion*. But in the case of naturally falling bodies, the form by which (*quo*) the generator moves is not itself a mover, even a secondary one: "In purely corporeal things … their forms cannot be movers, although they can be a principle of motion, as that *by which* something is moved, as in the motion of earth heaviness is the principle *by which* it is moved. Nevertheless, it is not the mover. (In rebus pure corporalibus esse non potest, quia formae eorum non possunt esse moventes, quamvis possint esse motus principium ut quo aliquid movetur, sicut in motu terrae gravitas est principium quo movetur non tamen est motor.)" *QDV*, q. 22, a. 3, c., (Leonine 22.3.1:618). This text is referenced by Weisheipl, "The Principle *Omne quod movetur*," 91, n. 61. Translation and emphasis mine.

41. See *ST* I, q. 118.

42. *QDV*, q. 22, a. 3, c. See fn. 40 above.

43. This new understanding of the mover principle casts some doubt on the second thesis (but

The foregoing can serve as an answer to a potential objection based on Aristotle's claim, endorsed by Aquinas, that causes in act are together/simultaneous (*simul*) with their effects in act.[44] This is true for two reasons: first, simply by definition the cause acts when the effect occurs because the act of moving is the same act as that of being moved, and that one act inheres in that which is moved, not in that which is doing the moving; hence it is trivially true that movers move when the mobile is in motion.[45] (Generally, however, in the case of physical movers causing

not the first) of my paper, "Aquinas on Will, Happiness, and God: The Problem of Love and Aristotle's *Liber de Bona Fortuna*," *American Catholic Philosophical Quarterly* 91, no. 1 (2017): 113–42. There, partly on the basis of the mover principle, I had argued that for Aquinas God is the first mover of the human will in an act distinct from that of causing the will's nature. But I now see that when Aquinas insists that God not only creates the will but moves it to its first will-act, this need mean no more than that God is the one who determines the will to will goodness in general, by being the one who creates the will's nature and conserves its *esse* by making it actively be the kind of thing it is. (Also, since God is the universal cause of *esse*, the will cannot produce *any* actually existing will-act unless God produces the will-act's *esse*.) However, with respect to many particular will-acts God would still be a mover in ways distinct from those of creating and conserving and concurring with the will. This would be the case certainly in all those will-acts inspired by the Holy Spirit in particular situations. Furthermore, a special act of moving on God's part would still be necessary, in principle, for anyone to love God more than himself, for two reasons. First, God must be a mover in the sense of one who removes an impediment, the impediment of a fallen human being's sinful focus on his own private good. Secondly and more importantly, God must direct the will toward Himself as the supernatural common good. The will by its nature is only directed to God as the natural common good (see *ST* I-II, q. 109, a. 3). Thirdly, despite the analysis of the mover principle in the present article, it may still be the case that the human will, even unstained by original sin, could not have loved God above self as the natural common good without God's distinct act of moving the will, because to be directed in act to the highest good requires the activity of the highest cause and is simply beyond the capacity of any created nature (see *ST* I-II, q. 109, a. 6 and cp. q. 9, a. 6. Further evidence for this position might be taken from I-II, q. 109, a. 1 and 2). In this sense and others, God moves the human will to its act, but the First Way is not concerned with this sort of extended sense of "movement."

44. Aristotle, *Physics* II.3, 195b16–21 and VII.2; Aquinas, *In II Phys.*, l. 6, n. 195 [9]; *In VII Phys.*, l. 3 and *ST* I, q. 104, a. 1. In *QDP*, q. 3, a. 11, obj. 5, Aquinas actually raises *Physics* VII.2 and its assertion of the contact between causes and effects (*simul sunt*) as an objection against his view that parents are the ones that generate offspring, since there is a time-delay between intercourse and the generation of offspring. He responds with the text quoted above, which restricts contact to the beginning of motion, using the same kind of language as he used in his commentary on *Physics* VII.2 (*In VII Phys.*, l. 3, n. 907 [11]: mover and moved are together "at least at the beginning of the motion, *saltem in principio motus*.") Not noticing this, and relying on *Physics* VII.2, Christopher Decaen interprets the "generator" that causes natural elemental motion as a heavenly body, but Aquinas's texts, as we have seen, will not bear this out. ("The Impossibility of Action at a Distance," in *Wisdom's Apprentice: Thomistic Essays in Honor of Lawrence Dewan, O.P.*, ed. Peter A. Kwasniewski, 173–200 [Washington, DC: The Catholic University of America Press, 2007], at 180–82.) But Decaen's broader point is probably correct: action at a distance is impossible, and the notion of contact must be broadened to include virtual contact. The generator, e.g., a prior fire, is in physical contact at the beginning of the generated fire's motion and in virtual contact later in the motion, where virtual contact means only that it is responsible for its motion, and has left in it the form from which such motion follows.

45. This is Aristotle's position in *Physics* III.3. See Aquinas, *In III Phys.*, l. 4, esp. n. 306–7 [10–11]:

motion also requires a new act inhering in the mover. To move a rock, for example, my hand must undergo motion. But this new act in the mover is not always simultaneous with the motion it causes, as in the example of the natural motion of an element caused by the prior act of its generator. Furthermore, such a new act in the mover is not essential to the very fact of causing motion, otherwise God could not cause motion while being eternal and entirely immovable.) Secondly, the cause is in "virtual contact" with its effect so long as its "virtue" (e.g., the substantial form left in the generated body and the semen left in the womb) remains at work in the effect. Such virtual contact may be quite thin, metaphysically speaking. If I throw a basketball at the backboard and it bounces back into the hoop, I cause it to rebound into the hoop and am in virtual contact with the ball as it reverses course. There is nothing magical, spiritual, or immaterial going on here, no "spooky action at a distance." It simply means that I am the one who determined the ball to rebound into the hoop by giving it a momentum (*impetus*).[46]

But time delay between the cause's direct contact with its patient and the realization of the effect is not possible in causes of being, only in causes of becoming—that is, movers. The reason for this disparity is that motion is something essentially extended in time as a continuum, whereas being is not.[47] If the being of a thing bears an essential relation to an efficient cause—as is the case with every being other than God, the only one whose existence is His essence—then the dependence of that being on its cause cannot be tied to any particular moment in time. But since motion is essentially temporal, its dependence on its cause can be tied to particular time, namely, the time of its beginning. Thus a cause, acting in a relatively short time, can sufficiently cause a motion toward some terminus which takes a relatively long time to be completed.

As we now see, in asserting the mover principle Aquinas certainly does not mean that everything currently in motion is currently being moved by a mover currently in contact with it. Rather, the sense of Aquinas's

---

"The act of the mover and of the moved are the same.... It is necessary that there be one act of both, namely of the mover and of the moved, for what is from the mover as from an agent cause, and what is in the moved as in a patient and recipient is the same.... For motion, insofar as it proceeds from the mover unto the mobile, is the act of the mover, and insofar as it is in the mobile from the mover, it is the act of the mobile." Translation mine.

46. See *In VIII Phys.*, l. 8, n. 1035 [7], quoted in fn. 35 above.

47. See *In VIII Phys.*, l. 21, n. 1155. The difference between causes of being and becoming will be discussed at greater length in chapter 2, p. 63–71 below.

mover principle is that for everything in motion, there is something else *responsible* for that motion. That something else may have acted in the past, with its effect still lingering in the present.

The Mover Principle and the Hypothesis
of a Beginningless Universe

But such an interpretation of the principle is in danger of assimilating Aquinas's argument to William Lane Craig's once again. If the mover principle merely states that for every motion there was some cause *in the past*, the regress of movers would proceed backward in time, and blocking the infinite regress would lead to the conclusion of a first moment in time for the universe's motion, would it not? But that cannot be Aquinas's argument, as he is quite clear about the impossibility of demonstrating that the world had a beginning in time.[48]

The solution to this difficulty lies in Aquinas's oft-noted distinction between essentially ordered and accidentally ordered causes. A full discussion of this distinction will be postponed until the next chapter on infinite regress, but in this context the following can suffice. For every motion there must be a proximate cause, *which may be exercising its causality now or have exercised it in the past*. If that proximate mover-cause is itself not an unmoved mover, it too will have a cause. But the proximate mover-cause can have a cause in two different senses. Either the fact that it has such a prior cause is an essential factor in its ability to cause the ultimate effect, or it is only accidentally related. For example, the fact that a father himself has a forefather is totally irrelevant to his ability to sire a son. Otherwise, Adam would have been unable to sire a son, since he had no forefather. Hence the series of parents, grandparents, great-grandparents, and so on, is an accidentally ordered series of causes. But when a hand moves a stick that moves a pebble, the stick cannot move the pebble in that way except insofar as it is itself being moved by the hand. Hence this is an essentially ordered series of causes.[49]

---

48. For example, *ST* I, q. 46, a. 2.

49. See *ST* I, q. 46, a. 2, ad 7. Aquinas's distinction between essentially ordered and accidentally ordered series of causes is often elaborated in terms of the simultaneity or non-simultaneity of the causes. But this is only a fallible sign of the type of order, not an essential part of the distinction between the types. (Michael Augros makes this same point: "Ten Objections to the *Prima Via*," 86–89 and 92–93, and *Aquinas on Theology and God's Existence*, 288–90.) Those who think that simultaneity is a necessary condition for a series of causes to be essentially ordered are actually in

Now it may happen that the proximate cause of some effect exercised its causality in the past, but the prior essential cause exercised its causality simultaneously with the proximate cause's causality. For example, Aquinas holds that when fire (which he regards as an elemental body) generates more fire out of a wick—as when one torch ignites another—the cause of the later fire's upward motion is the former fire, which in turn could only generate the later fire because it was being influenced concurrently by a "heavenly body," perhaps the sun or the stars.[50] The series of essentially ordered causes cannot be infinite, but consistent with such a finite series of essentially ordered causes is an infinite series of accidentally ordered causes extending backward in time, according to Aquinas.[51] Hence my interpretation of the mover principle—that everything in motion is moved by something else that either currently exercises causality or did in the past—need not lead to an argument that establishes a first in time, but only a first among essentially ordered causes.

THOMAS'S ARGUMENT FOR THE MOVER PRINCIPLE
IN THE *SUMMA THEOLOGIAE'S* FIRST WAY

What has been uncovered so far—by taking seriously the inductive argument for the mover principle in *SCG* and its context in Thomistic physical theory—provides a distinct advantage when analyzing the proof of the mover principle in *ST*'s First Way. (This proof corresponds to the third proof of the mover principle in G1.) Aquinas argues in *ST* that what is in motion is as such in potency, and it can only be moved by what is in act. But the same thing cannot be both in potency and in act in the relevant respects at the same time. Hence nothing can reduce itself from potency to act, that is, move itself. It should by now be clear that this argument envisions the reduction of first potency to first act by an external agent already in act, which in turn predetermines the reduction of second potency to second act, which occurs spontaneously. It does not claim that every reduction of potency to act requires a simultaneous, conjoined mover. Aquinas's argument is, then, more modest than it at first sight seemed.

------

agreement with Scotus (*De Primo Principio*, 3.11), not Aquinas. This point will be discussed at length in chapter 2, p. 60–71 below.

50. See for example *QDP*, q. 5, a. 8 and *ST* I-II, q. 109, a. 1, c., which was quoted and discussed above in this chapter, p. 31–33 "The Issue of Simultaneity." See also *ST* I, q. 115, a. 3, ad. 2.

51. *ST* I, q. 46, a. 2, ad 7.

Aquinas's argument in *ST* for the mover principle is commonly objected to on the basis of clear and manifest counterexamples. Aquinas
says that the mover must be in act with respect to the potency it actualizes. But if I throw a rock into a pond, I need not actually be in the
pond myself. Hydrogen and oxygen can be chemically combined to form
water, without water itself being present before the reaction. Or, as Anthony Kenny famously objects, "The principle that only what is actually
F will make something else become F does not seem universally true: a
kingmaker need not himself be king, and it is not dead men who commit
murders."[52]

The common and valid response to this objection is that Aquinas does
not in fact mean that, to reduce some potency to act, an efficient cause
must actually ("formally") have the same characteristic that it causes. The
example Aquinas uses in *ST*'s First Way—the example of something hot
in act heating something hot in potency—does give that impression. But
Aquinas certainly did not believe that someone who makes a soup is a
soup in ("formal") actuality. Aquinas distinguishes just two questions
later between univocal and equivocal causes, that is, between causes that
produce effects the same in kind with themselves, and those that produce
effects bearing some likeness to themselves but not of the same kind.[53]
An equivocal cause must have the act that it causes in a higher way than it
exists in the effect; otherwise it could not bring about that effect. (This is
sometimes referred to as possessing the act *virtually*, or in power, whereas
the univocal cause possesses the act *formally*.)[54] The soup maker possesses

---

52. Anthony Kenny, *The Five Ways*, 21.

53. *ST* I, q. 4, a. 2 and 3.

54. Among those who respond to the objection this way, see John Wippel, *The Metaphysical
Thought of Thomas Aquinas*, 420–21, fn. 59, & 447; Scott MacDonald, "Aquinas's Parasitic Cos-
mological Argument," 133–35; Timothy Pawl, "The Five Ways," 117–18. Edward Feser thinks that
Aquinas is likely only making a much weaker claim in the First Way: that whatever moves must be in
act, period. It need not have the actuality it brings about, either formally or virtually. Aquinas's point,
Feser thinks, is simply that what is potential does not exist and cannot produce an effect (*Aquinas:
A Beginner's Guide* [Oxford: Oneworld Publications, 2009], 68.) (The same claim is made by David
Oderberg, "'Whatever is Changing is Being Changed by Something Else': A Reappraisal of Premise
One of the First Way," in *Mind, Method, and Morality: Essays in Honour of Anthony Kenny*, ed. John
Cottingham and Peter Hacker, 140–64 [Oxford: Oxford University Press, 2010], at 160–62. Oderberg attributes the point to William Lane Craig and Christopher Martin.) But this certainly cannot
be Aquinas's point. Otherwise, his claim that a thing cannot be both in potency and act in the same
respect at the same time would be out of place. Anything in potency is also in act in some other way,
otherwise it would not exist at all and could not be moved or in motion. Unless a mover needed to
be in act *with respect to the effect it produces*, there would not even be a *prima facie* reason to rule out
the possibility of a thing in potency having the actuality needed to produce the effect to which it is
in potency, i.e., its being able to move itself.

the actuality of being a soup mentally, which is a higher way of having that actuality than physically being a soup. It is better to know soup than to be soup.[55]

This response, however, raises its own objection, one that dates back (at least) to John Duns Scotus, in the generations immediately following Aquinas,[56] and which is echoed in the contemporary literature.[57] If the cause need only virtually possess the characteristic to be effected, and not formally possess it, then why is the possession of the relevant actuality incompatible with being in a state of potentiality at the same time? Could not the same thing simultaneously be in a state of potency to F, not be F formally, and yet be virtually F? Why would the virtual possession of F be incompatible with being potentially F? Something that is virtually F is not F, but has the actuality of F in a higher way, just as the sun is not a maggot but—according to Aquinas—can generate maggots from putrefying matter, since it possesses the actuality of maggot-ness in a higher way than maggots do.[58] If what is virtually F need not be actually F, there seems to be no reason why it could not also be potentially F. And thus it seems possible for a thing to reduce itself from potency to act, that is, move itself, as an equivocal cause.

But Scotus's counter-objection loses its force when set against the results of the above analysis of the inductive argument for the mover principle in *SCG*. Aquinas is not claiming that every reduction of potency to act involves a mover currently in contact. He is arguing that the reduction of *first* potency to *first* act requires such a mover. What possesses first act/second potency already possesses a substantial and/or accidental form upon which a certain characteristic will follow unless impeded. Such a

55. In regard to the case of the production of water from oxygen and hydrogen, Aquinas would say that substantial change involves the influence of the celestial bodies (see *ST* I, q. 115, a. 3, ad 2—and the influence of the intelligent, incorporeal movers of the celestial bodies: see *QDP*, q. 5, a. 1), which possess the substantial forms of natural bodies in a higher way than they are found in those bodies themselves. A modern Thomist could save the principle that the cause always has the actuality it effects, either formally or virtually, by arguing that all chemical reactions, if they really do lead to new substantial, and not merely accidental forms, require God's direct involvement as equivocal cause. This is a good way to save the principle but does not leave it very convincing to non-Thomists, or more particularly to nontheists, who require that God's existence first be proven by means of this principle. A principle that presumed God's existence for its plausibility would not be very helpful in a proof of God's existence. For a rather different proposal for dealing with cases like the production of water from its elements, see fn. 59 below.

56. For Scotus, see *Questions on Aristotle's* Metaphysics, q. 14, especially n. 24–31, *Ordinatio* II, d. 2, p. 2, q. 6, and *Ordinatio* I, d. 3, p. 3, q. 2, n. 422, 512–527.

57. See William Rowe, *The Cosmological Argument*, 15–16. Scott MacDonald tries to respond to a version of this objection in "Aquinas's Parasitic Cosmological Argument," fn. 29.

58. Cf. *ST* I, q. 105, a. 1, ad 1.

form is a formal cause of the second act that follows on it, not an efficient cause. (One might say that the form/first act possesses the second act virtually, but perhaps that language should be reserved for cases of efficient causality.) But if a thing lacks the first act, the form, from which a given characteristic follows as second act, it certainly cannot provide itself with either the second or the first act, for it lacks the determination (first act) to have such acts. In order to have those acts, it must be determined by something else as an efficient cause. The efficient cause must have the relevant act, the act that determines the efficient cause itself to produce such a determination in something else, its patient. Hence what is in motion from first potency to first act must be moved by something else. Thus Aquinas's reasoning appears in every way sound.[59]

But there is an important objection to my reading of the argument in the First Way: in the clearly parallel argument for the mover principle in *SCG*, Aquinas appeals to the definition of motion, and seems to conclude from it that anything in motion (thus even a heavy or a light body in natural motion) must be in the sort of potency that would require its subject to be actualized by an external mover:

59. There is still the objection that when hydrogen and oxygen react to form water, the causes do not seem to possess the actuality of their effect either formally or virtually. The following response can be given: Certainly the reactants, together with environmental conditions, possess the determination to produce the effect that follows, and so in that minimal sense they are in act with respect to the result. But I think we can do better. Whenever water is produced intentionally in the laboratory it exists intentionally in the mind of the human bringing it into existence. But what about when it is produced in nature? It is a law of chemistry that reactions that reduce entropy, creating a state of more ordered energy, do not occur spontaneously. Only if energy is added to the system by an external agent can such a reaction proceed (as in the important case of photosynthesis, an endothermic reaction that produces higher-order molecules out of lower-order ones by means of the relatively low entropy energy coming from the sun in the form of light.) Reactions are only spontaneous if they involve a decrease in free energy, i.e., ΔG is negative. $\Delta G = \Delta H - T\Delta S$, where ΔH is the change in enthalpy—negative in exothermic or heat releasing reactions, positive in endothermic or heat absorbing reactions—and T is the absolute temperature—always positive—and ΔS is the change of entropy in the chemicals involved in the reaction. Thus spontaneous reactions either lead to lower-order products (ΔS is positive) or produce enough high entropy heat to more than offset the decrease in entropy resulting from the production of higher-order products ($\Delta H/T$—which corresponds to the entropy given to the environment by the chemicals in the form of heat—must be more negative than ΔS is.) In the latter case—which includes the formation of water from its elements—this could be conceived as some of the chemicals' internal energy (U) being used to form new bonds—lowering internal entropy—and then being released in the form of entropic heat. ($H = U + PV$, so negative enthalpy change—ΔH—correlates to a decrease in internal energy. P is pressure, V is volume. Regarding the science referenced in this explanation, see Darrell D. Ebbing, *General Chemistry*, 5th ed., [Boston: Houghton Mifflin, 1996], ch. 6, 9, and 18, esp. 232–8, 374–6, 748–53, 755–61, and 771–3.) Furthermore, in many cases, such as that of the formation of water at normal temperatures, an activation energy such as a spark is needed to get even a spontaneous reaction (in the chemist's sense) going. Thus there is always more energy in the cause than in the effect, even in natural chemical reactions.

In the *third way*, Aristotle proves the proposition [that everything in motion is moved by another] as follows. The same thing cannot be at once in act and in potency with respect to the same thing. But everything that is in motion (*movetur*) is, as such, in potency. For motion is *the act of something that is in potency inasmuch as it is in potency*. That which moves, however, is as such in act, for nothing acts except according as it is in act. Therefore, with respect to the same motion, nothing is both mover and moved. Thus, nothing moves itself.[60]

This argument, as well as the proof of the mover principle in *ST*'s First Way, has as its source Aristotle's *Physics* VIII.5. The definition of motion, however, is from *Physics* III.1. How is it to be reconciled with Aquinas's account of the inductive argument in his commentary on *Physics* VIII.4? To claim that the downward fall of heavy bodies or the upward rise of light bodies were not actually instances of motion would be to ignore plain reality for the sake of philosophical system. But if such motion is truly motion, by definition the body is in potency, and seemingly—according to this text from *SCG*—in the kind of potency that is incompatible with the simultaneous possession of the relevant act or form that could reduce that potency to act. In that case it would need continuous contact with an external mover.

The solution to this difficulty lies in the fact that Aquinas conceives of the natural motion of inanimate bodies as just the completion of the process of their generation.

> For just as the other accidents are consequent upon substantial form, so also is place, and thus also "to undergo motion to place." However the natural form is not the mover. Rather the mover is that which generates and gives such and such a form upon which such a motion follows.[61]

Just as a first fire generates a second fire (e.g., one torch lights another), so also the first fire makes the second one be hot, and of a certain color, and so on. But, says Aquinas, the first fire also makes the second fire be in a certain place, namely high up, which place is just a natural consequence of the second fire being fire. But since the second fire cannot be in two places at once, the actuality of being in the high up place is delayed. What follows immediately is *motion* to the high up place, as long as nothing impedes. But once the high up place is reached, there is no further motion, rather, the fire rests in the upward place.

---

60. *SCG* I, c. 13, n. 89 [9]. Translation emended.
61. *In II Phys.*, l. 1, n. 144 [4]. Translation emended. On this text, see above, fn. 19.

In fact, Aquinas argues in *De Potentia*, q. 5, a. 5, that motion, *in and of itself*, can never be a natural consequence of a material form. Only a certain place, quality, or size can be a natural consequence of such a form. *If* the body does not have its natural place, quality, or size, it will undergo motion toward them. If it does have them, it will remain at rest. Hence continuing cyclical motions such as the motions of the heavenly bodies require an external cause to sustain them, unlike the natural motions we have been considering.[62] This will become important in another context in a future chapter, but for now, it explains why *all motion, just as such, essentially involves a potency requiring the influence of an external mover for its reduction to act*. Nothing possesses essentially the determination to motion; everything is determined to motion by another. The text is worth quoting at length:

> The heavenly movement is not natural to the heavenly body in the same way as the elemental body's movement is natural to the elemental body. The latter movement has in the thing movable its principle not only material and receptive but also formal and active: because that movement follows upon the form of the elemental body, even as other natural properties result from essential principles: wherefore in these things the generator is said to be the mover inasmuch as it gives the form from which results the movement. But this does not apply to a heavenly body. Because as nature ever tends to one definite effect through not being indifferent to many, it is impossible that any nature tend to movement as such, since in every movement there is a certain absence of uniformity, inasmuch as the thing in motion passes from one mode of being to another, and uniformity in the thing in motion is contrary to the definition of movement. In consequence nature never inclines to movement for the sake of movement, but for the sake of some definite result to be obtained by movement: thus a heavy body is inclined by nature to rest in the centre, wherefore it tends to a downward motion, for the reason that by such a movement it will reach that place. On the other hand the heaven by its movement does not reach a "whereabouts" to which it is inclined by nature, because every "whereabouts" is the beginning and end of [its] movement: so that its natural movement cannot result, so to say, from a tendency of a natural inherent power, in the same way as the natural movement of fire has an upward tendency. Now circular movement is said to be natural to the

---

62. One might think that this claim is outdated, but it is actually a point of contact between Aquinas's physical theory and modern science. Everyone agrees that perpetual motion machines are impossible. Continuing cyclical operations require an energy source, such as fuel. Without an external energy source, every system progresses towards a state of equilibrium. This idea will be explored at greater length in a later chapter.

heaven, in so far as it has a natural aptitude for that kind of movement, so that it contains in itself the passive principle of that movement, while the active principle of this movement is some separate substance, such as God, or an intelligence, or a soul according to some. As to which of these it may be, it matters not to the question at issue. Accordingly, no argument for the permanence of this movement can be taken from the nature of a heavenly body.[63]

Since resting in its natural place, rather than motion, is the natural consequence of a body's nature,[64] in order to undergo natural motion two things are necessary for a body: a determination to a specific natural place, and a potency to being in that place due to the occupation of *another* place. No inanimate body determines for itself what its proper place will be, and no inanimate body determines itself to the actual occupation of an improper place.

Hence there could only be two reasons why a body would be *in motion* toward its natural place: first, that it was generated from another body, at rest in another place, as the second fire was generated from the heavy material out of which the torch, resting in its place, was constructed. Given that the second fire, when it is generated, is out of its place, it undergoes motion toward its natural place. Hence its natural motion is a direct consequence of its *generation*, rather than of its mere existence as a body of light nature. Hence it can only be in (natural) motion because it *was* in a state of first potency such that it could be reduced to a state of first act (a state of having the substantial form of fire) by something already in act. Hence, necessarily, there is a mover, namely, the generator. This mover, although it acts in the past, nevertheless terminates an *essentially ordered* series of causes, rather than an accidentally ordered series. This is because the body in motion, despite having in its nature a formal principle of such motion, does not have what is needed to account for the fact that it is in motion. For that, its prior generation out of place,

---

63. Aquinas, *On the Power of God* (*Quaestiones Disputatae de Potentia Dei*), trans. English Dominican Fathers (Eugene, OR: Wipf and Stock, 2004), q. 5, a. 5, c. Translation emended. Here Aquinas uses the term "active principle" differently than in his commentary on the *Metaphysics* and in the interpolated passage in his commentary on the *Physics*. There by active potency he meant a principle of causing change *in another*. The substantial form of a heavy body, and the active quality of heaviness that flows from it, are not principles of change or motion in other bodies, but active principles of motion in the body in which they inhere. See fn. 19 above.

64. In this regard Aquinas's position is still in tension with the modern principle of inertia. I address this below in chapter 6. The present chapter takes a first, crucial step towards reconciling Aquinas's natural philosophy with inertia by showing that it is not impossible for motion to occur without anything impelling.

and hence its generator, are necessary—and perhaps further factors still.

The second reason that such a body could be in natural motion to its proper place is that it is moved out of its place by some other agent and then allowed to return to its natural place on its own, as one might dig up a clod of dirt, fling it upward, and watch it fall back down. In this case the one throwing the clod is responsible for its downward motion, and hence is a mover.[65] But the generator would still also be a mover. For the clod would not fall back down upon being flung upward unless it were of a heavy nature; a light body flung upward would continue to rise. Since it is the generator that is responsible for the body having a heavy nature, it determines it to move downward. Both movers, however, the generator and the one flinging, act, each in turn, upon something in first potency: the generator acts upon a body not having the substantial form, and the one flinging acts upon a body not in first act with respect to an upward place (since it is not a light body.) Hence motion is always associated with the reduction of first potency to act—even if some motions are in and of themselves the reduction of second potency to act—and so every motion requires a mover separate from that which is moved.

The third argument for the mover principle in G1 then, is itself perfectly consistent with the interpretation of the mover principle that I have advanced. Everything *in motion* is moved by something else, but not always by something else in contact with it throughout the entirety of its motion. Rather, for everything in motion there is something responsible for its motion, whether the mover is currently acting, or acted in the past. Only so understood can the argument Aquinas presents be defended. And when so understood, it seems absolutely convincing.

---

65. Brian Carl has asked me perceptively in conversation whether the one flinging the clod is a *per se* or *per accidens* mover for the ensuing downward motion. The answer is that he is a *per accidens* mover, similar to the way in which, as Aquinas says, a wall is a *per accidens* mover of a ball rebounding off it, since the *impetus* towards motion did not come from the wall: *In VIII Phys.*, l. 8, n. 1035 [7]. For the text see fn. 35 above.

Chapter 2

The Impossibility of Infinite Regress

INTRODUCTION

The second premise in Aquinas's First Way is that an infinite regress of moved movers is impossible. This is a case of the more general proposition that an infinite regress of causes is impossible.[1] This principle, operative in Aquinas's first three ways and in cosmological arguments in general, has been the subject of intense debate in the modern and contemporary periods. Nevertheless, unlike the mover principle, it has continued to have many mainstream defenders. Furthermore, Thomistic scholars have generally done a good job explicating Aquinas's argument for it and his key distinction between "essentially ordered" and "accidentally ordered" causal series. I can therefore build on their work.

But my project requires advancing beyond other scholars in two important respects. First, Aquinas is usually regarded as adhering strictly to a condition of *simultaneity* for the causes in an essentially ordered series, although most scholars acknowledge that this condition plays little if any role in Aquinas's *argument* against infinite regress. I will show that although simultaneous causality is still the paradigm for Aquinas as it was for his predecessors, he is open to cases in which the causes in an

---

1. Aquinas argues against an infinite regress of any kind of efficient causes in his Second Way. The argument is basically the same as that given in the First Way for the more restricted version of the principle. Aquinas holds, in fact, that an infinite regress is impossible in *any* type of causality, efficient, final, formal, or material. See *In II Meta.*, l. 3–4.

essentially ordered series exercise their causality *successively*, rather than simultaneously.

Secondly, Aquinas's proofs for God's existence require him to defend two separate theses regarding causal regress, utilizing two very different types of argument. The first thesis is that an infinite regress of essentially ordered causes is impossible. Most Thomistic scholars have been entirely accurate in their understanding of Aquinas's argument for this thesis, and it alone appears in the First Way itself. The second thesis is that an infinite regress of accidentally ordered causes, although possible in principle, would have to depend for its continuance upon an essential cause or essentially ordered series of causes outside the accidental series. To defend this thesis Aquinas uses a version of what has been called the "composition" or "lumping" argument against infinite regress. This argument shows up in other versions of Aquinas's motion proof, particularly in G2. As I will argue in the following chapters, if the First Way is to succeed in establishing the existence of a supermundane mover or transcendent God, it must be extended with just such an argument, and so I will treat it here along with the first type of argument.

This chapter will be divided into five sections. First, I must explain Aquinas's main argument, presenting the distinction between essentially ordered and accidentally ordered causal series. A proper understanding of this distinction is the key to understanding Aquinas's arguments against infinite regress and his proofs for God's existence. Second, I must defend Aquinas's principle from objections raised against it by prominent opponents to cosmological arguments. Third, I must show that the causes in an essentially ordered series need not always exercise their causality simultaneously. This point follows from a proper understanding of essentially ordered series and is of the highest importance, as it will enable me in later chapters to apply Aquinas's argument to the natural world as it is now understood in the light of modern science. Fourth, I will consider and reject the claim some have made that Aquinas's argument depends on the impossibility of an actual infinite. Fifth and finally, I will consider Aquinas's argument for the dependence of infinite accidentally ordered series upon finite essentially ordered series.

In the course of this chapter, I will respond to the objection raised by Anthony Kenny and C. J. F. Williams, who argue that Aquinas begs the question by assuming that there must be a first mover.[2] I will clarify

---

2. C. J. F. Williams, "*Hic autem*"; Anthony Kenny, *The Five Ways*, 25–27 and 44.

what Aquinas means by the phrases "first mover" and "second mover" as used in his argument. I will then respond to Antony Flew, who objects to cosmological arguments that base themselves on the impossibility of infinite regress, for he claims that every explanation must always end with some "brute fact" or other and that there is no more reason to take God's existence as a brute fact than to take the forces of nature as brute facts. As I will argue, this objection is not to the point, since the argument against infinite regress is not the whole proof, but merely one step in it.

I will also consider the objection made by David Hume and Paul Edwards, who argue that in an infinite regress each and every item is adequately explained by the cause before it, and that the whole series is not a further item needing a cause in addition to its members.[3] In responding to this objection I will clarify that Aquinas's argument against infinite regress of essentially ordered causes, unlike that of Avicenna, Scotus, Clarke, or Leibniz, is not a composition or "lumping" argument. He is not "treating the world as a great big object" and arguing that it needs a cause.[4] Rather, Aquinas's point—a sound one—is that not even one individual thing is explained if it has no first cause in the sense of a cause at the head of an essentially ordered series. Hence Edwards's objection to Aquinas's argument in the First Way is not to the point.

However, the Hume-Edwards argument *is* relevant when it comes to Aquinas's second thesis about infinite regress (that an infinite accidentally ordered causal series would have to be sustained by an enduring, finite, essentially ordered causal series). Aquinas's argument for this thesis is a composition argument. But, as I will show, Aquinas has a direct and convincing response to the Hume-Edwards objection and succeeds in establishing his thesis. When a series of causes—even though its members be accidentally ordered to each other—continues forever, this cannot be by chance. And what is not by chance requires its own cause. Hence the perpetuity itself of the infinite accidental series *is* a separate item requiring its own explanation, distinct from that of each of the members of the series.

3. David Hume, *Dialogues concerning Natural Religion*, part IX; Paul Edwards, "The Cosmological Argument," in *The Rationalist Annual*, ed. Hector Hawton (London: Pemberton, 1959). This paper has been frequently anthologized, for example, in Brian Davies, OP, ed., *Philosophy of Religion: A Guide and Anthology*, 202–212 (Oxford: Oxford University Press, 2000). I will quote from Donald R. Burrill, ed., *The Cosmological Arguments: A Spectrum of Opinion*, 101–23 (Garden City, NY: Anchor Books, 1967) because it contains the complete article. Antony Flew also repeats the same objection: *God and Philosophy* (New York: Harcourt, Brace & World, 1966), 89–90.

4. P. T. Geach, "Aquinas," in G. E. M. Anscombe and P. T. Geach, *Three Philosophers*, 65–125 (Oxford: Basil Blackwell, 1967), 112. See also C. F. J. Martin, *Thomas Aquinas: God and Explanations* (Edinburgh: Edinburgh University Press, 1997), 141–43.

CLARIFYING THE ARGUMENT

In his first motion proof in the *Summa contra Gentiles*, Aquinas gives three arguments against an infinite regress of movers. The first is taken from Aristotle's *Physics* VII.1 and, like the argument for the mover principle also found there, is difficult and seems less promising. Although it would be good to analyze and evaluate Aquinas's presentation of this argument, I am not going to do that here. I will turn, rather, to Aquinas's other two arguments, which correspond closely to the argument given in the *Summa Theologiae*'s First Way. Aquinas, in fact, states a preference for these later two arguments, for he says that they constitute "a more certain way"[5] of proving the impossibility of an infinite regress than the first argument. Since the text of the First Way in *ST* has already been given at the beginning of chapter 1, the later arguments as found in *SCG* are presented here:

> The *second argument* … is the following. In an ordered series of movers and things moved (this is a series in which one is moved by another according to an order), it is necessarily the fact that, when the first mover is removed or ceases to move, no other mover will move or be moved. For the first mover

---

5. *In VIII Phys.*, l. 9, n. 1040 [4]. The first argument against infinite regress, that based on *Physics* VII.1, argues that in an infinite series of moved movers all movers would move at the same time, while the final mobile was in motion. When the final mobile undergoes motion over a finite distance in a finite time, all the infinite movers would collectively traverse an infinite distance. But an infinite motion cannot occur in a finite time. This is because a part of that motion would have to occur in each half of the finite time. If a part of the motion were infinite, then it would equal the whole motion, but a part cannot equal its whole. If each part were finite, they could not add up to an infinite motion. (See *SCG* I, c. 13, n. 92–93 [12–13] and *In VII Phys.*, l. 2 and *In VI Phys.*, l. 9, esp. n. 845 [5].) There are many drawbacks to this argument. It seems to be restricted in scope to local motion only and requires the contingent and counterfactual assumption that all the infinite movers make up parts of a single body (*In VII Phys.*, l. 2, n. 893–96 [3–6]). Furthermore, it requires that all the infinite movers be "together (*simul*)." Aristotle proceeds to argue for this premise in the succeeding chapters and Aquinas endorses it. But Aquinas qualifies it in the case of "pushing off" (see *Physics* VII.2) when he says that "it is necessary that the pusher be in contact with (*simul cum*) that which is pushed *at least in the beginning of the motion (saltem in principio motus)*, when the pusher moves that which is pushed away from itself or from another" (*In VII Phys.*, l. 3, n. 907 [11], emphasis added). This raises the possibility of something like a domino effect in which not all the movers act ("push off") at the same time and are never all in contact with one another, and so perhaps the argument in question needs to be restricted to cases of pulling and "pushing on" rather than "pushing off." Furthermore, the argument depends upon the premise that, of two infinites, one cannot be smaller than and a part of the other. Finally, even granting all this, the argument seems open to the objection that each previous mover in the series could be smaller than the succeeding one, such that they asymptotically approach a finite limit in their aggregate size. If that were the case, the infinite number of movers would not undergo a collectively infinite movement in a finite time. For all these reasons, I put this argument aside. I am not convinced that it cannot be made to work, but neither am I convinced that it can.

is the cause of motion for all the others. But, if there are movers and things moved following an order to infinity, there will be no first mover, but all would be as intermediate movers. Therefore, none of the others will be able to be moved, and thus nothing in the world will be moved.

The *third* proof comes to the same conclusion, except that, by beginning with the superior, it has a reversed order. It is as follows. That which moves as an instrumental cause cannot move unless there be a principal moving cause. But, if we proceed to infinity among movers and things moved, all movers will be as instrumental causes, because they will be moved movers and there will be nothing as a principal mover. Therefore, nothing will be moved.[6]

These two arguments are really the same, as Aquinas states more clearly in his *Commentary on Aristotle's* Physics.[7] But what Aquinas here calls the second argument corresponds most closely to the formulation used in the First Way. The third is helpful mainly because of its use of the notions of "instrumental" and "principal" causes.

To avoid seriously misunderstanding Aquinas's argument, one must note right away that he is not claiming that there could not be a series of causes stretching infinitely backward in time. Although Aquinas believes that the universe began because God reveals this and His Church teaches it, he does not think it possible to prove this on the basis of reason.[8] So not all kinds of infinite regress are impossible, only some. In an oft-quoted and important passage, Aquinas makes the following distinction between causal series:

> In efficient causes it is impossible to proceed to infinity *per se*—thus, there cannot be an infinite number of causes that are *per se* required for a certain effect; for instance, that a stone be moved by a stick, the stick by the hand, and so on to infinity. But it is not impossible to proceed to infinity accidentally as regards efficient causes; for instance, if all the causes thus infinitely multiplied should have the order of only one cause, their multiplication being accidental, as an artificer acts by means of many hammers accidentally, because one after the other may be broken. It is accidental, therefore, that

---

6. Aquinas, *SCG* I, c. 13, n. 94–95 [14–15].

7. *In VIII Phys.*, l. 9, n. 1041 [5]. He also makes it more clear there how the second argument has a "reversed order." The second argument "is the same argument as the preceding one as regards the force of the inference, differing, however, in the order of proceeding. He repeats it, however, for greater clarity.... Above he premised that everything in motion is moved by another, and that that by which it is moved moves either because of itself or because of something else prior moving it. This was to proceed by ascending. Here, however, conversely, he proceeds by descending, saying that every mover moves something and moves with something, either with itself or with another inferior mover." Translation mine.

8. *ST* I, q. 46, a. 2.

one particular hammer acts after the action of another; and likewise *it is accidental to this particular man as generator to be generated by another man; for he generates as a man, and not as the son of another man.* For all men generating hold one grade in efficient causes—viz. the grade of a particular generator. Hence it is not impossible for a man to be generated by man to infinity; but such a thing would be impossible if the generation of this man depended upon this man, and on an elementary body, and on the sun, and so on to infinity.[9]

The emphasized clause provides the reason why accidentally ordered series can regress to infinity while essentially ordered series cannot, and it is the primary distinguishing characteristic between these two types of series. When a father sires a son, the fact that he is able to do so is not dependent on the fact that he had a forefather. He can sire a son because he is a man, not because he is a son. Otherwise, the first man Adam could not have sired any sons, since he had no father. While it is true that a presently living father would not have existed if his forefather had not sired him, the causal activity of his forefather does not cause his causal activity. Hence the causal series constituted by parental lineage is accidentally ordered.[10] A hammer, in contrast, cannot produce a plowshare except insofar as it is put to work by a blacksmith. Perhaps by itself it could change something's shape—say, by falling on and denting another object—but it does not have within itself the ability to produce plowshares or other tools. Hence the series constituted by the blacksmith, the hammer, and the plowshare is an essentially ordered one.

Due to this difference between the types of series, the causality in essentially ordered series is transitive, but not in accidentally ordered series. The grandfather does not sire the grandchild, but the smith does shape

---

9. *Ibid.*, ad 7. Emphasis added. Scott MacDonald ("Aquinas's Parasitic Cosmological Argument," 139–140) misinterprets Aquinas's reference to many causes having "the order of only one cause (*non teneant ordinem nisi unius causae*)." MacDonald takes this to mean that each cause is only the cause of one thing, namely the immediately following effect, rather than transitively causing more remote effects. That reading would require Aquinas to have written something like *non teneant ordinem nisi* ad unam causam or even *ad unum effectum*. Aquinas refers here, rather, to cases in which many causes successively fulfill one role without there being any intrinsic need for more than one cause to fulfill that role. In his example, many hammers are used, not because the job itself requires many, but because several happen to break. (Aquinas does not say an infinite number of hammers are used because he is simply trying to illustrate what it means for causes to be accidentally ordered, not what it would mean for an accidentally ordered series to be infinite.) But MacDonald's point is correct anyways. The causality in essentially ordered series is transitive and in accidentally ordered series it is not. MacDonald's overall defense of Aquinas's argument is quite good in fact.

10. In *De Substantiis Separatis*, c. 15, Aquinas explicitly uses the language of *causing to cause*, or *not causing to cause*, to distinguish between the two types of causal series.

the plowshare, even if he never directly touches it during its fabrication.[11]

Given this understanding of essentially ordered series, Aquinas's argument is undeniably cogent. In essentially ordered series, all caused causes fail to explain their effect. This is because they do not have within themselves the ability to produce the effect; rather, they can only do so insofar as they are caused to cause it. The caused causes have the status of instruments, rather than that of principals. To explain the ultimate effect, some uncaused or principal cause is needed. To see this, a classic example will help: If a caboose is in motion, something must certainly be moving it. Perhaps the caboose is coupled to a boxcar that is pulling it. But the boxcar can only pull the caboose because the boxcar is itself in motion, and it can only be in motion insofar as it is being moved by something else. In other words, a boxcar cannot account for the motion of the caboose because a boxcar is only a moved mover. The same would be true of two boxcars, or three, or ten million, or even an infinite number of them coupled together. Boxcars are only instrumental movers, and they can never by themselves account for the motion of even one thing—the caboose—no matter how many of them there are. Boxcars cannot move anything unless they are themselves moved by an engine. An engine, on the other hand, is itself the kind of thing that *can* account for the motion of other things. It is a principal mover.[12]

The case is otherwise with accidentally ordered series. Consider successive generations of sheep; they constitute an accidentally ordered series of causes, each generation being brought into existence by the preceding one. According to Aquinas, it is possible to regress backward infinitely in the series of sheep generations. Why? Because each sheep in the series would be accounted for by its immediate parents, who in that respect would not be caused causes, but rather uncaused causes. For a single pair of parent sheep constitute the kind of thing that is itself capable of generating a lamb.[13] In terms of essentially ordered causes the regress stops

11. Aquinas uses this property of transitivity to characterize essentially ordered causal series in his commentary on the *Book of Causes*, lectio 1.

12. Two other classic examples are also helpful: no matter how long the paintbrush's handle, even if it were infinitely long, it could paint nothing without an artist to wield it. Again, no matter how many links there are in a chain, it could hold nothing up, unless it were itself hung on an immovable point. These illustrations appear, for example, in Mackie, *The Miracle of Theism*, 90 and Fr. Reginald Garrigou-Lagrange, OP, *God: His Existence and His Nature*, trans. Dom Bede Rose, OSB, vol. I (St. Louis: Herder, 1945), 265.

13. Unless, that is, some consideration reveals a causal deficiency in the parents and with it the need for some other causal factor to be at work in the generation of offspring. But this is by no means

there; the parent sheep themselves have parents who have caused them, but that is irrelevant to their present ability to produce a lamb. Hence, if the series of generations of sheep were infinite, every sheep in the series would be accounted for by the immediately prior sheep, and no sheep would be without adequate explanation. That would not, according to Aquinas, be an impossible situation. It would be like an infinite series of engines, rather than an infinite series of boxcars. What is impossible is for any one of the items in an accidentally ordered series not to have an adequate explanation by means of a finite essentially ordered series of causes, which in this case might be quite short: each sheep could be explained adequately by its immediate parents, for all we have said so far. Aquinas has another, rather different argument to show that an infinite accidentally ordered series would itself have to depend on another cause outside the series (and thus not on the parent sheep), but that argument is not at question here and will be put aside until the end of this chapter.

In arguing against an infinite regress of essentially ordered causes as part of a motion proof for God's existence, Aquinas's ultimate goal is not to establish that God must exist in order to initiate motion at the beginning of the universe, but rather that God must exist in order to explain motion *now*. If the universe had no beginning, God's existence would still be required to account for the continuance of motion. But how one is supposed to arrive at this conclusion is by no means yet clear. Aquinas's immediate goal is much more modest: there cannot be an infinite regress of moved movers; one must arrive at a first mover that is itself capable of causing and accounting for the motion at hand. Since whatever is in motion is moved by another, a first mover must not need to be in motion in order to cause motion. It would in that respect be an unmoved mover, even if it were in motion at other times and in other respects irrelevant to its ability to cause the motion in question.

RESPONDING TO OBJECTIONS

Aquinas's argument against infinite regress has, of course, had its critics. But a proper understanding of essentially ordered causal series, as opposed to accidentally ordered series, allows one to disarm the standard

---

assumed in the present context. Rather, I am for now presuming that no such deficiency exists. Aquinas, in fact, thinks that the sun and other heavenly bodies must be at work in the generation of sheep offspring, but this in no way affects the structure of his general argument against infinite regress.

criticisms. One well-known objection is that Aquinas begs the question by referring to "first movers" and "second movers" and asserting that second movers cannot move without a first mover. C. J. F. Williams and Anthony Kenny both raise this sort of objection.[14] Williams quotes directly the text in the First Way:

> But this cannot proceed to infinity. For in that way there would not be any first mover, and consequently neither any other mover, because secondary movers do not move [anything] except insofar as they are moved by a first mover.[15]

Williams's objection is succinct:

> The flaw in this argument is its use of the term *mouentia secunda* in an attempt to prove the impossibility of an infinite series of causes. For not until we know that such a series is impossible can we know that all movers are properly described either as "a first mover" or as "second movers". This, however, is precisely what the argument assumes. It equates "movers other than a first mover" and "second movers". It fails to recognize the possibility of a third class of movers, those, namely, which belong to an infinite series of moved movers. Thus to presuppose the impossibility of the infinite series in the premises of the argument is to commit *petitio principii*.[16]

It must be admitted that Aquinas's phrasing does make his argument appear to beg the question. But it should by now be clear that Aquinas's argument is quite sound. Any confusion can be cleared up by allowing Aquinas to tell us what he means by "first mover" and "second mover." This he does in his commentary on book VIII of Aristotle's *Physics*:

> Something happens to be a mover in two ways. In one way, when it does not move *because of itself*, that is, by its own power, but because it is moved by something else moving it. And this is a second mover. In another way something moves *because of itself*, that is, by its own power, not because it is moved by another.[17]

Aquinas goes on to refer to the latter type as a "first mover." If "second mover" means that which does not move on its own account or by its own power, and "first mover" means that which does move on its own account, then Aquinas does not beg the question in asserting that secondary

---

14. C. J. F. Williams, "*Hic autem*"; Anthony Kenny, *The Five Ways*, 25–27 and 44.
15. Aquinas, *ST* I, q. 2, a. 3.
16. Williams, "*Hic autem*," 403.
17. *In VIII Phys.*, l. 9, n. 1038 [2].

movers require a first mover. What he means amounts to the claim that a caboose will not undergo motion without an engine, no matter how many boxcars are coupled before it.

In this way Kenny's objection can be answered as well. He argues that Aquinas equivocates on "first mover." In asserting that second movers do not move without a first mover, Aquinas must by "first mover" mean "prior mover," otherwise he would beg the question. In asserting that in an infinite regress there is no first mover, he must by "first mover" mean "unmoved mover," otherwise he will not get his conclusion. But a syllogism in four terms is invalid; Aquinas commits the fallacy of equivocation, Kenny says.[18] But Aquinas does not equivocate. In both premises and in the conclusion "first mover" means "mover that moves by its own power."

Now one might think that Aquinas's argument, while establishing that there must be a first mover, does not really establish that there cannot be an infinite regress. Why couldn't there be an infinite number of intermediary causes between the first mover and the ultimate effect? Some of Aquinas's defenders are open to this possibility; as long as there has to be a first mover, Aquinas's First Way can proceed.[19] This is true, and Aquinas himself does indeed say, in his commentary on book II of Aristotle's *Metaphysics*, that even if, *per impossibile*, there were an infinite number of secondary causes, a first cause would still be required, for instrumental causes do not act without a principal cause.[20] But Aquinas then proceeds to argue that there cannot be an infinite number of intermediary causes. For if there is a first—the uncaused or principal cause—and a last—the ultimate effect in question, caused by the whole series—then the series of causes is bounded and finite. "Both of these [i.e., a first and a last] are opposed to the nature of the infinite, which excludes every limit, whether it be a starting-point or a terminus."[21] Further on in the same text Aquinas says "an infinite number of intermediates cannot exist when certain limits are held to exist, since limits are opposed to infinity."[22] Aquinas's point is

---

18. Kenny, *The Five Ways*, 25–27.

19. In the view of some, only Aquinas's general but wavering rejection of actual infinites stands in the way of essentially ordered series with an infinite number of intermediate causes (assuming an uncaused cause at the head of the series.) This is the view of Caleb Cohoe: "There Must Be a First: Why Thomas Aquinas Rejects Infinite, Essentially Ordered, Causal Series," *British Journal for the History of Philosophy* 21, no. 5 (2013): 838–56, at fn. 21 and 849–50. See also John Wippel, *The Metaphysical Thought of Thomas Aquinas*, 409 and n. 26; 447–48.

20. *In II Meta.*, l. 3. n. 303.

21. *In II Meta.*, l. 3, n. 303 (trans. John P. Rowan [Notre Dame, IN: Dumb Ox Books, 1995]).

22. *In II Meta.*, l. 3, n. 312.

that if a process of counting begins somewhere and ends somewhere, it necessarily counts a finite number. If the causal series begins with an uncaused cause and ends with a present effect, it cannot contain an infinite number of intermediate causes. A further important point follows directly from this line of reasoning: *Aquinas's argument is not that the unmoved mover stands outside the whole (essentially ordered) series and supports it, but that it stands at the head of the series.*

The structure of Aquinas's argument against infinite regress, then, is this: Secondary or instrumental movers do not of themselves have the wherewithal to cause motion. They only cause motion, instrumentally, if something that does have the wherewithal to cause motion sets them in motion. In an infinite regress there is no first or unmoved mover, that is to say, there is no mover that does itself have the wherewithal to cause motion. Hence an infinite regress of movers can cause no motion at all. This argument is sound.

Others, such as Antony Flew, object to cosmological arguments that base themselves on the impossibility of infinite regress, for they claim that every explanation must always end with some "brute fact" or other. Why should the regress end with God as a brute fact rather than with some other brute fact, such as the forces of nature? To argue to God we would need a strong version of the principle of sufficient reason, they say, but that principle is not demonstrable, and indeed false. Even if it were true, to end the regress of causes God would have to be a necessary being, the very idea of whom necessitates His own existence. But the failure of the ontological proof shows that this view is incoherent.[23]

Yet in regard to Aquinas's First Way at least, this objection is not to the point. The sub-argument against an infinite regress of moved movers cannot carry the whole burden of proving the existence of God.[24] It makes, rather, a quite modest claim. It does not establish that the transcendent God exists, but only that there cannot be an infinite regress of movers. The

23. Antony Flew, *God and Philosophy*, 82–84, 95–98. (Flew, of course, later came to accept God's existence.) J. L. Mackie and William Rowe also argue that cosmological arguments depend on the principle of sufficient reason, but they are content to say merely that that principle is neither self-evident nor demonstrable. See Rowe, *The Cosmological Argument* and J. L. Mackie, *The Miracle of Theism* (New York: Oxford University Press, 1982), ch. 5. (a) and (b). The idea that the cosmological proof covertly depends on, and falls with, the ontological argument stems from Immanuel Kant, *Critique of Pure Reason*, Transcendental Dialectic, The Ideal of Pure Reason, section five.

24. The contrary has been argued by Timothy Pawl, "The Five Ways," in *The Oxford Handbook of Aquinas*, ed. Brian Davies and Eleonore Stump, 115–31 (Oxford: Oxford University Press, 2012), at 118.

mover principle already necessitates that for every motion there is a mover; the sub-argument against infinite regress only establishes that for each motion there is a mover that itself has the wherewithal to cause motion, rather than being an instrumental cause; in other words, every motion requires a "first mover." Whether every motion has the same first mover or not, and thus whether there is one or many first movers, is not established by this sub-argument. Also not determined is whether the first mover is some physical substance whose existence is a brute fact—say some particle or field—or a transcendent being. The argument against an infinite regress is meant to do no more than just that, to establish that there cannot be an infinite regress of movers. To establish the existence of a transcendent God will require further argumentation, as I describe in chapters 3 and 4.

A different objection is raised by David Hume. Hume's intended target was Samuel Clarke's cosmological argument, but Paul Edwards elaborated Hume's objection and explicitly directed it at Aquinas.[25] Hume's passage is famous:

> In such [an infinite] chain, too, or succession of objects, each part is caused by that which preceded it, and causes that which succeeds it. Where then is the difficulty? But the *whole*, you say, wants a cause. I answer that the uniting of these parts into a whole, like the uniting of several distinct countries into one kingdom, or several distinct members into one body, is performed merely by an arbitrary act of the mind, and has no influence on the nature of things. Did I show you the particular causes of each individual in a collection of twenty particles of matter, I should think it very unreasonable should you afterwards ask me what was the cause of the whole twenty. This is sufficiently explained in explaining the cause of the parts.[26]

In an infinite regress, Hume and Edwards argue, every member of the series is explained by the previous one. There is no item that does not have a previous member, so there is no member that is without explanation. Nor is there any need to give another explanation for the existence of the whole series, because the series, so they reason, is nothing over and

---

25. Paul Edwards, "The Cosmological Argument."

26. Hume, *Dialogues concerning Natural Religion*, ed. Richard H. Popkin, 2nd ed. (Indianapolis: Hackett, 1998), 56. The same sort of argument was made in the Middle Ages by William Ockham (*Philosophical Writings*, ed. and trans. Philotheus Boehner, OFM, rev. Stephen F. Brown [Indianapolis: Hackett, 1990], 120–21, 124). Ockham was criticizing Duns Scotus's version of the cosmological argument and reasoned instead that only an infinite regress of conserving—as opposed to producing—causes was impossible. Hume criticizes cosmological arguments *tout court*.

above its members. Hence an infinite regress sufficiently accounts for everything that needs accounting for.

Hume's argument is dubious, for it seems that the question "Why should the causal series exist at all? Why is there something rather than nothing?" still needs an answer. Several authors have critiqued Hume on this score in promising ways, for example, Alexander Pruss and Michael Rota.[27] But Hume's objection is only relevant for forms of the regress argument that proceed by composition, that is, by lumping all the members of a causal series into a whole and then arguing that the whole needs a cause external to itself. Avicenna, Scotus, Clarke, and Leibniz make this type of argument.[28] But does Aquinas?

Peter Geach and C. F. J. Martin think so,[29] but there is no basis in the text of the First Way for their interpretation. Neither do any of the three sub-arguments against infinite regress in *SCG*'s first motion proof proceed by composition.[30] In the argument in question, Aquinas has not said that a moved mover explains the ultimate motion while leaving something else unexplained, either itself or the series as a whole. Aquinas argues that a moved mover *does not* explain the ultimate motion, because a moved mover is not the kind of thing that can account for the motion. A moved mover cannot account for its own causality, but can only cause motion insofar as it is moved by another. By regressing to infinity in an essentially ordered series, one will never have explained even one thing. This one cannot do unless one comes to a first mover that moves by its own power, whatever that first mover might be.[31]

---

27. Alexander R. Pruss, "The Hume-Edwards Principle and the Cosmological Argument" and Michael Rota, "Infinite Causal Chains and Explanation," *Proceedings of the American Catholic Philosophical Association* 81 (2007): 109–22. Rota, in particular, argues that an infinite regress fails as an explanation because it would follow that a part of the group—all members except the current one—must explain the whole group. That means that the explanation presupposes part of what it is supposed to explain.

28. For Avicenna, see *The Salvation*, Metaphysics, Second Treatise, ch. 12 in *Philosophy in the Middle Ages: The Christian, Islamic, and Jewish Traditions*, ed. Arthur Hyman, James J. Walsh, and Thomas Williams, 3rd ed. (Indianapolis, Hackett: 2010), 246; cp. *The Metaphysics of* The Healing, ed. and trans. Michael E. Marmura (Provo, UT: Brigham Young University Press, 2005), VIII.1, n. 4–7. For Scotus, see *Ordinatio* I, d. 2, p. 1, q. 1, n. 53 (translated by Allan Wolter, OFM, in John Duns Scotus, *Philosophical Writings*, 41–42). For Clarke see *A Demonstration of the Being and Attributes of God*, proposition 2. For Leibniz, see "On the Ultimate Origination of Things," and "Monadology," n. 31–32 and 36–38 (G. W. Leibniz, *Philosophical Essays*, trans. Roger Ariew and Daniel Garber [Indianapolis: Hackett, 1989], 149–50 and 217–18.)

29. Geach, "Aquinas," 112; C. F. J. Martin, *Thomas Aquinas: God and Explanations*, 134, 142–43.

30. *SCG* I, c. 13, n. 91–95 [11–15]

31. Scott MacDonald gives the same account in "Aquinas's Parasitic Cosmological Argument," 146.

However, in a later step in the second motion proof in *SCG*, Aquinas does use something resembling a "lumping" argument to prove that a certain type of infinite accidentally ordered series requires a finite essentially ordered series of causes to sustain it.[32] Hume's objection is relevant to this latter argument, but I will postpone its consideration until the end of this chapter.

NON-SIMULTANEITY IN ESSENTIALLY ORDERED CAUSAL SERIES

Duns Scotus's Marks of an Essentially Ordered Causal Series

In elucidating Aquinas's crucial distinction between essentially ordered and accidentally ordered causal series, several scholars have turned to Duns Scotus, who clearly and succinctly characterizes the distinction with three marks.[33] Scotus is, in fact, quite helpful here, but one must of course proceed with caution due to the possibility that Scotus and Aquinas do not completely agree on the issue. Here is Scotus's text:

> *Per se* or essentially ordered causes differ from accidentally ordered causes in three respects. The first difference is that in essentially ordered causes, the second depends upon the first precisely in its act of causation. In accidentally ordered causes this is not the case, although the second may depend upon the first for its existence or in some other way. Thus a son depends upon his father for existence but is not dependent upon him in exercising his own causality, since he can act just as well whether his father be living or dead. The second difference is that in essentially ordered causes the causality is of another nature and order, inasmuch as the higher cause is more perfect. Such is not the case, however, with accidentally ordered causes. This second difference is a consequence of the first, since no cause in the exercise of its causality is essentially dependent upon a cause of the same nature as itself, for to produce anything one cause of a given kind suffices. The third difference is that all *per se* and essentially ordered causes are simultaneously required to cause the effect, for otherwise some causality essential to the effect would be wanting. In accidentally ordered causes this is not so, because there is no need of simultaneity in causing inasmuch as each possesses independently of

---

32. *SCG* I, c. 13, n. 105–06 [25–26]; *In VIII Phys.*, l. 12, n. 1074 [6].

33. See, for example, William Rowe, *The Cosmological Argument*, 23–29; Edward Feser, *Scholastic Metaphysics: A Contemporary Introduction* (Heusenstamm, Germany: Editiones Scholasticae), 148–150; Patterson Brown, "Infinite Causal Regress," 512–513 and fn. 9, 515 and fn. 16.

the others the perfection of causality with regard to its own effect. For it is enough that one cause after the other exercises causality successively.[34]

Scotus thus identifies three properties of essentially ordered causal series: prior causes cause posterior causes to cause, prior causes have ontological superiority over posterior causes, and prior and posterior causes cause simultaneously. There is general agreement that Scotus's first mark holds true for Aquinas also, and that it is the key to his arguments against infinite regress.[35] I of course share this view. But the second two marks are also frequently accepted by scholars as representing Aquinas's view, particularly the third mark of simultaneity.[36] Some even assert that the characteristic of simultaneity plays a necessary role in Aquinas's argument against infinite regress,[37] although most deny this.[38] What I will argue for in this and the following sections is that, in the context of Aquinas's motion proof for God's existence, the second two marks hold only in a significantly qualified way. In particular, I wish to defend the possibility, on Thomistic principles, of an essentially ordered causal series whose causes exercise their direct causality successively, rather than simultaneously. But I first discuss the second mark.

Consider the following example of an essentially ordered series of causes of becoming: Aquinas asserts in many places that the astronomical bodies—which in his view are on a higher ontological plane than most terrestrial beings—are causally active in the generation of new substances here on earth.[39] He also asserts that in regard to the higher—or "perfect"—animals, the causality of parents of the same species is necessarily

34. Scotus, *Ordinatio* I, d. 2, p. 1, q. 1, n. 48–51, as translated by Allan Wolter in Scotus, *Philosophical Writings*, 40–41. See also *De Primo Principio* 3.11.

35. For examples, see Caleb Cohoe, "There Must Be a First," 839–40; John Wippel, *The Metaphysical Thought of Thomas Aquinas*, 422–24; Gaven Kerr, "Essentially Ordered Series Reconsidered," *American Catholic Philosophical Quarterly* 86, no. 4 (2012): 541–55, at 550; Edward Feser, *Scholastic Metaphysics*, 151–54; Scott MacDonald, "Aquinas's Parasitic Cosmological Argument," 138–146; Patterson Brown, "Infinite Causal Regression," 516.

36. For example, Feser, *Scholastic Metaphysics*, 148–50; William Rowe, *The Cosmological Argument*, 29; Cohoe "There Must Be a First," 842, 846–47; Brown, "Infinite Causal Regression," 515; Wippel, *The Metaphysical Thought of Thomas Aquinas*, 408;

37. John King-Farlow, "The First Way in Physical and Moral Space," *The Thomist* 39, no. 2 (1975): 349–74; Jason Eberl, *The Routledge Guidebook to Aquinas'* Summa Theologiae (New York: Routledge, 2016), 43. Although this is not Aquinas's reason for rejecting infinite series, it is Ockham's reason for rejecting infinite series of *conserving* causes: Ockham, *Philosophical Writings*, 123.

38. For example, Cohoe, "There Must Be a First," 846–50; Brown, "Infinite Causal Regression," 519–20; Feser, *Scholastic Metaphysics*, 153; Michael Augros, *Aquinas on Theology and God's Existence*, 288–90.

39. See, for example, *ST* I, q. 115, a. 3, ad 2.

required.[40] Hence, in Aquinas's view, the parents terminate an essentially ordered series of causes of becoming for their child, which regresses upward to the astronomical bodies, and beyond them to the angelic beings that move them.

In this case, the superiority of the more remote causes of becoming has to be qualified. Aquinas does not believe that the astronomical bodies, such as the sun and planets, are strictly speaking alive. He will sometimes speak of them as animated and as self-movers, but when expressly discussing the subject, he argues that their "souls" are not really souls, that is, forms of living bodies. Their "souls" are self-subsistent, immaterial beings—that is—angels, which move the astronomical bodies. These angels are souls only in the Platonic sense of a pilot in a ship.[41] The astronomical bodies do have their own substantial forms, which are not souls, and so the astronomical bodies are not living beings, strictly speaking.[42] If they are not alive, how can the astronomical bodies generate living beings on earth, which are not only not inferior to them, but actually superior? And how can they move the animal parents to act, when they are of an inferior nature to those parents?

Aquinas's solution to this problem is twofold. The astronomical bodies have forms that are in a certain respect more noble than the forms of living beings on earth, although he admits that simply speaking they are less noble.[43] In Aquinas's view, the astronomical bodies are more perfect in a physical or chemical sense than any bodies on earth, even the bodies of animals. More importantly, however, the astronomical bodies can only act toward the production of living beings insofar as they are themselves moved by angels, which are alive in a preeminent degree. In the generation of living beings on earth, the astronomical bodies act only as instruments.[44]

We can outline the essentially ordered series of causes of becoming, in the case of animal generation, as follows: the child animal is generated by gametes, acting as instruments of the animal parents, which are moved by astronomical bodies acting as instruments of immaterial, living angels, which are, finally, moved by God. (All of these beings belong to the essentially ordered series; the parents' parents, and the grandparents'

40. See *QDP*, q. 3, a. 11, ad 12 and its context.
41. *ST* I, q. 70, a. 3; *QDSC* a. 6.
42. *In VIII Phys.*, l. 21, n. 1152–53.
43. *QDV*, q. 5, a. 9, ad 13; *ST* I, q. 70, a. 3, ad 2.
44. *ST* I, q. 70, a. 3, ad 3; *QDP*, q. 3, a. 11, ad 13 and ad 14; *QDSC* a. 6, ad 12.

gametes, are accidentally ordered causes of the production of the grand-child, as are bygone revolutions of the astronomical bodies.) The ontological superiority of prior causes of becoming, then, is qualified. Gametes are not in themselves metaphysically superior to developing animals. Nor are animal parents metaphysically superior to their offspring. Nor are astronomical bodies higher than either the parents or offspring, except in a highly qualified sense. God is certainly superior to the angels, and angels to animals, so Scotus's second mark of essentially ordered series holds at the most important points, even on Aquinas's scheme. But at the physical level, many detours through less noble instrumental causes can be found in essentially ordered series of causes of becoming.

Temporal Succession in Essentially Ordered Causes of Becoming

I do not think that Scotus would deny much of this. But Aquinas and Scotus do diverge quite significantly on the issue of whether essentially ordered causal series must be simultaneous or not. Aquinas's position is nuanced. He, unlike Scotus, does allow for non-simultaneous efficient causation, but this can only take place insofar as a mover initially comes into contact with a mobile and leaves in it a form by means of which it moves it, even after losing physical contact with the mobile. Alternatively, the proper moving cause may set up an instrumental agent cause that acts as its proxy in causing motion.

As a motion proof, Aquinas's First Way deals with *causes of becoming*, rather than *causes of being*. This is an important distinction, and the applicability of Scotus's third mark varies in the two cases. The distinction can be seen, for example, in the following passage from the *Summa Theologiae*:

> Every effect depends on its cause, so far as it is its cause. But we must observe that an agent may be the cause of the becoming of its effect, but not directly of its being.... For the builder causes the house in its becoming, but he is not the direct cause of its being. For it is clear that the being of the house is a result of its form, which consists in the composition and order [of the materials], and results from the natural qualities of certain things.[45]

45. *ST* I, q. 104, a. 1, c. Translation emended. This text is clearly influenced by Avicenna, *The Metaphysics of* The Healing, VI.2. The distinction between causes of being and becoming is also made in Aquinas's *QDP*, q. 5, a. 1, among other places.

The house under construction will stop coming to be if its builder dies or stops working, but a house that already exists will not cease to exist if its builder dies. This is because the builder is a cause of becoming for the house, not of being. On the other hand, if the nature of the wood is destroyed by a severe infestation of termites, then the house *will* cease to exist. The nature of the wood is a cause of being for the house.

For Aquinas, efficient causes *of being* must indeed always be simultaneous with their effects. But efficient causes of becoming need not *always* be simultaneous with their effect. The possibility of non-simultaneous causality has already been demonstrated in the previous chapter, using the case of the natural motion of elemental bodies. I need now to illustrate how causal *series*—in particular, essentially ordered ones—can be successive. I am not the first person, however, to argue that Aquinas countenances successive causality. Fr. William Wallace, OP, has blazed a trail in an interesting article, focusing his attention on a passage from Aquinas's commentary on Aristotle's *Posterior Analytics*.[46] Wallace argues that Aquinas's theory of causality, while fundamentally Aristotelian, does grant a subordinate role, at least on a phenomenal level, to a more modern, Humean type of causality characterized by successive events (yet the connections between causes and effects remain essential on Aquinas's view, not accidental as on Hume's view).[47] I think Fr. Wallace was on the right track, but that Aquinas's account is not restricted to the phenomenal level. Aquinas's theory of causality is more modern than that of his predecessors or immediate successors such as Duns Scotus. The text that Fr. Wallace undertakes to study is important in that it distinguishes between causes of motion and causes of being and connects the successive character of mover causality to the essentially successive character of motion itself.

46. *In II Post. Anal.*, l. 10–12.

47. Fr. William Wallace, OP, "Aquinas on the Temporal Relation between Cause and Effect," *Review of Metaphysics* 27, no. 3 (1974): 569–84 (reprinted as "Cause and Effect: Temporal Relationships," in *From a Realist Point of View: Essays on the Philosophy of Science*, 99–114, 2nd ed. [Lanham, MD: University Press of America: 1983].) One should not press the comparison with Hume too far. For Hume, there is no discernible connection between causes and effects, whereas on Aquinas's view there is always an essential connection (except for chance effects of chance causes, which are accidentally connected.) Furthermore, Aquinas identifies causes of being in addition to causes of becoming. Causes of being are simultaneous with their effects throughout their duration. Finally, even causes of becoming/motion are in contact with what they move and are active simultaneous with the beginning of the motion, even if that motion can continue for a finite time and reach its completion after the cause has ceased impelling it. Yet there does seem to be something right about Hume's notion that causal series can be successive. Contemporary science seems very much to rely on this idea.

In his commentary, Aquinas explains that some demonstrative syllogisms use causes simultaneous with their effects as middle terms. Others, however, take as middle terms causes that are not simultaneous with their effects. In the former case, there must be a temporal parity between premises and conclusions. For example: "The earth *is* interposed between the sun and moon, therefore there *is* an eclipse." "The earth *was* interposed between the sun and moon, therefore there *was* an eclipse." In the case of causes not simultaneous with their effects, however, one must argue backward in time, from effect to cause. (One cannot demonstrate forward from cause to non-simultaneous effect in Aquinas's view; in part this is because a time lag between cause and effect presents an opportunity for outside factors to intervene before the effect comes about and prevent it from occurring, yet demonstrative conclusions must be certain and necessary.[48]) But in arguing backward from effect to cause, there is difficulty in going from one event at one instant to another event at a prior instant, for events occurring at particular instants cannot be consecutive to one another, just as no two points can touch each other.[49] Arguing from one discrete event to another might seem like an illegitimate jump insofar as what happens between them would be left out. But one can argue from ongoing processes/motions to prior moment-like events that established the sufficient conditions for the processes to occur, and then from those moment-like events to prior processes that brought about those moment-like events, and so on, like this: "Because this process is happen*ing*, that event must *have happened*. And since that happen*ed*, therefore, this other process must have been happen*ing* before it," and so on.[50]

Aquinas connects the fact that causes of motion are not always simultaneous with their effects to the essentially successive character of motion:

> Because in motion it is necessary to consider prior and posterior, in the causes of motion one should take cause and effect to relate as prior and posterior. Now it is clear that a natural agent cause accomplishes its effect by moving, and just as through the whole motion it brings the mobile to the terminus of the motion, so too through the first part of motion [the mobile] is brought to the second part, and so forth. Whence just as motion is the cause of the consequent rest, so too the first part of motion is the cause of the subsequent

---

48. *In II Post. Anal.*, l. 10, n. 512 [9].
49. See *In VI Phys.*, l. 1–5.
50. See *In II Post. Anal.*, l. 10, n. 510 [7].

part, and so forth. And this is the case whether this is considered as taking place in one mobile which is moved continuously from the beginning up to the end [of the motion] or as taking place in diverse mobiles, the first of which moves the second, and the second the third. And although the first mobile is in motion (*moveatur*) at the same time as the first mover causes motion, nevertheless *the first mobile continues to cause motion (remanet movens) after it ceases to be in motion (moveri)*, and at the same time as it causes motion, the second mobile is in motion. And in this way the mobiles are moved successively, of which one is the cause of the motion of another, as the Philosopher shows concerning projectiles in *Physics* VIII. *In this way it happens that the cause is not simultaneous with that of which it is the cause, inasmuch as, namely, the first part of motion is the cause of the second part, or the first moved object moves the second.*[51]

The series of causes of motion can be successive rather than simultaneous, as in the case of Aristotelian projectile motion. Since they do not believe in what we call inertia, Aquinas and Aristotle explain projectile motion by saying that when a person throws a rock, he moves not only the rock but part of the air. This part of the air, when it ceases to be moved by the hand, stops undergoing motion, but it continues for a time to cause motion in the rock and in the next part of the air. This next part of the air, after it stops undergoing motion, continues to move the rock and the next part of air, and so forth.[52] There is not just one motion in the flight of the rock; it is actually a series of motions, Aquinas says. But each bit of air has less force than the previous one, and eventually the process comes to an end and the rock remains at rest.

The *motion* of the first bit of air causes the motion of the second bit of air, which causes the motion of the third bit of air, and so on, and the motions of these bits are successive, not simultaneous. Aquinas does assert immediately after the quoted text that the immediate *agent*—for example, the first bit of air—causes motion at the same time as its patient—the second bit of air—undergoes motion. But he says that this is simply by definition: motion, as the act of the mobile, is the act in virtue

---

51. *In II Post. Anal.*, l. 10, n. 505 [2]. Translation mine. Emphasis added.

52. *In VIII Phys.*, l. 22. As explained in the previous chapter, this account is motivated for Aquinas by the violent, nonnatural character of such motion, as opposed to a generalized commitment to always finding simultaneous efficient causes. Later authors rightfully rejected this account, since sense experience demonstrates that air resists the motion of projectiles, rather than sustains it. See John Buridan, *Questions on the Eight Books of the Physics of Aristotle*, bk. VIII, q. 12 and Galileo, *Dialogue concerning the Two Chief World Systems—Ptolemaic and Copernican*, second day (trans. Stillman Drake, 2nd ed. [Berkeley: University of California Press, 1967], 148–153).

of which a mover is said to be a mover, so it is trivially true that when the patient undergoes motion, the mover is causing motion.[53] But the immediate mover can only cause motion because it itself undergoes motion, and Aquinas says clearly that it is *not in motion* for the same length of time as it causes motion in another. One still bit of air is said to move the projectile and the next bit of air because motion can only go on when the conditions for it obtain (one can consider the condition in question as the still bit of air crowding out the next bit, and think of Aristotelian projectile motion as a result of a compression wave). But these conditions themselves cannot obtain except due to a prior motion; it is not air as such but squeezed air that can propel the next bit of air and the projectile forward. For this reason, the prior *motion* of the prior bit of air is also a cause of the later motion. But that prior motion must in turn have begun when *its* conditions first obtained. The conditions of the prior motion obtained at the beginning of that prior motion, whereas the conditions for the later motion obtained only at the end of the prior motion. In this way, a successive series of causes is established. ("This motion *is* going on because that event *has* happened. That event has happened because that other motion *was* going on before it. That other motion *was* going on, because another event *had* happened before it.")

Aquinas concludes the text by comparing movers to causes of being:

> And much more is it necessary that the cause be simultaneous with its effect in those things which are outside [the sphere of] motion, whether one considers a terminus of motion (for instance, the illumination of air is simultaneous with the rising of the sun) or wholly immobile things and essential causes, which are causes of being itself.[54]

---

53. *In II Post. Anal.*, l. 10, n. 505 [2]: "However, although motion has succession in its parts, nevertheless it is simultaneous with the moving cause. For at the same time as the mover causes motion, the mobile is in motion (*movetur*), in that *motion is nothing other than the act of the mobile from the mover*, according to which the mover is said to move and the mobile to be in motion (*moveri*)." On reconciling the non-simultaneity of some proximate efficient causes with this reasoning based on the definition of motion, see chapter 1, p. 36–37 above.. Briefly, following Aristotle in *Physics* III.3 Aquinas holds that in the case of motion there are not two actualities, an action on the part of the cause and a reception on the part of the mobile. Rather, motion is a single act that can be looked at in two ways, as the act of the mobile *from* the mover, or the act of the mover *on* the mobile. This one act, a single act of both the mover and the mobile, exists in the mobile and not in the mover. (This is why God can cause changing effects in the world without Himself changing at all.) As long as the motion exists, *by definition* it is the act of the mover, even if the mover no longer exists. (Although in that case the motion would not be occurring in the mobile unless the mover left behind a form in it or an instrumental agent that serves as its proxy.)

54. *Ibid.*

Causes of being are always simultaneous with their effects, without quali-fication, for being is not intrinsically successive, unlike motion. But causes of becoming are often non-simultaneous with their effects.

Yet one might wonder whether *essentially* ordered series of causes of becoming could be non-simultaneous. Isn't the example analyzed above a case of an accidentally ordered series? No it is not. Aquinas's account of projectile motion is an example of an essentially ordered series of movers. The person "projecting" is, transitively, the cause of the rock reaching its destination, and the cause of the whole collection of motions. Recall a text cited in the last chapter:

> An instrument is understood to be moved by a principal agent as long as it retains the power impressed by the principal agent. For this reason an arrow is moved by the projector as long as the force of the impulse of the projector remains. In this way also that which is generated is moved by the generator in regard to heavy and light things as long as it retains the form given to it by the generator. Whence also semen is understood to be moved by the soul of the generator as long as the power impressed by the soul remains there, although it be physically divided. It is necessary, however, for the mover and the moved to be together in regard to the beginning of motion, not, howev-er, in regard to the whole motion, as appears in projectiles.[55]

In accidentally ordered series the causality is not transitive, and so if the archer were not part of an essentially ordered series, he could not be said to strike the target with the arrow. He could only be said to move the arrow just to the edge of his reach and to move the air adjacent to him. A later portion of the air would be what moves the arrow to strike the target. But the archer *is* the arrow's moving cause, all the way to the end of its flight. True, he is not the proximate efficient cause on Aquinas's view. A portion of the air is.[56] But the archer is a proper efficient cause nonetheless, and is in fact the first cause in an essentially ordered series.

---

55. *QDP* q. 3, a. 11, ad 5. Emphasis added. Translation mine.

56. This is different from the case of the generator of a heavy body and the natural motion of a body generated. In that case, the generator acts by means of a substantial form it leaves behind in the body generated and through the accidental form of heaviness that flows from the substantial form. These instruments of the generator cannot be instrumental *efficient* causes, since they are just forms, not determining agents. But in the case of projectile motion, the motion does not continue—on Aquinas's view at least—because of a form left behind in the projectile. Rather, it continues because the air pushes it. The air is not a formal cause intrinsic to the projectile, but an instrumental efficient cause, a determining agent, extrinsic to it. (The obvious way to save Aquinas's principles from the absurdity of his view of projectile motion is to consider the projector as imparting an accidental form, an impetus/momentum, on the projectile, from which motion flows as from a formal cause.)

In a pitched battle bowman Giles may fire his longbow at Sir Cedric, then have his head chopped off by Sir Gladwyn and die while his arrow is still sailing through the air. When the arrow strikes Sir Cedric mortally, it was Giles who killed him, not just the arrow. The arrow and the bits of air and the archer are efficient causes of Sir Cedric's death. They form an essentially ordered series, and yet they exercise their causality successively, rather than simultaneously. (Despite Sir Kenny's objection, sometimes murders *are* committed by dead men![57])

Consider also another example from Thomistic physics. Its analysis depends on the following distinction:

> Some of the forms that begin to exist in matter through the action of a corporeal agent are, when produced, perfect both in their specific nature and in their being in matter, like the form of their generator, the reason being that the matter does not retain contrary principles. And such forms remain after the action of their generator, until the time of their corruption. Other forms, however, when produced are perfect in their specific nature, but have not perfect being in matter. Thus heat in hot water has the perfect species of heat, but not perfect being—which depends on the hold that the form has on the matter—inasmuch as the matter retains the form that is contrary to the quality of heat. Forms of this description can remain for a short time after the action of the agent, but are prevented from remaining for long by the contrary principle that is in the matter. Again other forms when produced in matter are imperfect both in species and in being, as for instance light which is produced in the air by a luminous body. For light in the air is not a perfect natural form as light in the luminous body, but [exists] rather after the manner of an *intention*. Hence just as a man's likeness does not remain in a mirror save as long as the mirror is in front of him, even so neither does light remain in the air when the luminous body is no longer present.[58]

On Aquinas's view, being cold is a property of water flowing from its substantial form, just as other accidental features are properties of any given nature and flow from its substantial form. So water cannot become hot on its own nor can it remain hot on its own. If it is hot, it will undergo a natural alteration until it reaches its natural temperature. Hence heat in water does not have "perfect being in matter." On the other hand, if

---

57. Anthony Kenny, *The Five Ways*, 21.

58. *QDP* q. 5, a. 1, ad 6. Translation emended. *Intentional existence* is a difficult Thomistic concept. But it is sufficient for our purposes to grasp that, on Aquinas's view, when green light shines through the air, the air does not become green. Also, the mirror does not become human-shaped when the shape of human has intentional existence in the mirror.

water is heated until it boils, then the vapor will remain hot, on Aquinas's view, because the substantial form of water has been replaced with the substantial form of air, which is naturally hot.

Suppose, then, that on a chilly night a pot of water is placed over a fire and allowed to become very hot. Then the pot is removed from the fire and the fire is quickly put out. Then someone else, not knowing that it is hot, dips his hand into the pot of water and receives a burn. Later the skin starts to blister. The water and the fire constitute an essentially ordered series of causes of becoming for the blister. The fire must be part of the *essentially* ordered series, because water is not the kind of thing that can account for the burn or the blister. In Aquinas's view, neither is *hot* water the kind of thing that can by itself account for them. Water is cold by nature, hence hot water is essentially in motion with respect to quality; hot water, and the actions hot water can perform, have an essential connection to an external heat source, which in this case is the fire that acted previously. Furthermore, Aquinas says that active qualities like heat can only cause substantial change (in this case, the corruption of skin, turning it into dead material) by acting in virtue of the substantial form to which they belong.[59] When hot water causes a substantial change, however, the heat cannot act in virtue of the form of water, since that form is opposed to the heat. The heat must act in virtue of the substantial form of the fire from which it is derived. Since, then, the essentially ordered series of causes for a given effect is that series that begins with the principal cause that produces the effect by its own power and proceeds through the instrumental causes that produce the effect only by the power of the principal cause—and since, furthermore, the fire has in and of itself the heat that can produce the blister and the water does not—therefore the water must be an instrumental cause and the fire the principal cause in an essentially ordered series of causes of becoming. Hence, according to Thomistic physics, one could legitimately demonstrate in this fashion: "This skin is being burnt by hot water, therefore the water had become hot, therefore the water was previously being heated by something fiery."

The analysis demonstrates that, in an essentially ordered series of causes of becoming, the movers need not exercise their causality simultaneously. In some cases, a body can cause motion here and now precisely by virtue of the fact that it was moved in the past by some other cause.

---

59. *ST* I, q. 115, a. 1, ad 5 and *SCG* III, c. 69, n. 2453 [23].

Nevertheless, not *all* past movers belong to the essentially ordered series. Although the fire in my example was generated from wood, that fire does not heat and burn insofar as it was generated by wood, but insofar as it is fire. Furthermore, although the water might have been drawn from a cistern, and may be held in place by a metal cauldron produced by a blacksmith, the water does not burn or produce a blister insofar as it is drawn from a cistern nor insofar as it is contained by a cauldron produced by a blacksmith. Rather, it burns insofar as it is heated by fire. Hence far more past causes belong to the accidentally ordered series than to the essentially ordered one, even though some past causes do indeed belong to the essentially ordered series.

While essentially ordered causal series of becoming can stretch backward in time, they cannot stretch infinitely backward in time; they require a first cause. Although some successive causal series are essentially ordered, Aquinas does explicitly say, in the text from the commentary on the *Posterior Analytics* analyzed above, that all *cyclical* successive causal series *are* accidentally ordered. Aquinas gives the following example: the earth is watered because it rained, and it rained because clouds were generated, and clouds were generated because vapor rose, and vapor rose because the sun generated vapor from the earth and the sun generated vapor from the earth because the earth had been watered. Aquinas then states: "This cycle of causes, however, cannot be found according to the order which is found in causes *per se*, for in that case it is necessary to arrive at one first cause in any genus of causes, as proved in *Metaphysics* II. That, however, water is generated from fire, and fire again from water, is not *per se* but *per accidens*."[60] Whether the cycle has been completed once before, thirty times before, a billion times before, an infinity of times before, or never before is irrelevant to the causality presently being exercised. Hence the previous cycles are only accidental causes of the current process.

CAUSAL SERIES AND ACTUAL INFINITES

In my treatment of essentially ordered causal series, one loose end remains. A few authors maintain that Aquinas's primary reason for rejecting infinite regresses is that he believes that it is impossible for an actual infinite number of beings to exist simultaneously. Since causes in an essentially

---

60. *In II Post. Anal.*, l. 12, n. 523 [3]. Translation mine.

ordered series are simultaneous—so they say—an actual infinite would exist if such series could regress infinitely. But this is impossible, and so such series cannot regress infinitely.[61] I think this misconception is common among those who are not scholars of Aquinas's work. But it in fact reflects William of Ockham's thought, not Aquinas's.[62]

However, in just two texts, Aquinas does at least appear to argue against an infinite regress on such grounds:

> According to the philosophers, it is impossible to proceed to infinity in the order of efficient causes which act together at the same time, because in that case the effect would have to depend on an infinite number of actions simultaneously existing. And such causes are essentially infinite, because their infinity is required for the effect caused by them. On the other hand, in the sphere of non-simultaneously acting causes, it is not, according to the partisans of the perpetual generation theory, impossible to proceed to infinity. And the infinity here is accidental to the causes; thus it is accidental to Socrates' father that he is another man's son or not. But it is not accidental to the stick, in moving the stone, that it be moved by the hand; for the stick moves just so far as it is moved.[63]

> That the same effect be preceded by causes infinite *per se* or essentially is impossible, but accidentally it is possible. This is to say, an effect in whose notion (*ratione*) it be that it proceed from infinite causes is impossible. But it does happen to an effect that those causes be infinite whose multiplication matters nothing to it. For the sake of example: certain moving causes, such as a craftsman and a tool, are required *per se* for the being of a knife. And that these be infinite is impossible, because from this it would follow that an infinite number of things would exist in act (*infinita esse simul actu*). But that a knife made by a certain elderly craftsman, who has many times replaced his tools, should follow a successive multitude of tools is *per accidens*. And nothing prevents there being infinite tools preceding this knife, if the craftsman were sempiternal. And similarly in the generation of an animal, because the semen of the father is an instrumentally moving cause in respect of the power of the sun. And because such instruments, which are second causes, are generated and corrupted, it happens that they are infinite. And in this way also it happens that infinite days have preceded this day, because the substance of the sun is sempiternal according to them, and each of its revolutions is finite. And the Commentator [Averroes] posits this reason in *Physics* VIII, text 15 and 47.[64]

---

61. John King-Farlow, "The First Way in Physical and Moral Space"; Jason T. Eberl, *The Routledge Guidebook to Aquinas'* Summa Theologiae (New York: Routledge, 2016), 43.

62. William Ockham, *Philosophical Writings*, 123.

63. *SCG* II, c. 38, n. 1147 [13].

64. *In II Sent.*, d. 1, q. 1, a. 5, ad 5. I have translated this text from the Mandonnet edition, vol. 2, 39–40.

These two texts do appear to rule out an essentially ordered infinite regress on the grounds of simultaneity and the impossibility of an actual infinite. Yet neither of these two texts constitutes part of an argument for God's existence. They are both, rather, rebuttals of attempts to prove the non-eternity of the world. Those attempting to prove the non-eternity of the world had argued that the series of events constitutes a causal regress, and that if the world were sempiternal there would be an impossible infinite causal regress. While Aquinas does believe that the world had a beginning in time, he does not think this can be proved against philosophers who hold the world to be sempiternal. And so in both texts, after reporting a series of arguments for the non-eternity of the world, Aquinas states that they are insufficient and that philosophers would respond to them in the ways he will indicate:

> Now, these arguments, though not devoid of probability, lack absolute and necessary conclusiveness. *Hence, it is sufficient to deal with them quite briefly,* lest the Catholic faith might appear to be founded on ineffectual reasonings, and not, as it is, on the most solid teaching of God. *It would seem fitting, then, to state how these arguments would be countered by the partisans of the doctrine of the world's eternity.*[65]
>
> And because the philosophers have responses to the reasons given to the contrary, which I have said are not demonstrations, therefore, although their conclusion is true they also *are to be given responses [here], according as the philosophers themselves respond,* lest [these reasons] occur suddenly [or perhaps "improvidently" (*ex improviso*)] to someone disputing against those holding the eternity of the world.[66]

Hence in the two problem texts given above, Aquinas is giving the sorts of arguments that non-Christian philosophers would use and doing so in brief. If he were making a point on his own behalf, he would not argue in the same way. Now most philosophers Aquinas was familiar with certainly did hold that causes and effects, and essentially ordered series of causes, were simultaneous. Aquinas was something of an innovator in this regard.[67] Most such philosophers also categorically rejected actual infinites. And so the quickest way to point out the inadequacy of

---

65. *SCG* II, c. 38, n. 1142 [8]. Emphasis added.

66. *In II Sent.*, d. 1, q. 1, a. 5, ad 1. Emphasis added. I have translated this text from the Mandonnet edition, vol. 2, 38.

67. As indicated in the previous chapter, Aquinas's predecessors such as Avicenna and Averroes, and his successors such as Scotus, explained natural motion in terms of the efficient causal activity of the body itself, in virtue of its form. Aquinas, rather, identifies a previously acting generator as its efficient cause.

the argument in question was to present the stock response of classical philosophers: essentially ordered causes are distinct from accidentally ordered causes. Essentially ordered causes are simultaneous and accidentally ordered causes are successive. Essentially ordered causes cannot regress infinitely, for then an actual infinite would exist. Accidentally ordered causes can regress infinitely without generating an actual infinite.[68] Even though Aquinas does not agree that essentially ordered causes are always and everywhere simultaneous, that does not enable him to defend those arguing for the world's beginning against the philosophers. For there can still exist *accidentally* ordered non-simultaneous causal series, and there is nothing absurd, in his view, about such causes proceeding to infinity. Hence Aquinas simply lets the philosophers' rebuttal stand.

But the impossibility of a simultaneous, actual infinite is certainly not Aquinas's own method of arguing against infinite regress. He never uses this method in his cosmological arguments. Furthermore, as Caleb Cohoe and Patterson Brown have pointed out, if Aquinas's argument were based on the impossibility of actual infinites, he would never have said that even if, *per impossibile*, there were an infinite number of intermediate causes, there would still have to be a first cause at the head of the series.[69] Finally, Aquinas would not regard an argument based on the impossible occurrence of an actual infinite as a strong argument, for he himself displays real hesitance about the possibility or impossibility of a simultaneous, actual infinite.

In many places Aquinas argues that *actual* infinites are indeed impossible.[70] The theoretical possibility of the eternity of the world would involve only a potential, successive infinity, not an actual, simultaneous infinity. But among the arguments for the non-eternity of the world that Aquinas considers, there is one that gives him pause. Aquinas holds, of course, that each human has his own soul, and that each soul survives bodily death and is immortal. But if the world were sempiternal—so the argument in question goes—there would by now exist an actual infinite number of human souls, which is impossible. In response, Aquinas points out that this argument would not be very convincing to most

68. I, in fact, introduce my own students to the distinction between the two types of causal series by means of the presence or absence of simultaneity, although I ultimately believe this mark to be imprecise and inadequate. Yet it is the best path into the distinction. Precision can be provided for the students later.

69. Cohoe, "There Must Be a First," 849–50; Brown, "Infinite Causal Regression," 519–20.

70. Most famously and importantly, *ST* I, q. 7, a. 3 and 4.

philosophers, because many would just assert that souls do not survive, or that they are reincarnated, or that there is only one intellectual soul that all humans share (Averroes's view). But since he thinks that these are all *philosophical* errors, Aquinas is forced to conclude his reply to this argument, in the *Summa*, by saying that even if the human species might have needed a beginning, the world as a whole could be sempiternal.[71]

However, in his short treatise *On the Eternity of the World*, which most scholars think is later than the *Prima Pars*,[72] Aquinas ends his response to an identical objection by also stating that "it is not yet demonstrated that God cannot make infinite things exist in act." Aquinas, it seems, is not sure that actual infinites are impossible after all. Aquinas's hesitance is almost certainly based, at least in part, on "Al-Ghazali's" *Metaphysics*—which Aquinas mistakenly believed represented Al-Ghazali's own views[73]—where a distinction is made between ordered and non-ordered infinites. (Aquinas refers to these as essential and accidental infinites, respectively. These terms are not to be confused with "essentially *ordered*" and "accidentally *ordered*" infinite series.) The same text goes on to assert the simultaneous existence of an actual infinite number of separated human souls. An infinite number of human souls involves no order, since they do not have any causal or spatial relationship to one another, and so, this text argues, there is no impossibility that infinite souls exist. But the causes in an infinite series are ordered as prior and posterior, and wherever there is an order, there must be a first, which is incompatible with infinity, which has no limits.[74]

In *SCG*, in fact, Aquinas asserts that this position—that an accidental infinite number of human souls exists—is compatible with Aristotle's principles.[75] In his very late *Quodlibet* XII, question 2, Aquinas says that

71. *ST* I, q. 46, a. 2, ad 8.

72. See Torrell, *Saint Thomas Aquinas*, 184–87. The late dating is not unanimous.

73. See Thérèse-Anne Druart, "Al-Ghazali," in *A Companion to Philosophy in the Middle Ages*, 118–26, at 118. Jon McGinnis tells me in conversation that "Al-Ghazali's" *Metaphysics* is actually a text written by Avicenna and mistakenly attributed to Al-Ghazali in the Christian west during the Middle Ages.

74. *Algazel's Metaphysics: A Medieval Translation*, ed. J. T. Muckle, CSB (Toronto: PIMS, 1967), 40–43. Aquinas refers to this text and the distinction between kinds of infinites in a good number of places: *Quod.* IX, q. 1; *QDV* q. 2, a. 10; *ST* I, q. 46, a. 2, ad 8; *De Unitate Intellectus*, c. 5; and *SCG* II, c. 81, n. 1622 [9] and *ST* I, q. 7, a. 4, in both of which later texts Aquinas correctly ascribes the view that an actual accidental infinite is possible to Avicenna as well (on which see Jon McGinnis, "Avicennan Infinity: A Select History of the Infinite through Avicenna," *Documenti e Studi sulla Tradizione Filosofica Medievale* 21 [2010]: 199–222).

75. *SCG* II, c. 81, n. 1622 [9]. In his very early *Quod.* IX, q. 1 ad s.c., Aquinas categorically rejects

the existence of an infinite in act is not self-contradictory. Nevertheless, he says there, God could not produce an actual infinite, for it would be opposed to his wisdom and reasonableness.[76] Perhaps this should be regarded as a strong probable argument, and not as a demonstrative one.

Aquinas is only consistently confident that actual infinites cannot exist when the infinites in question are essential and imply order. Hence, even if Aquinas were to argue against essentially ordered infinite regress on the basis of the impossibility of an actual infinite—which he never does—his firmest basis for the premise that actual infinites were impossible would be that ordered series require a first item and are thus necessarily finite. Hence this hypothetical argument would end up reducing itself to the argument as I have presented it in this chapter, namely, that in an infinite regress there is no first cause, and if there is no first cause, there can be no secondary causes either.

THE DEPENDENT CHARACTER OF INFINITE ACCIDENTALLY ORDERED SERIES

As we have seen, Aquinas does allow for the possibility of infinite accidentally ordered causal series. If the world had no beginning, the series of generations could stretch backward forever. Yet Aquinas also believes that the perpetuity of such a series requires a sempiternal sustaining cause. This thesis does not appear in the First Way, but it does appear in other versions of the motion proof (for instance, in *SCG* I, c. 13, n. 105 [25]), and I will need it in later chapters. The argument is presented most amply in his commentary on book VIII of Aristotle's *Physics*:

> If there is a cause of the generation and corruption of those things which move themselves [e.g., of the animals], it is also necessary that there be a cause of this, namely, that their generation and corruption continue perpetually. But it cannot be said that the cause of this continuity is one of those immobile things which are not sempiternal. Nor can it be said that the causes

---

any kind of actual infinite as self-contradictory. But in the text from *SCG* Aquinas seems open to the possibility of an accidental infinite number of souls. But he again clearly rejects this as impossible in his later *ST* I, q. 46, a. 2, ad 8. Later again, in *De Aeternitate Mundi*, he seems open to the possibility once more. Perhaps his last word on the subject is in *Quod.* XII, where he is against the possibility of any actual infinite but leaves the door open a bit by saying that an actual infinite is not self-contradictory. If the *De Aeternitate Mundi* is an earlier work, from the period of *SCG*, Aquinas changed his mind only twice, but still manifested hesitance in the very late *Quod.* XII.

76. *Quod.* XII, q. 2, a. 2, c.

of the sempiternal generation and corruption of some self-movers are certain immobile movers which are not sempiternal, and that there are other causes of the others. He [i.e., Aristotle] explains this by adding that the cause of this continuous and eternal generation cannot be one of them nor all of them. That one of them cannot be the cause he shows thus: For that which is not sempiternal cannot be the cause of that which is necessarily sempiternal. That, however, all of them cannot be the cause he shows through the fact that if generation is perpetual all such corruptible principles are infinite and do not exist together (*non simul sunt*). It is impossible, however, for one effect to depend on infinite causes. Moreover, things which do not exist together (*non simul sunt*) cannot be the cause of something, although it is possible that of those things which do not exist together, certain ones dispose and others cause, as is clear in the case of successively falling drops which erode a stone. But if many things are the direct cause of something, they must exist together (*simul*).[77]

By self-moving beings Aquinas has in mind animate beings, but for present purposes that aspect of the argument is irrelevant. What one has here is the hypothesis of a beginningless and endless, infinite, accidentally ordered causal series. Each cause in the series comes to be and passes away. Hume and Edwards argue that each item in such a regress is explained by the cause immediately before it, and that no item is left without an explanation. The series as a whole is not a separate item needing its own explanation they say. As Paul Edwards argues, if five Eskimos are standing on the same corner in New York City, and one has a separate explanation of why each is in that place, one does not need a further explanation of why all five are there.[78] Aquinas, however, does seem to be asserting that the whole series, or rather its "endlessness," requires an explanation above and beyond the explanation of any one of its members. Why is there such a series at all, rather than motionlessness?

---

77. *In VIII Phys.*, l. 12, n. 1074 [6], translation emended. Aquinas continues: "Therefore, it is clear that if there are a thousand thousands of immobile moving principles, and if there are also many self-movers of which some are generated and some corrupted, and if among these some are mobile objects and others are movers, there still must be something over all of these which contains in its power everything which is generated and corrupted in the above way. This is the cause of their continuous mutation, as a result of which at one time they are and at another are not; and as a result of which some are the cause of the generation and motion of certain ones, and others are the cause of generation and motion of others. For every generator is the cause of generation in that which is generated. But corruptible generators receive their power of generation from some first incorruptible being. Therefore, if the motion as a result of which certain things at one time are and at another are not is eternal, as was shown above, and if an effect is eternal only if the cause is eternal, then the first mover must be eternal, if it is one. And if there are many first movers, they also are eternal."

78. Paul Edwards, "The Cosmological Argument," IV, 113–14.

How does one know that the perpetuity of the series requires its own cause, above and beyond those of its members? The answer lies in the distinction between *per se* and *per accidens* effects. In Edwards's example, the presence of the five Eskimos at the one spot is a chance, that is, *per accidens* event. *Per accidens* effects do not need their own cause above and beyond that of their components. If someone digs a grave and finds a treasure, the discovery is an accidental, that is, chance effect. It needs no cause above and beyond the cause of its components: the finder's act of digging and the owner's act of burying. Each of these has a cause: the finder's desire to make a grave, and the owner's desire to keep his money safe. If the perpetuity of the accidentally ordered series of causes discussed above were an accidental effect, then it would not need its own cause, as Hume and Edwards and Ockham argue. But *per accidens* effects cannot be perpetual.[79] What is chance or accidental is something that occurs on certain occasions, not all the time. If the continuation of the temporal series of causes and effects was by chance, then at each causal juncture it would be possible for the series to fail. In that case, given enough time it eventually *would* fail.[80] Once it failed, there could never be any new effects again. Hence if the temporal series of causes and effects is infinite, its perpetuity must be a *per se*, not a *per accidens* effect. But *per se* effects require a *per se* cause. There must, then, be a cause outside the whole ensemble, keeping the process going. Since the process goes on forever, its cause must be sempiternal.

Aquinas argues that no single member of the series could cause the whole series, and one could hardly disagree with him on this. He further asserts that the whole collection of members cannot cause the endless series either. But Humeans might push back and ask: why not? Can't an infinite number of temporal causes cause an infinite temporal effect? No, for three reasons. First, in that scenario there would be no reason why there is a series at all, rather than not. Secondly, because then the series would cause itself, since the infinite collection of members is causing the perpetuity of the series, and hence is causing the infinite collection of its members.[81] If the series were not perpetual, it would certainly need a

---

79. See, for example, *In I De Caelo*, l. 29, n. 9.

80. Unless the probability continually approaches zero as a limit as time goes toward infinity. I discuss this issue more thoroughly in chapter 7 below, section titled "Objections to the Entropic Argument: Universe-Entropy, Infinity, and Statistical and Statistical Mechanics," p. 251–255. However, as far as I can tell, especially from his commentary on *Physics* VI, Aquinas was unaware of asymptotes.

81. Cp. Rota, "Infinite Causal Chains and Explanation."

cause outside of it to start it. Hence, barring outside causes, none of the members of the series would exist unless the series were perpetual. Thus by causing the perpetuity of the series, the collection of the members is causing itself.

Thirdly, Aquinas reasons that the members cannot cause the series because they are infinite and do not act together (*simul*). One can put this in the following way: if the *per se* effect that is the perpetuity of the series were really caused *per se* by the whole infinite ensemble of its members, then the series would be essentially ordered, not accidentally ordered. And then the earlier arguments in this chapter would prove that the series could not be infinite. In an accidental causal series, it is irrelevant, as far as any individual cause is concerned, whether its causal act comes first in time, tenth, billionth, or infinitieth. This is what it means for the series to be accidentally ordered. Thus there is nothing about that causal act that explains why it is part of an eternal, infinite, causal series rather than a finite series. To actually contribute *per se* to producing the perpetuity of the series, however, it would have to *not* be irrelevant to the cause that it was operating after infinite others. It would have to act in virtue of the prior (and posterior) causes, which would cause it to cause the perpetuity of the series. For it surely cannot cause such perpetuity by its own power. Now not only is this contrary to fact, since the cause does not act in virtue of the prior (or posterior) causes, but it would not solve the problem even if it were true. For in that case, the causal series would be essentially ordered and could not be infinite. Otherwise there would be nothing that itself had the wherewithal to cause the perpetuity of the series, and each cause would act only as an instrumental cause. We would have an infinite series of boxcars with no engine.

In fact, despite all appearances, hardly anyone disagrees with Aquinas on this. Atheists, agnostics, and materialists *do* think that there is a sempiternal, essential cause of the perpetuity of the accidentally ordered series of changes in the universe. They call this cause "energy." The first law of thermodynamics states that in every physical event the total quantity of energy is always conserved. Energy makes stuff happen, and it is often said to be incapable of being generated or corrupted; it merely changes its form. It is an everlasting active cause. The perpetuity of the causal series is not, in fact, a chance event on this view. It is a necessary effect of an everlasting cause. This of course raises the question of whether energy is necessary through itself or through another. But we will also see in later chapters that this view is not in fact supported by modern science; it ignores the first law's counterpart, the second law of thermodynamics.

Hence Aquinas's second thesis concerning infinite regress is sound. An infinite, successive, accidentally ordered causal series must be sustained by an enduring, finite, essentially ordered causal series. Nor does Aquinas's argument exclude other compelling contemporary arguments against the Hume-Edwards objection.

CONCLUSION

Aquinas, then, has good grounds for arguing against the impossibility of an infinite regress. His reasoning holds up in the face of the arguments made against it by contemporary critics. The distinction between essentially and accidentally ordered causal series solves a host of problems, but this distinction is more subtle than it is sometimes made out to be. The causes in an essentially ordered series need not all act simultaneously. They can act successively, and this fact becomes very important when one attempts to reconcile the principles of Thomistic natural philosophy with the results of modern science. As I will argue in the coming chapters, even if one cannot demonstratively prove that the world had a beginning in time, one *can* show that the kind of physical phenomena presently occurring on earth depend essentially on certain astronomical causes, which in turn depend on certain prior causes, and ultimately lead to God as an unmoved mover of the universe. But first let us see how Aquinas concludes his First Way of proving God's existence.

Chapter 3

The First Way

A Modest Interpretation

INTRODUCTION

Having defended an unconventional understanding of the premises of Aquinas's First Way, I must now propose a new way of understanding how the proof concludes. In this chapter I will analyze the First Way in *ST* as an isolated argument, showing how it demonstrates its conclusion, but also how modest its conclusion actually is. It proves that for every motion there is a first mover that is already in act, formally or eminently, with respect to that toward which the mobile is in motion. It does not prove that this being is pure act, or even anything more than a natural cause. To show that an immaterial mover exists what is required is the extended motion proof G2, analyzed in the next chapter.

I begin with an overview of various conventional interpretations in the literature. Such interpretations present the First Way as moving vertically and arriving rather quickly at God understood as pure actuality or the pure act of existence. These interpretations depend on the simultaneity of movers, which I have already shown need not obtain. Moreover, they read too many metaphysical concepts into the First Way without adequate textual support and rob the proof of its "more manifest" character; they depend upon an idea that it is hard to convince anyone of unless he already believes in God, namely, that things would remain completely inactive, freeze in place, or even fall out of existence unless actualized by a being without any potentiality. Now things would indeed cease to exist and act instantly without God's conservation and concurrence, and Aquinas would recognize an argument for God's existence formed on this basis.[1] Yet this is a subtle metaphysical truth that many people cannot readily grasp. A proof that depended on it would not be particularly manifest. Such concepts make no appearance in the First Way.

I undercut all such interpretations by presenting texts in which Aquinas says clearly that the universe will not stop in place when its movers cease to act, rather, things will undergo motion toward their natural place. I then show that the First Way does not utilize the notion of pure act to prove that God exists, contrary to many versions of the conventional interpretation. God's existence has already been established before the concept of pure act emerges; it is not a condition for demonstrating His existence. Those who cannot follow the further, metaphysical argumentation required to show that God is pure act, or do not find it convincing, must nevertheless still admit the force of the prior proofs for God's existence.

In the second part of the chapter, I begin by comparing Aquinas's various versions of the proof for an unmoved mover (*ST* I, q. 2 is not the only place where Aquinas gives such an argument), noting their source in Aristotle's *Physics*. The versions divide into two main groups, and Aquinas regards the group to which the First Way belongs as showing only *that* a first mover exists, not *what* sort of being the first mover is.

In the next section I analyze the logic of the First Way itself. It shows that there is a principal mover for any motion that takes place, a mover

---

1. See Aquinas, *QDP* q. 3, a. 7 and *ST* I, q. 105, a. 5. As I read these texts of Aquinas's, God is the first cause of every operation of every creature insofar as i) He creates every finite nature, and ii) He conserves it in existence by continually causing in it the act of being. Existence (*esse*) is an *act*, so by continually causing this act—which is what is most intimate in things—God causes the creature to dynamically be what it is and thus impels it to act according to its own nature. God also iii) "applies" secondary causes to their action—as an artist applies his tools—by commanding the angels to move the heavenly spheres in choreographed fashion (or by just arranging things Himself) so as to set the elements to work in purposive ways, bringing every agent into contact with the proper patient and providing for the dispositions needed for creatures to act, all in accord with His detailed and perfect providence. This will become clearer below in chapter 4, section titled 'God or Angels?', p. 131–140, and chapter 5, 'The Need for an Organizing Principle,' p. 160–164. Finally, all things iv) act "in virtue of God's power" insofar as every one of their effects involves a new existence (*esse*) that can only be received from God—the universal cause of *esse*—and so God must concur in causing new *esse* every time a creature acts, otherwise the creature would be unable to act. Yet all of this is subtle metaphysical truth, depending on a prior demonstration of the real distinction between essence and existence, and not part of the more manifest First Way. I thank Michael Bolin for spurring me on to clarify my position on this, although he does not, I think, completely agree with me.

not caused to move by anything else, and that this mover is already in act with respect to that toward which it moves the mobile. It does not establish that there is only one unmoved mover, that is, that every instance of motion is caused by the same unmoved mover. Nor does the First Way establish that such a mover possesses any of the attributes that contemporary philosophers of religion associate with the term "god." For example, it does not establish that this being is intelligent, eternal, or omnipotent. The argument, in fact, does not immediately rule out the possibility that the unmoved mover is a natural, material cause. I argue in the third section that the proof is concerned with physical motion, not spiritual motion. It does not, by itself, establish the existence of a transcendent God.

Yet, as I show in the fourth section, Aquinas thinks that it is already appropriate to call this unmoved mover "god" in a minimal sense. It is not meaningless to say that elements or planets are gods, although it is false; when pagans and Christians disagree over what to call "god," Aquinas says that they use the term univocally. The First Way shows that there is a "god," but does not yet demonstrate to what being that term correctly applies. In the next chapter, however, I will show how Aquinas extends the motion proof to arrive at a much more robust conclusion. He does this with the Fifth and Third Ways in *ST*, and with the second motion proof in *SCG*.

Aquinas's procedure in natural theology has often been misunderstood. It is sometimes argued that Aquinas's proof fails to establish the existence of the Christian God but rather establishes, if anything, the existence of some other kind of being. But that charge is equivocal. Aquinas's strategy is to demonstrate the existence of a kind of being that has only the thinnest set of attributes that could warrant the name "god," and then to progressively determine more and more attributes that must belong to this kind of being (such as being immaterial, one of a kind, simple, etc.). Aquinas's First Way establishes the existence of a being that does not definitely have all the attributes that Christians believe God has but also does not definitely *not* have those attributes, nor does it definitely have any attributes that the Christian God does not. The concept of God is at first highly indeterminate and needs to be progressively determined by further argumentation.

WHAT'S WRONG WITH
THE CONVENTIONAL INTERPRETATION?

Interpretations in the Literature

My analysis of the First Way will be similar in some ways to Scott Mac-Donald's analysis.[2] He regards the First Way as a "parasitic cosmological argument"; that is to say, he regards it as incomplete by itself and only successful in proving God's existence if supplemented with further reasoning (in his view, probably with the Third Way). This cannot be quite right, because Aquinas concludes the First Way by claiming that God's existence has been demonstrated. I will claim, rather, that the argument proves God's existence, but only in a very minimal sense, and that proving His existence in a robust sense requires extending the argument with the Third Way, the Fifth Way, and G2.

However, the conventional interpretation of Aquinas's argument is rather different. It is said that the argument proceeds "vertically," utilizing the metaphysics of act and potency as a route directly to God, understood as pure actuality or even as the pure act of existence. The argument is supposed to establish that anything with an admixture of potency requires God to move it *metaphysically*, and if God stopped moving it, it would freeze instantly in place or even drop out of existence. I do indeed believe that things would drop out of existence instantly if God stopped sustaining them, but I do not believe that the First Way establishes this fact. I also believe that God's initiative is prior to every act of each creature, but once again, I do not believe that this has anything to do with the First Way.

2. Scott MacDonald, "Aquinas's Parasitic Cosmological Argument." After the writing of this book was far advanced, Michael Augros's excellent book *Aquinas on Theology and God's Existence* came out. It is the best treatment of the First Way that I have seen in the literature (other than the current one of course!). In many ways Augros and I agree, but there are some differences between us. Augros reads much of the argumentation from G2, which I consider in the next chapter, into the First Way itself. Since he considers this material to be implicit in the First Way, he thinks that the First Way establishes a stronger conclusion than I do. Augros makes no use of the minimal concept of god that Aquinas utilizes in his proof. Augros also considers the scope of the argument to include "spiritual motions," changes in conscious acts, while I restrict it to physical motion. Augros also does not argue for the universe's ability to continue in motion for a finite time after its mover stops moving it, something I do in the next section below. Another important difference is that Augros does not connect Aquinas's argument with modern science as I do. The connection with thermodynamics, discussed in chapters 4, 6, and 7, is crucial if the argument is to convince our contemporaries. Finally, he does not present as ample textual evidence as I do, or as carefully consider the relationship between Thomas's various texts. We in fact have many disagreements on the textual relationships between the various pieces of argument, but we agree on the overall reasoning that proves the existence of an immovable mover.

It will be helpful to consider some prominent versions of the conventional interpretation to see where they fall short. Then I will present clear texts in which Aquinas relates what would happen to the physical universe if it were no longer moved by immaterial beings. This will show quite clearly the untenability of the conventional interpretation and set the stage for my analysis of the First Way in this chapter and of G2 in the next.

Perhaps the best place to start is with the most traditional figure, Fr. Réginald Garrigou-Lagrange, OP. He believes that motion as such requires a mover constantly at work, for motion always involves a new actuality at every moment (e.g., a body in locomotion constantly occupies a new location), and that new actuality cannot come from the mobile itself, since it is in potency to that actuality.[3] In the same way, changing cognitive and appetitive acts ("metaphysical motions") require a mover constantly at work. The only thing that could stop the infinite regress of movers for any motion is something completely immobile and eternal, with no potency to be actualized. Such a being, purely in act, is pure existence, the transcendent God.[4] If God did not continually move things, they could not be in motion for even an instant.[5]

The analysis of the mover principle in the first chapter already demonstrates the untenability of Garrigou-Lagrange's interpretation. Besides its historical inaccuracy, his interpretation also requires denying the objective validity of the scientific principle of inertia, reducing it to a mere mathematical device.[6] Furthermore, his interpretation will be hard to square with Aquinas's denial that bodies would freeze instantly in place if their immaterial movers ceased moving them, as we shall see in the next section.

Fr. Joseph Owens, and John F. X. Knasas following him, see the first way as based upon the act of existence.[7] Existence is the actuality of all acts, what actualizes all things, and motion itself is something with the potential to exist. When it actually exists, it must receive existence from

---

3. Garrigou-Lagrange, *God: His Existence and His Nature*, vol. 1, 273.

4. Garrigou-Lagrange, *God: His Existence and His Nature*, vol. 1, 266–67.

5. Garrigou-Lagrange, *God: His Existence and His Nature*, vol. 1, 261–89.

6. Garrigou-Lagrange, *God: His Existence and His Nature*, vol. 1, 273–76 and fn. 24.

7. Joseph Owens, *St. Thomas Aquinas on the Existence of God: The Collected Papers of Joseph Owens, C.Ss.R.*, ed. John R. Catan (Albany, NY: State University of New York Press, 1980). For Knasas, see for example "Thomistic Existentialism and the Silence of the *Quinque Viae*," *The Modern Schoolman* 63, no. 3 (1986): 157–71, and *Thomistic Existentialism and Cosmological Reasoning*, 251–56.

something else that actualizes it. If that which actualizes the existence of motion is itself in potency to existence, then it also requires an actualizer. Since there cannot be an infinite regress, there must be a being that exists without the potency to exist, a being which is itself the pure act of existence. This being is God.

Although I accept this reasoning in itself, there are two problems with this interpretation. One, it is not plausible as an interpretation *of the First Way*, which does not even mention the act of existence. It resembles Aquinas's argument in *De Ente et Essentia* much more than it resembles the First Way. A cause of existence is a cause of being, which Aquinas distinguishes from a cause of becoming.[8] "Movers" are causes of becoming, not causes of being. Owens and Knasas have got the wrong "way." Secondly, the argument as they have described it is highly metaphysical, and it is quite a task to convince people of the need for a real distinction between essence and existence on which their argument is based. The argument would lose its status as the "more manifest way" if it were based on the act of existence. Aquinas has more ways of proving God's existence than one, each with different advantages, and Owens and Knasas rob us of all but one of those arguments.[9] Most importantly for my purposes, they rob us of the one that the empirically minded will find most convincing, the natural philosophical motion proof.

Edward Feser's account of the First Way is a modification of Owens's and Knasas's. He sees the consideration of motion with which the argument starts as doing no more than establishing the distinction between act and potency.[10] Once that is done, the argument turns to the existence of the mobile (rather than to the existence of the motion, as on Owens's interpretation), which is the actualization of the mobile's potency for existence. Since there cannot be an infinite regress, there must exist a purely actual actualizer, the pure act of existence, God.[11] The same problems that exist for Owens's and Knasas's interpretation exist also for Feser's interpretation.

All of these interpretations (those of Garrigou-Lagrange, Owens, Knasas, and Feser) clash with Aquinas's text in another way: they think that the proof establishes God's existence by establishing that pure act

8. E.g., *ST* I, q. 104, a. 1.
9. See Owens, "Aquinas and the Five Ways," in *St. Thomas Aquinas on the Existence of God*, 132–41.
10. See Feser, *Five Proofs of the Existence of God*, 24–25.
11. See Feser, *Aquinas*, esp. 74–76.

must exist. Yet in all of his works, Aquinas does not draw the conclusion that God is pure act until after the motion proof, and on the basis of further argumentation. One must first show that God exists and then show that He is pure act. One does not first show that pure act exists, and therefore that God does. I consider the relevant texts below (in the section titled "Is the Unmoved Mover Pure Act?", p. 96–100.)

Gaven Kerr has recently argued for a similar reading, although it is not clear whether he regards the existence of a being who is pure act as established in the First Way itself or subsequently but on its basis.[12] He holds that the argument shows that there must be a single source of all actuality manifested in any motion, a source that is not itself dependent on anything for its own actuality. How we get from each motion requiring a first, unmoved mover to the conclusion that every motion depends on the same first, unmoved mover, is not explained.[13] But Kerr seems to rely implicitly on the notion that motion depends upon God as the pure act of existence, of which there can be only one. Without fully identifying the two arguments, Kerr nevertheless assimilates the First Way to the argument in *De Ente et Essentia* and echoes Owens and Knasas in saying "it is not the case then that here we have several ways to God in Aquinas: the first way from motion and the more existential way(s) manifest in other places."[14]

Msgr. John Wippel's interpretation of the First Way is more historically plausible than the previous ones. He regards it as beginning with physical motion, but when it comes to justify the mover principle it broadens its scope to that of metaphysical motion. The argument establishes that there is an unmoved mover, a being that is not reduced from potency to act. Whether there is one or more than one unmoved mover—and whether this being is intelligent, and so on—will only be established by further argumentation he says.[15] But when Wippel proceeds to consider Aquinas's further arguments for divine unicity, infinity, and so on, he utilizes *as a premise* that God is pure act and states that this has been established by the First Way.[16] Yet being unmoved is not the same thing as being pure act. Being *immovable* is a bit closer, but being *unmoved* is not

---

12. Gaven Kerr, "A Deeper Look at Aquinas's First Way," *Nova et Vetera* 20, no. 2, English edition (2022): 461–84, at 476.

13. *Ibid.,* 475.

14. *Ibid.,* 477 and n. 29.

15. Wippel, *The Metaphysical Thought of Thomas Aquinas,* esp. 456–59.

16. Wippel, *The Metaphysical Thought of Thomas Aquinas,* 487, 491.

the same thing as being *immovable* either. Finally, Wippel, with so many others, holds that the mover must be simultaneous with what it moves,[17] and I have shown that this need not be the case.

In many ways David Twetten's interpretation excels others in its historical acumen. As he sees it, the First Way is based on metaphysical motion, on *change* of any kind, including changes in acts of intellect and will. All such changes require a continuously acting actualizer, and if that actualizer is itself changing *or changeable*, then it requires a further actualizer. The only way to end the regress is with an unactualizable actualizer, something entirely unchangeable. Such a being must in fact be uncaused and pure act, but these last two conclusions are not expressly drawn in the First Way and require further argumentation.[18] Although his interpretation is sophisticated, there are several problems with his analysis. First, Aquinas's motion proof is focused on physical and not metaphysical motion, as I will argue below. Secondly, Twetten's interpretation relies on simultaneity between mover and moved,[19] which need not obtain, as I have shown in the two previous chapters. Thirdly, Twetten does not justify the move from "unchanging changer" to "unchangeable changer." This cannot be justified by the First Way without the further argumentation found in G2 or the Third Way. Fourthly, Twetten must justify the claim that a change*able* but not chang*ing* mover would require a prior actualizer in order to cause motion.

All of the previous interpreters argue for a metaphysical (or "existential") reading of the argument. Recently, Fr. Michael Dodds has argued for a natural philosophical reading.[20] However, he too rests his interpretation on the idea of the simultaneity of efficient causes and effects.[21] He reasons that the characteristic motions of natural substances derive from their natures, determined for them by their substantial forms,[22] and that the continued existence of such forms depends upon "a cause of the form as such," a cause not of the becoming of the form, but of its very being.[23] Since the "existence of a form in matter implies no movement or change

17. Wippel, *The Metaphysical Thought of Thomas Aquinas*, 427, n. 72 and 408.
18. Twetten, "Clearing a 'Way' for Aquinas," 267–71.
19. See Twetten, "Back to Nature in Aquinas," and chapter 1 above.
20. Michael J. Dodds, OP, "From the Action of Creatures to the Existence of God: The First Way, Science, and the Philosophy of Nature," *Nova et Vetera* 19, no. 3, English edition (2021): 739–68, at 752–53 and n. 59.
21. *Ibid.*, 754.
22. *Ibid.*, 756.
23. *Ibid.*, 757.

except accidentally, and since no bodies act unless moved," "it follows of necessity that the principle on which the form depends directly must be something incorporeal,"[24] which is God. Unfortunately, in so interpreting the argument, Fr. Dodds has turned it into a metaphysical argument yet again, against his own intention. The argument no longer argues for a first mover, a cause of becoming, but for a first cause of being, something that holds things in existence every moment. Only a metaphysical argument can reach such a conclusion, not a natural philosophical one. Indeed, as I showed in chapter 1 above, Aquinas denies that the substantial form of a thing is a mover, that is, an efficient cause of motion, and so it cannot be part of the essentially ordered series of movers.[25] The First Way, basing itself on the series of *movers*, does not reason from a motion, to a substantial form, and then to a cause of being.

The following two sections will show how these interpretations clash with textual evidence outside the First Way. Afterward I will analyze the First Way itself, showing how it proves only a more modest conclusion than these interpretations propose.

Against the Conventional Interpretation: What Happens if God Does Not Move the Universe?

A very natural question that anyone might have, upon reading the First Way for the first time, is this: "What does Aquinas suppose would happen if God did not move the universe? Would it instantly freeze in place?" All of the previous interpretations imply that something like this would happen. Yet this seems hard to believe for our contemporaries, reared on the principle of inertia. It seems, rather, that something must act to *stop* motion. But if the universe can keep going without the continual action of a mover, then wouldn't one have to give up the motion proof, or fall back to arguing that God set the universe in motion in the beginning?

Fortunately, there are a couple of places where Aquinas explicitly addresses such issues: in his *Disputed Questions on the Power of God (De Potentia)*, question 5, a. 5–10, and his *Response to 43 Articles*. These texts are of the greatest interest for anyone attempting to make sense of the motion proofs for God's existence, and they have received very little attention. In the *Response to 43 Articles*, Aquinas gives his expert opinion

---

24. *Ibid.*, 760, quoting Aquinas, *QDP*, q. 5, a. 1, c.
25. See, for example, *In II Phys.*, l. 1, n. 144 [4] and *QDV* q. 22, a. 3, c.

on a series of questions he had been asked by his superior. In response to the first question ("article"), Aquinas states that in the order of nature God moves bodies not immediately but rather through the mediation of created spirits, although he can, whenever he pleases, move them directly by a miraculous act.[26] In response to the second and third articles, Aquinas states that created spirits move the heavenly bodies and thereby also move terrestrial bodies. In articles 12–15 Aquinas is asked whether the angels, by moving astronomical bodies, are the causes of all natural processes on earth. His response is that, yes, they are.[27]

Although none of this is demonstrated in the First Way, nor does the logic of the argument nor its conclusion depend on it, Aquinas's background belief (as evidenced by this text and many others) is that motion here on earth is caused by the movement of the astronomical bodies. These, in turn, are moved by intelligent angels, and these, finally, are moved by God's will. This is the essentially ordered series of moving causes, and breaking it anywhere precludes any *mover* causality from reaching terrestrial bodies. God could, of course, continue to move things supernaturally without the secondary movers that form part of the natural series, but a possible miracle of this kind plays no role in Aquinas's reasoning in the texts to be considered.

In the *De Potentia* text Aquinas considers what will happen at the end of the world. He does not believe that one can demonstrate by means of reason that the world *will* have an end, but faith teaches that it indeed will, and one can consider philosophically what would happen in such a scenario. In particular, Aquinas considers what would happen if the angels stopped pushing the planets and stars around.

The senses certainly do suggest at least some dependency of terrestrial motion on astronomical motion; the moon appears to cause the tides and the sun to cause plants to grow, for example. In the *De Potentia* text, Aquinas explains why he believes that the motion of the sun or any

---

26. *Resp. 43 Artic.*, art. 1 (Leon 42: 327, l. 60–328, l. 63, 70–77): "An Deus moueat aliquod corpus immediate. Ad quod respondendum uidetur quod ordo communis diuinitus institutus hoc habet ut corporea creatura ab ipso moueatur spiritu mediante…. Neque tamen diuina potentia est huic ordini alligata quin possit quandoque preter ordinem causarum secundarum aliquid agere cum sibi placuerit, sicut patet in operibus miraculosis. Dicit enim Augustinus XXVI Contra Faustum 'Appellamus naturam cognitum nobis cursum solitum nature, contra quem Deus cum aliquid facit magnalia uel mirabilia nominantur'."

27. *Resp. 43 Artic.*, art. 12–15: "To all those articles there is one response. For, since the heavenly bodies are the cause of the generation of inferior bodies—as is clear through the authority of Dionysius introduced above—it follows that the angels moving the heavenly bodies are also the cause of this generation." Translation mine.

other astronomical body requires an intelligent mover. This is certainly not apparent to the senses, and one might wonder why the regress of movers could not stop with the astronomical bodies. Why does a planet have to be moved by anything else, given Aquinas's understanding that natural motion flows spontaneously from the nature that a body has (as explained in chapter 1)? In Aquinas's view, neither an angel nor anything else pushes rocks down when they fall. Downward motion is just a natural consequence of what rocks are. Why couldn't orbital motion just be a natural consequence of what planets and stars are?

Aquinas considers this idea and his analysis shows how his view that planets and stars are moved by one or more external agent is actually required by the theses I have explored in chapter 1:

> The heavenly movement is not natural to the heavenly body in the same way as the elemental body's movement is natural to the elemental body. The latter movement has in the thing movable its principle not only material and receptive but also formal and active, because that movement follows from the form of the elemental body, even as other natural properties result from essential principles. Wherefore in these things the generator is said to be the mover inasmuch as it gives the form from which the movement results. But this does not apply to a heavenly body. Because as nature ever tends to one definite effect through not being indifferent to many, it is impossible that any nature tend to movement as such, since in every movement there is a certain absence of uniformity, inasmuch as the thing moved passes from one mode of being to another, and uniformity in the thing moved is contrary to the definition of movement. In consequence nature never inclines to movement for the sake of movement, but for the sake of some definite result to be obtained by movement. Thus a heavy body is inclined by nature to rest in the center, wherefore it tends to a downward motion, for the reason that by such a movement it will reach that place. On the other hand the heaven by its movement does not reach a "whereabouts" to which it is inclined by nature, because every "whereabouts" is the beginning and end of [its] movement, so that its natural movement cannot result, so to say, from a tendency of a natural inherent power in the same way as the natural movement of fire has an upward tendency. Now circular movement is said to be natural to the heaven insofar as it has a natural aptitude for that kind of movement, so that it contains in itself the passive principle of that movement, while the active principle of this movement is some separate substance, such as God, or an intelligence, or a soul according to some. As to which of these it may be, it matters not to the question at issue.[28]

---

28. *QDP* q. 5, a. 5, c. Translation emended.

Because it is cyclical, astronomical motion cannot be natural in the same way as the free fall of rocks. A planet does not (apparently) head to a definite place or condition and come to rest when it has attained that goal. Rocks, in their natural motion, do. A natural cause always tends toward its natural effect; it is determined to one result, which is its end or final cause. In modern terms, physical systems always tend toward an equilibrium condition, and once they reach it they do not spontaneously depart from it. Planets do not (apparently) act like a purely physical system.

There is no such thing as a perpetual motion machine. For a physical system to repeat a given cycle indefinitely, it must be continually supplied with energy by some external agent. In the case of an automobile engine, it is a person returning again and again to the gas pump. In the case of animals, it is through the ingestion of plants. For plants, it is the sun radiating energy toward the earth in the form of light (and the plants themselves are the source of fossil fuels). If the stars and planets really are continuing in motion indefinitely, repeating perfectly identical cycles, then they too must be moved by an external agent. Otherwise they would be winding down toward some equilibrium condition. (In fact, they are winding down very, very slowly, but this was not apparent to Aquinas, and it does not harm his argument, which is disjunctive as we will see in the next chapter.)

Unlike a natural agent, an intelligent being can repeat identical cycles as many times as it needs to for its own purposes. The stars and planets are moved externally by one or more immaterial intelligent beings. As Aquinas says in the text, this could be God, angels, or "sphere-souls," but his preferred opinion is that they are moved by angels. Aquinas believes that the angels will continue to move the sun and stars around and around as long as necessary for enough human beings to be generated to complete the number of the elect, at which point the angels will stop moving the stars. If their purpose required them to move the stars around forever, they would do so.[29]

It is not Aquinas's view, however, that the rest of the universe will instantly freeze in place when the causes sustaining its motion withdraw their influence and the heavenly bodies come to rest. Rather, the universe will not be able to continue in motion *forever* without that sustaining influence. It will wind down to equilibrium in a finite time. Whether that

---

29. *QDP* q. 5, a. 5, c.

time is five minutes or fifteen billion years is an empirical question, rather than one of principle. In the *De Potentia* text, what Aquinas says will happen, whether quickly or slowly, is as follows: animals, plants, and "mixed bodies" (what we would now call chemical compounds) will dissolve into their elements, because anything composed of contrary elements has within itself a principle of its own corruption (the contrary properties of the various elements present virtually within the mixed body work against each other and break the whole down into its elements).[30] After this dissolution, the four elements themselves will continue to exist and will retain their natural qualities, including heaviness and lightness by which they tend to their proper places. The four elements will return to their four, separate, proper places.[31] (For example, out of a fish that dies in the ocean all four elements will be generated; three of them will be out of place and will have to return to their places via locomotion. The water can stay put.) At that point, and only at that point, everything will rest in place, and no more motion will occur in the universe. The sun, planets, and stars, since they will then be motionless, will no longer act on the elements, and without their influence the elements will be unable to alter one another and produce any change.[32]

It is already clear from this text that it will take time for animals, plants, and minerals to dissolve into their elements and for these elements

30. *QDP* q. 5, a. 9: "Since they [minerals, plants, and brute animals] are composed of contrary elements, they contain within themselves an active principle of corruption.... Nor have they an internal principle to preserve them from corruption, because their forms are in themselves corruptible through not being self-subsistent but depending on matter for their being. Consequently they cannot remain for ever identically the same, nor specifically the same when generation and corruption cease" (a. 9, c.). "All God's works 'continue for ever' either in themselves or in their causes: in this way animals and plants will remain [at the end of the world] because the heavenly bodies and the elements will remain" (a. 9, ad 1.) Punctuation emended.

31. *QDP* q. 5, a. 7, c.: "It seems that it is to be said that, [when the motion of the heavens ceases,] the elements will remain in their substance with their natural qualities, but that generation, corruption and alteration resulting from their action on one another will cease.... The substance, however, of the elements will remain even as the substance of the heaven. The reason is that since the universe will remain forever, as we have proved already, it follows that whatsoever belongs to the perfection of the universe must remain as to its substance. Now this applies to the elements inasmuch as they are essential parts of the universe, as the Philosopher proves (*De Caelo et Mundo*, II). For if the universe is a circular body it must have a centre, and this is the earth; and given the earth which is heavy absolutely as occupying the centre, there must be its contrary, namely fire, which is light absolutely, because if one contrary exists in nature, the other must exist also. Now given the extremes, we must posit the middle, wherefore we must posit air and water, which are heavy in comparison with fire, and light in comparison with earth, one of which is nearer to the earth than the other." Translation emended. Cp. also a. 10, obj. 7 and ad 7: in the human body, and only in the human body, the elements' tendency to move back to their proper places will be restrained.

32. *QDP* q. 5, a. 7–8.

to return to their places, although the time required might be quite short on Aquinas's view. It would be unreasonable to think that the disparate elements could get to their places instantaneously. There would be motion in the universe as the elements returned to their places, even after the immaterial being or beings stopped moving the universe.

Fortunately, we also have in his *Response to 43 Articles* Aquinas's *explicit* acknowledgment that there would be motion for a time if the intelligent movers of the universe stopped moving it. In articles 20–24, Aquinas is asked about what would happen if the astronomical bodies ceased from motion ("*ordine naturae*," that is, what would happen in the order of nature, barring a divine miracle?) Would iron instantly ("*in instanti*") dissolve into its elements (art. 20)? Would every body composed of elements *instantly* dissolve into its elements (art. 21)? Would the whole world be resolved *instantly* into its elements (art. 22)? If there were no light from the stars, would all humans *instantly* die (art. 23)? If there were no light from the stars, would all irrational animals *instantly* die (art. 24)? Since Aquinas has already stated in response to the first article that in the order of nature God moves bodies indirectly, through the angels moving the planets (and that when He moves them directly it is called a miracle) these questions are tantamount to asking what would happen if God stopped moving the universe.

In response to these interesting questions (exactly the questions we want to hear the answer to!) Aquinas says the following:

> To all these [questions] there is the same response. For as has been said above, the higher [i.e., astronomical] bodies through their motion and rays are the cause of generation and corruption and of corporeal life in lower [i.e., terrestrial] bodies. Hence no one should doubt that if such a cause is removed its effect will be removed, especially since this seems highly consonant with the faith, according to which we posit that, putting aside the figure of this world, and the motion of the heaven ceasing through the divine will, only the elements made new will remain, as well as humans made immortal by the divine power. *Unless perhaps the force of the question lies in the words "in an instant"* (in instanti), *because the dissolution of these bodies into the elements, since it is a certain motion, cannot be in an instant; but* its beginning *can be in an instant* [i.e., the motion can instantly begin].[33]

---

33. *Resp. 43 Artic.*, art. 20–24, (Leon 42: 331, l. 322–35): "Ad omnia ista est eadem responsio. Sicut enim supra dictum est, superiora corpora per suum motum et radios sunt causa generationis et corruptionis et uite corporalis in inferioribus corporibus; unde nulli dubium esse debet quin remota tali causa remoueatur effectus, et precipue cum hoc ualde consonum fidei uideatur secundum quam

Aquinas is saying that when, by God's command, the angels stop moving the astronomical bodies, the astronomical bodies themselves will stop moving terrestrial bodies. These bodies will immediately begin to dissolve into their elements.[34] *But Aquinas states as clearly as one could wish that this dissolution will take a finite time, even though it only starts when the heavenly bodies stop moving.* But if it takes a finite time, after the heavens have ceased their motion, for compound bodies to alter and then corrupt,[35] then it will certainly also take a finite time for the elements generated out of the corrupted bodies to return to their proper places. Locomotion will have to occur, for the elements will be generated out of their proper places.[36]

---

ponimus quod, pretereunte figura huius mundi et motu celi cessante per uoluntatem diuinam, sola elementa innouata remanebunt et homines immortales effecti uirtute diuina. Nisi forte fiat uis in hoc quod dicitur 'in instanti', quia resolutio istorum corporum in elementa cum sit quidam motus non potest esse in instanti; sed principium eius in instanti esse potest." Translation mine. Emphasis added. This text is dated to 1271, late in Aquinas's career. For the dating, see Torrell, *Saint Thomas Aquinas*, vol. 1, 168–69.

34. The *De Potentia* texts referenced above make it clear that it is the cessation of the *locomotion* of the heavenly bodies, not of their shining light, that will cause compound bodies to dissolve. The heavenly bodies will continue to shine after the world ends (see *QDP* q. 5, a. 8), but there will be no compound bodies other than human bodies.

35. Substantial change itself is instantaneous, but it is the terminus of a process of alteration. See, for example, *In VI Phys.*, l. 8, n. 834, 839–40 [9, 14–15].

36. A reviewer reasonably objects that, since Aquinas's definition of time is the number of the motion of the heavenly sphere, time must come to an end when the heavenly sphere stops rotating. But there cannot be motion without time. Hence there could be no motion anywhere in the universe after the heavenly sphere stops undergoing motion. This is a weighty objection, but it has a solution. In *ST* I, q. 66, a. 4, ad 3, Aquinas responds to an objection arguing that time cannot begin at the beginning of creation, because the firmament is only created on the second day! Aquinas responds: "If the movement of the firmament did not begin immediately from the beginning, then the time that preceded was the measure, not of the firmament's movement, but of the first movement of whatsoever kind. *For it is accidental to time to be the measure of the firmament's movement, insofar as this is the first movement. But if the first movement was another than this, time would have been its measure, for everything is measured by the first of its kind.* And it must be granted that at once from the beginning, there was movement of some kind, at least in the succession of concepts and affections in the angelic mind. But movement without time cannot be conceived, since time is nothing else than the measure of priority and succession in movement." Time is the measure of the first movement (not first movement in time, but first in nature). It so happens that given the present constitution of the universe (as Aquinas's medieval cosmology saw it), the movement of the outermost heavenly sphere is the first movement. But given other constitutions, other movements would be the first movement, and time would be their measure. Will there be a new time after the heavenly sphere stops undergoing motion, just as there is a new heaven and a new earth? Aquinas states in *ST* I, q. 10, a. 5, ad 1 that "Spiritual creatures as regards successive affections and acts of intelligence are measured by time." In q. 14, a. 12, he states that "we must hold that God knows infinite things even by the knowledge of vision. For God knows even the thoughts and affections of hearts, which will be multiplied to infinity as rational creatures endure for ever." Hence in Aquinas's view there will always be change of some kind, and always time of some kind, even after the heavenly bodies cease circling. Michael Bolin also points out to me that on Aquinas's view time is not a prerequisite for motion, but rather a consequence of it.

We can see clearly now that in the First Way Aquinas *cannot* be arguing that an unmoved mover is needed to keep everything in motion every instant. For Aquinas does not believe that the universe would freeze instantly in place if its mover stopped moving it. In fact, Aquinas states in his response to the twenty-sixth article that it takes divine power to *prevent* the human body from corrupting (and hence undergoing the motion of dissolution) if the heavens cease rotating; the reasoning used applies to all compound bodies.[37] Insofar as the conventional interpretation holds that natural beings must be continually moved by an external mover as long as they are in motion, it clashes with Aquinas's understanding of physics and cosmology.

Is the Unmoved Mover Pure Act?

Another problem with the conventional interpretation (in all but Twetten's version) is that it sees the First Way as proving the existence of a being that is pure act. Yet Aquinas makes no mention in the First Way of "pure act." In justifying the mover principle he does argue that a mover must be in act in a way that what is in motion is not. It is often suggested that, when coupled with the ensuing argument against infinite regress, this implicitly proves that there must exist a being in no way in potency, but purely in act. However, the argument for the mover principle is not well suited for drawing such a conclusion.

Aquinas reasons in the First Way that "it is not possible that the same thing be at the same time in potency and act in reference to the same thing, but only in reference to diverse things. For what is hot in act cannot be at the same time hot in potency." The kind of potency about which he reasons, therefore, is incompatible with actuality, not composed with it. In later scholastic terms, the argument is about "objective potency" and not about "subjective potency."[38] In the relevant sense, a living sheep

---

37. *Resp. 43 Artic.*, art. 25–26, (Leon 42: 331, l. 355–332, l. 370): "Cum ergo dicitur cessante motu celi corpus hominis esse incorruptibile per naturam, si hec prepositio 'per' designat causam per se, falsum est: non enim ad hoc se extendit uirtus nature create ut causare possit incorruptionem corporis ex contrariis compositi. (The power of a created nature does not extend so far as to be able to cause the incorruption of a body composed out of contraries.) Si autem predicta prepositio designet causam per accidens, sic uerum est quodam modo quod dicitur, quia subtracta est uniuersalis causa corruptionis naturalis, scilicet motus celi. In hoc etiam sensu melius diceretur negatiue quam priuatiue, puta si sic diceretur: cessante motu celi corpus hominis, si remaneat diuina uirtute, non est iam corruptibile per naturam. Verum quia semper quod est per se potius est eo quod est per accidens, potius uidetur dicendum quod sit corruptibile per naturam."

38. For this terminology, see Suárez, *Metaphysical Disputations*, disp. 31, sect. 3, n. 2–3, translated

composed of prime matter (pure potency) and substantial form (act) no longer has any potency to be a sheep. Yet the sheep is certainly not what Thomists call "pure act," not even in respect of substance and prescinding from accidental perfections that the sheep could acquire. Hence the kind of real composition of act and potency represented, by, say, the union of substantial form and matter, or essence and existence, or substance and accident, is not even considered by the First Way. To end the regress of movers causing a given motion, one does not need a being without composition of ("subjective") potency and act, but one that is not purely in ("objective") potency to that toward which it moves another thing. At least, that is all the argument shows.

Aquinas does, however, proceed to conclude that God is pure act soon *after* the motion proof in both *ST* and *SCG*. In *SCG* in fact, he states that he will utilize the motion proof's conclusion that God is "absolutely unmoved" to demonstrate God's other attributes.[39] The conclusion that God is pure act is drawn just three short chapters away, in chapter 16. In *ST*, Aquinas draws the conclusion that God is pure act in the article immediately following the Five Ways, in I, q. 3, a. 1.

However, arguments are given in each case for the conclusion. It is not already established that God is pure act in the proofs for God's existence themselves. Aquinas does not merely say that we should notice that the conclusion was already drawn; he provides an additional argument, taking a step beyond the proofs for God. In other words, to establish that God exists one need not establish that pure act exists. Rather, one first establishes that God exists and then provides a further argument that He possesses the attribute of being pure act. If the later argument that God is pure act is rejected or criticized, that does not touch the proof that God exists, which stands on its own merits.

Furthermore, in *ST* Aquinas states that the conclusion that God is pure act follows from the fact that he has established that God is the

by Norman J. Wells as *On the Essence of Finite Being as Such and on the Existence of that Essence and their Distinction* (Milwaukee, WI: Marquette University Press, 1983), 67–68. See also Scotus, *Questions on the* Metaphysics *of Aristotle*, bk. IX, q. 1–2, n. 39–49. Scotus's understanding of potency is somewhat different from Aquinas's. For him, no potency, strictly speaking, is composed with its act. Scotus does not consider prime matter to be pure potency, but a minimal actuality with potency to becoming various corporeal substances. Once it receives a certain form, there is no longer a potency in matter to that form.

39. *SCG* I, c. 14, n. 119 [4]: "As a principle of procedure in knowing God by way of remotion, therefore, let us adopt the proposition which, from what we have said, is now manifest, namely, that God is absolutely unmoved (*omnino immobilis*)." This proposition is proved by G2, not G1.

"First Being."[40] Since act is by nature prior to potency, he reasons, the first being must be pure act. But which of the Five Ways establishes that God is the "first being?" Clearly the Fourth Way does, since its conclusion is that something exists that is most of all being, and the cause of being and goodness in all other things. The Fourth Way, if successful, provides the most solid basis for the argument that God is pure act. The Second and Third Ways also establish that God is a first being, although in a weaker sense: a first efficient cause or self-necessary being may not be before all other beings, since there may be other self-necessary beings, but no other being is prior to such a being. For a first efficient cause has no cause of its own being and cannot come to be, and the same is true of a self-necessary being. Hence any such being depends on no other, and by Aquinas's argument is without potency. (In terms of the Second Way and Third Way this conclusion is obvious in regard to potency to substantial existence, but more needs to be said to show that such a being cannot have potency in regard to accidents.)

Does the First Way establish that there is a first being? As I will show in the logical analysis of the First Way below, it only establishes that for each motion there is a first mover with the wherewithal to cause that motion, rather than being a merely instrumental cause. Whether there is one or more such first movers is not established, and without further argumentation it is not clear that such a noninstrumental mover is anything more than a natural cause, brought into existence at an earlier point in time and liable to go out of existence later. And perhaps an unmoved mover, which is not moved to cause motion, is in potency to other perfections that are irrelevant to its ability to cause the motion. Finally, barring further argumentation, it might also be the case that a first mover is conserved in being by something prior, without being moved by it. The First Way is certainly not the best candidate for establishing that a first being exists.

SCG presents a different case than *ST*. There Aquinas does draw the conclusion that God is pure act on the basis of His being "wholly immovable." But in *SCG* Aquinas can utilize the stronger motion proof G2, rather than just the weaker one, G1. The third stage of G2 shows that infinite

---

40. *ST* I, q. 3, a. 1, c. (Leon. 4:35): "Necesse est id quod est primum ens, esse in actu, et nullo modo in potentia. Licet enim in uno et eodem quod exit de potentia in actum, prius sit potentia quam actus tempore, simpliciter tamen actus prior est potentia: quia quod est in potentia, non reducitur in actum nisi per ens actu. Ostensum est autem supra quod Deus est primum ens. Impossibile est igitur quod in Deo sit aliquid in potentia."

accidentally ordered series would depend on a finite essentially ordered causal series. And the fourth stage of G2 shows that there is an everlasting being that moves the whole universe as final cause, commanding even the immaterial movers of the celestial spheres, if there be any. This being is more clearly the first being, possessing priority over all other beings that exist or have existed. These facts serve as the basis for arguments that God is pure act in *SCG* I, c. 16.[41]

It is thus possible to utilize Aquinas's motion proofs as a basis for establishing that God is pure act, and Aquinas himself does so. Yet that conclusion belongs outside of the proofs for God's existence, and the proofs do not depend on it. Furthermore, the First Way is too weak on its own to serve as a basis for drawing the conclusion of pure actuality. It must first be extended by G2 or by the Fifth and Third Ways. The conclusion that God is pure act is a highly important and fruitful metaphysical truth, yet God's existence as an immaterial, everlasting, immovable mover can be proven by natural philosophy (utilizing G2) without the need to wade into difficult metaphysical arguments.

We should not reduce the number of ways to God's existence, or require too much of all of them. Some of them have more robust conclusions than others (especially the Fourth Way and the *De Ente et Essentia* proof) but are correspondingly more difficult to grasp. The motion

41. Aquinas also draws the conclusion that God is pure act from the motion proof in the *Compendium Theologiae*. There Aquinas builds almost his entire philosophical account of the divine nature on a proof quite similar to the First Way. Now this is not in itself decisive; the *Compendium* is usually considered a more popular work, and the argumentation in it is less tight and more summary in form. (Torrell speaks of Aquinas, in authoring the *Compendium*, as taking on the role of a "popularizer": *Saint Thomas Aquinas*, vol. 1, 165. Wippel speaks of the *Compendium* as intended for "a broader audience": *The Metaphysical Thought of Thomas Aquinas*, 440.) However, the text should not be dismissed. He gives a single proof for God's existence that looks much like the First Way (*Comp.* I, c. 3), and goes on to argue that since God is the first mover, He must be immovable (c. 4), necessary in himself (c. 6), pure act (c. 9), and existence itself (c. 11). However, a close look at the motion proof in c. 3 reveals that the kind of extended argumentation found in G2 is needed by this argument. Aquinas states that "we see that all things in motion are moved by other things, lower things indeed by higher things, as the elements by celestial bodies, ... and among celestial bodies inferior ones are acted on by a superior one. (*Videmus enim omnia que mouentur ab aliis moueri: inferiora quidem per superiora, sicut elementa per corpora celestia; ... et in corporibus etiam celestibus inferiora a superiori aguntur*.)" (Leon. 42, p. 84, c. 3, l. 3–8. Translation mine.) Aquinas is there presupposing standard medieval physics and cosmology and the argument depends on it. He can ignore the problem of whether every regress of movers ends with the same mover or each with a different one because it is common scholarly opinion that terrestrial motion depends on astronomical motion, and that everything is subject to the motion of the outermost sphere. Hence everything must be moved by whatever moves the outermost sphere. Such a being cannot be affected by any other mover. Without the medieval cosmology of an enclosed universe of concentric spheres, the argument there would not justify as strong of a conclusion as Aquinas takes from it.

proofs are the more manifest ways because they belong to natural philosophy. They can prepare the ground for the metaphysician by showing that being extends beyond the material, and they are also valuable in their own right. Those who find metaphysical reasoning unconvincing should still find the natural philosophical demonstration of God's existence fully convincing.

THE FIRST WAY: SUCCESS AND LIMITATIONS

Aquinas's Versions of the Motion Proof

In *ST*, there is one motion proof for God's existence, the first of the famous five ways. In his earlier work *SCG*, Aquinas presents two motion proofs (G1 and G2), attributing both to Aristotle. Although attributed to Aristotle and based closely on his texts, these proofs are not quite identical to those found in Aquinas's commentaries on Aristotle's *Physics* and *Metaphysics* (those two works being the original sources of Aquinas's arguments.) In *SCG*, Aquinas more freely adapts and arranges the sub-arguments found in Aristotle's text to his own purposes. In his commentaries, Aquinas develops the various pieces of the arguments at greater length, but is more bound to Aristotle's own purposes and arrangement (although even in the commentaries Aquinas does take some liberties).

The first motion proof in *SCG*, G1, has the exact same structure as the First Way in *ST*. The most obvious difference is that instead of providing one sub-argument for each of the two premises—the mover principle and the impossibility of infinite regress—in G1 Aquinas provides three sub-arguments for each premise.[42] The same structure that is utilized in the First Way and in G1 is also found in the motion proof contained in Aquinas's commentary on book VII of Aristotle's *Physics*,[43] although there the proof is cast only in terms of local motion. *Physics* VII.1 is, in fact, the clear source of both *ST*'s First Way and *SCG*'s G1, which ought to be read in its light. Yet although the overall structure is the same in all three proofs, the sub-arguments offered for the premises are different in each. *Physics* VII.1 provides one sub-argument for each premise. G1 includes these same

---

42. Another difference is in the way the conclusion is worded. In *ST* the conclusion is that a first *unmoved* mover exists (*a nullo movetur*), whereas in G1 it is that a first *immobile* mover exists (*immobile*). *Immobile* could mean "unmoved," but "immovable" seems a safer reading. See chapter 4, fn. 11 below.

43. *In VII Phys.*, l. 2, n. 891 [1].

sub-arguments, but it supplements each with two further sub-arguments taken from *Physics* VIII.4–5. In the First Way, Aquinas retains only one sub-proof of each premise, but not the ones from *Physics* VII.1—these are more difficult to make work. Rather, he utilizes the more promising sub-arguments deriving from *Physics* VIII.5.

Contrasting with these proofs, the second motion proof in *SCG*, G2, is based closely in its whole structure on Aristotle's extended argument in *Physics* VIII. Thus we have two sets of motion proofs. On the one hand there are the First Way, G1, and the commentary on *Physics* VII. On the other hand, there are G2 and the commentary on *Physics* VIII. The structures of these two sets of proofs are clearly distinct. The ones deriving from *Physics* VII are quite short in their basic structure, even if the sub-proofs of the premises occupy quite a bit of space, as in G1. The *Physics* VIII version, including G2, is much more extended and involves explicit discussion of the possibility of sempiternal motion.

This taxonomy of motion proofs enables one to appreciate the significance of something Aquinas says in his commentary on Aristotle's *Physics* (which was probably written late in Aquinas's career, after *SCG* and *ST*'s five ways[44]). At the beginning of both *Physics* VII and *Physics* VIII Aquinas states in his commentary that the *Physics* VII motion proof establishes "*that there is a first motion and a first mover (esse primum motum et primum motorem)*," whereas the *Physics* VIII proof establishes "*what sort of thing the first motion and first mover is (qualis sit motus primus et primus motor.)*"[45] What holds of *Physics* VII holds of G1 and the First Way: they show that there is a first mover, but not what sort of being it is. This will be confirmed below by the logical analysis of the First Way itself. We need the *Physics* VIII/G2 version of the proof—analyzed in the next chapter—to show that the first mover is immovable, everlasting, and immaterial—in other words, that it is not a purely natural, mundane mover.

Logical Analysis of the First Way: Unmoved Movers

To see more clearly what the First Way on its own does and does not accomplish, it will be helpful to look once more at the structure of the argument as given in Aquinas's text:

44. See Torrell, *Saint Thomas Aquinas*, 231–33.
45. *In VII Phys.*, l. 1, n. 884 [1]; see also *In VIII Phys.*, l. 1, n. 965 [1].

The first and more manifest way [to prove God's existence] is the one that is taken from motion. For it is certain and evident to the senses that some things are in motion in this world. Now whatever is in motion is moved by another.... If, therefore, that by which it is moved be in motion, it is necessary that it also is moved by another, and that by another. But this cannot proceed to infinity.... Therefore it is necessary to arrive at some first mover which is moved by nothing (*primum movens, quod a nullo movetur*), and this all understand to be God (*et hoc omnes intelligunt Deum*).[46]

In its basic outline this argument is quite simple. The defense of the premises, omitted here, constitutes the bulk of the argument as a whole. But since we have now already grasped the premises, we can see readily what follows from them. If everything in motion is moved by another, and there cannot be an infinite regress of essentially ordered moved movers, there must be a mover that is not moved by anything else and not itself in motion.

But if one recalls the First Way's argument for the mover principle, not quoted here but analyzed extensively in chapter 1, one can get a bit more from the proof. That argument reasoned that everything in motion is moved by another because what is in motion is in potency, and what causes motion is in act, and the same thing cannot be in potency and act with respect to the same feature at the same time. Hence the conclusion of the First Way is not only that each motion is caused by an unmoved mover, but that that mover is already in act with respect to that toward which the mobile is in motion. The unmoved mover must formally or eminently possess the actuality that it effects, that is, it must have that actuality either in the same way or in a higher way.

---

46. *ST* I, q. 2, a. 3, c. Leonine edition (4:31): "Prima autem et manifestior via est, quae sumitur ex parte motus. Certum est enim, et sensu constat, aliqua moveri in hoc mundo. Omne autem quod movetur, ab alio movetur. Nihil enim movetur, nisi secundum quod est in potentia ad illud ad quod movetur: movet autem aliquid secundum quod est actu. Movere enim nihil aliud est quam educere aliquid de potentia in actum: de potentia autem non potest aliquid reduci in actum, nisi per aliquod ens in actu: sicut calidum in actu, ut ignis, facit lignum, quod est calidum in potentia, esse actu calidum, et per hoc movet et alterat ipsum. Non autem est possibile ut idem sit simul in actu et potentia secundum idem, sed solum secundum diversa: quod enim est calidum in actu, non potest simul esse calidum in potentia, sed est simul frigidum in potentia. Impossibile est ergo quod, secundum idem et eodem modo, aliquid sit movens et motum, vel quod moveat seipsum. Omne ergo quod movetur, oportet ab alio moveri. Si ergo id a quo movetur, moveatur, oportet et ipsum ab alio moveri; et illud ab alio. Hic autem non est procedere in infinitum: quia sic non esset aliquod primum movens; et per consequens nec aliquod aliud movens, quia moventia secunda non movent nisi per hoc quod sunt mota a primo movente, sicut baculus non movet nisi per hoc quod est motus a manu. Ergo necesse est devenire ad aliquod primum movens, quod a nullo movetur: et hoc omnes intelligunt Deum." Translation mine.

But as I explained above (in the section titled "Is the Unmoved Mover Pure Act?"), this is not the same as showing that the unmoved mover is pure act, completely lacking any admixture of potency. For the only kind of potency Aquinas is talking about in this argument is the potency that is *replaced by act* ("objective potency") rather than that which *enters into composition with act* ("subjective potency.") For he says in the text of the First Way that "it is not possible that the same thing be at the same time in potency and act in reference to the same thing, but only in reference to diverse things. For what is hot in act cannot be at the same time hot in potency." This is only true of objective potency. In the case of subjective potency, what is a sheep in act is also a sheep in potency at the same time. For a sheep is composed of prime matter—pure potentiality—and the substantial form of sheep, its actuality. Aquinas's argument for an external mover, since it is based on the impossibility of the simultaneous possession of both potency and act, shows that the mover must not be in objective potency to the act it causes; it does not show that the mover is not in subjective potency to the act it causes, for it can simultaneously possess the act necessary to move something toward that same act. Hence an unmoved mover, in order to be the first mover in the generation of a new sheep, for example, must actually be a sheep, formally or eminently, and not merely in ("objective") potency. This does not in itself show that the first mover must be lacking the potential principle of prime matter, or lacking any other admixture of subjective potency.

Proponents of the conventional interpretation will object: Potency is not of itself in act, and hence anything composed of potency and act depends on some naturally (rather than temporally) prior, actual being for its own actuality. If the cause of its being actual is not itself pure act, it too would depend on a prior being, and one cannot stop until one reaches pure act. Hence the First Way does show that something more than sheep generate sheep; it shows that a transcendent being does.

Certainly Aquinas would not disagree with this reasoning in itself, but it is not contained within the more manifest First Way. The First Way defines the act of moving as "the drawing out of something from potency into act. (*Movere enim nihil aliud est quam educere aliquid de potentia in actum.*)" This means that to move something—as the phrase is used in this proof—is to change it. This proof says nothing about a stable being composed of potency and act needing a continual cause of its actuality. The mere fact that the actuality of being a sheep, its substantial form, is the act of some potency (prime matter) from which it is really distinct does not mean that the sheep needs a continual mover to sustain it and make it act. Certainly one could extend the term "move" to include any metaphysical, external cause of any actuality of any potency, but the fact that any such actuality needs a simultaneous cause is far from manifest, needs an argument, and has nothing to do with the First Way. It is not manifest that once something exists in act, it needs a continual cause of its actuality.

The next thing to notice about the First Way is that nothing in the argument precludes the possibility that different motions are caused by different motionless movers. At the same time, nothing in the argument proves that different motions *are* caused by different motionless movers; they could all be caused by one and the same motionless mover. This argument, therefore, proves that there is *one or more* motionless movers. (Graham Oppy criticizes the First Way for failing to prove that a single unmoved mover causes every motion,[47] but he misunderstands Aquinas, who did not even intend to prove that stronger conclusion within the First Way itself. He addresses the issue of God's unity in q. 11, a. 3.)

The First Way, then, is beginning to look like quite a modest argument. The underlying reason for this modesty is that only Aquinas's first thesis about infinite regress appears in the proof, namely that essentially ordered causal series cannot be infinite. The second thesis is not utilized, that is, the thesis that infinite accidentally ordered causal series must be sustained by an essential cause or essentially ordered series of causes outside the accidental series. The absence of this second thesis prevents the First Way from definitively proving that anything more than natural movers exist.

To see how, take the case of the growth and development of sheep. This motion is caused by the generators of the child sheep, namely, the parent sheep. The essentially ordered series of causes cannot regress infinitely. Does it stop with the parent sheep, or does it continue back toward some more principal cause? Aquinas, of course, believes that the parent sheep act in virtue of the motion of a heavenly body, which in turn is moved by an immaterial being. Could anything in the argument of the First Way prove this or anything like it, however? Recall that in an essentially ordered series of causes the prior cause causes the posterior

---

47. Graham Oppy, *Arguing about Gods* (New York: Cambridge University Press, 2006), 103.

cause to cause, and the causality is transitive: the prior cause causes the ultimate effect. Can anything other than the parent sheep be shown to be responsible for the generation and development of the child sheep?

The fact that the sheep species exists means that the actuality that constitutes the wherewithal to generate children sheep (namely, the substantial form of sheep) is present in the world.[48] It cannot be shown that the parent sheep are essentially subordinate to a higher mover unless it can be shown that something causes—by nature or intention, not by chance—the whole sheep species to come into existence or to be preserved in existence. That something's causality would be responsible for all the characteristic features of sheep, including their generation and development. However, if the generations of sheep have proceeded without beginning and without end—as Aquinas thinks entirely possible on the basis of reason—then the species as a whole is not brought into existence. The generations of sheep would constitute an infinite, accidentally ordered causal series. Is the sheep species sustained in existence? To show that, one needs the second thesis against infinite regress. That thesis is absent from the First Way, but it is present in G2 in *SCG*, and something very much like it is present in the Third Way in *ST*, as I will explain in the next chapter. Alternatively, if one could show that the generation of new sheep and the preservation of the species requires the purposive coordination of noncognitive causes, of astronomical and environmental factors say, then one could show that the parent sheep are subordinated as movers to a higher, intelligent cause. That line of reasoning, however, belongs to the Fifth Way, the teleological proof, which I will take up in chapter 5. Hence, to show that anything more than parent sheep causes the child sheep—as part of an essentially ordered causal series—one needs the Fifth Way, the Third Way, or G2. These proofs extend and complete the First Way.

As I have said, then, the First Way establishes that for any given motion there is some mover that is not itself moved to cause the motion in question, a first, unmoved mover. It does not, however, establish that this unmoved mover is immov*able*. The argument's most famous critic, Anthony Kenny, was right to argue thus.[49] Accidentally ordered causal series

---

48. Or rather, one would presume that the requisite actuality was present until a metaphysical argument proved otherwise.

49. Kenny, *The Five Ways*, 23, 33; see also MacDonald, "Aquinas's Parasitic Cosmological Argument," 146–47.

can continue to extend backward when essentially ordered series come to a stop. Perhaps an unmoved mover, which brings a stop to the regress of essentially ordered causes of a given motion, and which itself has the wherewithal to account for that motion, was nevertheless moved in some way in the past. Perhaps it will be moved in the future.

Indeed—given the logic of the argument, the proof of the mover principle, and the argument against infinite regress—it could even be undergoing motion in the present, at the same time as it is acting as an unmoved mover, as long as it is undergoing motion in some respect irrelevant to its ability to act as a mover. To end the regress of causes the first mover must *of itself* have the actuality necessary to cause the motion in question, and hence it must not be in motion—and thus moved by another—with respect to that state of actuality. But for all that has been said so far, it might be acquiring some completely different, unrelated actuality at the same time as it is causing the motion in question. A magnet can move iron toward itself all on its own and thus act as a first mover;[50] it is irrelevant whether or not it is being heated by the sun at the same time as it draws the iron.[51] Furthermore, on the common understanding of gravity the earth is causing the moon to move in a circle around it, and no further explanation of the moon's orbit is needed beyond the moon's own natural force of inertia. At the same time the sun is heating the earth up, but that seems irrelevant to the earth's ability to move the moon.

Thus the logic of the argument is not able to demonstrate that an unmoved mover must be "supermundane" (i.e., something more than a natural mover within the world). Perhaps what have been called "mundane primary movers"[52] would suffice. There is nothing supernatural about a magnet, yet it seems to act as an unmoved mover. To all appearances, nothing moves it to move the iron; it can do this all by itself. Again, the earth at least seems to be a modern example of a primary, unmoved mover with respect to the moon's orbital motion. Consider one more modern

50. Lawrence Dewan helpfully points out that "first cause" or "first mover" is a *kind* of thing that we find instantiated multiple times, to varying degrees, in the world of our experience. God as we understand Him is first mover in the highest, absolute way, but He is not the only first mover we know of: "St. Thomas and Infinite Causal Regress," in *Idealism, Metaphysics and Community*, ed. William Sweet, 119–30 (Aldershot: Ashgate, 2001.) Unlike me, however, Fr. Dewan thinks that the First Way establishes the existence of an absolutely immovable first mover.

51. But Aquinas's own understanding is that magnetic attraction is caused by the motion of the heavenly spheres influencing the magnet: *QDV* q. 22, a. 13, c. This is certainly not established by the argument in the First Way.

52. MacDonald, "Aquinas's Parasitic Cosmological Argument," 147; Kenny, *The Five Ways*, 15.

example as well: Imagine two particles at rest in space. Each would gravitationally attract the other and thus cause it to begin undergoing motion. Each would be a first, unmoved mover with respect to the other, because the one's ability to move the other is not dependent on, but only concomitant with, its being moved by the other. Nor is any further cause of motion needed; each particle has within itself the wherewithal to attract the other.[53]

More important, however, is the fact that Aquinas considers the souls of animals and humans to be unmoved movers with respect to many motions. Animals are self-movers, but they do not violate the principle that everything in motion is moved by another, for they must be analyzed into a moved, bodily part, and an *immobile moving soul*. As non-extended, the soul itself cannot undergo motion *per se* in the proper, physical sense. It does undergo motion *per accidens*, Aquinas says, insofar as it is hylemorphically united to a body that undergoes motion in the proper sense; when a lion walks about, its soul "goes" with it. *Per se* the animal soul initiates and sustains motion by its perception and desire, without itself being moved by anything.[54] But since the souls of animals are as one with their bodies as the wax's shape is with the wax, these souls while not themselves bodies are not immaterial in any robust sense.[55] True, *human* souls are immaterial in a robust sense, but that thesis requires separate, difficult argumentation.[56]

The First Way, then, does not prove the existence of a supermundane or immaterial mover. It only shows that for every motion there is a mover

53. One might object that Aquinas does draw the conclusion that the first mover is not a body from the mover principle, in the article immediately following the First Way: "No body moves [another] unless it is moved, as is evident from induction. Now it has been already proved that God is the first immovable mover (*primum movens immobile*). Therefore it is clear that God is not a body" (*ST* I, q. 3, a. 1, c.) However, the term "immovable" does not show up in the First Way, and first appears in q. 2, a. 3, ad 2, in association with the Third Way. I will say more about this in the next chapter. But for now, it is sufficient to note that to draw his conclusion Aquinas also adds another premise not contained in the First Way, namely that no body moves without itself undergoing motion. (Aquinas does not mean that a body can only cause motion *at the same time* as it undergoes motion, but that it can only cause motion *in virtue of* undergoing motion; see the case of projectile motion as analyzed in chapter 2 above, p. 65–69, especially the text from *In II Post. Anal.*, l. 10, n. 505 [2], quoted there.) Since Aquinas appeals to induction, his premise requires careful consideration of the whole breadth of the physical universe, verifying that the various kinds of physical substances all must undergo motion in order to move other bodies. Note also that the conclusion that the first mover is not a body does not require that it be supermundane, for as I explain in the text the souls of animals are immovable movers and are not bodies, and yet they are hylemorphically one with their bodies.

54. *SCG* I, c. 13, n. 101–103 [21–24]; *In VIII Phys.*, l. 9–11.

55. *In II De Anima*, l. 1, n. 234.

56. *ST* I, q. 75, a. 2.

that already possess the actuality—formally or eminently—toward which the mobile is in motion. Such a mover cannot, then, be in motion toward the same actuality. And to be a first mover, it must not be acting as the instrument of any higher agent. Whether such a first mover is a natural or transcendent cause, and whether there is one or more than one, is left an open question.

Spiritual Motions?

Some Thomists will say that a soul's appetitive and apprehensive acts should be regarded as motions in the sense in which that word is used in the motion proof for God's existence, and that a soul cannot, therefore, terminate the regress of movers, since it is not unmoved in its moving.[57] But this is not correct. In his motion proofs, Aquinas uses the term "motion" for physical motion. Aquinas does allow for cognitive and appetitive acts to be called "motions" in an extended sense, but with Aristotle he distinguishes between the "act of the perfect" and the "act of the imperfect." Physical motion (locomotion, alteration, growth and decrease, and generation and corruption) is the "act of the imperfect." The Aristotelian definition of motion—"the act of that which is in potency as such"[58]— only applies to such acts. Motion in this proper sense can only belong to that which is extended and divisible, that is, to bodies.[59] Appetitive and apprehensive acts, whether sensory or intellectual, are "acts of the perfect" and belong to souls. In his motion proof, Aquinas uses "motion" to signify the act of the imperfect, that is, physical motion.

This is evidenced by many facts. First, in the parallel argument G1 in *SCG*[60] Aquinas explicitly appeals to the definition of motion that applies

---

57. Cf. Twetten, "Clearing a 'Way,'" 267–68; Wippel, *The Metaphysical Thought of Thomas Aquinas*, 453 and 449–452; Garrigou-Lagrange, *God: His Existence and Nature*, vol. I, 261–62, 266. These interpretations are coherent, insofar as they restrict the term "motion" to *changes* in apprehensive and appetitive acts, and thus preserve for God His unmoved status. But the texts of Aquinas's motion proofs indicate that he has in mind only proper, physical motion. Augros, who shares the view of these authors on this point, claims that *ST* I, q. 2, a. 3, ad 2 shows that Aquinas has spiritual changes in mind in the First Way (*Aquinas on Theology and God's Existence*, 266–67). But that text does not clearly connect such changes to the First Way, rather than the Third Way. (I discuss the text in the next chapter.) Furthermore, even if one applies the term "motion" to *changes* in such acts, to "move" a soul or anything else would mean to change its acts; merely sustaining an act/potency composite in act is not to move it, even in the extended sense of motion.

58. Aristotle, *Physics* III.1

59. *SCG* I, c. 13, n. 90 [10]: "Aristotle understood motion strictly, according as it is the act of what exists in potency inasmuch as it is such. So understood, motion belongs only to divisible bodies."

60. *SCG* I, c. 13, n. 83–96 [3–16].

only to the act of the imperfect.[61] Second, in one of his arguments for the mover principle and in one of his arguments against infinite regress in G1, he explicitly states that everything in motion is an extended, divisible body.[62] Third, he explicitly tells us in G1 that Aristotle, whom he is following, restricts the term "motion" in his proof to the act of the imperfect, and thus reasoned to the existence of an *unmoved* mover, unlike Plato who used "motion" in a broad sense so as to include the act of the perfect and thus reasoned to the existence of a first *self-mover*.[63] God does indeed have a spiritual act. Hence if "motion" in Aquinas's First Way were taken in a broad sense so as to include spiritual acts, its conclusion would be that a first self-mover exists, not a first unmoved mover.

Since cognitive and appetitive acts do not count as motions, animal souls are unmoved movers. Just because such acts are really distinct from the potencies of the organisms to which they belong (that is, really distinct from the powers of their soul) does not mean that they are motions, nor are they, just as such, subject to the mover principle. Hence animal souls, in virtue of possessing such acts, can move animal bodies and thereby move other bodies without themselves being in motion (except *per accidens*). The First Way certainly does not prove or argue that such acts require the continuous, actualizing activity of a higher mover. To establish that conclusion would require separate, metaphysical argumentation.

However, although it is clear that Aquinas restricts G1 to physical motion, it is not impossible that in the First Way he intends to include *changes* of cognitive and appetitive acts (rather than the mere existence of such acts) under the term motion. Although the briefer First Way closely parallels the longer G1, in *ST* Aquinas does not explicitly utilize the Aristotelian definition of motion nor explicitly restrict motion to divisible bodies. But even if one did include *changes* of cognitive and appetitive acts within the bounds of the First Way and subject them to the mover principle, one still would not reach a completely immovable or

---

61. *SCG* I, c. 13, n. 89–90 [9–10].

62. *SCG* I, c. 13, n. 85, 92 [5, 12].

63. *SCG* I, c. 13, n. 90 [10]; cf. n. 89 [9]. See also *ST* I, q. 9, a. 1, ad 1 & q. 18, a. 3, ad 1. (See *In III De Anima*, l. 12 for the language "act of the perfect" and "act of the imperfect.") But the difference between Plato and Aristotle is only verbal, Aquinas tells us. Plato's self-mover is only in motion in the sense that it has intellectual and volitional acts. Aristotle's unmoved mover—God in Aquinas's view—does indeed have such acts. But Aquinas has chosen to use Aristotle's terminology and uses the term "motion" only to mean the act of the imperfect—i.e., physical motion—which only extended, divisible, bodily beings can undergo. (Plato reasons to a first self-mover in *Laws* X, but Aquinas had no direct access to that text.)

supermundane mover. When the desires within an animal soul are *not* changing, the soul is an unmoved mover, possessing in itself the causal ability to move its body. (These desires might have a cause of their being, but not a mover, since they are not changing.) Nothing in the argument precludes the possibility that the soul with such a desire ends the regress of essentially ordered movers, while being preceded by other accidentally ordered movers. (In fact, the natural desires of the soul *do* bear an essential connection to an external agent since these desires are the consequence of another's command, but the First Way by itself does not establish this. It emerges from *teleological* considerations, of the sort I will consider in later chapters.)

Secondly, when the desires are changing, one will need to look for a cause of the change, which will lead one to an unmoved mover *for that change in desire*. This might be a more basic inclination, such as the desire for survival and reproduction, or the desire for happiness. Or it might be an external sensible or intelligible good that the animal has newly come to be aware of and attracted to. In fact, following Aristotle in *De Anima* III.10, Aquinas says that desire is a moved mover (moved in the improper sense of motion, the act of the perfect) and the external good is an unmoved mover.[64] Now such an external good or more basic desire may have itself undergone a change in the past, or may undergo a change in the future, but need not be changing at the same time as it causes motion. It may thus be an unmoved mover and a first mover, ending the regress of essentially ordered movers responsible for a given motion, without being absolutely immovable or supermundane. For example, in the generations of sheep the natural desires of parent sheep lead to the coming into existence of new sheep and the coming to be of the same sorts of desires in the next generation. The parent sheep, for all that has been argued so far, can be taken to be first, unmoved movers in the production of new sheep.

Thus the First Way (and G1, which strictly parallels it) does not establish that an unmoved mover need be supermundane. For all that has been said so far, animal souls and even inanimate physical causes might be the

---

64. *In III De Anima*, l. 15, n. 831 [14]: "The mover, however, is twofold, one unmoved (*immobile*) and the other a moved mover. In the motion of an animal, therefore, the mover which is not moved is the actual good which moves the appetite according as it is understood or imagined. But the moved mover is the appetite itself, because everything which desires is moved insofar as it desires, and to desire is itself a certain act or motion, according as motion is the act of the perfect, as has been said concerning the operation of sense and intellect. What is moved, however, is the animal." Translation mine.

unmoved movers primarily responsible for motion in the universe.[65] In
fact such movers are not unmoved and do not end the regress of essentially ordered causes, for they are set on their path by a higher mover. But
demonstrating that requires additional argumentation not contained in
the First Way, and so the First Way cannot claim to have demonstrated
the existence of a *transcendent* God.

Qualified Success of the First Way:
God in a Minimal Sense

There is a serious objection to my analysis of the First Way's conclusion: If
animal souls and other natural entities could count as unmoved movers,
how could Aquinas take himself to be justified in concluding his argument with the claim that all understand an unmoved mover to be God?
The answer is that the term "god" does not denote as much as it is usually
taken to denote. In *SCG* III, c. 38, Aquinas tells us that although the existence of God is not self-evident, it takes very little reasoning to reach
the conclusion that there is a God, and so almost everyone has a very
rudimentary knowledge of (and not just belief in) God:

> There is a common and confused knowledge of God which is found in
> practically all men; this is due either to the fact that it is self-evident that
> God exists, just as other principles of demonstration are—a view held by
> some people, as we said in Book One—or, what seems indeed to be true,
> that man can immediately reach some sort of knowledge of God by natural
> reason. For, when men see that things in nature run according to a definite
> order, and that ordering does not occur without an orderer, they perceive in
> most cases that there is some orderer of the things that we see. But who or
> what kind of being, or whether there is but one orderer of nature, is not yet
> grasped immediately in this general consideration.... But this knowledge
> admits of a mixture of many errors. Some people have believed that there
> is no other orderer of worldly things than the celestial bodies, and so they
> said that the celestial bodies are gods. Other people pushed it farther, to the
> very elements and the things generated from them, thinking that the natural
> motions and operations which these elements have are not present in them
> as the effect of some other orderer, but that other things are ordered by them.
> Still other people, believing that human acts are not subject to any ordering
> other than human, have said that men who order others are gods. And so,
> this knowledge of God is not enough for happiness.[66]

---

65. In regard to inanimate bodies being unmoved movers, see the qualifications in fn. 53 above.
66. *SCG* III, c. 38, n. 2161, 2163 [1, 3]. Translation emended.

If planets (which many people in the classical world thought of as animated), emperors, or even elements were in fact ultimately responsible for the order and motion of things, they would be gods—but they are not ultimately responsible, so they are not gods. The First Way can conclude to the existence of God by means of an implicit disjunction: one or more primary—in the sense of noninstrumental—movers exist. If any primary mover is not subject to any higher mover it would be a god. If it is moved by a higher mover, then the higher mover would be a god. Either way, one or more gods exist.

If the desires and perceptions of sheep were controlled ultimately by the elements, then the elements would be the gods of sheep. If nothing prior to sheep had control over their desires and actions, then they would be gods. If there were some Greek superman in charge of sheep, then it would be the god of sheep. So too with humans: if a human were in ultimate control of his own destiny, then he would be a god. If a Roman emperor were in ultimate control of his subjects' destinies, then the Roman emperor would be a god. (We have a hard time even taking such talk seriously, but it certainly was taken seriously by the ancient authors with whom Aquinas was in dialogue.) But none of this is in fact true. The basic desires and inclinations and natural tendencies of all things, as well as the results of all undertakings, are in the hands of the one, transcendent God. But this has not yet been established by the First Way.

According to standard and widely accepted classical beliefs about cosmology and physics, the motions and activities of things here on earth were caused by the motions of the planets, and these planets were understood to be either themselves alive, or to be moved about by immaterial beings. When Aquinas concludes the First Way by saying that all understand a first, unmoved mover to be "god," the most plausible candidates would have been the transcendent God, an immaterial agent moving a planet, or a living planet itself. No one in the ancient world would hesitate to apply the term "god" to any of these candidates. In fact, the planets *were* considered gods in the ancient world. That this is the subtext of the First Way is confirmed by the more popular presentation of the motion proof in Aquinas's *Compendium Theologiae* (c. 3), where explicit mention is made of the heavenly bodies. Yet in the more precise argument in *ST*, no mention is made of the planets because nothing in the logic of the proof actually picks out any specific mover at all. The argument only shows that there is one or more first movers/gods. It shows nothing about what sort of thing or things a first mover or god is.

If the term "god" did not have a quite general, somewhat indeterminate signification, then when a polytheist asserted that his idol was a god, or a Roman his emperor, and a Christian asserted that it, or he, was not, they would not have been contradicting one another since they would have been using the term "god" in different senses. But Aquinas says that they are using the term in the same sense.[67] The term "god," by itself, does not denote an omnipotent, omniscient, immaterial, or even intelligent creator of all things. It denotes the source of the order of things, that which is highest among things, that which is the principle of things and different from all other things that are not such a principle; or, to be more precise, it denotes a nature to which such attributes belong, whatever that nature may be.[68] Aquinas argues powerfully that such a nature must in fact be one, immaterial, eternal, immutable, infinite, and so on,[69] but all such argumentation is subsequent to the basic task of establishing that such a nature does in fact exist, which is all that the First Way in *ST* I, q. 2 does by itself. It proves that there is a first mover. G2 will show what sort of thing the First Mover must be.

67. *ST* I, q. 13, a. 10, ad 1: "It is evident that a Catholic saying that an idol is not God contradicts the pagan asserting that it is God; because each of them uses this name *God* to signify the true God. For when the pagan says an idol is God, he does not use this name as meaning God in opinion, for he would then speak the truth, as also Catholics sometimes use the name in the sense, as in the Psalm, 'All the gods of the Gentiles are demons.' (Psalm 95:5)"

68. *ST* I, q. 13, a. 8, c. and ad 2: "Thus the name *God* signifies the divine nature, for this name was imposed to signify something existing above all things, the principle of all things and removed from all things; for those who name God intend to signify all this."

69. *ST* I, q. 3–13.

Chapter 4

An Eternal Mover for a (Potentially) Eternal Motion

Completing the Argument with G2

INTRODUCTION

I have argued that the First Way establishes only a very modest conclusion, namely that for every motion there is something primarily responsible, and that anything that fundamentally determines some motion to occur—whether it be an element, a planet, or an immaterial intelligence—is a god. But Aquinas is interested, of course, in demonstrating a much more robust and interesting conclusion. Aquinas provides three paths by which to supplement the weak version of the motion proof (contained in the First Way and G1) and complete its work: one is with the Third Way in *ST*, another is with the Fifth Way, and a third is with G2 in *SCG*. This last proof remains explicitly a proof *from motion* and demonstrates the existence of an immaterial, everlasting, immovable mover. G2 will be the primary focus of this chapter.

After considering textually how Aquinas himself connects these proofs, as well as the logical relationship between the argument in the First Way and G2's first and second stages, I turn to an analysis of G2's crucial third stage. G2 depends on a special disjunctive move and a counterfactual hypothesis: either motion in the universe as a whole is sempiternal, or it has a beginning in time. In the latter case, it is clear that

God, understood as an immaterial being outside the universe, must exist to initiate motion. But Aquinas is more interested in proceeding on the first assumption, that the universe and its motion are sempiternal. If God's existence as an immaterial, immovable mover is established on this, the least favorable and in his view counterfactual assumption, then His existence has been demonstrated in the strongest possible way. No matter what the case may be—whether the universe is sempiternal or temporally finite—God has to exist.

Aquinas's argument, in brief, is this: if an immaterial, immovable, everlasting being did not keep moving the universe, it could not continue in motion *forever*. It would necessarily wind down toward an equilibrium condition,[1] in which all compound bodies have dissolved into their elements and the elements have returned to their natural places and rest. This process would take time, but it could not last forever. No natural causes, no "mundane primary movers," could keep the universe in motion perpetually.

After explaining G2, I will provide a concise analysis of Aquinas's Third Way, pointing out the ways in which it parallels G2. The first stage of the Third Way, in arguing that not every being can be generable and corruptible because otherwise at some point there would be nothing, makes effectively the same point as G2's third stage. For an everlasting succession of possible beings would be an infinite accidentally ordered causal series. Such an infinite succession would have to be sustained by a necessary, that is, everlasting cause.

My interpretation of the motion proof keeps it within the discipline of natural philosophy, but some scholars (particularly Owens and Knasas) have argued that no natural philosophical—as opposed to

---

1. I use the anachronistic term "equilibrium" throughout this book in glossing and explaining Aquinas's argument. This is a scientific term, and I use it intentionally so as to forge a link between Aquinas's argument and contemporary science. My use of the term in analyzing St. Thomas's argument is validated as follows. Aquinas holds that natural things are naturally purposive and head toward their natural place, quality, and size spontaneously, and then rest in their natural condition. At the most basic level, the final cause of a natural thing is whatever it is determinately inclined to by its nature, the result it always heads toward and reaches, barring outside impediments. (See, e.g., *ST* I, q. 44, a. 4, c. and I-II, q. 1, a. 2.) In contemporary physics and chemistry, any system spontaneously heads toward an equilibrium condition—different systems at different rates—and then remains in that equilibrium condition until outside influences disturb it. Hence "equilibrium" is the physicist's word for what a Thomist calls "natural final cause," or "natural place," etc., at the lowest level of the inanimate. (I am not the first to make this connection. See Pierre Duhem, "Physics of a Believer," in *The Aim and Structure of Physical Theory*, trans. Philip P. Wiener, 273–311 [Princeton: Princeton University Press, 1991], at 309–310 [originally published in French in 1905.])

metaphysical—form of the motion proof can get beyond "sphere-souls," even in the context of medieval cosmology. In other words, even if Aristotelian physics were actually true, the motion proof as I have interpreted it would still only establish that the astronomical bodies had souls and were animated, perpetual self-movers. Aquinas does, indeed, raise these issues in G2, and so in the third section of this chapter I consider the problem of angels and sphere-souls. I show that Aquinas does not consider his motion proof to establish the existence of such entities, although, in accordance with his time, he takes their possibility very seriously. Aquinas's motion proof proceeds, once again, on a disjunction. Either motion in the universe depends on sphere "souls"/angels moving the astronomical bodies, or it depends on God directly moving these bodies. In the former case, the "souls" are really completely immaterial angels, and the moving that they do presupposes that the angels themselves are caused to move by an even more transcendent God. This follows from considerations that will connect the First Way to the Fifth Way. In any case the existence of God or gods, as completely immaterial, immovable, and eternal, has been established by the motion proof in its extended form, preparing the way for metaphysics.

My interpretation of the motion proof has a distinct advantage over others, in addition to being more historically accurate. The principles employed in this argument are easily reconcilable with science. One need neither deny nor relativize the principle of inertia; what the argument needs is not the thesis that motion cannot continue without a mover, but rather the thesis that there cannot be a perpetual motion machine. In other words, it needs the second law of thermodynamics. Science is not a problem for Aquinas's motion proof but rather an asset for it. Since it is at home with modern science, and since it provides an alternative to the kalām cosmological argument in that it need not take on the burden of proving the finitude of past time, the proof of an unmoved mover warrants the serious consideration of contemporary philosophers. Many opponents have rejected the motion proof out of hand as hopelessly dependent on outdated and debunked Aristotelian physics.[2] On my interpretation, it is every bit as relevant as the Second and Third ways.

2. For example, J. L. Mackie, *The Miracle of Theism*, 87.

HOW THE PROOFS ARE RELATED

Reaching a Supermundane Mover: Textual Indicators of Aquinas's Procedure

I am not the only one to claim that the First Way needs to be extended by Aquinas's other proofs. Scott MacDonald too has argued that the First Way is an incomplete proof. (Not making use of Aquinas's minimalist understanding of the term "god"—as I have done above—MacDonald sees it as simply unable to prove God's existence.) He too claims that it must be extended with further argumentation. Pointing to Aquinas's reply to the second objection in the text of the Five Ways, MacDonald suggests that Aquinas intended to complete the First Way with the Third Way.[3] This is roughly speaking correct, but the precise nature of the connection between these two proofs needs to be clarified.

It will be helpful to look at the text itself. First the objection:

> It is superfluous to suppose that what can be accounted for by a few principles has come to be by many. But it seems that everything we see in the world can be accounted for by other principles, supposing God did not exist. For all natural things are reduced to one principle which is nature; and all voluntary things can be reduced to one principle which is human reason or will. Therefore there is no need to suppose God's existence.[4]

This objection certainly indicates that Aquinas intends to prove the existence of God in more than a minimalist sense, for otherwise natural principles and humans with authority would be gods enough, as noted at the end of the previous chapter. Let us look at Aquinas's response:

> Since nature works for a determinate end under the direction of a higher agent, whatever is done by nature must needs be traced back to God, as to its first cause. So also whatever is done voluntarily must also be traced back to some higher cause other than human reason and will, since these can change or fail (*mutabilia sunt et defectibilia*); for all things that are changeable and capable of failing (*omnia mobilia et deficere possibilia*) must be traced back to an immovable and self-necessary (*immobile et per se necessarium*) first principle, as was shown.[5]

---

3. MacDonald, "Aquinas's Parasitic Cosmological Argument," 154.
4. *ST* I, q. 2, a. 3, obj. 2, translation emended.
5. *ST* I, q. 2, a. 3, ad 2, translation emended.

The First Way in *ST*, by itself, establishes that there is one or more unmoved movers. The objection wonders if natural causes would suffice. In response, Aquinas traces natural causes back to God as an intelligent agent by means of the *Fifth Way* (not appealing immediately to the Third Way, as MacDonald had argued). But *human* agents are given special consideration. In their case, is Aquinas making an appeal to the First Way? Or to the Third Way? Or to both? MacDonald uses this text as evidence that the First Way is linked to the Third Way and completed by it. The language of *deficere possibilia* and *per se necessarium* corresponds to the Third Way. The language of *mobilia* and *immobile* reminds one of the First Way, but the First Way never speaks of anything immovable (*immobile*), only of something not moved by anything (*a nullo movetur.*)

For reasons that will emerge more clearly when I analyze the Third Way below, Aquinas must be appealing here, in the special case of human agents, to the Third Way, which shows that the (accidentally ordered) series of changing beings depends essentially on something necessary and everlasting and hence immutable. The First Way does not show this. And the issue of voluntary, human action is not within the scope of the First Way anyways. The First Way is about *motion* in the proper, physical sense. One can extend the kind of argumentation found in the First Way to cover motion in an improper sense (acts of sensation, intellect, and will), as Aquinas does much later in *ST* (I-II, q. 9, a. 4–6). Yet the First Way itself is not concerned with human acts of will. What it is concerned with (primarily or exclusively) is natural, physical motion.

But the Third Way is relevant to the First Way nonetheless. As I have shown, the unmoved mover that the First Way concludes to might be no more than an animal soul. An animal or human soul moves in virtue of desire, and its desires, while not motions, are contingent and changeable. Moreover, animals are generable and corruptible and hence "possible beings." Their souls "can change or fail." To prove God's existence in a robust sense, Aquinas must prove that such beings, and any other natural unmoved movers, depend upon an immov*able*, everlasting, necessary being. The only reasoning present in *ST* I, q. 2, a. 3 that can get Aquinas from a being "moved by nothing"—the conclusion of the First Way—to a being entirely "immov*able*" is that found in the Third Way, and the connection between them is manifested in the reply to the second objection just quoted.

I will take up the Fifth Way in the next chapter and the Third Way later in this chapter. But there is yet another way that Aquinas utilizes to complete the proof found in the First Way, one that remains more explicitly in the domain of motion. The First Way is equivalent to G1 in *SCG*, and there the proof is completed with G2. Since G2 more clearly manifests the presuppositions of Aquinas's position, I will consider it before considering the Third Way. But to make headway, I will first need to clarify the logical relationship between Aquinas's First Way and G2. Clarifying this logical relationship will involve a partial analysis of the first two stages of G2, and this will prepare the ground for the crucial analysis of how G2's *third* stage completes G1 and the First Way.[6]

The Logical Relationship between the First Way and G2's First and Second Stages

G1, like the First Way, proceeds by arguing against the possibility of an infinite regress of moved movers, thus establishing that there is a mover not moved by anything else and thus not in motion, *per* the mover principle. In place of the argument against infinite regress, G2 substitutes a difficult *reductio ad absurdum* argument against the proposition "every mover is moved."[7] This proposition, if true, would be true either *per se* or *per accidens*. But reasons are given that it cannot be true *per accidens* and that it cannot be true *per se*, and hence that it is not true at all. Hence some mover must be unmoved. I am not confident that this argument works, nor am I convinced that it does not work. I will not analyze it in this book.[8] But the conclusion of this, the first stage of G2, is that there is some mover that is not moved by anything external (*aliquod primum quod non movetur aliquo exteriori*).[9]

Aquinas continues in the second stage of G2:

> Granted this conclusion—namely, that there is a first mover that is not moved by an exterior moving cause—it yet does not follow that this mover is absolutely unmoved (*penitus immobile*). That is why Aristotle goes on to say that the condition of the first mover may be twofold. The first mover

---

6. I follow Norman Kretzmann in dividing G2 into four stages. See *The Metaphysics of Theism*, 64–83.

7. *SCG* I, c. 13, n. 97–99 [17–19].

8. Norman Kretzmann attempts to analyze it in *The Metaphysics of Theism*, 65–72. There is also an analysis by Andrew Bailey, "Thomas' Lesser Way: A Critique," *Ars Disputandi* 6, no. 1 (2006): 6–16.

9. *SCG* I, c. 13, n. 100 [20].

can be absolutely unmoved (*penitus immobile*). If so, we have the conclusion
we are seeking: there is a first unmoved mover (*primum movens immobile*).
On the other hand, the first mover can be self-moved. This seems probable, because that which is through itself is prior to what is through another.
Hence, among things moved as well, it seems reasonable that the first moved
is moved through itself and not by another. But, on this basis, the same conclusion again follows. For it cannot be said that, when a mover moves himself, the whole is moved by the whole. Otherwise, the same difficulties would
follow as before: one person would both teach and be taught, and the same
would be true among other motions. It would also follow that a being would
be both in potency and in act; for a mover is, as such, in act, whereas the
thing moved is in potency. Consequently, one part of the self-moved mover
is solely moving, and the other part solely moved. We thus reach the same
conclusion as before: there exists an unmoved mover (*movens immobile*).[10]

Together the first two stages of G2 reach the conclusion that an unmoved (immovable?[11]) mover exists. They do so by utilizing in the second stage the same act and potency argument that the First Way uses
to establish the mover principle and by providing in the first stage an
alternate *reductio* argument to accomplish the same thing as the argument against infinite regress in the First Way. There is thus an equivalence
between the entirety of the First Way and the first two stages of G2. *The
First Way and G1 its counterpart only establish as much as the first two stages of G2, nothing more.*

As noted in the last chapter, many defenders of Aquinas's First Way
have claimed on the basis of the argument from act and potency that the
argument is metaphysical and not limited in its scope to physical motion. They say that the First Way establishes the existence of a being who
is pure act.[12] But the wording with which the *third stage* in G2 begins
reveals what has been left unaccomplished by the first two stages of G2—
and thus by the First Way and G1 in their entireties:

---

10. *SCG* I, c. 13, n. 101–02 [21–22]. Translation emended.

11. Pegis translates *immobile* as "unmoved" in the above quoted passage, rather than "immobile"
or "immovable." I have in general taken *immobile* to mean "immovable," although I am not completely convinced that this is correct. The term *mobile* is routinely used by Aquinas to mean "that which is
in motion," as for example in his commentary on *Physics* VI. *Immobile* seems at times to mean simply
"something not in motion." Examples are *SCG* III, c. 139, n. 3144 [17] ("Corpus autem, vivificatum
per animam, ex seipso movetur: sed corpus mortuum vel immobile manet, vel ab exteriori tantum
movetur") and *In III Sent.* d. 35, q. 1, a. 1 co. ("Aquae autem immobiles congregatae in lacunis dicun-
tur aquae mortuae.") However, the word *immobile* often does seem to mean "immovable."

12. See above, chapter 3, p. 84–89.

But because in self-moving beings familiar to us, namely in animals, although the moving part, which is to say the soul, is immovable (*immobilis*) *per se*, yet is moved *per accidens*, Aristotle further shows that the moving part of the first self-moving being is not moved either *per se* or *per accidens*.[13]

Nothing in the logic of the First Way or in G1 has ruled out the *possibility* of ending the regress of movers with an animal soul, which is incapable of being itself in motion strictly speaking. If this had already been sufficiently disproved, Aquinas would not need to continue on in the third stage of G2 to rule out this possibility. The premise that does all the work in this third stage is the counterfactual hypothesis that motion in the universe is sempiternal. Without this premise and a special disjunctive move, the motion proof cannot arrive at the existence of God in the sense of a supermundane mover:

> For, since self-moving beings known to us, namely, animals, are corruptible, the moving part in them is moved *per accidens*. But corruptible self-moving beings must be reduced to some first self-moving being that is everlasting (*sempiternum*). Therefore, some self-moving being must have a mover that is moved neither *per se* nor *per accidens*. That, however, it is necessary that, according to the position of Aristotle, some self-moving being is everlasting, is clear. For if, as Aristotle supposes, motion is everlasting, … there must therefore be some perpetual (*perpetuum*) self-moving being.[14]

The argument will be supplied and analyzed in the next section, but what I want to emphasize here is that without some consideration of the possibility of perpetual motion in the universe as a whole the motion proof is incomplete. Much will need to be clarified. Aquinas does not in fact think that motion is everlasting. Nor is God part of an everlasting self-moving being. But what is important here is to see that nothing in the logic of the First Way in *ST*, or G1 in *SCG*, has ruled out the possibility of ending the regress of movers with mundane primary movers, with natural causes such as animal and human souls (although by the same token nothing in the First Way or G1 has required that the regress does end with such mundane primary movers).

---

13. *SCG* I, c. 13, n. 103 [24], translation emended. Pegis continues to translate *immobile* as "unmoved."

14. *SCG* I, c. 13, n. 104–5 [24–25], translation emended.

PROVING A SUPERMUNDANE GOD

Two Strange Premises: G2 as a Doubly Disjunctive Argument

G2's third stage proceeds explicitly on the basis of two assumptions: that motion in the universe is sempiternal and that the regress of movers is *likely* to arrive at a *self-mover*. The kind of self-mover that Aquinas has in mind in this third stage, as will become clear shortly, is an astronomical body with an angel united to it as its mover. This might make G2 seem wildly implausible as a contemporary argument. To avoid seriously misunderstanding Aquinas, we need to note carefully that both premises (the sempiternity of motion and the "animation" of the astronomical bodies) are *hypothetical* and each merely one part of its own *disjunction*. Aquinas clarifies this at the end of G2 by considering two objections that his modern readers will almost certainly have:

> Two considerations seem to invalidate these arguments (*praedictos … processus*). The first consideration is that, as arguments, they presuppose the eternity of motion, which Catholics consider to be false.… The second consideration is that the demonstrations given above presuppose that the first thing undergoing motion (*primum motum*), namely, a heavenly body, is self-moving. This means that it is animated, which many do not admit.[15]

As regards the animation of the astronomical bodies, Aquinas thinks it probable that they are in fact animated, although not in the true, hylemorphic sense. I will say more about this below, but for now Aquinas's own response to the second objection suffices:

> The reply to this consideration is that, if the first [physical] mover is not held to be self-moved, then it must be moved immediately by something absolutely immovable (*penitus immobili*). Hence, even Aristotle himself proposed this conclusion as a disjunction: it is necessary either to arrive immediately at an immovable separate first mover (*primum movens immobile separatum*), or to arrive at a self-mover from which, in turn, an immovable separate first mover (*movens primum immobile separatum*) is reached.[16]

The logic of Aquinas's argument does not either establish or rule out that the regress of movers terminates in a self-mover. It takes seriously the possibility of ending with a self-mover, *as a mere possibility*. Either motion in the universe reduces to an entirely unmoved mover or it ends

---

15. *SCG* I, c. 13, n. 109, 111 [29, 31], translation emended.
16. *SCG* I, c. 13, n. 112 [32], translation emended.

with a self-mover, which is moved by an unmoved moving part and—as we shall see—a separate, immovable being that moves it as a final cause. So although the argument involves the proposition that astronomical bodies are animated, it does so only as a hypothesis, not as an assertion. Aquinas regards the hypothesis as likely, but if the contemporary mind regards it as certainly false, that in no way harms the argument, since it is disjunctive.

Aquinas responds as follows to the other objection regarding the sempiternity of motion:

> The most efficacious way to prove that God exists is on the supposition that the world is sempiternal. Granted this supposition, that God exists is less manifest. For, if the world and motion have a first beginning, some cause must clearly be posited to account for this origin of the world and of motion. That which comes to be anew must take its origin from some innovating cause; since nothing brings itself from potency to act, or from non-being to being.[17]

This is an extremely important move, the force of which has not always been appreciated.[18] The motion proof is disjunctive in this regard as well: either motion in the universe had a beginning or it did not. If God's existence follows from both assumptions taken individually, then it is proved that He most certainly exists.[19] Now if motion did begin in the universe, it follows readily that an immaterial, immovable, eternal being exists outside the universe as its cause, and that such a being warrants the name God.[20] Aquinas is interested, however, in proceeding on the

---

17. *SCG* I, c. 13, n. 110 [30].

18. Michael Augros has appreciated its force: *Aquinas on Theology and God's Existence*, 295–96.

19. Aquinas draws here upon the work of Moses Maimonides, who accepts Aristotle's argument for an unmoved mover but reconciles it with his own belief in a temporal beginning to the universe by appending to Aristotle's argument this disjunctive move: if the universe has a beginning, then God obviously exists. If it has no beginning, Aristotle's argument proves that God exists. Either way, God exists. See Maimonides, *The Guide of the Perplexed*, p. 2, ch. 2.

20. See *In XII Meta.*, l. 5, n. 2499. Aquinas does not say very much about what kind of conclusions one could draw about God's attributes from the hypothesis that the universe had a beginning, presumably because he did not think anyone following mere reason would find enough evidence to render such a beginning likely. But it seems reasonable enough to conclude that such a being is immaterial, immovable, everlasting, and even eternal. For if the initiating cause of the universe were not eternal in the sense of completely outside of time, it could not have initiated the universe. For its action would have had to take place at a specific time, yet it could not have had any reason to start the universe at one time rather than another. For if there were time prior to the existence of the universe it would have been completely empty time, and every moment would have been exactly like any other. If something else caused the unmoved mover to start the universe when it did rather than at some other time, or if some propitious condition arose then and not earlier, then there must have

hypothesis that motion and the universe are sempiternal. What then? The answer to this question is found in the text of the third stage of G2.

The Crucial Step: G2's Third Stage

In the third stage of G2, Aquinas argues as follows:

> Since self-moving beings known to us, namely, animals, are corruptible, the moving part in them is moved *per accidens*. But corruptible self-moving beings must be reduced to some first self-moving being that is everlasting (*sempiternum*). Therefore, some self-moving being must have a mover that is moved neither *per se* nor *per accidens*.
>
> That, however, it is necessary that, according to the position of Aristotle, some self-moving being is everlasting, is clear. For if, as Aristotle supposes, motion is everlasting, the generation of self-moving beings that are generable and corruptible must be endless. But the cause of this endlessness cannot be one of the self-moving beings, since it does not always exist. Nor can the cause be all the self-moving beings together (*nec simul omnia*), both because they would be infinite and because they are not simultaneous [or "because they are not together": *tum quia non simul sunt*]. There must therefore be some perpetual self-moving being, which causes the endlessness of generation among these lower self-moving beings. Thus its mover is moved neither *per se* nor *per accidens*.
>
> Again, we see that among beings that move themselves some begin to be in new motion as a result of some [other] motion which the animal does not itself cause, for example, the digestion of food or alteration of air. By such a motion the self-moving mover is moved *per accidens*. From this we may infer that no self-moving being is moved everlastingly whose mover is moved either *per se* or *per accidens*. But the first self-mover is everlastingly in motion; otherwise, motion could not be everlasting, since every other motion is caused by the motion of the first self-mover. The first self-moving being, therefore, is moved by a mover which is not moved either *per se* or *per accidens*.[21]

The counterfactual hypothesis that motion is sempiternal is what allows Aquinas to get beyond mundane primary movers and establish the existence of a supermundane mover. It does so by two, closely related arguments, which are also found paired together in Aquinas's commentary

---

been some kind of motion going on, and the beginning of motion was not really a beginning after all. See *ST* I, q. 46, a. 1, obj. 6 and ad 6. If such a being is eternal/outside of time, then it cannot possibly undergo change and is thus immovable.

21. *SCG* I, c. 13, n. 104–6 [24–26], translation emended.

on *Physics* VIII.[22] The first is that the cycle of generation and corruption, birth and death, continues forever on this hypothesis. No member of this cycle can cause it to continue forever, because no member exists forever. There must, therefore, be some everlasting being outside this whole cycle to keep it going forever.

Notice three things about this argument: first, unlike Aquinas's primary arguments against infinite regress, it is a composition or "lumping" type argument. Second, it serves a different purpose than those arguments. Those arguments established that an *essentially* ordered series of causes cannot regress infinitely. This argument intends to establish that an infinite *accidentally* ordered series of causes requires an essentially ordered cause outside the series to sustain it.[23] It does not claim that an accidentally ordered series must have a beginning; it assumes, in fact, that it does not. But the accidentally ordered series must be sustained by a separate, finite, essentially ordered series of causes. The third thing to notice is that this argument is closely related to the Third Way in *ST*. The reasoning in both is that if every entity involved in a process is possible, that is, generable and corruptible, the process as a whole cannot continue forever. To do so, the process must depend on an everlasting, necessary being. I will say more about this in the next section.

The second argument for an everlasting mover in G2's third stage focuses, not on the *existence* of mundane primary movers, but on their *activity of moving*. It points out that even though the souls of animals cannot be moved *per se*, they can be moved *per accidens*. In other words, they are affected by the motion that their bodies undergo. Physical changes in the bodies of animals prompt different perceptions and desires in their souls. In some conditions, their souls cause motion in their bodies, but in other conditions, they cause rest. The soul of a lion with an empty stomach that perceives a gazelle will cause its body to undergo motion toward the gazelle. Upon catching and eating the gazelle, the lion has nothing further to do and goes to sleep. The sun moves, shifting the shade, and the lion is prompted to move himself to get back into the shade. Once the food has been digested, the lion begins to prowl once again. Since its soul can be affected by motions in its body caused by external agents, it cannot cause motion perpetually. Sometimes it is put out of a condition to cause

---

22. *In VIII Phys.*, l. 12–13.

23. See above, chapter 2, section titled "The Dependent Character of Infinite Accidentally Ordered Series," p. 76–80. Cp. Duns Scotus, *Ordinatio* I, d. 2, p. 1, q. 1, n. 53–54.

motion. So if there is to be perpetual motion, there must be a mover that is not affected by motions occurring in a body to which it is united. In other words, there must be a supermundane mover.

At the end of chapter 2 above I demonstrated, against the Hume-Edwards objection, that Aquinas's argument here is cogent. An infinite temporal succession of accidentally ordered causes depends upon a perpetual first cause outside the whole series. Yet I think an understanding of what Aquinas has in mind when speaking of self-movers familiar to us and of perpetual self-movers will render Hume's objection moot in any case.

What Aquinas has in mind with these two arguments is that motion here on earth seems at first and at second glance to occur in endless cycles ("seems" because he actually thinks, on the grounds of religious faith, that it began and will end). Motion is always going on, but in a sense nothing ever changes. Each animal species continually reproduces after its own kind.[24] To live and reproduce, some species eat other animals, others eat plants, but in every case the food chain ends with plants. Plants themselves continually reproduce at recurring seasons. They depend upon light and rain for their life and growth, and for both these things they depend upon the sun, since the heat of the sun evaporates water and produces weather patterns. Hence life on earth depends on the energy provided by the sun.

Yet if the sun stayed in one place relative to the earth, life would come to an end; the earth would become a barren dessert on one side and a frozen wasteland on the other. Life and the familiar weather patterns depend on the relative *motion* of the sun and the alternation of night and day, winter and summer. (Even the tides depend upon the motion of the moon, as the ancients were aware.) If motion on earth is to be perpetual, the sun must be in perpetual motion. Hence Aquinas is on good grounds in arguing from the hypothetical endlessness of the cycle of generations to an everlasting mover in the heavens. But since everything in motion is moved by another, Aquinas claims that the sun itself must be moved by an everlasting mover, either directly by God, or by a soul or angel somehow conjoined to it. (In the latter case, favored by Aquinas, the sun and other stars and planets would be perpetual "self-movers" and, in a loose sense, animated.)

In his proof for a transcendent unmoved mover, Aquinas is not arguing

---

24. None of the paleontological evidence for the transformation of species over geological time-periods was available to Aquinas.

that God must exist to set the universe going in the beginning, nor is he arguing that God must exist to keep the universe in motion every instant. What Aquinas has in mind is more like the idea that unless a basketball player keeps dribbling a ball, it will bounce less and less until it comes to rest on the court. If the ball is to keep bouncing forever, a player needs to dribble it forever, and for that to happen there needs to be a player who does not need to eat or rest, and who is not subject to the process of ageing. In short, there needs to be an everlasting and *immovable* mover. And given that all material agents are susceptible to change, this mover must be immaterial. Furthermore, such a mover cannot cause motion as a natural cause does, but rather as an intelligent agent. All natural causes are determined to one, finite effect: they head toward thermal equilibrium. On their own, physical systems always come to rest. But intelligent beings can adjust and readjust means to ends in order to keep a system in motion indefinitely. (The next chapter will shed more light on this last idea.)

Strictly speaking, an immaterial mover is required to sustain not only everlasting motion but also perfectly uniform, unabating motion (although in the latter case one cannot immediately infer that the mover is *everlasting*, only that it is immaterial). Aquinas endorses Aristotle's argument at the end of the *Physics* (VIII.10), where Aristotle reasons that perpetual motion, lasting for an infinite time, requires infinite power in its mover. He argues further that infinite power cannot reside in a body or bodily faculty, and thus that the first mover (or movers) of the astronomical bodies must be immaterial.[25] Aquinas, while not believing that the motion of a heavenly sphere is actually everlasting, maintains that an immaterial mover with infinite power is nevertheless required to sustain it, for "there is no evidence that the passing of time has slowed down the motion of the heavens."[26] Physical movers always wear down over time, and cannot sustain unremitting motion. Horses grow tired and slow down; automobile engines wear out and decrease in performance; batteries decrease in voltage and eventually go dead. This principle is verified both by common experience and by current science, which states that although the energy in any closed system remains constant, the amount of that energy available to do work inevitably decreases over time.[27]

---

25. See *SCG* I, c. 20 and *In VIII Phys.*, l. 21 and 23.

26. *SCG* I, c. 20, n. 187 [32] and *De Substantiis Separatis*, c. 2 (Leon. 40 D: 46, l. 197–212).

27. These are the first and second laws of thermodynamics, the conservation of energy principle and the entropy principle, respectively.

In Aquinas's day there was no observable evidence that the heavens were winding down; today there is considerable evidence, but Aquinas's disjunctive argument remains effective. Given the limits of observation when dealing with something as large as the universe, it is theoretically possible that the universe is not really winding down toward high-entropy equilibrium. Perhaps some cyclical process is going on in unobservable regions, and the universe (or "multiverse") is maintaining a constant rather than increasing level of entropy. In that case, however, an everlasting, immaterial, immovable mover is needed to sustain the universe in motion forever; physical systems cannot evade decay into equilibrium on their own. It seems more likely, however, that the universe is winding down toward thermal equilibrium (the "heat death," see chapter 7 below.) Yet even here there are two possible scenarios. The universe could be wound back up periodically from outside so as to be everlastingly winding down, like a grandfather clock that is prevented from ever stopping. In that case an everlasting, immovable, immaterial mover must exist to periodically wind the universe up. On the other hand, the universe could have been wound up once and for all at the beginning of time and be now winding down to a final state; in *that* case an immaterial, eternal, immovable mover must exist to get the universe started in the beginning. In any case, an immaterial, immovable, everlasting mover certainly exists.

The regress of essentially ordered movers causing a given motion need be neither horizontal, nor vertical; it can be "diagonal." A given motion here on earth might, in Aquinas's view, be traceable straight up to an astronomical body and to its immaterial mover (God, soul, or angel), simultaneously moving it and the terrestrial body through it, as when ice is melted by the sun. But a terrestrial motion might in fact be caused by a previously acting terrestrial "generator" that brought the mobile into being and made it heavy or light, as we saw in chapter 1. That generator would in turn have been moved simultaneously by an astronomical body.[28] Aquinas thinks of the astronomical body as being itself moved simultaneously by an angel, since its motion is absolutely constant. But if there were some evidence that the motion of the heavenly body was

---

28. The kind of chemical changes that occur on earth are those that occur at the current earth temperature range. Chemical reactions are highly dependent on temperature, and the earth's temperature would be radically different without the heat streaming to it from the sun. Hence the sun and its motion are part of an essentially ordered series of causes for many or even most of the motions going on here on earth.

slowing down, then the mover that caused its motion might in fact have acted further back in the past, winding up the clockwork of the heavens. That immaterial mover of the heavens may or may not have periodically wound up the heavens an infinite number of times previously, but that would be irrelevant to its causation of the current terrestrial motion; that motion would be caused whether the immaterial mover had wound up the heavens for the first time, for the billionth time, or for the "infini-tieth" time. Hence the essentially ordered series of movers responsible for a present terrestrial motion could extend backward a finite distance into the past, without excluding the possibility of an infinite accidentally ordered series of moving causes preceding it.

The Third Way and G2

Before moving on to G2's fourth and final stage, I want to elaborate on the connection between the Third Way and G2's third stage. We have seen that in *ST* Aquinas appeals to the Third Way to explain why voluntary human actions must ultimately depend on the transcendent God. Scott MacDonald sees the Third Way as that argument by which Aquinas intends to complete the First Way, and he is not entirely wrong in this, although for the general case of natural motion Aquinas appeals directly to the Fifth Way, rather than to the Third Way.

Now in the Third Way Aquinas reasons that "possible" beings must be supported by necessary beings and that beings necessary through another must be caused by a being necessary in itself. Let us look at the argument:

> The third way is taken from possibility and necessity, and runs thus. We find in nature things that are possible to be and not to be, since they are found to be generated, and to be corrupted, and consequently they are possible to be and not to be. But it is impossible for these always to exist, for that which is possible not to be at some time is not. Therefore, if everything is possible not to be, then at one time there was nothing in existence. Now if this were true, even now there would be nothing in existence, because that which does not exist only begins to exist by something already existing. Therefore, if at one time nothing was in existence, it would have been impossible for anything to have begun to exist; and thus even now nothing would be in existence—which is clearly false. Therefore, not all beings are merely possible, but there must exist something the existence of which is necessary.
>
> But every necessary thing either has its necessity caused by another, or not. Now it is impossible to go on to infinity in necessary things which have

their necessity caused by another, as has been already proved in regard to efficient causes. Therefore we must admit the existence of some being having of itself its own necessity, and not receiving it from another, but rather causing in others their necessity. This all men speak of as God.[29]

Here Aquinas uses "possible" to mean "generable and corruptible," and "necessary" to mean "always in existence."[30] Terrestrial bodies are possible beings, for they last a finite time, being generable and corruptible. In Aquinas's worldview the most obvious necessary beings are the astronomical bodies, which he regards as not generable and not corruptible. There are also immaterial intelligences, that is, angels. Both the angels and the astronomical bodies are necessary through another, not in themselves, and—as the Third Way goes on to argue—they must be caused by a being necessary in itself, namely, God.

Although it is a more abstract argument than G2, there are clear parallels between the Third Way's first step and G2's third stage. The reasoning in both is that a series of generable and corruptible beings cannot continue forever without an everlasting being to sustain it. Contingent, terrestrial beings depend upon heavenly, necessary beings. The formulation of the arguments is different, however. The Third Way argues that if a being is corruptible, then given infinite time it will be corrupted at some point.[31] If all beings are corruptible, then it must be possible for all beings to corrupt at the same time. (They might of course each corrupt at a different time, but it is sufficient for Aquinas's argument for it to be merely possible for them all to corrupt at the same time.) And if that is possible, it must happen at some point, given infinite time. If the universe has already been around for an infinite amount of time it would have already happened at some point in the past that every being was corrupted at the same time. In that case, there would have been nothing at all and there would still be nothing, contrary to fact. If there has not been an infinite time in the past, perhaps the simultaneous corruption of all things has simply not happened yet, even though it is possible for it to happen in the future. But in that case, a necessary being would have to exist to get the universe started. (It is thus apparent that the disjunctive

---

29. *ST* I, q. 2, a. 3, c. Translation emended.

30. See Timothy Pawl, "The Five Ways," 121 and fn. 47.

31. Aquinas's own reasons for holding this principle seem to be those found in his commentary on *De Caelo* I.12 (*In I De Caelo*, l. 26–29). A more modern defense of the principle is that if the probability of a certain event does not approach zero as a limit as time tends toward infinity ($\lim_{t \to \infty} p(E) \neq 0$), then the event is bound to happen, given enough time.

move that considers the possibility of a beginningless universe is implicit in the Third Way.)

How do we know that if every being is corruptible it is also possible for all beings to corrupt at the same time? The only thing that could prevent this from being possible is if one substance cannot corrupt without another being generated at the same time. The only thing that could make *that* necessary are the combined facts that matter cannot exist without a substantial form and that matter itself cannot be corrupted; thus matter cannot lose one form without gaining another. But this is just to say that matter is in a sense a necessary being (really a principle of being), and thus that not all beings are possible.

But how does one know that matter is not the self-necessary being to which the argument concludes? Because matter is a purely passive principle, and an active principle must give it form. Without a perpetual, necessary, active principle, matter would come to rest and remain motionless, possessing a single substantial form perpetually (the substantial form of some element.) No generation and corruption could take place, and there would be no possible beings. Hence generable and corruptible beings must depend in addition upon necessary active causes (in Aquinas's view the heavenly bodies and the angelic intelligences.) These in turn, if they are necessary through another, must be caused by a being necessary in itself. (Further, metaphysical argumentation may also be brought in to rule out the possibility that prime matter, heavenly bodies, or angelic intelligences are necessary in themselves, but such argumentation is not presented in the text of the Third Way itself.)

The Third Way, then, closely parallels G2 and is valid given Thomistic philosophy of nature. Many contemporaries doubt that the proof concludes to God in the relevant sense because they think of matter and energy as necessary in themselves and of energy as an active principle. These seem to guarantee the perpetuity of generation and corruption. But as I will show in the sixth and seventh chapters, this rests on a misunderstanding of modern science and a failure to consider the second law of thermodynamics.

GOD OR ANGELS? THE FOURTH STAGE OF G2

Those in favor of a metaphysical interpretation of the motion proof have often argued that natural philosophy cannot get beyond sphere-souls. If it were a natural philosophical argument, the motion proof would establish the existence, not of God, but of sphere-souls.[32] I have shown above what the first three stages of G2 actually establish: so far, the argument has proved that *either* a completely separate, wholly immovable being exists—not a sphere soul but a transcendent being—*or* that an immovable mover is united to an astronomical body as its mover—something that could be thought of as a "sphere-soul." So does the argument not succeed in establishing the existence of God, but only that there are, at least, "sphere-souls"?

Notice several points right away. First, if the only thing that the argument could succeed in establishing was the existence of everlasting, intelligent "souls" of the stars and planets, and nothing higher existed, those souls/angels would count as gods by Aquinas's lights, because they would be the principles and directors of motion in the universe (see the end of chapter 3 above). If something higher did exist, then that would be god, and either way god or gods would exist.

Secondly, the "sphere-souls" would themselves be immaterial beings, for to cause everlasting motion they must be moved neither *per se* nor *per accidens*, and thus cannot be the forms of mobile bodies. They are united to the astronomical bodies not really as their souls but as their movers. (This will be made clearer presently.) Hence, even before the fourth stage, the natural philosophical argument contained in G2 has succeeded in proving that one or more immaterial, everlasting, immovable movers exist, and has thus extended the concept of being beyond the material in preparation for the science of metaphysics.

However, Aquinas does intend to establish the existence of God as wholly separate and not confined to any body. Hence he proceeds in the final and fourth stage of G2 to argue that even if there are intelligent, moving parts in astronomical "self-movers," another, completely independent, immaterial mover also exists, one that is not part of any "self-mover." This line of argument enables him to conclude that there is only one God

---

32. See Wippel, *The Metaphysical Thought of Thomas Aquinas*, 429–431, 456–57; Owens, "The Conclusion of the *Prima Via*," in *St. Thomas Aquinas on the Existence of God*, 142–68, at 150–51 and 167, as well as Owens, "Aquinas and the Proof from the 'Physics,'" *Mediaeval Studies* 28 (1966): 119–50, at 148–49; Twetten, "Clearing a 'Way' for Aquinas," 262–63; Garrigou-Lagrange, *God: His Existence and His Nature*, vol. I, 266. John F. X. Knasas sees the natural philosophy argument as concluding only to an everlasting celestial sphere, not to a sphere-soul: *Thomistic Existentialism and Cosmological Reasoning* (Washington, DC: The Catholic University of America Press, 2019), 176–77 and Knasas, "The *Suppositio* of Motion's Eternity and the Interpretation of Aquinas' Motion Proofs for God," in *God: Reason and Reality*, ed. Anselm Ramelow (Munich: Philosophia Verlag, 2014), 147–78, at 159–162.

over all. But to understand Aquinas's reasoning, we need to have a still clearer picture of his cosmology.

Aquinas sees the universe as an enclosed sphere, with the earth at its center. Immediately surrounding the earth is the sphere of the moon, and surrounding that sphere are a series of other spheres one within the other, containing the sun, the planets, and, outermost of all, the "fixed stars," those forming the constellations. The outermost sphere rotates once daily, carrying the sun, moon, planets, and stars with it, producing the alternation of night and day here on earth. Among the other spherical motions the most important is the motion of the ecliptic, which is tilted with respect to the daily motion and is completed in the space of one year. The motion of the ecliptic produces the alternation of the seasons by carrying the sun more northerly in the summer and more southerly in the winter.[33]

Aquinas thinks of these spheres as self-movers, and sometimes speaks of them as animated or as having souls.[34] He argues, however, that their "souls" cannot be the substantial forms of the astronomical bodies. These astronomical bodies are not living organisms,[35] for the very simple reason that they have no observable organs.[36] Since soul is defined by Aquinas as the substantial form of a living, naturally organized body, the "souls" of the celestial spheres are not really souls in a strict Aristotelian sense. They are only souls in an improper sense, the same sense in which Plato thought, incorrectly, that souls were connected to bodies here on

33. For these and other details, see, among other places, *In XII Meta.*, l. 9–10 and l. 6, n. 2511, which show how astute Aquinas was about the details of astronomy as known in his day. Aquinas displays greater understanding of this science than Aristotle does in his text.

34. E.g., *SCG* I, c. 13, n. 111 [31].

35. *ST* I, q. 70, a. 3: "From what has been said, then, it is clear that the heavenly bodies are not living beings in the same sense as plants and animals, and that if they are called so, it can only be equivocally" (c.). "The heaven is said to move itself in as far as it is compounded of mover and moved; not by the union of the mover as the form with the moved as the matter, but by contact with the moving power, as we have said" (ad 5). Cf. also *QDSC* a. 6, c.: "In this way, therefore, it is to be denied that the celestial bodies are animated in the way in which those inferior bodies are animated. Nevertheless it is not to be denied that the celestial bodies are animated, if by animation nothing else is understood than the union of mover and mobile." Translation mine. See also ad 11: "Heavenly bodies are said to be animated because spiritual substances are united to them as movers, and not as forms." See also *QDV* q. 5, a. 8, ad 12.

36. *QDP* q. 6, a. 6, c.: "If a spiritual substance does not have in itself any other power than intellect and will, it would be united to a body to no purpose (*frustra*), since these operations are completed without the body. For every form of a body effects some action corporeally. If, however, they have other powers … it is necessary that such substances be united to organized bodies, so that they might execute the actions of such powers through determinate organs." Translation mine. See also *QDSC* a. 6, c.

earth; the angel that moves a celestial sphere is in it only the way a pilot is in a ship.[37] Yet the angel *is* confined to its sphere;[38] it is finite, and its range of influence is limited to its sphere; while moving the sphere it cannot act in any other location.[39] Yet the angel is not naturally united to its sphere, in such a way that it would be an incomplete being if separated from it, as the human soul is when separated from its body.[40]

This background understanding of the "sphere-souls" is relevant to G2, for it sheds light upon a strange passage found at the very end of its third stage. After arguing that perpetual motion requires a mover that is moved neither *per se* nor *per accidens*, Aquinas reasons:

> Nor is it against this argument that the movers of the lower spheres produce an everlasting motion and yet are said to be moved *per accidens*. For they are said to be moved *per accidens*, not on their own account, but on account of their movable subjects, which follow the motion of the higher sphere.[41]

Without the context just provided this would sound like a piece of scholastic obfuscation, distinguishing between the *per se per accidens* and

37. *QDSC* a. 6, c.: "For Plato, as has been said above, said that not even the human body is animated except insofar as the soul is united to the body as mover." See also *ST* I, q. 70, a. 3.

38. In *QDSC* a. 6, ad 11, Aquinas uses the term *inclusa* to describe the "soul's" relation to the celestial body.

39. See *QDSC* a. 6, ad 7: "A spiritual substance which moves the heaven has a natural virtue determined to the motion of such a body." Translation mine. *ST* I, q. 52, a. 2, c: "An angel's power and nature are finite, whereas the Divine power and essence, which is the universal cause of all things, is infinite. Consequently God through His power touches all things, and is not merely present in some places, but is everywhere. Now since the angel's power is finite, it does not extend to all things, but to one determined thing.... Hence, since the angel is in a place by the application of his power to the place, it follows that he is not everywhere, nor in several places, but in only one place.... Neither, if any angel moves the heavens, is it necessary for him to be everywhere. First of all, because his power is applied only to what is first moved by him. Now there is one part of the heavens in which there is movement first of all, namely, the part to the east; hence the Philosopher attributes the power of the heavenly mover to the part which is in the east. Secondly, because philosophers do not hold that one separate substance moves all the spheres immediately. Hence it need not be everywhere." The angels have a power limited in kind and place, but they do have a power infinite in a way (*SCG* II, c. 49, n. 1252 [6]). More importantly, since they are immaterial their power is not diminished in acting; they do not grow weary nor do the bodies they move react on them and alter them. Hence they can move the heavenly spheres for an infinite time. Nevertheless, the infinite and/or perfectly uniform motion of a heavenly body demonstrates that its *first* mover is of infinite power, but not necessarily that its proximate mover is. Hence if the immaterial movers of the heavenly bodies are not their first movers, they would not need to have truly infinite power.

40. *QDSC* a. 6, ad 9: "The soul which moves corruptible animals is united to them according to being. But the spiritual substances which move the heavenly bodies are united to them according to motion only." Ad sc 2: "One angel is assigned (*deputatur*) to guard one human being as long as he lives. Whence it is not unfitting if [one] is assigned (*deputatur*) to move a celestial body as long as it is moved." (Cp. sc 2.) Translations mine. See also fn. 42 below.

41. *SCG* I, c. 13, n. 107 [27], translation emended.

the *per accidens per accidens*, or something like that. But given the background context one can see that Aquinas is responding to the objection that the lower spheres (such as those of the moon and Venus) are moved by their movers perpetually, and yet these lower spheres are carried around not just by their own motion, but by the daily motion of the outer sphere and the yearly motion of the ecliptic. Hence in addition to being moved *per se* by their particular motion, they are moved *per accidens* as a plank is moved in a ship. But if its "soul" is united to each sphere, and the sphere undergoes motion, wouldn't the "soul" be moved *per accidens*, just as the soul of an animal is moved *per accidens* by what affects its body? In that case, how could it cause motion perpetually, if Aquinas has concluded that what is moved *per accidens* cannot cause perpetual motion?

Aquinas's response depends on the fact that the soul of an animal is united to it in being, as its form, whereas the "soul" of the sphere of the moon and other celestial bodies is not united to it in being. It is not its form, only its mover, and so it is not affected by the motion that the sphere undergoes and is not really moved even *per accidens*.[42] (Furthermore, even if the moving part of the hypothetical perpetual self-mover, its "soul," really were its substantial form, then it could not cause perpetual motion without the aid of another, truly immaterial mover. For as we have seen, perpetual motion—or even just unremitting motion—requires a mover with infinite power, and no bodily being can have infinite power.[43])

We can turn now to the final fourth stage of G2:

> Now, God is not part of any self-moving mover. In his *Metaphysics*, therefore, Aristotle goes on from the mover who is a part of the self-moved mover to seek another mover—God—who is absolutely separate. For, since everything moving itself is moved through appetite, the mover who is part of the self-mover moves because of the appetite of some appetible object. This object is higher, in the order of motion, than the mover desiring it; for the one desiring is in a manner a moved mover, whereas an appetible object is an absolutely unmoved mover. There must, therefore, be an absolutely unmoved separate first mover. This is God.[44]

---

42. *In VIII Phys.*, l. 13, n. 1082 [6], paralleling *SCG* I, c. 13, n. 107 [27]. Note especially: "The reason for this diversity is that the movers of the higher orbs are not constituted in their being by a union to bodies, and their connection is invariable. Therefore, although the bodies of the orbs are moved, their movers are not moved *per accidens*. But the souls which move animals are constituted in their being by a union to bodies."

43. See above, this chapter, section titled "The Crucial Step: G2's Third Stage," p. 127 as well as *In VIII Phys.* l. 21 and 23, and *In XII Meta.* l. 8, n. 2548–50.

44. *SCG* I, c. 13, n. 108 [28].

The unexpected move from efficient causality to final causality prepares the way for my next chapter, which will consider the connection between the motion proof and the Fifth Way. But the present argument is obscure, and a number of considerations are required to make it clear. If the mover part of the perpetual self-mover is not its substantial form and not naturally united to it, as Aquinas believes, in what sense could it constitute part of a self-mover? It can do so only in an improper sense, namely, that the immaterial mover "belongs" to the sphere in the sense that its power is limited to moving the heavenly sphere; it cannot act anywhere else, at least as long as it *is* moving the heavenly sphere.[45] Since the motion of each heavenly sphere is continuous, and either everlasting or of exceedingly long duration, its proximate mover is confined to its sphere.

But no motion is for its own sake according to Aquinas; every motion must tend to some end that it can attain. Why, then, would an immaterial mover apply its power to moving a heavenly sphere and confine itself there? The motion certainly does not perfect the heavenly spheres, for according to Aquinas's cosmology they are incorruptible and unalterable, and one place in the sky is as good as another for them. The end served by their motion is the generation and corruption of mixed bodies and living organisms here on earth, above all the generation of human beings.[46] But if the immaterial mover of a sphere is confined to its sphere, and cannot move other spheres or directly move particular terrestrial bodies at the same time, then the success of its own work would depend in part upon the action of other movers. For what the motion of each sphere effects depends upon the location of terrestrial bodies relative to it and to each other and depends upon the concurrent influence of other heavenly bodies. This means that the mover of a sphere is drawn by an end outside itself, something that it lacks and desires. The end that it seeks to achieve cannot be a benefit that it has freely and gratuitously chosen to bestow on its own initiative, because that end is beyond its power. The end is, rather, ordained by a higher being whose power embraces the whole, and the immaterial mover of the sphere moves out of love for this higher being, desiring to participate in its life by fulfilling its generous plan.[47] It is, therefore, moved metaphorically and is in a sense a moved mover.

---

45. *ST* I, q. 54, a. 2.

46. *QDP* q. 5, a. 5, c. and ad 6.

47. This explains Aquinas's statement in G2's fourth stage (*SCG* I, c. 13, n. 108 [28]) that "since everything moving itself is moved through appetite, the mover who is part of the self-moving being moves because of the appetite for some appetible object." If the "soul" is not the form of the sphere

The mover of a heavenly sphere is, then, limited and confined to its sphere *by the command of a superior immaterial being, and that superior being is God*. The mover part of the perpetual self-mover is a moved mover in the sense that it is drawn to move its sphere out of love and obedience to a completely independent, immaterial being. If this were not the case, the sphere's mover would not be confined to it and would not be a "soul" in even a Platonic sense; it would itself be, rather, a completely separate, independent mover, and would be the kind of supermundane God whose existence Aquinas is trying to prove.

Aquinas clearly regards the motion in the universe as orderly, rather than chaotic and random. The astronomical bodies move like clockwork, and their movements support life here on earth. The prime mover must be responsible for this orderly motion. Since this order appears to encompass the universe as a whole, there must be some being responsible for overseeing the motion of the universe as a whole. This being could not in any sense be confined to a single body in the universe, but would be, rather, completely separate, not part of any "self-mover." Any mover that *was* confined to a single body so as to constitute part of a "self-mover" would need to have its activity coordinated with that of other movers so as to maintain the order in the universe. Hence any immaterial angel whose activity was confined to a single sphere would need to be directed by a higher immaterial being that was not so confined. Thus God, a completely separate, immaterial, eternal, immovable mover of the whole universe, must exist, either to move the universe directly Himself or to direct the angels to move its various parts in a coordinated way.

There is further, textual support for this interpretation. Fr. Stephen Brock shows that when Aquinas comes to explain, in his commentary on Aristotle's *Metaphysics*, how the first unmoved mover moves in the order of final causality—moves "as loved"—he indicates that the sphere "souls" wish to fulfill the plan that the unmoved mover conceives in His intellect.[48]

---

but only its mover, why in causing motion would it have to desire anything outside itself? Why could it not move gratuitously, to share its own goodness, as God does? And if it could not, why would God be able to do so when He moves the sphere, either directly or by commanding its "soul"? In short, what makes the difference between the sphere "soul" and God, such that one is moved by an appetible object but the other is not? The answer seems to lie in the localized power of the angelic mover and the universal power of God.

48. Fr. Stephen Brock, "The Causality of the Unmoved Mover in Thomas Aquinas's *Commentary on Metaphysics* XII," *Nova et Vetera* 10, no. 3, English edition (2012): 805–32.

Now it is said that the first mover causes motion as something appetible because the motion of the heavens has this mover as its end or goal, for this motion is caused by some proximate mover which moves on account of the first unmoved mover in order that it may be assimilated in its causality to the first mover and bring to actuality whatever is virtually contained in it.[49]

Now assimilation to a being that wills and understands (as he shows God to be) is in the line of will and understanding, just as things made by art are assimilated to the artist inasmuch as his will is fulfilled in them. This being so, it follows that the necessity of the first motion is totally subject to the will of God.[50]

For the whole order of the universe exists for the sake of the first mover inasmuch as the things contained in the mind and will of the first mover are realized in the ordered universe.[51]

In fact, after summarizing the motion proof from the *Physics* in his commentary on *Metaphysics* XII, Aquinas, following Aristotle, completes the argument by turning to reasoning from design of the sort exemplified in the Fifth Way:

And just as the order of the family is imposed by the law and precept of the head of the family, who is the principle of each of the things which are ordered in the household, with a view to carrying out the activities which pertain to the order of the household, in a similar fashion the nature of physical things is the principle by which each of them carries out the activity proper to it in the order of the universe. For just as any member of the household is disposed to act through the precept of the head of the family, in a similar fashion any natural being is disposed by its own nature. Now the nature of each thing is a kind of inclination implanted in it by the first mover, who directs it to its proper end; and from this it is clear that natural beings act for the sake of an end even though they do not know that end, because they acquire their inclination to their end from the first intelligence.[52]

Aquinas believes that the absolutely first unmoved mover is a being who is His own end, who needs and seeks to acquire nothing for Himself. This being is God, who governs and establishes order in the universe as a whole out of gratuitous love for His creatures, not because He seeks to acquire anything but because He wishes to give Himself to them. To execute His plan, God instills in physical things their natural inclinations

---

49. *In XII Meta.*, l. 7, n. 2521. (John P. Rowan, trans., *Commentary on Aristotle's* Metaphysics [Notre Dame, Ind.: Dumb Ox Books, 1995].)

50. *In XII Meta.*, l. 7, n. 2535.

51. *In XII Meta.*, l. 12, n. 2631.

52. *In XII Meta.*, l. 12, n. 2634.

and moves the celestial spheres either immediately by Himself or through angels acting under His command.[53] The angels are moved by God insofar as they love Him and desire to fulfill His commands.[54] Aquinas argues that there must be one God supreme over all things, material and immaterial, because the universe is an ordered whole, a unified system. Such unity of order requires unity in its orderer, a commander-in-chief, so to speak.[55] The other immaterial beings—the various ranks of angels—move in the way that subordinate officers or soldiers do.

It turns out, then, that Aquinas's motion proof brings one to the Fifth Way even if one travels the G2 path. The argument from order to an ordering intelligence will be considered at much greater length in the next chapter. But anyone who is hesitant to follow Aquinas's reasoning in this section and in stage four of the G2 argument should consider the context. Aquinas has argued that *either* one or more beings exist that are completely independent, immaterial, immovable, and everlasting, efficiently causing motion in the universe, *or* the primary physical components of the universe (which Aquinas thinks of as "the celestial bodies") are moved by angels confined to them. In the latter case, these angels are themselves "moved" by the command of a completely independent, immaterial being. We are not likely to take the hypothesis of quasi-animated astronomical bodies seriously, and so are left with the conclusion that one or more completely independent, immaterial, immovable, everlasting beings exist, in other words, God or gods. The third stage of G2 has already shown this much. A teleological argument, if successful, could further show that there is only one God. (If one does take the possibility of

---

53. See *ST* I, q. 22, a. 3.

54. But even this picture does not require that every sphere "soul" be moved immediately by God even as a proximate final cause. Aquinas is, in fact, inclined to believe that there is a different immaterial being—completely independent of any body—directing and commanding each of the sphere "souls." See, for example, *De Substantiis Separatis*, c. 2 (Leon 40 D: 44, l. 57–66): "Not only the first mobile—which is the first heaven—is moved in an eternal motion, but also all the inferior orbs of the celestial bodies. Whence also each of the celestial bodies is animated by its own soul, and each has its own separate appetible object, which is the proper end of its motion. In this way, therefore, there are many separate substances not united at all to any body. There are also many intellectual substances united to the celestial bodies." Translation mine. See also *QDSC* a. 6, c.: "In this way, therefore, there will be a twofold order of spiritual substances, certain of which will be the movers of the heavenly bodies, and will be united to them as movers to mobiles.... Certain, however, will be the ends of these motions, and these will be wholly separate, and not united to bodies." God is the supreme immaterial being, directing and orchestrating all the rest, the only one that is not caused in His existence, and the only one not directed to an end outside Himself, but there is a whole host of angelic beings between Him and the physical universe.

55. *In XII Meta.*, l. 12, n. 2661–63 and 2629–31.

angel-animated-spheres seriously and rejects the argument from them to a completely independent being, then those angels would count as gods. In either case, the proposition "one or more god exists" would be true.)

CONCLUSION

Aquinas's argument for an unmoved mover is much more elaborate than the conventional interpretation takes it to be. It requires a disjunctive logic: either the universe has a beginning or it is sempiternal. If it has a beginning then a nonphysical, immaterial, immovable, eternal being must exist to initiate it. If the universe is perpetually in motion, then an immaterial, immovable, everlasting being must exist to sustain it. Material causes simply cannot sustain perpetual, unabating motion. Hence an immaterial mover must exist. This is already a significant accomplishment. But the remaining chapters will take us still farther.

Chapter 5

The Living God

Uniting the First and Fifth Ways

We have seen in the previous chapter that Aquinas's motion proof leads finally to the teleological proof. In the text of the *Summa Theologiae*, Aquinas appeals to the Fifth Way to exclude the possibility that natural causes might be sufficient to account for what occurs in the universe (*ST* I, q. 2, a. 3, obj. 2 and ad 2), something that the First Way, all by itself, could not accomplish. The longer G2 version of the motion proof does establish the existence of one or more immaterial movers, yet after doing so it too steps over into the order of final causality, ending with an appeal to Aristotle's *Metaphysics* XII and the concept of God as the one who establishes order in the cosmos. It is necessary, then, to come to grips with Aquinas's Fifth Way and other presentations of his teleological proof. The work of the previous chapters has already established that there exist one or more immaterial, everlasting, immovable beings causing motion in the cosmos. The present line of inquiry will establish in addition that there is only one God, and that He is living and intelligent.

In his Fifth Way, Aquinas argues that nature is intrinsically purposive and that this purposiveness depends upon a transcendent intelligent agent. The proof is quite compressed and requires elaboration. According to a prominent interpretation, promoted by Edward Feser but advocated earlier by Fr. Garrigou-Lagrange, the Fifth Way relies merely on the regularity with which causes produce their effects. The proof, Feser says, relies on neither complexity, nor probability, nor beneficial adaptation. The point is simply that a given cause produces a given effect, regularly if not always, and that it could not do so unless it tended to that effect as to its end. But nothing can tend to a not yet existent end unless some intelligent being foresees that end and directs the cause toward it.[1] Marie George, however, argues against Feser's interpretation, maintaining that although simple phenomena of the kind Feser points to do involve final causality, in the Fifth Way Aquinas has in mind the kind of phenomena in which there is beneficial adaptation of parts to wholes and means to ends, exhibited especially by biological organisms.[2] Robert Koons and Logan Paul Gage also lend support to the role of complexity in Aquinas's argument.[3]

In this chapter I will argue that both Feser and George are right, each in his or her own way. Although Aquinas does regard every case of regular causality in nature as proof that God exists—as Feser maintains—he does not regard this line of argument as particularly effective at convincing naturalists of the Empedoclean or Democritean variety (or, in present day terms, at convincing scientifically minded atheists). To convince reductionists that nature acts for an end, one needs to show that the natures of things not only intrinsically tend toward specific results, but that those

---

1. See Edward Feser, *Aquinas*, 110–20, 16–23, and 36–51.

2. Marie George, "An Aristotelian-Thomist Responds to Edward Feser's 'Teleology,'" *Philosophia Christi* 12, no. 2 (2010): 441–49, at 445, 448 and "On the Occasion of Darwin's Bicentennial: Finally Time to Retire the Fifth Way?" *Proceedings of the American Catholic Philosophical Association* 83 (2009): 209–25, at 216–17. George also maintains that, although Aquinas certainly believes in intrinsic final causality, the Fifth Way itself is neutral as to whether the final causality found in nature is intrinsic to the natures of things or externally imposed. Marie George and Ed Feser carried on their debate in the following articles: Edward Feser, "Teleology: A Shopper's Guide," in *Neo-Scholastic Essays*, 28–48 (South Bend, IN: St. Augustine's Press, 2015), originally published in *Philosophia Christi* 12, no. 1 (2010): 142–59; George, "An Aristotelian-Thomist Responds to Feser"; Edward Feser, "On Aristotle, Aquinas, and Paley: A Reply to Marie George," accessed October 12th, 2021, Evangelical Philosophical Society Site Article, 2011 (http://www.epsociety.org/library/articles.asp?pid=83&mode=detail); Marie George, "'Intrinsic' and 'Extrinsic' Teleology: Their Irrelevance to Aquinas's Fifth Way and to Paley's Argument from Design," accessed October 12th, 2021, Evangelical Philosophical Society Site Article, 2015 (http://www.epsociety.org/library/articles.asp?pid=285&mode=detail). George had proposed her own account of the Fifth Way in "Finally Time to Retire the Fifth Way?" See also Marie George, "Thomistic Rebuttal of Some Common Objections to Paley's Argument from Design," *New Blackfriars* 97, no. 1069 (2016): 266–88 and "What Would Thomas Aquinas Say about Intelligent Design?" *New Blackfriars* 94, no. 1054 (2013): 676–700, as well as Edward Feser, "Between Aristotle and William Paley: Aquinas's Fifth Way," *Nova et Vetera* 11, no. 3, English edition (2013): 707–49.

3. Robert C. Koons and Logan Paul Gage, "St. Thomas Aquinas on Intelligent Design," *Proceedings of the American Catholic Philosophical Association* 85 (2011): 79–97, at 86. It should be noted that whereas Koons and Gage support the Intelligent Design (ID) movement George does not. See George, "What Would Thomas Aquinas Say about Intelligent Design?"

results are essentially *good.* George has made her point well in this regard. In his Fifth Way and other teleological proofs for God's existence, Aquinas bases his argument on the fact that the elements and their activities are moderated and coordinated in such a way that they produce, preserve, and benefit higher things, especially living organisms. I will label this characteristic "beneficial adaption." This is what most of all demonstrates that "the work of nature is the work of intelligence (*opus naturae est opus intelligentiae*)."[4]

Each of the interpretations has its advantages and its drawbacks. Feser's interpretation allows one to sidestep the issue of evolution through chance mutation and natural selection. Since such a process obviously depends upon law-like regularity in biochemistry, it would presuppose intrinsic purposiveness and the work of intelligence. But some people see no need for an intelligence behind law-like regularity, regarding it rather as a "brute fact." I don't know what arguments one can bring to bear to convince such people. George's interpretation, on the other hand, depends upon characteristics that much more obviously involve purposiveness and intelligence. Yet it cannot sidestep the issue of Neo-Darwinism, which seems to provide an alternative explanation of the empirically observed characteristics. But just as, with the First Way, historical accuracy requires tackling issues of physics head on, so too with the Fifth Way one cannot avoid raising issues in the philosophy of biology if one is to be fair to Aquinas's own text. Hence I advocate George's interpretation.

However, since tackling the issue of Neo-Darwinism adequately would require another book of its own, I can do no more than make a few comments on it, sticking rather to the historical task of explaining Aquinas's Fifth Way in its original context. However, my discussion in chapter 8 of contemporary scientific evidence that the universe is fine-tuned for the possibility of life will provide a down payment for the contemporary defense of Aquinas's teleological argument.

My order of proceeding in this chapter is as follows: In the first part, I will begin with a presentation of the Fifth Way and provide a preliminary analysis of its basic structure. I will then consider the qualified validity of Feser's interpretation of the Fifth Way. Then I will expound the bases and validity of George's claim that Aquinas has more in mind than mere

---

4. On the source of this adage, see Weisheipl, "The Axiom '*Opus naturae est opus intelligentiae*' and its Origins," in *Albertus Magnus Doctor Universalis: 1280/1980*, ed. Gerbert Meyer, OP, and Albert Zimmermann, 441–63 (Mainz: Matthias Grünewald Verlag, 1980).

causal regularity, and that the premise of his argument is that the causal powers of substances are regularly coordinated and moderated so as to promote the well-being of themselves and of others, in ways that their own natures do not guarantee. Finally, I will clarify the presuppositions of Aquinas's argument by elaborating on key aspects of his philosophy of physics, chemistry, and biology: inanimate beings, left to their own devices, always tend toward extremes, and order and moderation can only be effected by life and intelligence. In the second part of the chapter, responding to an objection from Anthony Kenny, I will show how Aquinas can justify his claim that the regularity with which natural beings achieve their ends both shows that they themselves are not intelligent *and* that they depend upon the activity of a transcendent intelligence.[5] I will show that the varied ways in which the same material causal factors are coordinated so as to achieve *different* beneficial ends in different contexts, but with regular success, depends upon a being having the characteristic of life in the highest degree, namely, immaterial intelligence. Then I will show how Aquinas argues from the teleological unity of the cosmos to the unity of God. As an epilogue to this chapter, I will connect the First and Fifth Ways by expounding further on Aquinas's philosophy of biology, according to which living things are defined by their ability to move themselves; I will explain how the different classes of life are arranged hierarchically according to the degree of their participation in the paradigm of self-motion, namely intelligent self-determination. The first mover is actually a self-mover. He is unmoved in that He undergoes no motion in the strict sense (the act of the imperfect); He is a self-mover in that He determines Himself to His own, unchanging activity (the act of the perfect).

The ultimate conclusion of this chapter and of the first part of the book is that Aquinas's philosophy of nature—in virtue of the combined motion and teleological proofs—leads in a sound and convincing way, given its historical context, to the existence of one, immaterial, everlasting, immovable, living, intelligent, and self-determining God. This is a quite significant and robust conclusion, a true preamble to faith.[6] In the philosophy of nature, however, Aquinas does not prove that God either is *or is not* omniscient and omnipotent. If God's omniscience and omnipotence can be established philosophically, it is only by thoroughly

---

5. Kenny, *The Five Ways*, 118–19.
6. See *ST* I, q. 2, a. 2, ad 1.

metaphysical means that are beyond the scope of this book. Yet no one need be alarmed that my conclusion is less robust than that God is the pure act of existence. For nothing I have said rules out the possibility that God is indeed self-subsisting existence, nor that such could be proved demonstratively in the science of metaphysics (as I in fact hold).

INTERPRETING THE ARGUMENT

A First Look at the Fifth Way

Aquinas' fifth proof for God's existence in the *Summa Theologiae* runs as follows:

> The fifth way is taken from the governance of the world. We see that things which lack knowledge, namely, natural bodies, act for an end, and this is evident from their acting always, or more often, in the same way, so as to obtain the best result. Hence it is plain that they tend to an end rather than arriving at it by chance (*non a casu, sed ex intentione perveniunt ad finem.*)
>
> Now whatever lacks intelligence cannot move towards an end, unless it be directed by some being endowed with knowledge and intelligence, as the arrow is shot to its mark by the archer. Therefore there is something intelligent by which all natural things are directed to their end; and this being we call God.[7]

There are parallel arguments in other texts. Worth mentioning are the following: the teleological argument is found in the prologue to Aquinas's *Commentary on John's Gospel*, n. 3. There Aquinas calls the argument "the most efficacious way (*via efficacissima*)," which I interpret as "the way by which average people are normally convinced of God's existence." Indeed, we saw in chapter 3 a text in which Aquinas speaks of a basic, natural, but inferential knowledge of God that almost everyone achieves, insofar as any ordinary person perceives order in the universe

---

7. *ST* I, q. 2, a. 3, c.: "Quinta via sumitur ex gubernatione rerum. Videmus enim quod aliqua quae cognitione carent, scilicet corpora naturalia, operantur propter finem: quod apparet ex hoc quod semper aut frequentius eodem modo operantur, ut consequantur id quod est optimum; unde patet quod non a casu, sed ex intentione perveniunt ad finem. Ea autem quae non habent cognitionem, non tendunt in finem nisi directa ab aliquo cognoscente et intelligente, sicut sagitta a sagittante. Ergo est aliquid intelligens, a quo omnes res naturales ordinantur ad finem: et hoc dicimus Deum." Translation revised. When Aquinas says that natural bodies that lack cognition *ex intentione perveniunt ad finem*, the word *intentio* means that they are actually tending toward the very result that they arrive at, rather than it just happening to work out that way: "to intend is to tend to something (*intendere est in aliud tendere*)" (*ST* I-II, q. 12, a. 5, c.; note the context as well.) Cf. Marie George, "Intrinsic and Extrinsic Teleology," 3–5, and fn. 11.

and knows that something or someone must be responsible for it.[8] But the teleological argument in its most well-developed form is found in *De Veritate*, q. 5, a. 2, a text that I will consider below.[9] There is also a similar argument at the end of *SCG* I, c. 13.

As commonly noted, the Fifth Way involves two stages,[10] and I have broken it into two paragraphs accordingly. The first stage argues that nature is intrinsically purposive; purposiveness is not restricted to human affairs. This is established by means of the fact that natural beings display beneficial adaptation with regularity, for example, rain makes plants grow and wings enable birds to fly. By chance something could serve a function quite well—for example, a rock might fall from a cliff and kill a wolf chasing a deer—but whatever occurs with regularity does not occur by chance. The second stage of the argument reasons that such final causality in the natural world must be due to the agency of an intelligent being. Since it is clearly not due to the agency of human beings, and since the beings that compose the natural world are clearly not themselves intelligent, their purposiveness must be due to a transcendent intelligence. Hence God exists.

Anthony Kenny sees a quantifier fallacy in the conclusion.[11] Even if the argument itself were sound, the only conclusion it could support is that each natural body lacking intelligence is directed to its end by an intelligent being. It is not proved that every natural body is directed to its end by the *same* intelligent being. Kenny is right about the logic of the argument but wrong about Aquinas's intention. That there is only one God is not established until nine questions later in *ST*, namely, in q. 11, a. 3. There Aquinas gives, among other arguments, one based on the teleological *unity* of the whole cosmos. This argument extends and completes the Fifth Way, and I will consider it below.

Certainly many deny that nature is intrinsically purposive, and thus

8. *SCG* III, c. 38. See chapter 3 above, section titled "Qualified Success of the First Way: God in a Minimal Sense," p. 111–113. The most relevant excerpt is the following: "When men see that things in nature run according to a definite order, and that ordering does not occur without an orderer, they perceive in most cases that there is some orderer of the things that we see. But who or what kind of being, or whether there is but one orderer of nature, is not yet grasped immediately in this general consideration."

9. In *QDV* q. 5, a. 2, Aquinas is not technically arguing for God's existence, but rather for His providence, but this merely shows how robust the teleological argument's conclusion is.

10. See, for example, C. F. J. Martin, *God and Explanations*, 179–80; Fr. Reginald Garrigou-Lagrange, OP, *God: His Existence and His Nature*, vol. I, 347; Timothy Pawl, "The Five Ways," 124–25.

11. Kenny, *The Five Ways*, 97.

object to the first stage of Aquinas's argument. This stage requires a defense. But the second stage is in some ways more difficult. If natural beings are *intrinsically* purposive, why must their purposiveness be accounted for by an extrinsic, intelligent being? Why can't nature just be the sort of thing that is purposive, in and of itself? C. F. J. Martin, for example, thought that this was the hard part of Aquinas's argument: "Every unconscious teleology, every case of something being for something without awareness of what it's for, is dependent on some conscious teleology, on some mind which is aware what that thing is for. It seems obvious to me that just in so far as one is disposed to admit the existence of unconscious teleology, one will be disposed to deny this claim."[12]

Before defending the two stages of the argument, I will first compare Edward Feser's and Marie George's interpretations of the Fifth Way and show how the textual evidence supports George. This will set the stage to show that Aquinas's argument is sound by making it clear what the purposiveness appealed to in the first stage consists in. It is that natural beings regularly achieve ends that are clearly good and beneficial, and that, furthermore, these ends are such that their own natures do not suffice to achieve them. They only achieve these ends when coordinated with other natural beings, and their own natures do not suffice to effect this coordination. The inference from such purposiveness to intelligent agency will be confirmed when I explain the difference between chance, natural purposiveness, and intelligent agency.

Regularity and Intelligibility as Evidence of Intelligence

Edward Feser understands the purposiveness appealed to in the Fifth Way as causal regularity, plain and simple:

> Aquinas' view is that efficient causes would not be intelligible without final causes. This is what he means when he says in the Fifth Way that "things which lack intelligence, such as natural bodies, act for an end, and this is evident from their acting always, or nearly always, in the same way, so as to obtain the best result." He is not especially interested here in the fact that hearts typically pump blood, that eyes enable us to see, and other such biological facts (though these would naturally be included as instances of the more general phenomenon he is interested in). It is the existence of *any causal regularities at all* that he takes to require explanation.... For Aquinas, the

12. Martin, *God and Explanations*, 199–200.

fact that A regularly brings about B, as B's *efficient* cause, entails that bringing about B is in turn the *final* cause of A. For if we did not suppose that A inherently "points to" or is "directed towards" the generation of B as its natural end, then we would have no way to account for the fact that A typically does generate *B* specifically, rather than C, or D, or E, or indeed rather than no effect at all.[13]

Feser cites *ST* I, q. 44, a. 4, c. and I-II, q. 1, a. 2, c, among other texts.[14] He is right to do so, as we can see:

> Every agent, of necessity, acts for an end.... An agent does not move except out of intention for an end (*ex intentione finis*). For if the agent were not determinate to some particular effect, it would not do one thing rather than another. Consequently, in order that it produce a determinate effect, it must, of necessity, be determined to some certain one, which has the nature of an end. And just as this determination is effected, in the rational nature, by the rational appetite, which is called the will, so in other things it is caused by their natural inclination, which is called the natural appetite.[15]

Such texts also help justify Feser's claim that the kind of teleology that Aquinas has in mind in the Fifth Way is intrinsic; by their very own natural inclinations, natural bodies tend toward ends.[16] But if purposiveness is intrinsic to natural bodies, why must they be directed to their ends by an intelligent agent? The answer, Feser says, is that a final cause exercises its causality even before it exists. (For example, desiring to eat a sandwich, I begin to assemble the ingredients; the not yet existent sandwich exercises final causality over my actions.) A final cause cannot exercise

---

13. Feser, *Aquinas*, 112–13.

14. Feser, "Between Aristotle and William Paley," 715 and fn. 11. Another important text cited by Feser is *SCG* III, c. 2 (particularly, n. 2 and 8).

15. *ST* I-II, q. 1, a. 2, c., punctuation emended.

16. Feser, *Aquinas*, 115–16. George argues in "Intrinsic and Extrinsic Teleology" that it is irrelevant to the Fifth Way whether purposiveness is intrinsic or extrinsic in nature. Her analysis of the syllogisms composing the Fifth Way is, on one level, convincing. The immanence of purposiveness does not show up in any of the premises, nor is it necessary for Aquinas to secure his conclusion, since he certainly thinks that extrinsic purposiveness also requires the activity of intelligence, as his very example of the arrow and archer shows. However, Feser is right that Aquinas's broader philosophy requires that the purposiveness in question in the Fifth Way be intrinsic. For God accomplishes everything by His divine art. But the divine art can utilize four different means: nature, creaturely art, chance, and miracle. The first syllogism of the Fifth Way is meant to rule out the possibility that the purposes regularly achieved in nature are by chance. It also excludes cases of creaturely art, because that requires the activity of creatures with knowledge, e.g., human beings. Aquinas certainly does not have in mind repeated miracles on God's part. So when Aquinas argues that natural bodies not possessing knowledge act always or for the most part so as to obtain what is best, he is implying that the purposes are achieved by nature. Thus the purposiveness is indeed intrinsic, as Feser argues.

any causality except insofar as it influences an efficient cause. But a not yet existent final cause can only influence an efficient cause by means of its preconception in the mind of an intelligent being.[17] Since the final causality operative in the natural world is intrinsic to the very natures of things, the intelligence at work in the natural world must therefore be responsible for the very natures of things. This intelligent being must cause and conserve the very being of these natures and must thus be pure act, existence itself.[18]

Fr. Garrigou-Lagrange adds that it is not enough that the final cause pre-exist in conscious knowledge, it must, rather, pre-exist in reason or intelligence. For animals perceive ends and means, but do not understand the relationship between ends and means, and so are guided in their actions by natural instincts that must be caused in them by an intelligent being.[19] Only reason can understand what an end is, and what means are, and freely determine what ends are to be pursued and by what means.

Demonstrating a great deal of perspicacity, Fr. Garrigou-Lagrange also relates the Fifth Way to the issue of the contingency of the very laws of nature, which are not *logically* necessary, although they are *metaphysically* necessary. Descartes dreamed of explaining the whole structure of the world by means of mathematical laws that could not even be conceived to be other than they were, but that is not possible. There is an unavoidable *logical* contingency to the laws of nature. Leibniz, and Plato in his *Phaedo* and *Timaeus*, had the right idea: the structure of the universe must ultimately be explained in terms of the *good*. God has chosen to establish the laws/causal relationships we in fact observe because they achieve His goals well.[20] (Yet I hasten to add that Leibniz was wrong to think that this world had to be and was the best of all possible worlds. Since the created world can only be finitely good, "best of all possible worlds" is a contradiction in terms. Although God has structured the natural world in a way that is very good, He could have established it differently, in other very good ways.[21] He has *freely* decided on this sort

17. Ibid., 116–17.

18. Ibid., 117–19. Note that Feser says here that "obviously all of this goes beyond what Aquinas says in the text of the Fifth Way itself, which, like the other ways, is intended only as a summary."

19. Fr. Garrigou-Lagrange, *God: His Existence and His Nature*, vol. I, 367–68, citing the continuation of the text from *ST* I-II, q. 1, a. 2, quoted above. See also *QDP* q. 1, a. 5, c.

20. Fr. Garrigou-Lagrange, *God: His Existence and His Nature*, vol. I, 357–59, 346.

21. See, for example, *QDP* q. 1, a. 5, c.: "Now the natural end of the divine will is the divine goodness, which it is unable not to will. Creatures, however, are not proportionate to this end, as though without them the divine goodness could not be made manifest, which manifestation was

of world. The full strength, Leibnizian Principle of Sufficient Reason is not in fact true, although a weakened version is true and essential to philosophical reasoning.)

I think that there is a lot of truth in the kind of argument Feser and Fr. Garrigou-Lagrange propose, and that Aquinas would recognize it as one of his own. The fact that there is any order and regularity *at all* in the universe means that the universe is intelligible, and intellig*ibility* is the mark of the work of intellig*ence*. Stanley Jaki has argued that it was no accident that science arose in Christian Europe, where the belief that a rational God had created the whole universe out of nothing was strong. Only on the basis of that belief could scientists be confident that the world was intelligible through and through and would prove tractable to human investigation.[22] Even Immanuel Kant argued that, despite the *a priori* forms of human intuition and the *a priori* concepts of the human understanding that according to him structure human experience, the empirical world need not have been so orderly. The world might have been so chaotic that it was impossible to identify any laws of nature. Hence we ought to think of the world of experience as purposive and as the product of intelligence. (Although, in his view, this is only a regulative, rather than constitutive principle; in other words, we cannot say that it really is so, only that given the limitations of the human intellect we will always find it helpful to think in such terms, for heuristic purposes.)[23]

Some people are impressed by this argument for God's existence. Others are not. Some are led by similar considerations to something like pantheism or the idea that matter is in itself incipiently conscious (consider the cases of Albert Einstein and Thomas Nagel[24]). Others, in response to Feser's argument, will simply say that if a natural cause is *intrinsically* directed to a certain result, then there must be something within the unconscious cause itself that determinately produces that result. Why

---

God's intention in creating. For even as the divine goodness is made manifest through these things that are and through this order of things, so could it be made manifest through other creatures and another order: wherefore God's will without prejudice to his goodness, justice and wisdom, can extend to other things besides those which he has made."

22. Stanley Jaki, *The Road of Science and the Ways to God* (Chicago: The University of Chicago Press, 1978).

23. See Immanuel Kant, *Critique of Judgment*, Introduction to the Second Edition, V and *Critique of Pure Reason*, Appendix to the Transcendental Dialectic, A670/B698–A673/B701, A675/B703–A679/B707, A685/B713–A688/B716, A653/B681–A654/B682.

24. Albert Einstein, *Essays in Science*, trans. Alan Harris (New York: Philosophical Library, 1934), 11; Thomas Nagel, *Mind and Cosmos*, 31–32, 4–5, 56–57.

multiply causes needlessly by introducing an intelligent agent? The effect is not an end or purpose, just a result, and it is a "brute fact" that such a cause produces such a result.

I think Feser's argument is sound and demonstrates the existence of the creator God; I think that the wise will see its force. However, it is not quite the argument Aquinas has in mind in the Fifth Way.

Beneficial Adaptation: Textual Evidence

Edward Feser grounds the Fifth Way on the mere existence of causal regularity. But Marie George has successfully criticized Feser's interpretation, pointing out that in the first stage of the Fifth Way Aquinas argues that the fact that natural bodies act for an end "is evident from their acting always, or more often, [*semper aut frequentius*] in the same way, *so as to obtain the best result.*"[25] The final clause would be superfluous on Feser's interpretation, since it is based on *mere* regularity. Certainly there are places where Aquinas makes an argument for final causality in nature solely on the basis of regularity,[26] sometimes using the very same wording as in the first stage of the Fifth Way but leaving off the final clause about the good. (*In II Phys.*, l. 13, n. 256 [2]: "Those things which happen always or for the most part [*semper vel frequenter*] happen for an end.") But Aquinas does not think that this is the most convincing line of argumentation:

> With regard to those things to which it can extend by virtue of its essential principles, nature does not need to be determined by another, but only with regard to those things for which its own principles do not suffice. Consequently, *philosophers, in saying that the work of nature is the work of an intelligence, were not led by observing the effects of heat and cold considered in themselves,* since even those who said that natural effects were necessitated by matter referred all the works of nature to the agency of heat and cold. But they were led by observing those effects which were beyond the power of these qualities of heat and cold, such as the arrangement of members in the body of an animal in such wise that nature is safeguarded.[27]

As George points out, for Aquinas biology is the center of the debate between those who affirm and those who deny purposiveness in nature (Aquinas is opposing the pre-Socratic philosopher Empedocles, who put

---

25. George, "An Aristotelian-Thomist Responds to Feser," 444–45.

26. Such as in the passages cited above: *ST* I-II, q. 1, a. 2, c. and I, q. 44, a. 4, c.

27. *QDP* q. 2, a. 3, ad 5, emphasis added. Punctuation emended. Cited by George in "Finally Time to Retire the Fifth Way?" fn. 36.

forward an ancient theory of natural selection, as well as the ancient atomists Democritus and Leucippus):

> Those who held that nature does not act for the sake of something tried to confirm their position by denying that in which nature is most clearly seen to act for the sake of something. That which most strongly demonstrates that nature acts for the sake of something is the fact that in the operation of nature a thing is always found to come to be as good and as suitable as it can be (*quanto melius et commodius esse potest*). Thus, the foot is made in a certain way by nature so that it may be suitable (*aptus*) for walking. Hence if it falls short of this natural disposition, it is not fit (*aptus*) for this use. And the same is true of other instances.[28]

In addition to the argument from causal regularity then ("nature acts always or more frequently in the same way"), Aquinas employs another, stronger argument, namely an argument from goodness. (The difference is illustrated by the fact that in *SCG* III, c. 2, Aquinas argues that every agent acts for *an end*, and then goes on to demonstrate in chapter 3 that every agent acts for *a good*, using different arguments.[29]) When Aquinas uses the phrase "nature acts always or more frequently in the same way *so as to obtain what is best*," or its equivalent, he routinely appeals not to causal regularity but to the benefit deriving from natural structures and processes.[30] It is this latter argument that he uses in the Fifth Way. Nature displays goodness in that natural beings regularly act in such a way as to preserve and perfect (i.e., fully actualize) themselves and to fulfill functions for the benefit of other beings. This is true both in regard to the parts of a whole possessing substantial unity and in regard to the parts of a whole possessing unity of order,[31] in other words, both in regard to the articulated parts of a living organism and in regard to the distinct substances that make up the ordered universe.

The argument from goodness that constitutes the first stage of the Fifth Way is presented in a slightly expanded form in *SCG* III, c. 3. There the note of biological self-preservation is again stressed:

---

28. *In II Phys.*, l. 12, n. 252 [3]. Emphasis added. Cited by George, "An Aristotelian-Thomist Responds to Feser," 445.

29. See George, "An Aristotelian-Thomist Responds to Feser," 444.

30. Or, in one case, to the similarity between nature's operation and human artifice, but with a reference backward to a passage in which the same phrase was explicated in terms of the benefit of biological structure: *SCG* III, c. 64, n. 2388 [5], with a reference to *SCG* III, c. 3.

31. On this distinction, see *In I Eth. Nic.*, l. 1, n. 5.

That which results from the action of an agent, but apart from the intention of the agent, is said to happen by chance or by luck. *But we observe that what happens in the working of nature is either always, or mostly, for the better. Thus, in the plant world leaves are arranged so as to protect the fruit, and among animals the bodily organs are disposed in such a way that the animal can be protected.* So, if this came about apart from the intention of the natural agent, it would be by chance or by luck. But this is impossible, for things which occur always, or for the most part, are neither chance nor fortuitous events, but only those which occur in few instances. Therefore, the natural agent *tends* toward what is better, and it is much more evident that the intelligent agent does so. Hence, every agent intends the good when it acts.[32]

That natural bodies are intrinsically purposive is on display above all in living organisms: in the way in which the differentiated parts of developing animals and plants grow spontaneously in a timed and coordinated sequence without any conscious effort on the part of the organism; in the different functions that each of these parts performs for the good of the whole organism (e.g., the foot serving for transportation, the teeth for cutting and grinding food, the heart for circulating blood); in the way in which bodies spontaneously heal from wounds and put themselves back together; and in the way in which social animals such as bees work together for the good of the colony and the males and females of all sexual organisms interrelate for the sake of reproduction. As Leon Kass argues, for these reasons "we must regard living things as purposive beings, as beings that cannot even be looked at, much less properly described or fully understood, without teleological notions."[33] Even materialists who reject any kind of teleology in the universe at large acknowledge that living beings must be looked at through the lens of purposiveness (though they prefer the word "teleonomy" to "teleology," believing that the purposiveness of living beings must ultimately be the product of random interactions among bits of nonpurposive inanimate matter.[34])

---

32. *SCG* III, c. 3, n. 1886 [9]. Emphasis added. Punctuation emended. Cp. *SCG* III, c. 64, n. 2388 [5].

33. Leon Kass, *Toward a More Natural Science: Biology and Human Affairs* (New York: The Free Press, 1985), 254–58.

34. Addy Pross, *What is Life? How Chemistry Becomes Biology* (Oxford: Oxford University Press, 2016), 9–10, 17: "There is another facet to the organized complexity of living systems that has been strikingly evident to humankind for thousands of years—life's purposeful character. That purposeful character is so well defined and unambiguous that biologists have come up with a special name for it—teleonomy. The 'teleonomy' word was introduced about half a century ago to distinguish it from the 'teleology' word with its cosmic implications.... Teleonomy, as a biological phenomenon, is empirically irrefutable. The term simply gives a name to a pattern of behavior that is

But Aquinas also has in mind the relationships between inorganic beings, and between inorganic and organic beings. In his *Commentary* on Aristotle's *Physics*, he considers the Empedoclean claim that rain does not fall to make the crops grow, since sometimes rain spoils crops on the threshing floor. Aquinas says that rain *is* purposive, and that it spoils crops infrequently—by chance—but promotes their growth for the most part—by nature. To be precise, he says, rain does not fall to make *crops* grow, specifically, but to continue the cycle of life in general—generation and corruption, growth and decay.[35] Feser and Oderberg point out that there are many natural cycles in the physical world, such as the oxygen/carbon dioxide cycle, the water cycle, and so on. These display a higher level of purposiveness than mere causal regularity, in that each stage in the process prepares the way for the next.[36] The result is naturally beneficial for the things involved.[37] Rain, for example, certainly does not promote life merely by chance. It is not for nothing that scientists get excited about any evidence of liquid water on other planets. But to promote life on land, rain must be neither too plentiful (think of Noah's ark) nor too scarce (think of the Sahara desert). Furthermore, rain is produced when the sun evaporates water, but neither heats the planet so much that all water is turned into and remains vapor, nor so little that all water is frozen into ice. In Aquinas's view, such cycles of inorganic causes, moderated and adjusted to promote the conditions for life, prove that nature is purposive.

Aquinas reasons that the kind of purposiveness that is found in nature cannot be explained by purely natural causes. Physical agents are determined to a single effect and produce that effect whenever or wherever they can, whether it benefits anything or not. To render the operation

---

unambiguous—all living things behave as if they have an agenda. Every living thing goes about its business of living—building nests, collecting food, protecting the young, and, of course, reproducing. In fact, within the biological world that's how we broadly understand and predict what goes on.... In the non-living world, by comparison, understanding and prediction are achieved on the basis of quite different principles. No teleonomy there, just the established laws of physics and chemistry.... If we wish to understand life, we will need to provide a rationale for life's teleonomic character in the same chemical terms we use to explain the global characteristics of inanimate systems."

35. *In II Phys.*, l. 12, n. 252–54 [3–5].

36. Feser, *Aristotle's Revenge*, 38–39; David S. Oderberg, "Teleology: Inorganic and Organic," in *Contemporary Perspectives on Natural Law: Natural Law as a Limiting Concept*, ed. A. M. González, 259–79 (Aldershot: Ashgate, 2008), at 266–73.

37. Neither Feser nor Oderberg think that it makes sense to speak of anything as good *for* a nonliving being, yet they believe that nonliving beings do serve purposes outside themselves. I disagree with the first part of their claim and agree with the second.

of such agents regularly beneficial, a higher kind of principle must be at work. It is not the mere regularity of nature, but the coordination of natural things—the fact that different parts or things fulfill functions for others—that serves as the ground of Aquinas's proof. Although natural beings achieve what is good while operating in accord with their nature—and in accord with what we would now call the laws of physics and chemistry—they can only do so insofar as they are directed by a higher, intelligent cause.

That this is the correct way to read Aquinas's Fifth Way is decisively confirmed by the *De Veritate* presentation of the proof:

> Some of the very ancient philosophers admitted only a material cause.... Later philosophers admitted an efficient cause, but said nothing about a final cause. According to both schools, everything was necessarily caused by previously existing causes, material or efficient. This position, however, was criticized by other philosophers on the following grounds. *Material and efficient causes, as such, cause only the existence of their effects. They are not sufficient to produce goodness in them so that they be aptly disposed in themselves so that they could continue to exist, and toward others so that they could help them (ad causandum bonitatem in effectu secundum quam sit conveniens et in se ipso ut permanere possit et aliis ut eis opituletur). Heat, for example, of its very nature and of itself can break down other things, but this breaking down is good and helpful (conveniens et bona) only if it happens up to a certain point and in a certain way. Consequently, if we do not admit that there exist in nature causes other than heat and similar agents, we cannot give any reason why things happen in a good and orderly way (convenienter fiant et bene).* Moreover, whatever does not have a determinate cause happens by accident. Consequently, if the position mentioned above were true, all the harmony and usefulness (*omnes convenientiae et utilitates*) found in things would be the result of chance. This was actually what Empedocles held. He asserted that it was by accident that the parts of animals came together in this way through friendship—and this was his explanation of an animal and of a frequent occurrence. This explanation, of course, is absurd, for those things that happen by chance, happen only rarely; *we know from experience, however, that harmony and usefulness are found in nature either at all times or at least for the most part (huiusmodi convenientias et utilitates accidere in operibus naturae aut semper aut in maiori parte).* This cannot be the result of mere chance; it must be because an end is intended.
>
> What lacks intellect or knowledge, however, cannot tend directly toward an end. Consequently, since natural things have no knowledge, there must be some previously existing intelligence directing them to an end, like

an archer who gives a definite motion to an arrow so that it will wing its way to a determined end. Now, the hit made by the arrow is said to be the work not of the arrow alone but also of the person who shot it. Similarly, *philosophers call every work of nature the work of intelligence.* Consequently, the world is ruled by the providence of that intellect which gave this order to nature; and we may compare the providence by which God rules the world to the domestic foresight by which a man rules his family, or to the political foresight by which a ruler governs a city or a kingdom, and directs the acts of others to a definite end.[38]

This is the same argument as the Fifth Way, but its presentation is much more explicit and developed. It consists of the same two stages: nature is purposive because it displays *goodness* and not mere regularity, and such purposiveness can only be accounted for by an intelligent agent. Marie George, then, is correct: the purposiveness in question in the Fifth Way involves coordination of parts and causes toward an overarching good, and biology is the focal point.

Things Fall Apart

What evidence can Aquinas provide for the claim that purely natural causes cannot by themselves account for what is observed in nature, that things display a purposiveness that demands an intelligent agent? Don't we discover what natural causes are capable of by observing what they do? Doesn't that imply that natural causes do account for natural occurrences, including any natural occurrences that seem or even are purposive?[39] The answer comes from observing the same things in different contexts, a procedure that allows us to distinguish what comes from a thing by itself and what comes from it with the aid of another. What we discover is that, cut off from intelligent, biological, or astronomical influences, physical and chemical beings tend to fall apart and come to rest, that is, they tend toward thermal equilibrium and maximal entropy. Spider webs and bird nests fall apart unless maintained by their living occupants. The same thing is true of houses when not cared for by their intelligent occupants. Water tends to pool and come to rest at the lowest point, and

---

38. *QDV* q. 5, a. 2, c. Punctuation emended. Emphasis added. Although Aquinas is professedly arguing not for God's existence but for His providence, Msgr. Wippel treats this text as one of Aquinas's arguments for God's existence, and connects it closely with the Fifth Way: *The Metaphysical Though of Thomas Aquinas*, 480, 410–13. I am in agreement with him.

39. This objection was suggested to me by Michael Bolin.

air enclosed in a room tends to become still and stuffy. But when placed within its normal context in the natural world, air is constantly on the move, whether as a gentle breeze or a driving wind. Water is always flowing toward the sea, undulating in the ocean, rising as vapor, or falling as rain. These effects are caused by the heat radiating from the sun.[40]

When Aquinas claims in the first stage of the *De Veritate* version of his teleological argument that material and efficient causes alone cannot account for the goodness and harmony found in nature, he is in possession of a rich philosophy of physics, chemistry, and biology on which he can draw to make his point. Although for Aquinas nature is purposive all the way down, in the animate and inanimate realms, there is something deficient about inanimate purposiveness. Natural beings are "determined to one," they pursue a single goal in a single way. They act regularly, but without any ability to moderate themselves. They are orderable, but order must be imposed on them. Left alone, they tend toward excess, for they act as strongly as they can and for as long as they can, thus reaching and resting in an extreme condition beyond which they can no longer move.[41]

Recall that in the *De Veritate* version of the teleological argument Aquinas says that "heat, for example, of its very nature and of itself can break down other things, but this breaking down is good and helpful only if it happens up to a certain point and in a certain way. Consequently, if we do not admit that there exist in nature causes other than heat and similar agents, we cannot give any reason why things happen in a good and orderly way." This passage is echoed in Aquinas's commentary on Aristotle's *De Anima*. Responding to the suggestion that the growth of living things could be explained by physical causes—for example, digestion by the action of an internal fire—Aquinas comments as follows:

> All food has to be cooked [or better, "digested"], and this is done by fire, so that fire does play a part in nutrition, and consequently in growth also; not indeed as the principal agent (which is the soul) but as a secondary, instrumental agent.... The principal agent in any action is that which imposes the

---

40. The orbit of the moon and the spinning of the earth on its axis also contribute to oceanic and atmospheric effects.

41. *In VIII Phys.*, l. 21, n. 1150: "For this is the difference between an intellectual agent and a material agent. The action of a material agent is proportionate to the nature of the agent. For a thing produces heat to the extent that it is itself hot. But the action of an intellectual agent is not proportionate to its nature, but to the apprehended form. For a builder does not build as much as he can, but as much as the intelligibility of the conceived form requires." See also *SCG* I, c. 20, n. 180, 183 [25, 28].

term or natural limit (*terminus et ratio*) upon what is done; thus in artificial things like boxes or houses the limit or term is fixed, not by the instruments used in the work, but by the art itself. The instruments, as such, are quite indifferent as to whether they are used to produce a thing of this shape and quantity or of that. A saw, as such, can be used to cut wood for a door or a bench or a house, and in any quantity you please; and if it cuts wood in this or that particular shape and quantity, this is due to the man who uses it. Now in nature each thing obviously has certain limits (*certus terminus, et determinata ratio*) to its size and its increase; each thing grows to a certain fixed pattern. For as each species of thing requires its proper accidents, so it needs its proper quantity, though some margin must be left to material differences and other individual factors. Men are not all equal in size. But there is a limit both to their largeness and their littleness; and *whatever determines this limit is the true principal cause of growth. But this cannot be fire, because the growth of fire has no naturally fixed limits; it would spread to infinity if an infinite amount of fuel were supplied to it. Clearly, then, fire is not the chief cause of growth and nutrition, but rather the soul.* And this is reasonable enough, for the quantitative limits of material things are fixed by form—the specific principle—rather than matter. Now the soul of a living being is to the elements it contains as form is to matter; the soul, then, rather than fire, sets the term and natural limit (*terminus et ratio*) to size and growth.[42]

Fire, of itself, acts in a regular and predictable way: it heats things and sets them on fire; it spreads. Like any purely physical cause, it will act this way as long as possible, until something blocks it from proceeding any further. But living things display *ratio*—in Aristotle's text, λόγος— not necessarily in the sense of possessing the ability to reason themselves (neither plants nor animals do), but rather in the sense of displaying reasonableness in their structures and activities. They are organized, articulated, measured, and coordinated. There is within them something that transcends the purely physical and chemical.

It is worth fleshing out this tendency toward extremes that Aquinas sees as characteristic of purely natural causes. According to Aquinas, each natural element is characterized by a set of contrary qualities: fire is hot, dry, and light; air is hot, wet, and (relatively) light; water is cold, wet,

---

42. *In II De An.* l. 8, n. 331–32 [8–9], translated by Kenelm Foster, OP, and Silvester Humphries, OP (Notre Dame, Ind.: Dumb Ox Books, 1994). Emphasis added. When fire or any other element exists on its own outside an organism, it has a form, and its matter is prime matter. Hence it too has a natural quantity consequent upon its form. But the only quantity determined by its nature is its density/rarity, not its actual volume. Its volume is determined by the amount of (designated) matter that takes on the elemental form, and could be of any measure whatsoever.

and (relatively) heavy; earth is cold, dry, and heavy.[43] Heavy bodies will undergo motion as far toward the center of the universe as they can, until they either reach the center or are blocked by a heavier body. Light bodies will head toward the circumference of the universe until they hit the dome of the sphere of the moon.[44] Hot bodies heat things as much as they are able, which depends on how hot they are; cold bodies cool things as much as possible; wet bodies get other bodies as wet as possible, and dry bodies dry other bodies as much as possible.

Although these qualities are moderated to some extent in mixed bodies that are generated out of contrary elements,[45] every mixed body must eventually be corrupted and dissolved back into its elements.[46] It is not that the elements are actually present in mixed bodies and pull apart as they move in contrary directions.[47] Rather, they are present virtually, insofar as the qualities that characterize them and through which they act

---

43. See Aristotle, *On Generation and Corruption*, II.3, 330b4–6.

44. Aristotle says in *De Caelo* IV.5, 312b3–5 that "in its own place every body endowed with both weight and lightness [i.e., water, air, and mixed bodies] has weight—whereas earth has weight everywhere—but they only have lightness among bodies to whose surface they rise." (Richard McKeon, ed., *The Basic Works of Aristotle* [New York: Random House, 2001].) All bodies other than fire and those in which fire predominates move as far down as they possibly can. Fire and those bodies in which fire predominates move as far up as they possibly can. Unfortunately, Aquinas did not comment on this portion of *De Caelo*. He does say, however, in *In II De Caelo*, l. 26, n. 526 that all heavy bodies—and not only earth is heavy—tend toward the center of the universe. For "it is proved in book III of Euclid [*Elements*, III.19] that if any line touch a circle [as tangent], and another straight line is drawn perpendicular to the tangent line at the place of contact, it is necessary that that line, if extended, cross the center of the circle. And in this way it is evident that all heavy bodies are moved towards the center of the earth, in such a way that, if there were nothing impeding, coming from diverse directions they would meet in the center of the earth, because each of them would be moved according to a straight line falling perpendicularly on the tangent line and at the place of contact. And in this way it is necessary that all heavy bodies are borne to the one middle point of the whole world and earth." If someone sits on a boulder, holds a bottle out, and pours its contents over the edge, the water will move straight down toward the center of the earth, perpendicular to its surface, even though water's natural place is above earth and it could settle above earth by moving a few inches laterally, rather than many feet downward. (This would happen even at places below sea-level, such as Death Valley in California.) The tendency of each heavy element and mixed body is to go down as far as possible until something blocks it, just as every physical and chemical tendency is toward an extreme.

45. See Aquinas, *De Mixtione Elementorum* (Leon. 43.156.123–125, 131–134): "The active and passive qualities of the elements are contrary to each other, and are receptive of more and less.... A certain middle quality is constituted out of them which is the proper quality of a mixed body, differing nevertheless in diverse bodies according to the diverse proportion of the mixture." Translation mine.

46. See, e.g., *QDP* q. 5, a. 9: "Since [animals, plants, and mixed bodies] are composed of contrary elements, they contain within themselves an active principle of corruption.... Consequently they cannot remain forever identically the same, nor specifically the same when generation and corruption cease." Punctuation emended.

47. See *In II De An.* l. 8, n. 328.

are present in mixed bodies.[48] Why, then, must mixed bodies inevitably corrupt, on Aquinas's view? It is not merely that other, contrary bodies will act upon and destroy them; rather, unlike the elements they have an active principle of their own corruption within them.[49] The reason the mixed bodies must corrupt is that the mean qualities characterizing them in virtue of their substantial forms constitute a state of relative disequilibrium, and therefore the mixed bodies—or their several parts—tend to slide toward extreme qualities that dispose them to corrupt into their elements: "It is impossible that there be anything mixed in which one of the contraries does not predominate, for many reasons.... And in this way it is necessary that corruption follows eventually in any mixed body whatever."[50] If it were not for the motion of the heavenly bodies—which is caused by intelligent beings according to Aquinas—the natural world would separate into the four elements severally congregated in their proper spheres.[51] The order that would exist would be of the lowest kind, representing a case of thermal equilibrium or maximal entropy.

The Need for an Organizing Principle

The motion of the heavenly spheres is what keeps motion going on earth and produces mixed bodies. But if the heavenly spheres were merely moved, rather than being moved in an intelligently orchestrated way, fruitless rather than beneficial motion would occur on earth:

> Because we have shown that the actions and virtues of natural bodies are caused by their specific forms, it follows that they are further reduced, as

48. *De Mixtione Elementorum* (Leon. 43.157.146–149): "The virtues of the substantial forms of the simple bodies are preserved in mixed bodies. The forms of the elements are therefore in mixed bodies, not indeed in act but virtually." Translation mine.

49. *QDP* q. 5, a. 7: "Corruption occurs in mixed bodies otherwise than in the elements. Mixed bodies contain within themselves the active principle of corruption, through being composed of contraries, whereas the elements have an outside contrary but are not composed of contraries, wherefore they do not contain an active principle of corruption, but only a passive principle, inasmuch as their matter has an aptitude to receive another form than that which they actually have." Punctuation emended. Cf. a. 8 and 9.

50. *In II Sent.*, d. 19, q. 1, a. 4, ad 2 (as numbered in Mandonnet ed., but responding to obj. 3), translation mine. See also c.: "There is a fourfold mode by which animal bodies are corrupted ... The second is common to all mixed bodies, due to the inordinate excess of some one of the contraries." Translation mine. The following text also suggests this view: "In a mixed body the qualities of one element are impeded through the qualities of another, which cannot be said [to occur] at the consummation of the world, where violence will wholly cease." *QDP* q. 5, a. 7, c. Translation mine.

51. *QDP* q. 5, a. 5–10. See chapter 3 above, section titled "Against the Conventional Interpretation: What Happens if God Does Not Move the Universe?", p. 89–96.

to higher principles, to the virtue of the heavenly bodies, and yet further to intellectual separate substances [which move the heavenly bodies]. A certain vestige of both principles is apparent in these works of natural things. For that such works of nature occur with a certain change, and according to a certain space of time, comes from a heavenly body, through whose motion the measure of time is defined. *But from the separate intellectual substances it is found in the works of nature that they proceed by determinate ways to determinate ends in a most congruous order and mode, just as also those things which come to be by art, in such a way that the whole work of nature seems to be the work of a certain wise being, due to which nature is said to operate wisely.*[52]

It is well known that Aquinas believes that the higher causes of natural effects here on earth are the motions of the heavenly bodies, which in turn act in virtue of the immaterial intelligences/angels. Yet Aquinas states that the angels cannot directly cause alteration or substantial change in any bodies, but only local motion.[53] By local motion, the angels apply natural causes to produce certain effects that the natural causes could not produce on their own, as a cook applies heat skillfully to produce a dish that fire could not produce on its own.[54] The angels provide for the natural order here on earth by moving the heavenly bodies in choreographed fashion.

As long as they are circling around, the astronomical bodies will stir the pot, as it were, putting the elements out of equilibrium and causing cycles of change that produce and dissolve mixed bodies. But these natural processes will only be orderly, beneficial, and such as to support life if the heavenly bodies are moved in a very intelligent, precisely choreographed fashion, and in turn move the elements in just the right way. A carpenter's tools, although fit for producing tables, chairs, desks, and other fine things, cannot move themselves. Unless they are set in motion by something, they will do nothing. But merely being set in motion is not enough. A saw set in motion by a monkey might mix things up, but it would not be particularly constructive. Only when set in motion by a skilled, intelligent being, and applied in the proper way, can any such tool produce positive results.

Yet all this is not to deny that it is within the natures of the elements

---

52. Aquinas, *De Operationibus Occultis Naturae*, emphasis added. Leon. 43.184.165–185.181, but reading "sicut in altiora principia in virtute celestium corporum" with δ so as to produce a sensible reading. The alternate reading of P[64] would also give the same sense.

53. *ST* I, q. 110, a. 2–3.

54. *ST* I, q. 110, a. 2, ad 3; a. 3, ad 2.

themselves, or of the mixed bodies, to act for an end. They certainly are intrinsically purposive. Nor is it metaphysically possible for their end not to be at least minimally good for them.[55] Insofar as the elements seek their proper places, for example, Aquinas says that they achieve what is good for them, a fuller actualization.[56] (Aquinas thinks that each element is best conserved in its proper place.[57]) The point is just that the *immediate* natural ends of the elements constitute the lowest level in the scale of purposiveness. The character of the good is hard to make out in their activities. It consists simply in this: that the elements participate in existence, and together constitute a stable cosmos that exhibits a kind of mathematical beauty (i.e., forming concentric spheres). To regularly achieve any more robust purposes, they must be organized by a higher principle.

55. *ST*, I, q. 5, esp. a. 5, c.: "Upon the form follows an inclination to the end, or to an action, or something of the sort. For everything, insofar as it is in act, acts and tends towards that which is in accordance with its form, and this belongs to weight and order. Hence the essence of goodness, so far as it consists in perfection, consists also in mode, species, and order." Punctuation emended.

56. Ed Feser thinks that for Aquinas nonliving beings never act for their own good or perfection, and that to do so is a defining mark of life ("On Aristotle, Aquinas, and Paley: A Reply to Marie George," 2–3; *Aquinas*, 135; *Aristotle's Revenge: The Metaphysical Foundations of Physical and Biological Science* [Neunkirchen-Seelscheid: Editioned Scholasticae, 2019], 375–76). Aquinas explicitly states the opposite. In addition to the following footnote, see, for example, *ST* I, q. 60, a. 3, c.: "Everything naturally seeks to procure what is good for itself, as fire seeks to mount upwards. (*Unumquodque naturaliter appetit consequi id quod est sibi bonum; sicut ignis locum sursum.*)" But although Feser is imprecise on this point, he has identified a real difference. Living beings manifest articulated self-perfection, which radically transcends the kind of self-perfection that inanimate things are capable of. Steven Baldner has recognized that for Aquinas every substance tends toward its own perfection, but thinks that this is no longer tenable in contemporary cosmology ("Thomas Aquinas and Natural Inclination in Non-Living Nature," *Proceedings of the American Catholic Philosophical Association* 92 [2018]: 211–22). But Thomas McLaughlin has argued that it is still plausible to maintain that nonliving substances act for their own good ("A Defense of Natural Place in a Contemporary Scientific Context," *Proceedings of the American Catholic Philosophical Association* 93 [2019]: 101–15), and I agree with him. Consider the example of hydrogen, which naturally coalesces gravitationally in space into massive nebulae. In this state hydrogen can glow and manifest itself, becoming more actual than when it exists as dispersed atoms or molecules. Or consider the example of water: a single water molecule is not liquid or wet, but when water collects—as it naturally does—then it exhibits the properties of water in full actuality. As Aquinas holds, what is good for each thing is (1) its preservation, (2) its full actualization, and (3) its service to a higher being and to the order of the universe. (See *ST* I, q. 6, a. 3 and q. 65, a. 2.)

57. See Aquinas, *In IV Phys.*, l. 1, n. 412 [7]: "Each of these things is carried to its own proper place if not impeded. Heavy things are carried downwards, and light things upwards. From this it is clear that place has a certain power of conserving that which is located in place. And because of this, that which is located in place tends toward its own place by a desire for its own conservation." *QDP* q. 5, a. 5, ad 7: "The body of the heavens is not perfected by place, as inferior bodies are, which are conserved in their proper place." (Translation mine.) See also Weisheipl, "Space and Gravitation," *The New Scholasticism* 29, no. 2 (1955): 175–223, at 181–86.

But Aquinas holds further that all creatures, even inanimate ones, possess a *natural* inclination to play their part for the common good of the whole universe;[58] they are naturally adapted to promote the health of ecosystems and the well-being of humans. How then can such higher levels of purposiveness exceed the limitations of purely natural causes? The answer is that many natural inclinations can only be fulfilled with the help of outside influences. Aquinas holds, for example, that it is natural for the heavenly bodies to revolve, but only in virtue of a passive principle, not in virtue of an active principle; they must be moved by immaterial beings.[59] He also says that even though fire possess the active principle of heat in virtue of its substantial form, it cannot heat or burn other things unless moved by the heavenly bodies (nowadays we might say that something needs to be "energized" to fulfill its tendencies).[60] Animals possessed of sight certainly have a natural inclination to see, but can only do so if the sun shines on them. In general, even when a natural thing has a natural inclination to—and even an active principle productive of—a certain end, it can only achieve that end when given the right sort of aid. Immature plants and animals grow spontaneously, but they can only do so in the proper soil or climate, and, in the case of many animals, only if provided with warmth and food by their parents. Something similar is found in human experience. Sometimes, in just the right context, one discovers that one has a natural talent that one never knew one had. External factors can bring out one's natural inclinations. Hence, even though all inanimate beings are naturally inclined to the service of the common good of the universe, they can only fulfill this inclination insofar as they are moved by a higher principle. They must be energized,

58. See, e.g., *ST* II-II, q. 26, a. 3, c.: "The fellowship of natural goods bestowed on us by God is the foundation of natural love, in virtue of which not only man, so long as his nature remains unimpaired, loves God above all things and more than himself, but also every single creature, each in its own way, i.e., either by an intellectual, or by a rational, or by an animal, or at least by a natural love, as stones do, for instance, and other things bereft of knowledge, *because each part naturally loves the common good of the whole more than its own particular good. This is evidenced by its operation, since the principal inclination of each part is towards common action conducive to the good of the whole."* Emphasis added. See also *ST* I, q. 60, a. 5; I-II, q. 109, a. 3; and I, q. 65, a. 2.

59. *QDP* q. 5, a. 5, c.: "Circular movement is said to be natural to the heaven, insofar as it has a natural aptitude for that kind of movement, so that it contains in itself the passive principle of that movement, while the active principle of this movement is some separate substance."

60. *QDP* q. 5, a. 8, ad 5: "It is proper to fire to heat, supposing that it have any action at all. But its action depends on another [namely the movement of the heavenly bodies], as has been said." Translation mine. In a. 7 Aquinas had argued that heat must remain in fire after the heavens stop revolving, because it is a proper quality of fire, flowing from its nature. See also a. 8, ad 1 and a. 7, ad 13 and *ST* I-II, q. 109, a. 1, c.

and the natural active and passive principles of each kind of substance must be coordinated with those of the others if the universe is not to devolve into chaos and entropy.

The elements are naturally suitable material for the production of mixed bodies and living organisms; they are naturally amenable to organization, and they can dispose prime matter to receive the substantial forms of higher kinds of bodies. But the elements do so in a rather imperfect way, retaining a tendency to lose the higher levels of order that they receive, a tendency toward entropy; the bodies composed of them have a limited power of existence and must dissolve after a finite time.[61] That the elemental bodies regularly promote the conditions for life and even compose the bodies of living organisms can only be due to the influence of a higher principle, without which they would not display the same level of purposiveness and goodness that they do.

Aquinas, then, has made a cogent argument that nature is intrinsically purposive *and* that it must be directed by a higher, intelligent cause to display such purposiveness. But some important objections must be addressed before the argument can rest.

RESPONDING TO OBJECTIONS

Kenny's Critique

Anthony Kenny, after expressing his uncertainty as to whether some form of the argument from design could or could not work as a proof for God's existence, does not hesitate to throw out Aquinas's version:

> Aquinas' own version of the argument, however, can be more briefly dealt with. For he seems to have sawn off the branch he was sitting on when, at *In Phys.* II, 259, he discussed the apparent intelligence of spiders and swallows. He says: "it is obvious that they act by nature and not by intelligence because they always perform in the same manner: every swallow makes its nest in the same way, and every spider weaves its web like every other, which they would not do if they acted with intelligence and skill, since not every builder builds a house in the same manner." But if it is only irregular adaptive behavior which calls for intelligence, then we do not need to look for any intelligence other than human, since only humans, according to Aquinas,

---

61. See above, fn. 46 and 49. Also, *In II Sent.*, d. 19, q. 1, a. 4, c.: "Material things have a finite power for being (*virtutem finitam ad essendum*), whence it is necessary that all things are corrupted within a certain period of time, as is said in *On Generation and Corruption* II." Translation mine.

exhibit irregular adaptive behavior. On the other hand, if even regular adaptive behavior calls for intelligence, Aquinas has given us no reason why we should not call the swallows and the spiders intelligent themselves, rather than looking for an intelligence to direct them from outside the universe.[62]

Kenny has put his finger on an important point. In Aquinas's view, the regularity with which something happens proves that it is natural, and the regularity with which beneficial results occur proves that nature is intrinsically purposive. Intrinsic purposiveness is supposed also to prove that an intelligence is at work. (Despite what Kenny says, certainly rocks, plants, and even animals are not themselves rational beings,[63] and so if an intelligence is needed one must look for a transcendent one.) But how can regularity of beneficial adaptation prove that a being is purposive and thereby that an intelligence is at work, if regularity proves that the purposive being is not intelligent? Kenny thinks that Aquinas has contradicted himself. Does regularity imply intelligence or the lack of it?

But Aquinas has not contradicted himself. Rather, there is simply a difference between that which determines a purpose for itself and that which is determined to a purpose by another. A being that regularly acts in the same way so as to achieve the same purpose over and over again is intrinsically purposive. A being that rarely acts in such a way as to achieve any purpose, achieves a purpose, when it does, only by chance. But a being that regularly achieves some purpose, but different purposes by different means on different occasions—yet still with frequent success—is intelligent.

As we have seen, Aquinas thinks that the elemental materials out of which everything in the visible universe is constructed tend on their own only toward the simplest goals (in modern terms, toward thermal equilibrium). Yet out of these same materials many different substances are generated—minerals, plants, animals, human beings—which tend toward many different ends, but each constantly toward its own unique end. Furthermore, within every single living substance many different tissues and organs are constructed from the same elements, which fulfill many different functions. (Out of mostly carbon, hydrogen, oxygen, nitrogen,

---

62. Kenny, *The Five Ways*, 118–19.

63. Some of the higher animals are astonishingly "intelligent," but certainly not rational in the strict sense. For an excellent account, sensitive to contemporary research into animal behavior, see Alasdair MacIntyre, *Dependent Rational Animals: Why Human Beings Need the Virtues* (Chicago: Open Court, 1999), ch. 2–6.

phosphorus, and sulfur are constructed nucleotides, amino acids, carbohydrates, lipids, and the cells, tissues, and organs composed of them.) Nature is determined to one. The adaptation of the same materials to many different ends by many different means requires that a self-determining intelligence work upon them. Since such varied, beneficial adaptation is present in the body of each living organism, and within the inorganic universe as a whole, some intelligent being must be at work.

Yet although living organisms display the work of intelligence within themselves—insofar as the materials out of which they are composed are adapted to many different functions—nevertheless they are not themselves possessed of intelligence (except for humans.) If their bodily structures and their instincts were due to their own intelligence rather than to a transcendent intellect, then they would possess the ability to set for themselves new ends and pursue them by new means. Although some remote participation in this ability is found among nonhuman living organisms, strictly speaking they lack the capacity to determine themselves.[64] Animals act on predetermined instincts and do not possess free will. Hence a superior intelligent being must be responsible for their bodily structures and instincts.

Someone who is not a materialist reductionist could argue that since a living organism is one substance with one nature, the adaptation of the same elements to use in many different tissues, and the use of the same tissues to compose many different organs and members, does not require any intelligent maker. Such adaptation is just intrinsic to the nature of a living being, and that's all there is to it. But this cannot be correct. For the nature of any living organism is such that it demands an efficient cause. No individual organism can exist on its own; it must receive its nature from its parent. Yet no member of the species can cause the species itself to exist, for then it would cause its very own existence. But the species itself does need a cause. In the generations of any biological species we have an accidentally ordered causal series; if it is finite it has an initiating cause, and if it is infinite it has a sustaining cause, as argued in chapters 2 and 4. Hence any species of organism is caused to exist. Must its cause be intelligent?

The potentiality for a living substantial form exists within prime matter, but to draw the form out into act requires a coordination of

---

64. Cf. *ST* I-II, q. 13, a. 2, obj. 3 and ad 3.

substantially distinct causes (e.g., the various elements, the sun, etc.) And the same elements must be put to use in different ways in different parts of the organism's body. The body must be organized if it is to be capable of life.[65] This can only come about through an intelligent agent that is free to act differently with the very same materials and instruments and can coordinate their influences. Hence the intrinsically purposive natures of living organisms are caused to exist by a transcendent intelligent being. This transcendent agent can utilize natural causes, even a process of evolution. (Aquinas in fact held that the intelligently guided motion of the heavenly bodies could generate primitive life forms out of non-living materials.[66]) Yet the natural causes must certainly be coordinated by an intelligent being.

Note that Feser's and Garrigou-Lagrange's defense of the second stage of the Fifth Way—that final causes cannot exercise influence except insofar as they are preconceived in the mind of an intelligent being, who can adjust means to ends—is much more convincing on my interpretation of the proof than on theirs. If the Fifth Way were an argument from mere causal regularity, it would be tempting to hold that it is just a brute fact that certain effects necessarily flow from the natures of certain physical things, or, in other words, that the laws of physics are just brute, meaningless facts. Water when cooled necessarily forms the crystalline structure of ice. But, one might say, why think of the effect as a purpose, rather than just a result? On the other hand, organisms consist of many distinct parts and the parts consist of distinct tissues, each with their own active and passive qualities (or, to use modern terms, of many distinct bio-chemicals with their own chemical properties). That all of these distinct causal factors, tending toward different effects, should be coordinated so as to preserve themselves, serve each other, and promote the well-being of the whole organism of which they are parts requires the activity of an intelligent being who can comprehend them all and adjust them to their ends. That elemental matter should ever acquire such complex, animate forms at all implies the work of intelligence.

The argument is even stronger if one has a case in which distinct *substances* are coordinated with and benefit one another. Since they share no nature in common, and are not parts of some greater substance, their

---

65. See Aristotle's *De Anima* II.1, and Aquinas's commentary on it.

66. *In VII Meta.*, l.6, n. 1403, George makes this point in "Finally Time to Retire the Fifth Way?" 213–14.

coordination cannot be due merely to intrinsic principles. Disparate substances such as water, the sun, trees, and animals can only be coordinated by an intellect that can take account of each and adjust them to one another so as to promote a common good as end. Aquinas holds, in fact, that such a unity of order is observable in the universe as a whole. The heavenly bodies in their motions are ordered harmoniously to produce night and day, the seasons, weather patterns, the motion of the tides, and so on, here on earth. In so doing they serve to promote life. Plants serve animals as food, and both plants and animals serve human needs. The corruption of one organism serves the generation of another, whether immediately as food, or more slowly as compost. As Aquinas says in his commentary on book XII of the *Metaphysics*, the universe is like an army, with God its general, or like a household, with God its head, or like a kingdom with God its ruler. He directs things toward their common end by instilling in them their natural inclinations and by directing the motion of the heavenly bodies.[67]

Hence, despite Kenny's objection, the Fifth Way can successfully argue that noncognitive natures are purposive, and that these natures can only tend toward their ends if directed by an intelligent being.

Neo-Darwinism

In the introduction to this chapter I noted that the Neo-Darwinist theory of evolution poses a challenge to Aquinas's Fifth Way that cannot be sidestepped. I also noted that responding to this objection adequately would require a book of its own. Here, however, I will provide some indication of the directions in which I think a response should go.

Neo-Darwinism poses a challenge because it seems to provide a way to explain the clearest case of natural purposiveness—living organisms and their activities—in a way that requires no purposiveness and no intelligence. According to Neo-Darwinism, the characteristics of living beings (their "phenotypes") are determined by their DNA. While living organisms tend to pass on their DNA faithfully to their offspring, purely random mutations do occur by chance. These mutations have no intrinsic tendency to help or harm organisms. But a few of these mutations, by chance, benefit the organisms that receive them. Given the intense competition within the biological realm for limited resources, any beneficial

67. *In XII Meta.*, l. 12, n. 2629–37, esp. 2634.

mutation will enable an organism to leave more offspring than its relatives that do not possess the mutation. Over time the proportion of members of the species with the mutation to those without the mutation will increase. Since the total number of such organisms that the environment can support is limited, eventually the members of the species without the mutation will disappear, and the species as a whole will have changed its character. In this way species will improve over time as beneficial mutations accumulate. Species will therefore appear to be purposively designed to thrive in their environment, yet their structures and behaviors will in fact be due entirely to chance.

In response to this challenge, it is important to note first that large-scale evolution, the occurrence of which is quite certain, does not itself imply that Neo-Darwinism is true. Neo-Darwinism is one theoretical explanation for how large-scale evolution could occur. There are other theories of evolution, including forms of Neo-Lamarckism, which draw attention to apparently purposive, nonrandom forms of genetic change.[68] Such theories provide for a richer understanding of biological teleology. But since Neo-Darwinism is the presumptive theory of evolution in contemporary culture, I will proceed on the hypothesis that its explanation of the mechanism of evolution is substantially correct. It turns out that even Neo-Darwinian evolution presupposes a level of intrinsic purposiveness sufficient for the success of Aquinas's Fifth Way.

Neo-Darwinian evolution depends upon the fact that living organisms are in fact striving to survive and reproduce, in other words, that they are intrinsically purposive. It also depends upon the highly teleological (or "teleonomic") molecular processes of DNA replication, transcription, and protein synthesis, as well as the teleological process of physiological development. Without this base level of purposiveness, the chance mutation of a molecule of deoxyribonucleic acid would have no biological effect at all. It would not affect a phenotype, it would not be inherited, and it would not drive evolutionary change. Neo-Darwinism does not, then, expel intrinsic purposiveness from its biological bastion (although it does reduce its scope, interpreting everything in terms of the goal of survival and reproduction alone).

Neo-Darwinism also does not negate the need for an intelligent agent. Why not? On the one hand, it is not in fact necessary that an intelligent

68. For example, James Shapiro, *Evolution: A View from the 21st Century* (Upper Saddle River, NJ: FT Press Science, 2011)

designer directly produce each species by a creative act. Natural history certainly indicates that later species developed from earlier ones by a natural process. On the other hand, in order for such things as living organisms to exist at all, the conditions of the universe have to be just right. Contemporary physics and cosmology have uncovered a great deal of evidence that the universe is fine-tuned for the possibility of life, as even many atheists admit. The seemingly contingent parameters that define the strengths of physical forces, as well as the initial conditions of the universe, have to fall within a very narrow range in order for life to be possible. It is *a priori* very improbable that they would fall into this range, but they in fact do. This suggests that they were determined by an intelligent agent whose purpose was to bring living organisms into being. I will examine contemporary fine-tuning arguments at greater length in chapter 8 below.

The fine-tuning of the parameters of the universe, however, does not itself guarantee that life *will* arise. It provides the environment in which life *could* come to be and thrive, but does not itself create life. The production of the first living organism required the intervention of an intelligent being. Neo-Darwinism does not provide an alternative explanation, for the mechanism of chance mutation and natural selection presupposes that there already are living organisms with DNA to begin with, and that these organisms are reproducing and competing. Neo-Darwinism cannot explain how the first life-form came into existence. For that, a higher cause is needed.

Some argue that life arose by mere chance, when just the right molecules happened to come together in just the right way. However, our planet only formed 4.5 billion years ago, and only became at all habitable 4 billion years ago when its molten surface cooled and stopped being bombarded by asteroids. The fossil record indicates that microbial life appeared 3.5–4 billion years ago, almost as soon as it possibly could. There was simply not enough time for life to arise *by chance*, even if it were not otherwise impossible on philosophical grounds. (The atheist astronomer Fred Hoyle famously compared the odds for such an occurrence to the chances of a hurricane assembling a Boeing 747 when passing through a junk yard.)

Despite nearly one hundred years of research, scientists have still found no definite, viable chemical pathway to assemble the molecular systems necessary for life. Living cells are, of course, immensely complex. At any given time, there are billions or even trillions of atoms within a cell, and they must have just the right kind of configuration if a cell is to remain alive. Even supposing, for the sake of argument, that having the right kind of atoms with the right sort of spatial relationships to one another were a sufficient condition for life, the odds are very much against a living cell ever arising by chance. To be sure, the various monomers out of which biomolecules are composed are easily synthesized, and probably do form in natural, nonbiological contexts. But producing the little bits *out of which* biomolecules are formed, which living cells are themselves in turn composed of, is a far cry from producing living cells. It is unclear how these monomers could be put together so as to form a living cell. We know the configuration of these molecules within already living cells tolerably well, but we do not know how they could get from a state of separation into such a configuration. Not only do we not know how this could have happened in nature, we do not even know how to do it with intelligent, human intervention. It is thus unreasonable to suppose that a living organism did arise on the earth by chance in such a short space of time. It is more reasonable to suppose that the first life-form was produced deliberately, by an intelligent being, and then evolved from there.

Finally, it is in fact impossible on philosophical grounds for life to be generated by purely inanimate causes.[69] A living organism represents a higher *kind* of actuality than any physico-chemical substance or system. The principle of proportionate causality prohibits the generation of a living thing by purely inanimate causes, since the total cause must possess the actuality of the effect formally or eminently. Another way to put this is that a living organism cannot be reduced to molecules and their configurations; it possesses a substantial unity and engages in activities that are different in kind from anything that physico-chemical systems perform (as is evident above all in the cases of conscious perception and self-conscious rationality). Hence, in order for a living organism to be generated out of chemical constituents, a different kind of agent with a higher kind of actuality must supply what is lacking. In short, only an intelligent being of the right sort could produce the first living organism. (As a further point, the evolution of *human* beings would have required another creative act, due to our immaterial soul, but this truth requires difficult philosophical argumentation.[70])

69. See the discussion in David Oderberg, "Synthetic Life and the Bruteness of Immanent Causation," in *Aristotle on Metaphysics and Method*, ed. Edward Feser (New York: Palgrave Macmillan, 2013), 206–35.

70. I also believe that the evolution of the first sense-perceptive life required a divine act, since

THE UNITY OF GOD

The Fifth Way establishes the need for intelligent agency, but it does not show that there is only one intelligent being ultimately responsible for all that is. Perhaps each kind of organism was produced by a different intelligent being, for example. However, if the universe as a whole possesses systematic natural purposiveness, a unity of order, then God's unity can be established. This is exactly how Aquinas argues in *ST* I, q. 11:

> It can be shown from three sources that God is one.... [Aquinas first gives two metaphysical arguments, one from God's simplicity, the other from the infinity of His perfection.] ... Third, this is shown from the unity of the world. For all things that exist are seen to be ordered to each other since some serve others. But things that are diverse do not harmonize in the same order, unless they are ordered thereto by one. For many are reduced into one order by one better than by many, because one is the *per se* cause of one, and many are only the accidental cause of one, inasmuch as they are in some way one. Since therefore what is first is most perfect, and is *per se*, not *per accidens*, it must be that the first which reduces all into one order should be only one. And this one is God.[71]

The teleological argument for God's existence in *SCG* is quite similar:

> Contrary and discordant things cannot, always or for the most part, be parts of one order except under someone's government, which enables all and each to tend to a definite end. But in the world we find that things of diverse natures come together under one order, and this not rarely or by chance, but

------

merely vegetative life does not possess sufficient actuality to effect sense-perceptive life. In my opinion, evolution was a purposive but natural process, requiring supernatural intervention at only three points: the production of the first living cell, the production of the first sense-perceptive organism, and the production of human beings. (To be precise, each new human being has an immaterial soul created directly by God.) Nevertheless, unlike some other Thomists, I believe that there are more than three philosophical species of living beings (plant, animal, and human). While Eastern and Western Bluebirds probably belong to the same philosophical species despite belonging to distinct biological species (in other words, their differences are probably accidental, not essential), nevertheless penguins are, I believe, an essentially distinct philosophical species from bluebirds, and elephants and mice are even more clearly distinct philosophical species from one another. Thomists have wondered how one species could produce another species that was essentially, and not merely accidentally distinct, since the cause must possess the actuality it produces in the effect. The answer is that the *total* cause of any effect has to possess the actuality of that effect formally or eminently. Now just as hydrogen, oxygen, and a spark eminently possess the actuality of water—which is one, distinct substance of a different kind than either hydrogen or oxygen—so too a mother and father of one species of animal, plus certain environmental factors, eminently possess the actuality to generate a new species of animal.

71. *ST* I, q. 11, a. 3, c. Translation emended. See also *ST* I, q. 103, a. 3, c.

always or for the most part. There must therefore be some being by whose providence the world is governed. This we call God.[72]

Some consider this argument to be weak (John Wippel, for example).[73] However, presuming such a universal order is observable in the cosmos (contemporary fine-tuning arguments can be helpful here, see chapter 8 below), I think the argument is quite strong. For things to pursue a common end they must have a common cause. One person is certainly capable of ordering multiple distinct things toward a single goal. This is precisely what any inventor of a machine or general of an army does, for example. On the other hand, two or more people can certainly work together toward a single end, but if one considers the matter carefully, this always presupposes some preexisting unity among the co-workers. The most obvious case is when multiple people work together because they have been directed to do so by a superior, for example, colleagues working on an assignment from their boss. On the other hand, equals could spontaneously decide to work together toward a common end without being commanded to do so. But this can only happen insofar as they share a single human nature, with shared natural inclinations toward common goals, which provides some basis for their interest in cooperating. (Humans and eels do not spontaneously work together toward a common goal, and if they ever were to pursue a common goal, it would only be due to humans training eels to act in unusual ways.) But humans only share a common nature because they have a common cause (a shared ancestor, and ultimately, God.) Without a common, single cause, any coordination of different substances toward a common end could only be by chance, and not a regular occurrence. Aquinas can, then, conclude to God's unity from the teleological unity of the cosmos, and his teleological proof (extended by this "third stage") establishes that all of nature is governed by one, transcendent, intelligent, self-determining being.

CONNECTING THE FIRST AND FIFTH WAYS

Before bringing the first part of this book to a close, I want to reflect on how the First and Fifth Ways can be connected in a fruitful manner to shed light on the claim that God is *alive*. As we saw in the previous

72. *SCG* I, c. 13, n. 115 [35].
73. Wippel, *The Metaphysical Thought of Thomas Aquinas*, 488, 434.

chapters, since everything in motion is moved by another, and since the universe cannot be a perpetual motion machine, it must be moved by an immaterial, everlasting mover. The Fifth Way shows that the motion in the universe is directed by an intelligent being. Certainly we think of intelligent beings as alive. Yet not all living things are intelligent. What, fundamentally, does it mean to be alive? And is such a characteristic, whatever it is, proper to God? The following sections will answer this question, showing that life is, most fundamentally, the power of intelligent self-determination, and that all living things are alive precisely to the extent to which they participate analogously in this characteristic. To act as the universe's first mover, God must possess the characteristic proper to life in the highest degree, but without the limitations of materiality that accompany all manifestations of life in the natural world. These considerations will set the stage for chapter 8 in the second part of the book, where I consider how contemporary science supports the natural philosophical conclusion that God is living and intelligent.

Life as Self-Motion

Living things are fundamentally different from nonliving things. Aquinas defines life as self-motion,[74] and self-motion is certainly one of the clearest manifestations of life. If one were to sit down pensively on what appeared to be a rock, and then discovered that it moved underneath one, one would conclude that it was alive (perhaps a giant tortoise instead of a rock).

74. David Oderberg and Edward Feser interpret Aquinas's definition of life as self-motion to mean that living beings engage in "immanent causation," whereas nonliving beings can only engage in "transeunt" causation. (David Oderberg, "Synthetic Life and the Bruteness of Immanent Causation," in *Aristotle on Method and Metaphysics*, ed. Edward Feser, 206–35 [New York: Palgrave MacMillan, 2013], at 213–14; Feser, *Aquinas*, 134–36; *Aristotle's Revenge*, 375–76.) Like Marie George ("On the Meaning of 'Immanent Activity' according to Aquinas," *The Thomist* 78, no. 4 (2014): 537–55), I have reservations about the suitability of this way of making the distinction. I showed in fn. 56 and 57 above that acting toward self-perfection is a characteristic common to both living and nonliving beings, but they see it as a defining characteristic of immanent activity. And there is another problem with how Oderberg and Feser set up the distinction between living and nonliving things. They say that only living beings initiate from within themselves causal processes that also terminate in themselves (this is what defines immanent causation according to them.) But I have shown that on Aquinas's view, elements have an intrinsic, formal, active principle of motion toward their own proper place. They are not pushed by anything. In one sense, however, their claim is true, for elemental bodies are not efficient causes of their own motion, only formal causes. Nonliving beings can only be efficient causes of motion in other bodies, whereas living beings can be efficient causes of their own motion.

Aquinas explains why he considers self-motion the defining feature of all life as follows:

> Life manifestly belongs to animals, for it is said, in *De Vegetab*. I, that in animals life is manifest. We must, therefore, distinguish living from lifeless things by comparing them to that by reason of which animals are said to live: and this it is in which life is manifested first and remains last. We say then that an animal begins to live when it begins to move of itself, and as long as such movement appears in it, so long it is considered to be alive. When it no longer has any movement of itself, but is only moved by another, then its life is said to fail, and the animal to be dead. Whereby it is clear that those things are properly called living that move themselves by some kind of motion, whether it be motion properly so called, as the act of the imperfect, i.e., of a thing in potentiality, is called motion, or movement in a more general sense, as when said of the act of the perfect, as understanding and sensing are called motion, as is said in *De Anima* III. Accordingly, *all things are said to be alive that determine themselves to motion or operation of any kind*, whereas those things that cannot by their nature do so, cannot be called living, unless by a similitude.[75]

But this account of life raises an objection: certainly animals move themselves. They perceive desirable objects and get up and pursue them. They stop if they lose interest or change course if they happen upon something more desirable. But plants are alive too. Do they move themselves? Although they do not walk about, they do grow. But if plants can be said to move themselves and live in virtue of having an intrinsic active principle of quantitative motion, why can't elements be said to move themselves and live in virtue of having an intrinsic active principle of local motion, by which they spontaneously move toward their proper place without anything external impelling them?

Aquinas responds to just such an objection:

> To bodies, whether heavy or light, motion does not belong except insofar as they are displaced from their natural conditions, and are out of their proper place. For when they are in the place that is proper and natural to them, then they are at rest. Plants and other living things move with vital motion, in accordance with the disposition of their nature, but not by approaching thereto [i.e., to their natural disposition] or by receding from it, for insofar as they recede from such motion, so far do they recede from their natural disposition. And moreover, heavy and light bodies are moved by an extrinsic mover, either the generator which gives the form, or that which removes an

---

75. ST I, q. 18, a. 1, c., translation emended. Emphasis added.

impediment, as is said in *Phys*. VIII. They do not therefore move themselves, as do living bodies.[76]

This is an important distinction. Heavy and light bodies, even though they move spontaneously with nothing pushing them, are not said to move themselves because they are *set* in motion by their generator, in the sense that they are determined by it to undergo motion in a certain direction. They proceed as far as they are able and then come to rest—in their natural place unless impeded—and they do not undergo further motion without an external force. Plants and all other living organisms, however, remain in motion as long as they live. Plants do not walk about, but they continually nourish themselves and grow, taking in material and releasing it into the environment. They do not cease undergoing motion when they reach their proper condition; they continue in motion. Insofar as they stop undergoing motion, they depart from their proper condition and die. Furthermore, plants, unlike inanimate bodies, *determine themselves* to motion, albeit in a limited sense:

> [Even] plants are alive; for they all possess some intrinsic power or principle of growth and decay. Now this principle is not mere nature. Nature does not move in opposite directions, but growth and decay are in opposite directions; for all plants grow not only upwards or downwards, but in both directions. Hence a soul, not nature, is clearly at work in them.[77]

Plants certainly are not conscious, free beings. But they grow in all directions, not just one, and they set for themselves a limit and shape to their own growth, unlike fire that will grow to whatever extent the available fuel makes possible. Each plant has a characteristic shape and size (with a certain degree of play room) and utilizes the available resources to construct its own body accordingly. Plants even respond to external stimuli, growing in different directions depending on where sunlight or water is available, for example. Plants maintain their own orderly patterns of growth, nutrition, and reproduction in the face of external forces. In a sense, they constitute perpetual harmonic motion machines.

But only in a sense. For one, they are not machines; living beings possess substantial unity, but machines possess only a unity of order. For another, machines can only undergo motion insofar as and as long as their

76. *ST* I, q. 18, a. 1, ad 2.
77. *In II De An.* l. 3, n. 256–57.

energy source proceeds toward a state of equilibrium (while the spring relaxes, the weight runs down, or the fuel burns up, for example). Yet living organisms do not simply move toward a state of equilibrium and rest there; rather, they maintain themselves in a state of nonequilibrium. They acquire new energy sources on their own, by obtaining and assimilating food. Unfortunately, however, they cannot sustain truly *perpetual* motion, for over time they wear out and die. This is due to their materiality; they are subject to external physical causes that weaken and destroy them,[78] and they are composed of contrary elements present virtually within them. They do, however, attain to immortality in a certain sense by reproducing themselves, in such a way that the cycle of generations would continue forever,[79] if the astronomical bodies perpetually revolved and forever sustained the conditions for life.[80]

The *quasi* perpetual motion characteristic of living beings casts light on the argument for the unmoved mover. In the last chapter I argued that Aquinas's extended motion proof relies on the assumption that there is perpetual, or at least undiminishing motion in the universe. To cause perpetual or unabating motion the unmoved mover must be immovable and thus immaterial. Now insofar as it causes unending cycles of orderly motion, the unmoved mover possesses the characteristic of living things but to a higher degree. Organisms do not merely remain in motion as long as they live, but the motions they undergo display *ratio*, that is, they are ordered, systematic, and adaptive. Motion in the universe as a whole displays the same orderly, adaptive, continuous characteristic. Its motion cannot stem from merely natural causes, but must be caused by a mover who can cause motion of the sort characteristic of living beings. (This is why Plato thought that the universe was itself alive, animated by a world soul.[81])

But there is a problem with this analysis. Living beings move *themselves*. If the unmoved mover moves, not itself, but the universe, does it make sense to think of it as alive? Aquinas answers this question by deepening our understanding of the meaning of self-motion.

78. See *In I De Gen.* l. 17, n. 118 [6].
79. *In II De An.* l. 7, esp. n. 317.
80. See *QDP* q. 5, a. 9.
81. See the *Timaeus*, 30B–C.

Life as Participation in Intelligence

According to Aquinas, self-motion is an analogical concept, with God as
its primary analogate. Life consists in varying degrees of self-determination,
but only intelligent life is fully self-determining. This is brought out clearly
in a text worth quoting at length, from *ST* I, q. 18, a. 3:

> Life is in the highest degree properly in God. In proof of which it must be
> considered that since a thing is said to live insofar as it operates of itself and
> not as moved by another, the more perfectly this power is found in anything,
> the more perfect is the life of that thing. In things that move and are moved,
> a threefold order is found. In the first place, the end moves the agent, and the
> principal agent is that which acts through its own form, and sometimes it
> does so through some instrument that acts by virtue not of its own form, but
> of the principal agent, and does no more than execute the action.
>
> Accordingly, there are things that move themselves not in respect of the
> form or end—which are [rather] inherent in them by nature—but only in
> respect of the executing of the movement, the form by which they act and
> the end of the action being alike determined for them by their nature. Of this
> kind are plants, which move themselves according to their inherent nature
> with regard only to executing the motions of growth and decay.
>
> Other things have self-motion in a higher degree, that is, not only with
> regard to executing the motion but even as regards the form, the principle
> of motion, which form they acquire of themselves. Of this kind are animals,
> in which the principle of motion is not a naturally implanted form, but one
> received through sense. Hence the more perfect is their sense, the more per-
> fect is their power of self-motion.... Yet although animals of the latter kind
> receive through sense the form that is the principle of their motion, nev-
> ertheless they cannot of themselves propose to themselves the end of their
> operation or motion, for this has been implanted in them by nature, and by
> natural instinct they are moved to any action through the form apprehended
> by sense.
>
> Hence above such animals there are those which move themselves even
> in respect to their end, which they determine for themselves. This can only
> be done by reason and intellect, whose province it is to know the propor-
> tion between the end and the means to that end, and duly coordinate them.
> Hence a more perfect degree of life is that of intelligent beings, for their
> power of self-motion is more perfect....
>
> But although our intellect moves itself to some things, yet others are
> supplied by nature, as are first principles, which it cannot doubt, and the
> last end, which it cannot but will. Hence, although with respect to some
> things it moves itself, yet with regard to other things it must be moved by

another. Wherefore, that being whose act of understanding is its very nature, and which, in what it naturally possesses, is not determined by another, must have life in the most perfect degree. Such is God, and hence in Him principally is life.[82]

The ultimate cause responsible for any motion is the end, the final cause. The end is the cause of causes, as scholastics would say. Self-motion in the truest sense is the ability to set for oneself one's own end. For any motion, whatever sets the end and determines the means to it is the true first mover. Yet there is a full spectrum of perfection when it comes to self-motion.

Violent motion is caused entirely by outside forces, and what undergoes violent motion cannot be a first mover. Natural inanimate motion flows from an internal principle instead, but inanimate bodies are only moved insofar as they are set in motion by others, and do not continue in motion beyond the terminus toward which they were bound. Furthermore, regular, beneficial motion cannot flow from natural inanimate principles left to themselves. Inanimate bodies cannot serve the common end unless they are coordinated with others by the movement of a higher principle. Plants, as living beings, can sustain motion and coordinate their parts and activities, but only in certain predefined ways; their nature is reasonable without actually possessing reason. Their nature must have been bestowed upon them by a higher principle. Only in that way could their natures be internally well-ordered, and properly coordinated with other living and nonliving natures. At the next level, animals consciously move themselves, and in a loose sense even exhibit voluntary behavior.[83] Furthermore, they display, to a limited extent, an ability to order and arrange their environment (e.g., spiders construct webs). But animals are not truly free and self-determining, acting rather on instinct. In their own physiological structure, and in their purposive relations with external beings, they too must be set in order by a higher principle.

Only rational beings can determine ends for themselves and freely impose order on the world outside them so as to achieve those ends. Humans possess rational, self-determining life, and construct varied and ever new artifacts and machines out of the simple materials provided by the natural world. But there are limitations to human self-determination. Our basic inclinations are determined for us by nature, and we determine

82. *ST* I, q. 18, a. 3, c. Translation emended.
83. *ST* I-II, q. 6, a. 2.

ourselves only within the framework they establish.[84] The true first mover must be a being that is living in the highest possible degree, totally self-determining.

The various levels of life must be understood as participating, in analogical ways, in the primary life of divine intelligence. Humans, with their conditioned but real autonomy, clearly exhibit the characteristic of intelligence. Perception, the defining characteristic of animals, consists in a lower degree of cognition, resembling intelligence but falling short of it. Plants can only grow, nourish, and reproduce themselves insofar as they nonconsciously discriminate between good and bad, for example, growing their roots toward moisture, their leaves toward sunlight, budding in the appropriate locations, and so on. In so doing, they exhibit a remote participation in intelligent life.

Since the natural world as a whole undergoes continual harmonic motion and is not itself alive, it must be moved by an intelligence distinct from the universe. The unmoved mover of the universe, although immaterial, displays the characteristic of the kind of life that humans have, namely, the ability to move itself in internal acts of intelligence and will so as to freely set ends for the universe and move the external world in orderly and beneficial ways conducive to these ends. The unmoved mover is alive in the highest degree.

A Summary of Aquinas's Natural
Philosophical Approach to God

We are now in a position to put everything together and draw the ultimate conclusions of the first, historical part of this book. Observing the natural world, one finds that inanimate things tend toward rest and entropy. Rocks stay put unless moved by an external force, for example by being lifted and dropped. Rocks do not spontaneously form designs on the ground or set themselves up as trail markers. Water pools and stagnates. Once set in motion machines will continue for a certain amount of time while their fuel burns up or their spring relaxes, and so on. But they too come to rest eventually, and they also tend to go out of order and need maintenance, repair, and replacement. Living things, on the other hand, move themselves,[85] and rather than moving chaotically, they do so

---

84. *ST* I-II, q. 10, a. 1, c.

85. They do not violate the principle that everything in motion is set in motion by another.

in functional, patterned ways. They are like perpetual harmonic motion machines, although much more versatile. The lowest level of life, plant life, can organize and energize itself, but the highest level of observable life, human life, can organize the world outside itself and set it in harmonic motion. Humans build machines and set them in motion.

The natural world as a whole appears to undergo perpetual, harmonic motion. If isolated, water tends toward rest, but in the wider world it continually flows until it reaches the sea, and then returns to the sky by a process of evaporation, then falls again as rain and flows to the sea. Air inside a closed compartment or room can be oppressively still, but as part of the atmosphere it is nearly always in motion. There are constant weather patterns, seasonal changes, and geological processes going on around us. The world as a whole seems as if alive, but only *as if* according to Aquinas.[86] Really, it is set in motion by the heavenly bodies (e.g., the sun and the moon). Many of the ancients considered the heavenly bodies to be alive, for they appear to move themselves. But Aquinas, as we have seen, rightly considers them not to be organisms, for they do not possess organs. They can only remain in motion and continue to move things here on earth insofar as they are moved by another, truly *living* being. Causing perpetual (or at least unabating) harmonic motion in the world external to itself, this mover possesses the characteristics of the highest kind of life: intelligence and self-determination.

The universe has the marks of a well-designed and well-maintained machine. This is not to deny that it is full of intrinsically purposive beings. But the universe is not a single substance; like a machine it only possesses a unity of order. Like a machine it cannot self-assemble. There is one difference, however: its parts have a natural—even if only passive—inclination to be assembled. Nevertheless, like any machine, it must be caused by an intelligent being.

According to Aquinas's combined motion and teleological proofs for God's existence, there is either a single immaterial, unmoved mover setting the various parts of the universe in motion such that they achieve their proper ends and the common good—and this being would be the

---

Living beings are composed of parts, one of which can move another. Most fundamentally, living beings possess a soul, the power of which—informing an already organized body—acts on external nourishment and converts it into biological tissues and organs, thus growing and maintaining the living body, replacing the material that is consumed by the "internal heat" of the organism. See *In I De Gen.*, l. 17, n. 118 [6].

86. See *ST* I, q. 18, a. 1, ad 3.

one and only God—*or* there are multiple immaterial unmoved movers (angels) moving the various parts of the universe in coordinated fashion. But in the latter case, these movers must each be responding to the directions of the same, higher intelligence, by whose plan the universe as a whole is orchestrated. This higher intelligence would "move as loved," and He would be the one true God. Either way, whether He acts directly or by means of His angels, one God must exist.

This being, coordinating the entire universe, is the living God. He knows and loves through Himself, without being determined to action by any other being. Thus He is in motion in the loose, extended sense of motion; as self-moving He is, in the highest sense, alive. But since He is immaterial, He is not subject to motion in the strict physical sense; He is unmoved. Yet He does cause physical motion in the universe. Being immaterial, He is not subject to corruption, decay, or weariness, and can cause motion forever. Able to encompass the entire universe, He and He alone can coordinate the whole, and keep it in perpetual harmonic motion, or, if He prefers, set it in finite motion in a wisely orchestrated fashion so as to sustain biological life for a long time and to achieve His ends. He is the living, intelligent, self-determining, immaterial, immovable mover, the one eternal God, to whose providence we are all in debt.

Together, the First Way, G_2, and the Fifth Way constitute Aquinas's natural philosophical path to God. This natural philosophical path is good and convincing in its historical context. Yet although I have hinted many times at how this argument can be applied in a contemporary scientific context, it is time to take up that project in earnest. In the second part of the book, I will delve into the history of science to show how Aquinas's argument can be made convincing here and now.

PART II

Defending Aquinas's Argument Today

Chapter 6

Classical Mechanics

Assessing the Motion Proof

In the first part of the book, I have expounded Aquinas's motion proof for God's existence in its historical context. I have argued that the proof belongs to the philosophy of nature, rather than to metaphysics, and is very much concerned with the physical characteristics of the universe as Aquinas understood it. Most saliently, Aquinas's motion proof depends on his view that motion cannot continue undiminished for an indefinite amount of time without an external agent. Any purely natural motion, occurring without a conjoined mover, has a predetermined terminus and comes to an end when the mobile either reaches its destination or is blocked by an impediment. *Living* physical beings do maintain themselves in motion, but can only do so for a finite time before they wear out and die. Motion here on earth can only continue on from age to age because the motions of the sun and other astronomical bodies cause ever renewed changes in terrestrial bodies. The astronomical bodies themselves, not being alive, cannot undergo motion indefinitely and with undiminishing speed as they appear to do unless they are moved by one or more immaterial, living movers who are not subject to decay or weariness. On the other hand, if, in spite of appearances, astronomical motions are in fact heading toward a predetermined destination, then their motion must also have had an absolute beginning, since otherwise they would have undergone motion for an infinite time and have already arrived at their destination. In short, Aquinas argues that motion in the universe must be either started, or continuously maintained—or both started *and* continuously maintained—by an immaterial deity, with the empirical evidence pointing to motion's continual maintenance, and Scripture revealing its absolute beginning.

In the second part of this book I wish to defend Aquinas's argument in light of modern physics. After 750 years certainly much has changed. In many significant respects, it is no longer reasonable to think of the physical universe as Aquinas did. His view that the whole universe is encased in a vast sphere that rotates once daily is no longer tenable, nor are there series of concentric spheres carrying the planets around. Nor are the "fixed stars" fixed in place. Most importantly, however, the principle of inertia has been well established. It is commonly supposed, and not without reason, that this principle wrecks Aquinas's argument. For according to this principle motion can continue forever without a mover.

Now I have shown in chapter 1 that, contrary to appearances, there is no formal contradiction between the mover principle—everything in motion is moved by another—and the principle of inertia. For the mover principle holds only that for any given motion there is a responsible agent, even if that agent set the body in motion at some time prior and is no longer impelling it. Yet my work is not yet done, for the principle of inertia still threatens the motion proof insofar as inertial motion continues *forever* if unimpeded. For Aquinas, natural motions stop at predetermined termini, and violent motions only continue so long as external agents impel. Aquinas's motion proof for God's existence is based (as I showed in chapter 4) on the *impossibility* of perpetual motion without an immaterial agent. Inertia contradicts this premise.

To accomplish my goal I must, then, provide an account of the motion proof that reconciles it with modern physics, or, conversely, an account of modern physics that reconciles it with the motion proof. In fact, I will do a little bit of both, adapting Aquinas's motion proof to modern physics and illuminating modern physics by means of its own history. I take the principle of inertia as true, and in a realist sense: if unimpeded, motion can continue as long as time itself endures. So I must recast Aquinas's proof somewhat. Yet it turns out that the necessary adaptation does not affect Aquinas's argument nearly as much as one might have thought. A proper understanding of physics leaves the basic structure of Aquinas's proof intact: perpetual *orderly* motion—perpetual motion outside thermal equilibrium—is impossible without an immaterial mover. In addition, modern observations incline the balance of probability firmly toward the other disjunct of Aquinas's disjunction: Aquinas held that, apart from revelation, it seems likely—but is not certain—that the universe has been around forever, yet modern observations strongly suggest—but do not prove—that the universe had a temporal beginning at the big bang roughly 14 billion years ago.

In this chapter I will reconcile Aquinas's motion proof, and his natural philosophy in general, with the laws of Newtonian mechanics. I begin with a consideration of Aquinas's Achilles Heel, namely, his Aristotelian understanding of projectile motion, according to which the air propels projectiles along. This theory was demolished by figures such as John Buridan and Galileo. The principle of inertia eventually took its place. Yet, as I will go on to show, Sir Isaac Newton, the central figure in the scientific revolution and the one whose formulation of inertia is used universally today, was himself a proponent of the same kind of argument as Aquinas's motion proof. According to him, motion, at least of the present kind, *cannot* continue forever without divine intervention. To show why this is so, I will consider seventeenth and eighteenth century work on the collision of bodies and the conservation of "quantity of motion" (what we call momentum, mv, where m represents mass and v represents velocity). It turns out that the quantity of motion in any interacting system cannot remain constant in an absolute sense but must decrease over time. Motion is dissipated by friction and other phenomena in which heat is generated.

Leibniz and many others, however, dreamed of a universal and inviolable law of the conservation of *vis viva* (mv^2), yet they were without experimental support until the development of the science of thermodynamics in the nineteenth century, to which I turn in chapter 7. In the 1840s James Prescott Joule and others demonstrated that a definite quantity of work can produce a definite quantity of heat, and vice versa. This led to the first law of thermodynamics, the principle of the conservation of energy.[1] According to this law energy never increases nor decreases in any physical process, but only changes its form, from potential to kinetic, mechanical to thermal, thermal to electrical, and so forth. In this

---

1. Leibniz's term *vis viva* was replaced by the later term *energy*, which was coined by Young. Energy comes in various forms, the central one of which, kinetic energy ($\frac{1}{2}mv^2$), is nearly equivalent to *vis viva* (mv^2). Kinetic energy is characteristically contrasted with potential energy. The term "kinetic energy" was coined by Kelvin, and "potential energy" by Rankine.

way advances in physics seemed to threaten the motion proof for God's existence yet again. Even without any external agent, the universe simply continues in motion forever, its store of energy morphing continuously. Over infinite time, must not all possibilities be actualized? No God would, then, it seems, be needed to account for the current motion observed in the universe.

Yet in the 1850s the second law of thermodynamics was established by Rudolf Clausius and William Thomson (Lord Kelvin). According to this law, heat cannot be consumed so as to do work (converted into usable forms of energy) without a simultaneous transfer of heat from a body at a higher temperature to a body at a lower temperature. Due to friction and other factors, more and more energy takes the form of heat over time, and heat constantly tends toward equalization of temperature. Once in a condition of thermal equilibrium, energy is locked away in an unusable form. To utilize such heat energy, as much energy or more must be consumed by doing work *on* the system in equilibrium as one gains *from* the system. Hence the second law of thermodynamics is also commonly expressed in this form: "entropy" (a term coined by Clausius) must always increase (or in an ideal situation remain constant) and can never decrease in any closed system. If it is a closed system, the amount of energy in the universe may remain constant, but the amount of usable energy must continually decrease.

Clausius, Kelvin, and Hermann von Helmholtz explicitly applied the second law to the universe as a whole. According to them, the known laws of physics indicated that the universe would eventually end in a "heat death," where all energy is in the form of heat, and temperature is equalized throughout the universe. The universe thus cannot have existed for an infinite time, or it would already be in thermal equilibrium by now. Twentieth century developments in cosmology lead to the same conclusion: in infinite time, the universe must either dissipate into heat death, or collapse into a "singularity" (a condition in which all matter is scrunched into a point) in either case reaching maximal entropy.

This suggests (as does Hubble's observations of galactic redshift and Penzias's and Wilson's discovery of the cosmic microwave background, as well as the Borde-Guth-Vilenkin theorem) that the universe had an absolute beginning in time. Yet, strictly speaking, this is not a necessary conclusion. The entropy of any *closed* system must increase over time, but if the universe is not a closed system—if God is at work in it—then it could have its entropy reduced so as to remain in motion forever.[2] Philosophically, then, the argument for the unmoved mover must still be made disjunctively, just as Aquinas made it:[3] either the universe had a beginning or it has existed forever. If it had a beginning, God must have given it a store of available energy to get it started. If it has existed forever, God must maintain its store of available energy, decreasing its entropy. If neither of these alternatives were in fact the case, then the universe would by now already be in a condition of heat death or have collapsed to a black hole, neither of which is true.

In chapter 8 I will turn to the "Maxwell's demon" thought experiment and connect the consideration of entropy with modern information theory. Drawing on the work of Szilard, Landauer, Schrödinger, and others, I will elucidate the connection between entropy reduction and life. I will also consider contemporary evidence that the universe is fine-tuned for life. This chapter will lend support to Aquinas's understanding of the unmoved mover as a living, intelligent being.

THE CHALLENGE OF INERTIA

Aristotle's Achilles Heel: Projectile Motion and Inertia

Aristotle's theory of projectile motion—adopted also by Aquinas—is infamous. When a person (the "projector") throws a stone or some such object (the "projectile"), the object continues in motion for a certain span of time after leaving the projector's hand. We have been conditioned to see nothing special about this: the stone is in motion, so it will continue to progress after losing contact with the projector until the resistance of the air has consumed all its momentum. Yet Aquinas and Aristotle lived long before the development of the principle of inertia. Hence they had to ask themselves why the projectile continued in motion without anything appearing to impel it. At first glance, Aquinas's understanding of natural motion suggests a ready answer. In the case of natural motion, the generator, in giving to a body its substantial form, causes its motion

2. Although the second law is commonly applied to the universe as a whole by cosmologists, some question whether the concept of entropy can be applied to the universe. I will address this issue in chapter 7 below, section titled "Objections to the Entropic Argument: Universe-Entropy, Infinity, and Statistical Mechanics," p. 245–248.

3. That is, unless one has other philosophical arguments against the possibility of infinite time, as does William Lane Craig. I make no judgments for or against the validity of his philosophical argument against infinite time, but I do not need any such argument to make my case.

toward its natural place, which flows from the imparted form as from an instrumental formal cause even after contact with the generator has been lost (see chapter 1). So too, why may not the projector impart to the projectile an accidental form or power, from which forward motion flows as from an instrumental formal cause, even after contact has been lost?[4] Yet Aquinas explicitly rejects this possibility:

> It is not, however, to be understood that the power (*virtus*) of the violent mover impresses on the stone that is moved by violence some power (*virtutem*) through which it is moved, as the power of the generating agent impresses on the generated [substance] a form from which natural motion follows. For in this way violent motion would be from an intrinsic principle, which is contrary to the notion of violent motion. It would also follow that the stone, by the very fact that it is moved locally by violence, would be altered, which is contrary to sense.[5]

Although natural motion can continue to its destination without anything impelling, violent motion cannot. And so Aquinas follows Aristotle in holding that projectile motion continues insofar as the air pushes the projectile along. The projector in moving the projectile also imparts motion to that part of the air that is in immediate contact with both, and this part of the air then pushes the projectile along after it leaves the projector and also imparts motion to the next part of the air, which then in turn pushes the stone further and also imparts motion to the next part of the air, and so forth. But each successive part of the air has a weaker force than the previous one, until no force is left and the projectile stops.[6]

But Aquinas's objections to the idea of an "impressed force" are not overwhelming. If the impressed force were not itself natural to the body, then the motion that flowed from it would also not be natural to the body. If the impressed force were even contrary to the nature of the body, then the motion that flowed from it would be contrary to the nature of the body. For a rock, forward impulse is presumably nonnatural but not

4. Such an account is given by Aquinas for the motion of iron toward a magnet (lodestone). The magnet alters the medium, and through it makes contact with the iron, altering it in such a way that it begins to move toward the magnet (*In VII Phys.*, l. 3, n. 903 [7]): "In another way something can be said to pull something else because it moves it to itself by altering [it] in some way, due to which alteration it happens that that which is altered undergoes motion according to place. And in this way the magnet is said to pull iron. For just as the generator moves heavy and light bodies insofar as it gives to them the form through which they are moved to a place, just so also the magnet gives some quality to iron through which it is moved to it."

5. *In III De Caelo*, l. 7, n. 591 [6]. Translation mine.

6. *In VIII Phys.*, l. 22, in addition to the continuation of *In III De Caelo*, l. 7, n. 591 [6].

unnatural, whereas upward impulse would definitely be unnatural. As for the objection that the hand would have to alter the stone by moving it, there does not seem to be anything impossible about this; Aquinas himself believes something similar about a magnet, namely that by its mere proximity it can alter iron in such a way that it begins to undergo motion toward the magnet (see fn. 4). If the quality in question in the case of projectile motion is nothing other than what we call "momentum," why can't the projector impress it on the stone?

Yet the projector does not alter the projectile by its proximity or contact, but by its motion; it is only because the hand is itself in motion, and thus the stone as well, that the stone will continue to undergo motion once the hand falls away. At the root of Aquinas's resistance there probably lies an unwillingness to accept the idea that motion of itself tends to continue, an idea at the heart of the later concept of inertia. This would open up the possibility that motion of itself could continue indefinitely, rather than heading toward a definite terminus. This would cast doubt on his account of heavenly motion and on the motion proof.

Nevertheless, there were arguments conclusively disproving Aristotle's view of projectile motion even in the ancient world, leveled by John Philoponus (sixth century AD).[7] Philoponus's text was not available in the thirteenth century, but a few generations after Aquinas, John Buridan (early to mid-fourteenth century) also cogently argued against the Aristotelian account of projectile motion. If the projectile is carried along by the air, then why couldn't the projector just beat the air and set the projectile in motion, rather than lifting and throwing it? Also, one should be able to throw a feather farther than a stone, since the force of the rushing air would more easily move a lighter weight than a heavier one, yet this is certainly not the case. The air does not propel projectiles; in fact, it resists them, and this is why stones can be thrown farther than feathers, since the air more easily resists a feather than a stone. Furthermore, when a boat is pulled upstream with a significant velocity, once let go it continues to move upstream for a space of time, and a sailor onboard does not feel the air impel him, but rather resist him. The reason why projectiles continue in motion, according to Buridan, is that the projector imparts to the projectile an "impetus" that moves the projectile in the direction it was projected (forward, or

---

7. James Weisheipl, OP, "Natural and Compulsory Movement," 29. Philoponus thinks that the projector must impart some force to the projectile body and even refers to it with the term "energy" (ἐνέργεια).

in a circle, as in the case of a millstone or spinning top). This impetus is unnatural for the body, and the body's own gravity and the resistance of the air act against it, until it is consumed and the projectile stops.[8] Some Medieval and Reformation Thomists (e.g., Domingo De Soto and Capreolus) accepted the theory of impetus but interpreted impetus as a formal instrumental, rather than efficient instrumental cause of projectile motion, in analogy with the substantial form as cause of natural motion.[9]

This account of projectile motion is much more satisfying than Aquinas's, and it raises a serious problem for the motion proof. We can see this in Buridan's own text:

> Since it does not appear from the Bible that there are intelligences to whom it pertains to move the heavenly bodies, one could say that there seems no need to posit such intelligences. For it might be said that when God created the world He moved each of the celestial orbs however He pleased; and in moving them He impressed an impetus that moves them without His moving them any more, except in the way of the general influence, just as He concurs in co-acting in everything that is done. For He rested on the seventh day from every work He had achieved by committing to others their reciprocal actions and passions. And those impetuses impressed upon the heavenly bodies were not afterwards lessened or corrupted because there was no inclination of the heavenly bodies to other motions nor was there the resistance that would corrupt or restrain that impetus.[10]

If one were not already assured that the world had a beginning, then there would be no reason, on this view, to think that anything needed to either set or maintain the astronomical bodies in motion. They could just simply have an impetus for circular motion, have always had it, and continue to have it forever. Hence one would have to argue for God's existence on other grounds, not on the grounds of the sempiternity of heavenly motion, as Aquinas did.[11]

8. Weisheipl, "Natural and Compulsory Movement," 31–32.

9. Weisheipl, "Natural and Compulsory Movement," 32–33.

10. John Buridan, *Questions on the Eight Books of the "Physics" of Aristotle*, book 8, q. 12, in *Philosophy in the Middle Ages*, 3rd ed., Arthur Hyman, James J. Walsh, and Thomas Williams (Indianapolis: Hackett, 2010), 703–4. For the full discussion, see *Super Octo Libros Physicorum Aristotelis*, 120rb–21rb (Paris, 1509). See also Erwin N. Hiebert, *The Historical Roots of the Principle of Conservation of Energy* (Madison, WI: The State Historical Society of Wisconsin, 1962), 65.

11. Similarly Francisco Suárez, SJ, (1548–1617) argues that the motion of the heavenly bodies "appears in many ways to be ineffective for demonstrating that there is in reality some immaterial substance, let alone for demonstrating a first and uncreated substance." (*Metaphysical Disputations*, disp. XXIX, sect. 1, n. 7, in *The Metaphysical Demonstration of the Existence of God: Metaphysical Disputations 28–29*, trans. John P. Doyle [South Bend, Ind.: St. Augustine's Press, 2004]). One of the

Buridan's impetus theory, while it modified Aristotelian physics, did not do away with it. The impetus account of projectile motion was thoroughly convincing, but Buridan's speculations about astronomical motion did not bring an end to the classical and Aristotelian view that the terrestrial and heavenly realms were utterly different.[12] Terrestrial bodies moved in straight lines, celestial ones in circles. Terrestrial bodies came to rest, celestial ones were in perpetual motion. Terrestrial bodies were generable and corruptible, celestial ones ingenerable and incorruptible. Terrestrial bodies were imperfect, celestial ones perfect. It seemed reasonable, and there was a strong tradition of holding, that the terrestrial bodies moved spontaneously, while celestial ones were moved by immaterial intelligences. The revolution in physics was really sparked by a revolution in astronomy.

In 1543 Copernicus's book *On the Revolutions of the Celestial Spheres* was published, advocating a heliocentric rather than geocentric astronomy. On this view, the earth is a planet just like Mars, Jupiter, and so on, and is in motion. If that were the case, then the same account must be given for terrestrial and astronomical motion. Furthermore, if everything around us, and we ourselves, were in motion and yet did not perceive this at all, motion must be in some strong sense relative (but not necessarily absolutely relative, as Newton later made clear). The received Aristotelian physics and cosmology would have to be reworked from the ground up, which led eventually to the modern principle of inertia.[13]

---

reasons he gives for its ineffectiveness is that a person could hold that circular motion resulted from an impetus natural to the heavenly bodies, and that no external mover was needed to maintain them in motion. Aquinas thinks this is impossible, since nature is determined to one, yet Suárez considers it merely improbable (it being more likely that they are pushed around by intelligences). Since the heavens were in fact created, such an impetus would be an instrument by which the Creator moves the astronomical bodies, yet the need for the heavenly bodies to have been created would have to be demonstrated otherwise, and only by metaphysical, not natural philosophical means. (*Metaphysical Disputations*, disp. XXIX, sect. 1, n. 7 and 13.)

12. Anneliese Maier maintains that no medieval author before or after Buridan believed that *terrestrial* motion could continue forever without a mover, even if all external resistance were, *per impossibile*, removed. According to her, terrestrial bodies were held to naturally resist not just vertical motion away from their proper place, but lateral motion as well, whereas celestial bodies gave no such resistance to the impetus. She understands Buridan the same way, but acknowledges that this is not as clear in his case: "The Significance of the Theory of Impetus for Scholastic Natural Philosophy," in *On the Threshold of Exact Science: Selected Writings of Anneliese Maier on Late Medieval Natural Philosophy*, ed. and trans. Steven D. Sargent (Philadelphia: University of Pennsylvania Press, 1982), 76–102.

13. Inertia and impetus are conceptually different. On Newton's account, inertia itself is innate to bodies and never changes. A body's motion changes, but not its inertia. On the late medieval account impetus is a *force* impressed on a body, from which force motion flows, and impetus remains in

The modern principle of inertia was given its definitive formulation by Isaac Newton in his *Principia* (1st ed. 1687), who was the first to reconcile terrestrial and astronomical physics in a thorough and convincing way. But one finds a window through which to view the historical transition in Galileo's *Dialogue concerning the Two Chief World Systems—Ptolemaic and Copernican* (published 1632). This book was an extended defense of the heliocentric worldview. Galileo argues against the distinct and special status of heavenly bodies in day one of the *Dialogue*, providing evidence that the heavenly bodies are subject to alteration and imperfection (e.g., sunspots). In the second "day" of the *Dialogue* Galileo gives arguments against the Aristotelian account of projectile motion that are similar to John Buridan's.[14] The refutation of the Aristotelian account of projectile motion is relatively brief, however, since by the seventeenth century it is old ground. The central topic of the second day of the *Dialogue* is a consideration of how bodies would behave in moving frames of reference.

If the earth is in motion, terrestrial objects are in a moving frame of reference, and if it were not for inertia, they would behave very differently than we observe them to behave. The ancient astronomer Ptolemy, not believing in inertia or impetus, objects that if the earth were spinning on its axis, all objects in the air would appear to move rapidly toward the west, as the earth outstripped them in its eastward motion (toward the rising sun).[15] Similarly, Aristotle objects that if the earth were spinning

---

the body until an outside force changes or removes it, or, in some versions, until the impetus expends itself or is diminished by the body's own nature. (This contrast between inertia and impetus is visible in Newton, *Principia*, Definitions 3 and 4.) But as we see above, Buridan already had the concept of a perpetual impetus that was not self-expending, as evidenced by the case of the perpetual motion of the astronomical bodies. Buridan's proposed astronomical impetus is circular, rather than rectilinear, but a version of the theory that posited a rectilinear and non-self-expending impetus in both the terrestrial and astronomical realms would be phenomenologically equivalent to the theory of inertia. Yet there is another difference between late scholastic impetus and the modern concept of inertia, the most important one of all: Impetus operates within the framework of the given natures of different bodies, with their different natural motions, and preserves the distinction between natural and violent motion. Although impetus is impressed from outside—e.g., a rock moves horizontally because it was thrown—bodies will also spontaneously undergo natural motion without being impelled, e.g., rocks will spontaneously fall. Inertia entails that a body in motion *or rest* will continue in constant motion or rest without an external force. Bodies do not undergo spontaneous, natural motion. The modern concept of inertia abstracts completely from the distinction between natural and violent motion. This issue will be explored in this chapter below, section titled "Newtonian Mechanics and Thomistic Natural Philosophy," p. 212–222.

14. Galileo, *Dialogue concerning the Two Chief World Systems—Ptolemaic and Copernican*, 2nd ed., trans. Stillman Drake (Berkeley: University of California Press, 1967), second day, 149–53.

15. Ptolemy, *Almagest* I, 7.

on its axis, objects thrown straight upward would not land in the same spot from which they were thrown, because the earth would move beneath them while they were aloft.[16] Galileo responds at length to such arguments against the motion of the earth in the second day of the *Dialogue*.[17] If it were not for the fact that objects already in motion tended to continue in that motion, and for the fact that all objects participating in the same sort of motion are at rest from one another's perspective, such objections against Copernicanism would be decisive. It seems that anyone who denies the reality of inertia must adhere to geocentricism. By refuting the Aristotelian account of projectile motion, and arguing for a sort of proto-principle of inertia, Galileo clears the ground for the possibility that heliocentrism is true.

A natural hypothesis for anyone trying to make sense of heliocentrism is that objects in circular motion, orbital or rotational, tend to continue in uniform circular motion; in other words, that there is circular inertia. In some passages Galileo seems to advocate for circular inertia.[18] However, heavy bodies on earth clearly move downward in straight lines, and projectiles tend to move in a straight line tangent to whatever curve they are projected on, as when a stone is whirled in a sling and then released. If a unified terrestrial and celestial physics is required, these facts have to be worked into one's account of orbital motion. (Furthermore, Kepler [1571–1630] showed that planets do not move in circles, but rather ellipses, some more and some less elongated, although Galileo did not accept this.) The way to do this is to analyze curves into two simultaneous rectilinear motions, one tangential to the curve (rectilinear inertia), and another toward the center (gravity).

Galileo gets very close to doing this. In the second day of his *Dialogue*, the character Salviati responds to a Ptolemaic argument against the rotation of the earth that objected that bodies on the surface of a

---

16. Aristotle, *De Caelo* II.14, 296b22–27.

17. Galileo summarizes the arguments to which he will respond in the second day, 124–27.

18. There is some debate about Galileo's understanding of inertia or impetus. It is generally agreed that he was close to the modern concept, but that he did not clearly formulate it. Some claim that he believes in only circular inertia (Alexandre Koyré, *Galileo Studies*, trans. John Mepham [Atlantic Highlands, NJ: Humanities Press, 1978], part III, ch. 2 and 3), others that he utilized both circular and rectilinear impetus/inertia (Stillman Drake, "Galileo Gleanings – XVII: The Question of Circular Inertia," in Stillman Drake, *Essays on Galileo and the History and Philosophy of Science*, ed. N. M. Swerdlow and T. H. Levere, vol. 2, 69–85 [Toronto: University of Toronto Press, 1999]). Descartes clearly formulates rectilinear inertia in print in the *Principles of Philosophy*, part 2, n. 39 (published in 1644), but it already appeared in his unpublished work *The World* (ch. 7), which he worked on from 1629 to 1633, until the condemnation of Galileo prompted him to abandon it.

spinning earth would fly off toward the sky, like stones whirled in a sling. But Salviati reasons that if the earth were spinning, bodies on its surface would undergo circular motion about its center, and thus remain stationary relative to the earth. This is because a body's rectilinear impetus, tangential to the surface of the earth, and the body's natural acceleration toward the earth's center would combine to produce a circular motion.[19] Furthermore, on the third day of his *Discourses on Two New Sciences*, Galileo demonstrates that uniform forward motion combined with uniform acceleration downward results in a parabolic trajectory for projectiles. However, Galileo does not clearly enunciate the modern principle of universal rectilinear inertia, and it would take Isaac Newton to describe precisely how inertia, combined with gravitation according to an inverse square law, could produce circular motion about a center and the various elliptical orbits of the planets and comets.

Galileo himself did not have conclusive evidence that the earth moves around the sun. He thought that this was established by the motion of the tides, which supposedly could only be caused by the earth's annual motion around the sun.[20] His account was fallacious, and the classical view that they are caused by the attraction of the moon is in fact correct.[21] However, once conclusive evidence for the motion of the earth around the sun became available, inertia was further demonstrated as a necessary consequence. Stellar parallax was finally observed in 1838, proving that the earth is in motion around the sun.[22] Further evidence of the motion of the earth, and thus for inertia, can be observed in the apparent rotation of a Foucault pendulum, developed in the mid-nineteenth century. These

19. Galileo, *Dialogue concerning the Two Chief World Systems*, second day, 189–95. Galileo's mathematical analysis here is problematic. For discussion see Koyré, *Galileo Studies*, 188–96.

20. This is the topic of day four of the *Dialogue concerning the Two Chief World Systems*. See also the Introduction by William Shea to Galileo, *Selected Writings*, trans. Willam R. Shea and Mark Davie (Oxford: Oxford University Press, 2012), xix.

21. See, for example, Aquinas, *De Operationibus Occultis Naturae*: "Aqua enim maris fluentis et refluentis talem motum sortitur preter proprietatem elementi ex uirtute lune, non per aliquam formam aque impressam sed per ipsam lune motionem, qua scilicet aqua mouetur a luna." (Leon. 43.183.53–58.) The moon is in fact the predominant factor, but the motion of the earth relative to the sun does modify the tides somewhat.

22. Parallax is the phenomenon of an object's apparent motion against a more distant background caused by change in the observer's position. One can easily observe an example of this by holding up one's thumb before one's face and closing first one eye, then the other. Objects in the background appear to move relative to one's thumb. Stellar parallax occurs when nearer stars are seen to move against the backdrop of more distant stars by making observations six months apart, when the earth is on opposite sides of the sun. But given the immense distances at which stars lie, very sensitive telescopes were required to observe this.

large pendula are suspended on a bearing that can rotate freely; swinging back and forth in straight lines, in the course of a day they spin around relative to the building in which they are located, without any motor or other mechanism to rotate the bearing.[23] This is inexplicable if the earth is not itself rotating around the pendulum.[24]

Although some philosophers question whether inertia is objectively real, and not rather a conceptual commitment or mathematical device,[25] I believe that the senses reveal that bodies in motion really do tend to continue in motion in a straight line at a constant rate. Despite the fact that no bodies undergo motion completely free of forces, however slight, they clearly *tend* to move uniformly in straight lines, even if that tendency is always more or less impeded (humans tend toward happiness, but are always more or less impeded in their motion toward it.)[26] This is observed in projectiles, in objects whirled in slings, in objects slid across smooth surfaces, and is legitimately inferred from the motion of the earth around its own axis and around the sun. Since the earth is in motion, bodies would not stay put on its surface nor fall straight down if the motion they shared with the earth did not tend to continue uniformly.

23. How long a Foucault pendulum takes to complete a full rotation depends on the latitude at which the pendulum lies. At the poles it takes exactly twenty-four hours, at the equator it does not rotate. At middle latitudes it takes longer than twenty-four hours. See https://en.wikipedia.org/wiki/Foucault_pendulum, accessed 5/13/2021. Since the supports of the pendulum are affixed to the earth, they can only swivel neatly around the swinging pendulum at the poles.

24. There is also the evidence of the equatorial bulge, caused by the spinning of the earth. This had been predicted by Newton, and was detected by a French team headed by Maupertuis in 1736. Finally, there is the astronomical phenomenon of the aberration of light, but the significance of this discovery was tied up with the issue of the nature of light, which remained problematic for quite some time.

25. Fr. Weisheipl considers the law of inertia to be a mathematical device that does not capture the reality of material nature. See *Nature and Motion in the Middle Ages*, 70, 33–48 and 267–72. Norwood Russell Hanson considers it to be, in some respects, a basic, conventional postulate of science, and in other respects an idealization of certain empirical phenomena. But it is neither self-evident nor demonstrated: "The Law of Inertia: A Philosopher's Touchstone," *Philosophy of Science* 30, no. 2 (1963): 107–21. Fr. William Wallace, OP, also questions the reality of inertia in his early work "Newtonian Antinomies against the *Prima Via*," *The Thomist* 19, no. 2 (1956): 151–92, at 176–81.

26. Fr. Weisheipl, Fr. Wallace, and Norwood Russell Hanson object that no bodies are ever observed or could ever be observed to move uniformly at a constant rate, since no bodies are ever force free (Hanson, "The Law of Inertia," 111–113; Weisheipl, *Nature and Motion in the Middle Ages*, 37, 49–50; Wallace, "Newtonian Antinomies against the *Prima Via*," 178–79.) But counterfactuals such as "if bodies were not acted on by external bodies, then they would move uniformly" can be objectively true, even if their antecedents are false. In fact, Aquinas argues that conditionals with *impossible* antecedents can be objectively true. See, for example, *SCG* I, c. 13, n. 87 [7] and *In VII Phys.*, l. 1, n. 889 [6]. It is not clear to me whether or not the antecedent of the conditional in question is impossible (namely that a body be force free) but it is certainly false. (Hanson argues that the antecedent is impossible.)

Furthermore, inertia/impetus seems to be the only way to explain the apparent rotation of Foucault pendula.

Fr. William Wallace objects that inertia is merely a limit concept. It is neither self-evident nor strictly demonstrable, although it can be given some basis in experience. We observe motions on earth and find that the less resistance there is in a medium through which a body moves, and the less friction there is between the body and the surface it moves over, the longer it remains in motion, and the more uniformly it moves. The deceleration approaches zero as the resistance approaches zero. We thus conclude that at the limit, where resistance is zero, the deceleration would actually be zero. But Fr. Wallace objects that what is true in the approach to a limit is not always true at the limit. As the number of sides a regular polygon has approaches infinity, the difference between the polygon and the circle in which it is inscribed approaches nothing. Yet during the approach to the limit the shape is a polygon, while at the limit it is no longer a polygon. A polygon cannot have an infinite number of sides. During the approach the polygon is becoming more like a circle. At the limit, the polygon has not become entirely like a circle, because there is no polygon.[27]

But this argument fails to convince. For inertia has, in addition to backing from terrestrial experience, even stronger support from astronomical knowledge. Planets, comets, stars, and space craft such as Voyager 1 and 2 move nearly uniformly for unimaginably vast periods of time. (I say "nearly" because there is some slight resistance from particles in space, and forces are at work on these bodies.) What are we supposed to think would happen if there were precisely zero resistance in space, rather than nearly zero? It seems entirely *ad hoc* to claim that they would eventually come to rest, to claim that there is an unobservable, tiny natural deceleration in every body that would prevent it from moving uniformly forever. Experience, both terrestrial and astronomical, leads us naturally to conclude that some positive cause of deceleration must act if the body is to stop. I therefore take the principle of inertia (or constant, rectilinear impetus) to be true, and in a realist sense.[28]

---

27. Fr. Wallace, "Newtonian Antinomies against the *Prima Via*," 179–80.

28. According to general relativity, all inertial motion is gravitational motion and *vice versa*; they are the same thing looked at from different frames of reference. If this is true inertia is still objectively real, but natural philosophy must give a unified account of it and gravity, somewhat different from the account it gives if inertia and gravity are separate as Newton holds. I will consider this issue in this chapter below, p. 220–222.

Sempiternal Motion without an Immaterial Mover?

If the principle of inertia is correct, then as far as the philosophy of nature is concerned, motion can continue forever without any mover to maintain it. Inertial motion is not directed toward a determinate terminus in which the body rests; inertial motion continues indefinitely without any particular goal. Furthermore, Newton's third law—that for every action there is an equal and opposite reaction—suggests that in any collision or interaction between bodies, quantity of motion (*mv*) is conserved. Accordingly, it seems that, contrary to Aquinas's motion proof, motion in the universe can continue *forever* without the aid of any cause outside the universe. In our post-Newtonian age, people tend to conceive of the universe as a collection of particles bouncing around freely in an open space like little billiard balls, interacting through collisions and gravitational forces, endlessly moving, changing, reconfiguring. Nothing external need move the bodies in space, because nothing short of a miracle can stop them from undergoing motion.

Given this basic world-image, modern day Epicureans can argue for the existence of an infinity of worlds of all different sorts in our universe (or "multiverse"), coalescing and dissolving over vast periods of time. In the same vein, the empiricist David Hume argues as follows:

> Instead of supposing matter infinite, as *Epicurus* did, let us suppose it finite. A finite number of particles is only susceptible of finite transpositions; and it must happen, in an eternal duration, that every possible order or position must be tried an infinite number of times. This world, therefore, with all its events, even the most minute, has before been produced and destroyed, and will again be produced and destroyed, without any bounds and limitations.... Why may not motion have been propagated by impulse through all eternity, and the same stock of it, or nearly the same, be still upheld in the universe?[29]

Not only must motion continue forever, but it can remain orderly and beneficial for vast stretches of time, and after succumbing to chaos for a much greater amount of time, it can again and again fall into orderly patterns:

> Suppose ... that matter were thrown into any position by a blind, unguided force; it is evident that this first position must, in all probability be the

---

29. David Hume, *Dialogues concerning Natural Religion*, ed. Richard H. Popkin, 2nd ed. (Indianapolis: Hackett, 1998), part VIII, 49–50.

most confused and most disorderly imaginable.... Thus the universe goes on for many ages in a continued succession of chaos and disorder. But is it not possible that it may settle at last, *so as not to lose its motion and active force (for that we have supposed inherent in it)*, yet so as to preserve a uniformity of appearance, amidst the continual motion and fluctuation of its parts? This we find to be the case with the universe at present. Every individual is perpetually changing, and every part of every individual; and yet the whole remains, in appearance, the same. May we not hope for such a position or rather be assured of it from the eternal revolutions of unguided matter; and may not this account for all the appearing wisdom and contrivance which is in the universe?[30]

In many ways, Descartes's cosmology is similar, but more optimistic: bodies move inertially in straight lines, and the same quantity of motion in the universe must always be conserved. In virtue of these laws, out of a hypothetical chaos an infinite number of solar systems must coalesce all over the universe, having the same basic features as ours.[31] Whereas the present world order arises by chance on Hume's account, for Descartes, it is a natural and inevitable result of necessary, mathematical laws.

Now Descartes himself used God's immutability as an argument for the conservation of quantity of motion; God's general, constant, and unchanging influence accounts for the overall amount of motion, and the interactions of bodies according to God's laws account for the particular, changing distributions of motion.[32] When later generations found Descartes's argument unconvincing, conservation of quantity of motion was accepted on its own experiential credentials and its mathematical elegance. It appeared to many that God was not necessary to account for the universe's motion; it was simply impossible for motion ever to stop.

If, then, Newton's three laws of motion are true, and if astronomical bodies are subject to the same basic laws as terrestrial bodies and move continually in conic sections in virtue of the combined action of inertia and gravitation, can any argument from motion to an unmoved mover still be made? Could not the universe just have always existed, and always have been in motion, with no immaterial being to sustain it? Could not the order of the world around us have arisen either as a natural or as a chance consequence of the necessary laws of physics?

---

30. Hume, *Dialogues concerning Natural Religion*, part VIII, p. 51. Emphasis added.

31. *The World, or Treatise on Light,* an unfinished work written in 1629–33, but only published posthumously in 1664. See especially ch. 6, 7, 8, 9, and 15.

32. In addition to *The World*, ch. 7, see *Principles* II, ch. 36–42.

THE MOTION PROOF VINDICATED BY
NEWTONIAN MECHANICS

Conservation of Momentum: Scalar vs. Vector

A proper understanding of some basic principles of classical physics, how-ever, will show that such a conclusion would be unjustified. The *absolute* value of the quantity of motion in a system of bodies actually tends to de-crease over time, and a cause is required to sustain it at the same level. The best way to understand this is to look at the historical development of the law of conservation of momentum, beginning with Descartes and ending with Newton. What we now call momentum was referred to at the time as "quantity of motion," and it is measured by mass times velocity. But it turns out that very much depends on whether one understands the term "velocity" as a scalar or as a vector quantity, or, to put it more simply, whether one allows velocity to have a sign, that is, to count velocity in the opposite direction as a negative quantity.

In his *Principles of Philosophy* (1644), Descartes puts forward three "laws of nature." The first two state, together, the law of inertia: (1): rest *and* motion tend to persist, and (2) motion persists in a straight line. Des-cartes's third law deals with collisions, and asserts an equality in the total quantity of motion before and after: "The third law: if a body collides with another body that is stronger than itself, it loses none of its mo-tion; but if it collides with a weaker body, it loses a quantity of motion equal to that which it imparts to the other body."[33] Here Descartes states that quantity of motion never increases nor decreases in any collision. By "quantity of motion" he understands the product of a body's size and its speed. Descartes does not distinguish mass from quantity of extension (roughly, volume.)[34] But even setting this difference aside and treating Descartes's quantity of motion as equivalent to mass times velocity, his version of the conservation of momentum law does not agree with the modern, Newtonian law, as I will show.

Following the statement of his third law, Descartes explains what will happen in accord with this law in different sorts of collisions.[35] The rules for impact that he proposes are manifestly contrary to experience. For

33. Descartes, *Principles* II, 40.
34. Richard J. Blackwell, "Descartes' Laws of Motion," *Isis* 57, no. 2 (1966): 220–34, at 225–26.
35. Descartes, *Principles* II, 45–52. See Erwin N. Hiebert, *The Historical Roots of the Principle of Conservation of Energy*, 66–67.

example, he says that if two bodies, one of which is "ever so little bigger," head in opposite directions with equal velocities and collide with each other, then the slightly bigger one will carry the other along with it, and both would move with equal velocity in the same direction. Each body would have the same speed before and after the collision, but the slightly smaller body would have its direction reversed, whereas the slightly larger body would continue to move just as before. Descartes acknowledges that his rules for collision conflict with observation, but claims that they must be true anyways, since they are self-evident and clearly and distinctly perceived by reason. He attributes the conflict to the fact that collisions in the concrete are complicated by all sorts of extraneous factors.[36]

Descartes's falsified rules for collision follow from his version of the conservation of momentum (as well as from his failure to account for any aspect of relativity of motion in cases of impact). He understands the quantity of motion that is conserved to be a scalar quantity. Velocity in any direction is treated as equivalent and as a positive quantity in each case.[37] Hence (substituting mass for size) Descartes's third law states that $p = m|v| = C$, where p stands for momentum or quantity of motion, m stands for mass, v stands for velocity, the vertical bars indicate the absolute value of the quantity (i.e., it is treated as positive no matter what the direction of motion), and C is a constant.[38] This law is simply not true, not even in the idealized condition of perfectly elastic bodies moving in a frictionless medium.

In 1668–69 however, summaries of correct rules for the collision of bodies by John Wallis, Christopher Wren, and Christian Huygens were published in the *Philosophical Transactions of the Royal Society* in England.[39] Huygens's statement is the most helpful: "The quantity of motion of two bodies can increase or decrease through impact; but always there remains the same quantity in the same direction, when the quantity

---

36. Descartes, *Principles* II, 52–53. Descartes's acknowledgment of the conflict between his rules for collision and sense experience is much more direct in the later French edition of the *Principles* (also published in his lifetime).

37. Cf. Blackwell, "Descartes' Laws of Motion," 225, fn. 13.

38. See Carolyn Iltis, "Leibniz and the *Vis Viva* Controversy," *Isis* 62, no. 1 (1971): 21–35, at 21–22.

39. For the context of this episode in the history of science, see Gemma Murray, William Harper, and Curtis Wilson, "Huygens, Wren, Wallis, and Newton on Rules of Impact and Reflection," in *Vanishing Matter and the Laws of Motion: Descartes and Beyond*, ed. Dana Jalobeanu and Peter R. Anstey, 153–91 (New York: Routledge, 2011). See also Hiebert, *The Historical Roots of the Principle of Conservation of Energy*, 72–73, but Hiebert states misleadingly that Huygens did not indicate in his 1669 communication to the Royal Society that mv^2 is conserved in elastic collisions. See Murray, Harper, and Wilson, "Huygens, Wren, Wallis, and Newton," 170.

of the contrary motions is subtracted."[40] In mathematical terms, $m|v|$—quantity of motion in Descartes's then current sense—can increase or decrease in a collision, but mv[41] (where v has a direction and can thus be counted as either positive or negative) remains constant. To illustrate my meaning, suppose that two bodies, each having 1 unit of mass and 10 units of velocity, collide head on. Before the collision, body A has $m|v|$ equal to 10 as does body B, so their total $m|v|$ equals 20. But since they travel in opposite directions, for body A mv equals 10, whereas for body B mv equals –10. Hence their total mv equals zero. Hence, according to Huygens's law—which is the correct one and was adopted by Newton—if body A and B rebounded each with speeds of 5 units (which can actually happen), then their quantities of motion would be, respectively, –5 and 5, and their total quantity of motion (mv) would be 0, exactly what it was before collision. Yet their total $m|v|$ would now equal 10, *half of its original value*. If, on the other hand, body A and B each rebounded with speeds of 20 units (this particular case is not one that can happen in the real world), mv for A would be –20, and mv for B would be 20, and the total mv would still be zero, satisfying Huygens's and Newton's law. But the total $m|v|$ would now be 40, twice its original value.[42] Although the conservation of momentum is indeed a law of nature for all collisions, quantity of motion in Descartes's absolute sense is certainly not conserved in collisions.

For the outcome of even an ideal, perfectly elastic collision to be determined, more than the law of the conservation of momentum is necessary. This law leaves the resulting velocities largely undetermined, as is clear from the fact that the two different hypothetical outcomes of the same collision just discussed both satisfy the law. The law of the conservation of momentum must be complemented by one of the following two laws: the relative velocity of the two bodies before impact equals their

40. Christian Huygens, "A Summary Account of the Laws of Motion, Communicated by Mr. Christian Hugens in a Letter to the R. Society, and since Printed in French in the *Journal des Scavans* of March 18, 1669. st. n.," *Philosophical Transactions* 4, no. 46 (1669): 925–28, at 928, as translated by Curtis Wilson in Murray, Harper, and Wilson, "Huygens, Wren, Wallis, and Newton on Rules of Impact and Reflection," 156. In actual, concrete situations, whether quantity of motion in Descartes's sense ($m|v|$) is conserved, decreased, or increased, depends on the frame of reference in which one calculates it. By varying one's frame of reference, one can change the same physical collision from one in which quantity of motion in Descartes's sense is decreased to one in which it is increased, and vice versa. Yet in any frame of reference, quantity of motion in Huygens's and Newton's sense will be conserved, not increased nor decreased.

41. Here I use mv and treat v as a scalar quantity, but one that can be positive or negative, rather than $m\mathbf{v}$ where velocity is a vector quantity, in order to match the seventeenth century account. The full analysis utilizing the mathematics of vectors was developed later.

42. See Newton, *Principia*, Corollary 3 to the Laws of Motion.

relative velocity after impact, and the sum of each body's mass times the *square* of its velocity is equal before and after the collision. The former rule can be called the conservation of relative velocity. The latter rule is equivalent to what is now known as the conservation of kinetic energy: $\frac{1}{2}m_A v_A^2 + \frac{1}{2}m_B v_B^2 = C$. (In the late seventeenth and eighteenth centuries, this would be known as the conservation of *vis viva*, a term coined by Leibniz.[43]) Huygens states only the latter law in his summary account in the *Philosophical Transactions*, but the former is also stated in his unpublished work *The Motion of Colliding Bodies*.[44]

But one must be careful to distinguish, as Descartes did not, between elastic and inelastic collisions, and between perfectly and imperfectly elastic ones. The law of the conservation of momentum holds for any collision, but the laws of conservation of relative velocity and of kinetic energy only hold for perfectly elastic ones. When bodies collide, they must each deform and reduce their velocity rapidly so as not to interpenetrate one another. In perfectly inelastic collisions, once one body's velocity has reached equality with the other's, no further change in velocity occurs. The two bodies "stick together" and proceed as one. (Imagine throwing a Velcro covered bean bag at a stuffed animal sitting on a table.) In elastic collisions however, after reducing their velocities to equality the two bodies "spring" back into shape, such that some of their lost velocity is restored.[45] (Imagine throwing a basketball against a wall; the side facing the wall will squish a bit before the ball as a whole rebounds, but it quickly regains its spherical shape.) In perfectly elastic collisions all of the lost velocity is restored, and the law of conservation of relative velocity holds. In imperfectly elastic collisions, some of it is restored, but not all. In the same way, kinetic energy is only conserved in perfectly elastic collisions; it always diminishes in imperfectly elastic collisions, and never increases in any collision of any kind.[46]

43. Carolyn Iltis, "Leibniz and the *Vis Viva* Controversy," 25; Leibniz, "A Specimen of Dynamics," in Leibniz, *Philosophical Essays*, trans. Roger Ariew and Daniel Garber, 117–38 (Indianapolis: Hackett, 1989), at 121. Iltis also refers to Leibniz's unpublished work of 1691 titled "Essay on Dynamics on the Laws of Motion, in which it is shown that not the same quantity of motion is preserved, but the same absolute force, or rather the same quantity of moving action," in *New Essays concerning Human Understanding*, trans. Alfred Gideon Langley (New York: Macmillan, 1896), appendix IV. This last essay is very clear and helpful.

44. See Richard J. Blackwell, trans., "Christian Huygens' *The Motion of Colliding Bodies*," *Isis* 68, no. 4 (1977): 574–97, at 579, proposition 4.

45. The discussion of Leibniz in "A Specimen of Dynamics," 131–32 is helpful.

46. Technically, the colliding objects might rebound with greater kinetic energy if another

For Isaac Newton, the law of the conservation of momentum follows from his third law of motion,[47] that for every action there is an equal and opposite reaction (together with his second law of motion, that the "change in motion is proportional to the motive force impressed"[48]). In the *Principia*, Newton confirms his third law with experiments he performed on colliding pendulums. In a passage that illuminates the law of the conservation of momentum, he states:

> Lest anyone object that the rule which this experiment was designed to prove presupposes that bodies are either absolutely hard or at least perfectly elastic and thus of a kind which do not occur naturally, I add that the experiments just described work equally well with soft bodies and with hard ones, since surely they do not in any way depend on the condition of hardness. For if this rule is to be tested in bodies that are not perfectly hard, it will only be necessary to decrease the reflection in a fixed proportion to the quantity of elastic force. In the theory of Wren and Huygens, absolutely hard bodies rebound from each other with the velocity with which they have collided. [N. B.: This is the law of the conservation of relative velocity.] This will be affirmed with more certainty of perfectly elastic bodies. In imperfectly elastic bodies the velocity of rebounding must be decreased together with the elastic force, because that force (except when the parts of the bodies are damaged as a result of collision, or experience some sort of extension such as would be caused by a hammer blow) is fixed and determinate (as far as I can tell) and makes the bodies rebound from each other with a relative velocity that is in a given ratio to the relative velocity with which they collide. I have tested this as follows with tightly wound balls of wool strongly compressed. First, releasing the pendulums and measuring their reflection, I found the quantity of their elastic force; then from this force I determined what the reflections would be in other cases of their collision, and the experiments which were made agreed with the computations. The balls always rebounded from each other with a relative velocity that was to the relative velocity of their colliding as 5 to 9, more or less. Steel balls rebounded with nearly the same velocity and cork balls with a slightly smaller velocity, while with glass balls the proportion was roughly 15 to 16.[49]

Real world objects have an experimentally determined coefficient of elasticity (or coefficient of restitution), somewhere between 0 and 1,

---

source contributes its energy during the collision. For example, the bodies might be coated with a volatile material, and the collision trigger an explosion that releases stored chemical energy.

47. Newton, *Principia*, Axioms, or the Laws of Motion, Corollary 3, in Newton, *Philosophical Writings*, ed. Andrew Janiak, 2nd ed. (Cambridge: Cambridge University Press, 2014), 95–96.

48. Newton, *Principia*, Axioms, or the Laws of Motion, Law 2, in *Philosophical Writings*, 91.

49. Newton, *Principia*, Scholium to the Laws of Motion, in *Philosophical Writings*, 103.

which determines how much of their relative velocity before collision they will preserve afterward. The more elastic a body is, the less energy it will lose in a collision. A well-inflated basketball is highly elastic, but it will still not rise precisely to the height from which it falls after bouncing off the court. A deflated basketball has a very low coefficient of elasticity and hardly rebounds at all from the floor. *Since no real-world bodies are perfectly elastic, some motion is lost in any collision.* Newton himself treats this as an issue having cosmological significance, as we will now see.

Query 31 to the Opticks:
Newton as Advocate of the Motion Proof

In a remarkable passage added to the end of the Latin edition of his famous work the *Opticks* (1706), Newton suggests a remarkable cosmological argument for the existence of God, one that closely parallels Aquinas's motion and teleological proofs as I have interpreted them.[50] This is significant because he does so while giving full attention to the modern principle of inertia:

> The *vis inertiae* [force of inertia] is a passive principle by which bodies persist in their motion or rest, receive motion in proportion to the force impressing it, and resist as much as they are resisted. [Author's note: Notice that Newton here ties all three laws of motion to inertia.] By this principle alone there never could have been any motion in the world. Some other principle was necessary for putting bodies into motion; and *now* [*that*] *they are in motion, some other principle is necessary for conserving the motion.* For from the various composition of two motions, it is very certain that there is not always the same quantity of motion in the world. [Author's note: Newton then describes how quantity of motion varies over time in the case of mutually bound, rotating globes moving through space.] ... By this instance it appears that motion may be got or lost. But *by reason of the tenacity of fluids, and attrition of their parts, and the weakness of elasticity in solids, motion is much more apt to be lost than got, and is always upon the decay.* For bodies which are either absolutely hard, or so soft as to be void of elasticity, will not rebound from one another.

50. For a discussion and historical context, see David Kubrin, "Newton and the Cyclical Cosmos: Providence and the Mechanical Philosophy," *Journal of the History of Ideas* 28, no. 3 (1967): 325–46. Kubrin argues that Newton may in fact have believed in an eternal, cyclical cosmos, but that the rebirth of the system of the world after its destruction could only occur through God's guidance of natural phenomena. This serves to underscore my point that Newton's argument for an unmoved mover, like Aquinas's, does not depend on proving that there was a beginning in time. It can proceed disjunctively: either the system of the universe had a beginning initiated by God, or it is sustained forever by God.

Impenetrability makes them only stop. If two equal bodies meet directly in a vacuum, they will by the laws of motion stop where they meet and lose all their motion, and remain in rest, unless they be elastic and receive new motion from their spring. If they have so much elasticity as suffices to make them rebound with a quarter, or half, or three quarters of the force with which they come together, they will lose three quarters, or half, or a quarter of their motion. *If it be said that they can lose no motion but what they communicate to other bodies, the consequence is that in a vacuum they can lose no motion, but when they meet they must go on and penetrate one another's dimensions.* If three equal round vessels be filled, the one with water, the other with oil, the third with molten pitch [a residue of tar], and the liquors be stirred about alike to give them a vortical [rotating] motion; the pitch by its tenacity will lose its motion quickly, the oil being less tenacious will keep it longer, and the water being less tenacious will keep it longest, but yet will lose it in a short time.[51]

Newton states here that due to the less than perfect elasticity of bodies in the real world, the viscosity of liquid and gaseous fluids, and, one can add, friction between moving surfaces, quantity of motion taken in an absolute sense is always upon the decrease. Momentum is conserved only in a relative sense, namely, that the difference between motion in one direction and motion in the contrary direction is always the same. Quantity of motion in a system of two bodies may begin, for example, as $10-10=0$, and steadily proceed to $9-9=0$, $8-8=0$, $7-7=0$, and so on, in which case the absolute value of the quantity of motion decreases from 20 to 18, to 16, to 14, and so forth. Newton continues:

Seeing therefore the variety of motion which we find in the world is always decreasing, there is a necessity of conserving and recruiting it by active principles, such as are the cause of gravity, by which planets and comets keep their motions in their orbits, and bodies acquire great motion in falling; and the cause of fermentation, by which the heart and blood of animals are kept in perpetual motion and heat … and the sun continues violently hot and lucid, and warms all things by its light. For we meet with very little motion in the world, besides what is owing to these active principles. And if it were not for these principles, the bodies of the earth, planets, comets, sun, and all things in them, would grow cold and freeze, and become inactive masses; and all putrefaction, generation, vegetation, and life would cease, and the planets and comets would not remain in their orbits.[52]

51. Newton, *Opticks*, part III, query 31, in Newton, *Philosophical Writings*, 182–83. Emphasis added. This query was added in the 1706 Latin edition as query 23; in the 2nd English edition (1718) more queries were added, but the query in question remained at the end, thus becoming query 31. A presentation by Tom McLaughlin first introduced me to this important text.

52. Newton, *Opticks*, part III, query 31, in Newton, *Philosophical Writings*, 184.

The three laws of motion do not conserve the same quantity of motion in the universe, but the force of gravity and the cause of heat, whatever it may be, serve to keep the levels of motion up. Now gravity can only add motion to a system of bodies as long as the bodies stand at a distance to each other. As they fall toward each other their quantity of motion increases, but once they collide and rest together—after perhaps a few bounces, as when one drops a stone on rocky ground—all the motion generated by gravity is gone, and no potential for further motion is present. However, if inertial sideways motion is properly adjusted to gravitational centripetal acceleration, orbital motion may be achieved and maintained:

> All material things seem to have been composed of the hard and solid particles above mentioned, variously associated in the first creation by the counsel of an intelligent agent. For it became him who created them to set them in order. And if he did so, it's unphilosophical to seek for any other origin of the world, or to pretend that it might arise out of a chaos by the mere laws of nature; though being once formed, it may continue by those laws *for many ages.* For while comets move in very eccentric orbits in all manner of positions, blind fate could never make all the planets move one and the same way *in orbits concentric, some inconsiderable irregularities excepted,* which may have arisen from the mutual actions of comets and planets upon one another, and *which will be apt to increase, till this system wants a reformation.* Such a wonderful uniformity in the planetary system must be allowed the effect of choice. And so must the uniformity in the bodies of animals ... Also the first contrivance of those very artificial parts of the animals, the eyes, ears, ... and the instinct of brutes and insects, can be the effect of nothing else than the wisdom and skill of a powerful ever-living agent, who being in all places, is more able by his will to move the bodies within his boundless uniform sensorium, and thereby to form and *reform the parts of the universe,* than we are by our will to move the parts of our own bodies. And yet we are not to consider the world as the body of God.[53]

Newton is here making a number of related points. One is that God gets the universe started. It is unclear whether this is an argument, or merely a statement. I am going to set this point aside. Newton is, however, certainly making a design argument for God's existence: the regular and beneficial order observed in nature requires an intelligent agent as cause. In the *Principia* he makes much of the concentric orbits of the planets

---

53. Newton, *Opticks,* part III, query 31, in Newton, *Philosophical Writings,* 185–86.

as evidence for God;[54] the Kant-Laplace hypothesis and its modern descendants can now explain the origin of the solar system by physical laws, but Newton's argument is not defeated, only pushed back: fine-tuning of physical constants and initial conditions is necessary for structure formation in the universe.

But it is the third consideration of Newton's that I am interested in here: Although the laws of physics can preserve the present order in the solar system "for many ages," it cannot do so forever. Irregularities in the orbits must slowly increase over time, "till this system wants a reformation." In fact, the moon is slowly receding from the earth, at a rate of about 3.8 cm per year, and the earth's rotation is slowing down, so that in a century a day will be 2 milliseconds longer than it is today.[55] If disorder in the motions of the solar system must increase over time, then the present world order cannot continue forever unless God sustains it, maintaining orderly motion in the solar system. The same thing is true for the universe as a whole. If there is to be perpetual orderly, orbital motion, God must exist to sustain it. Otherwise one of two things will eventually happen: either planets and stars will collide with each other and clump together, as gravitational attraction wins the victory, or inertial motion will win out and they will fly away from each other, escaping the force of gravity—which approaches zero as a limit as bodies recede from each other.

Newtonian mechanics corroborates Aquinas's motion proof for God's existence, and Isaac Newton himself is in fact a supporter of it (even if he did not recognize the similarity between his account and Aquinas's argument.) Motion in the universe either had an absolute beginning or it did not. If it did, God must exist to get it started. If it did not, God must exist to sustain it. Either way, the present world order can only be accounted for if there is an immaterial and intelligent mover outside the universe as a whole and at work in it. The difference is only in this: according to Newtonian mechanics, even without God's intervention motion of some kind might continue forever—for example, a body might sail off into the blackness of space—but not motion of the orderly, beneficial kind. For Aquinas, however, no motion of any kind can continue forever without God's moving activity.

---

54. Newton, *Principia*, book III, General Scholium, in *Philosophical Writings*, 110–111.

55. "Is the Moon moving away from the Earth? When was this discovered?" accessed 6/21/2019, http://curious.astro.cornell.edu/about-us/37-our-solar-system/the-moon/the-moon-and-the-earth/111-is-the-moon-moving-away-from-the-earth-when-was-this-discovered-intermediate.

Conflicting Worldviews: Leibniz and Newton

Descartes, as we have seen, believed that the same absolute value of quantity of motion was always conserved in the universe. We have also seen that he was incorrect in this. In criticizing Descartes's view, Leibniz introduced a concept that was to become increasingly important as time went on: *vis viva*, "living force," equal to mass times the square of the velocity.[56] (Nowadays we speak of *kinetic energy*—a term introduced by William Thomson—and equate it with $\frac{1}{2}mv^2$.) It is not the absolute value of quantity of motion, but *vis viva* that is conserved in all collisions and interactions according to Leibniz. (Notice that neither *vis viva* nor kinetic energy, involving the square of a velocity, have any sign or direction associated with them; they have absolute, scalar values.) Although Leibniz understood that *vis viva* is *not* observably conserved in any collision, he also knew that the more elastic bodies are, the more nearly their *vis viva* is conserved in collisions. He believed that, despite appearances, *vis viva* must actually be rigorously conserved in reality. He reasoned that the apparently lost *vis viva* is merely transformed, becoming the microscopic motions of the tiny parts of colliding bodies.[57]

Leibniz, in fact, also ties this point of physics to broad, cosmological issues. He directly attacks Newton's view, in Query 31 of the *Opticks*, that motion diminishes over time and that God must reform the universe if it is to keep going forever. In the letter that initiated his public correspondence with Samuel Clarke, Leibniz argues:

> Sir Isaac Newton and his followers have also a very odd opinion concerning the work of God. According to their doctrine, God Almighty wants to wind up his watch from time to time; otherwise it would cease to move. He had not, it seems, sufficient foresight to make it a perpetual motion. Nay, the machine of God's making is so imperfect according to these gentlemen that he

56. Leibniz, "A Brief Demonstration of a Notable Error of Descartes and Others concerning a Natural Law," (1686) in *Philosophical Papers and Letters*, ed. Leroy E. Loemker, 2nd ed. (Dordrecht: D. Reidel, 1969), 296–302; ibid., "A Specimen of Dynamics," in *Philosophical Essays*, 117–38.

57. See Erwin N. Hiebert, *Historical Roots of the Principle of Conservation of Energy*, 88–90 and Leibniz, "Essay on Dynamics on the Laws of Motion," 668–70, esp. 670: "When the parts of the bodies absorb the force of the impact, as a whole, as when two pieces of rich earth or of clay come into collision, or in part, as when two wooden balls meet, which are much less elastic than two globes of jasper or tempered steel; when, I say, some force is absorbed by the parts, it is as good as lost for the absolute force ... But this loss of the total force, or this failure of the third equation [i.e., conservation of *vis viva*], does not detract from the inviolable truth of the law of the conservation of the same force in the world. For that which is absorbed by the minute parts is not absolutely lost for the universe, although it is lost for the total force of the concurrent bodies."

is obliged to clean it now and then by an extraordinary concourse, and even to mend it as a clockmaker mends his work.... According to my opinion, the same force and vigor remain always in the world and only passes from one part of matter to another, agreeably to the laws of nature and the beautiful pre-established order.[58]

Clarke (who was speaking for Newton[59]) responds critically:

The notion of the world's being a great machine, going on without the interposition of God as a clock continues to go without the assistance of a clockmaker, is the notion of materialism and fate and tends ... to exclude providence and God's government in reality out of the world. And by the same reason that a philosopher can represent all things going on from the beginning of the creation without any government or interposition of providence, a skeptic will easily argue still further backward and suppose that things have from eternity gone on (as they now do) without any true creation or original author at all but only what arguers call all-wise and eternal nature.[60]

Clarke—himself very much a theist—is arguing that if theists like Leibniz claim that motion and order in the universe can sustain themselves forever into the future, then they leave the door wide open for atheists (or Spinozists[61]) to claim that motion and order have been able to sustain themselves forever in the past; an immaterial God would not be needed, not even to set the universe in motion originally. Clarke, on the other hand, agrees with Newton in holding that motion tends of itself to diminish and to grow disordered, and that if the universe is to continue indefinitely God's providential moving power is necessary.

Leibniz responds by claiming that "they who fancy that active force lessens of itself in the world do not well understand the principal laws of nature."[62] Clarke replies: "This is a bare assertion without proof. Two bodies void of elasticity meeting together with equal contrary forces both lose their motion," and he makes a reference to Query 31 of Newton's *Opticks*.[63] Leibniz's final response is as follows:

58. Leibniz, Correspondence with Clarke, First Paper, in *Philosophical Papers and Letters*, 675–76.

59. See A. Rupert Hall and Marie Boas Hall, "Clarke and Newton," *Isis* 52, no. 4 (1961): 583–85, as well as Domenico Bertoloni Meli, "Newton and the Leibniz-Clarke Correspondence," in *The Cambridge Companion to Newton*, ed. I. Bernard Cohen and George E. Smith, 1st ed. (Cambridge: Cambridge University Press, 2002), 455–64, at 459–60.

60. Samuel Clarke, First Reply, in Leibniz, *Philosophical Papers and Letters*, 677.

61. I thank Joe Zepeda for his suggestion as to Clarke's intended reference. Hobbes may also be in Clarke's mind.

62. Leibniz, Fourth Letter, in *Philosophical Papers and Letters*, 690.

63. Samuel Clarke, Fourth Reply, in Leibniz, *Philosophical Papers and Letters*, 695.

I can very well answer the objection here brought against me. I have affirmed that active forces are preserved in the world. The author objects that two soft or unelastic bodies meeting together lose some of their force. I answer, 'No.' 'Tis true their wholes lose it with respect to their total motion, but their parts receive it, being shaken internally by the force of the concourse. And therefore that loss of force is only in appearance. The forces are not destroyed but scattered among the small parts. The bodies do not lose their forces, but the case here is the same as when men change great money into small. However, I agree that the quantity of motion [i.e., in Descartes' sense] does not remain the same ... But I have shown elsewhere that there is a difference between the quantity of motion and the quantity of force.[64]

By quantity of force, Leibniz has in mind *vis viva* (measured by mv^2.) But Leibniz has no empirical evidence that *vis viva* is conserved in collisions. The evidence at the time pointed in the opposite direction in fact. Leibniz's conservation law was a consequence of his metaphysics, and despite many merits, Leibnizian, rationalist metaphysics is not a convincing system. For the time, Newton and Aquinas appear to have the upper hand. But Leibniz's view will have another chance when the science of thermodynamics arises in the nineteenth century, a development with which I will deal in the next chapter.

NEWTONIAN MECHANICS AND
THOMISTIC NATURAL PHILOSOPHY

Thomistic Inertia

I could turn at this point straight to the topic of thermodynamics, but my claim that Aquinas's proof is supported by Newtonian mechanics would remain unsatisfying unless I indicated how the principle of inertia itself might be reconciled with Thomistic natural philosophy. The motion proof still works, given Newton's laws of motion and collision, but the very idea that motion could, in principle, continue forever with no terminus seems to be opposed to some basic tenets of Thomistic natural philosophy. I will take up this issue in the present section, providing a teleological interpretation of inertia that is consistent with Thomistic principles.

Certainly Aquinas himself would have denied the principle of inertia

---

64. Leibniz, Fifth Paper, in *Philosophical Papers and Letters*, 713. See also Erwin N. Hiebert, *Historical Roots of the Principle of Conservation of Energy*, 88–90.

if someone in the thirteenth century had happened to propose it to him. In that sense, the principle is contrary to Thomas's doctrine. But being a Thomist does not mean agreeing with everything St. Thomas said. Otherwise, Thomism would be a dead letter. I will show that Thomistic philosophy of nature can be adapted so as to receive the principle of inertia, while remaining faithful to its own basic structure and deepest principles. One need not reduce inertia to a mere mathematical device devoid of physical reality (as does Fr. Weisheipl).[65]

For Thomists, the principle of inertia raises questions about the reduction of potency to act; I addressed this issue at length in chapter 1 and I will not repeat the discussion here.[66] But there are two further issues that the principle of inertia raises from a Thomistic perspective. One is that, according to Aquinas, every motion has a definite terminus or goal,[67] and no motion tends toward a terminus infinitely distant, for it is impossible for something to be in motion toward a terminus that it cannot possibly reach.[68] Inertial motion, however, either tends toward nowhere at all, or toward a point infinitely distant, depending on how one wants to look at it. Secondly and more importantly, inertia threatens to render the distinction between natural and violent motion incoherent, whereas this distinction is fundamental to Thomistic philosophy of nature. Motion can be natural in two senses: one, that it flows spontaneously from a body's nature, and two, that it is toward the body's natural place or condition. Correspondingly, motion is violent either insofar as it is imposed by an external source without the mobile body contributing anything, or insofar as it is away from a body's natural place and condition. But according to the principle of inertia, all motion is initiated by an external force, and all motion continues due to the body's own nature. Hence it appears that all motion is violent, and that all motion is natural. Furthermore, according to the principle of inertia, a body is indifferent to rest or motion and indifferent to motion in this direction or that direction, toward this terminus or that terminus. Hence it appears that no motion is either natural or violent. In short, the distinction between natural and violent motion breaks down.[69]

---

65. Weisheipl, *Nature and Motion in the Middle Ages*, 33–48.

66. Unlike, for example, Thomas J. McLaughlin in "Aristotelian Mover Causality and the Principle of Inertia," *International Philosophical Quarterly* 38, no. 2 (1998): 137–51, I believe that inertial motion does involve the reduction of potency to act, but that this does not require a conjoined mover. See chapter 1 above.

67. Aquinas, *QDP* q. 5, a. 5, c.

68. See, for example, *SCG* III, c. 2: "nihil enim movetur ad id ad quod impossibile est pervenire."

69. Koyré points out that inertia destroys the distinction between natural and violent motion

I will take up this second issue first. Galileo, of all people, provides a reflection that can reveal to a Thomist the way out of difficulty. Early in day one of the *Dialogue*, Salviati, Galileo's mouthpiece, proposes that it is natural for *all bodies*, not just heavenly ones, to move in a circle. He is echoing, but developing, Copernicus's defense of the physical possibility of his heliocentric theory.[70] Here Salviati uses the language of natural and violent motion and proposes something like Buridan's curvilinear impetus. Later in the *Dialogue*, he argues against the distinction between natural and violent motion, moving closer to the modern concept of inertia.[71] But for a Thomist, Salviati's early account in day one is rich and suggestive:

> If all integral bodies in the world are by nature movable, it is impossible that their motions should be straight, or anything else but circular; and the reason is very plain and obvious. For whatever moves straight changes place and, continuing to move, goes ever farther from its starting point and from every place through which it successively passes.... By means of [straight motions], just as well-arranged bodies would become disordered in moving, so those which were previously badly disposed might be arranged in order. But after their optimum distribution and arrangement it is impossible that there should remain in them natural inclinations to move any more in straight motions, from which nothing would now follow but their removal from their proper and natural places; which is to say, their disordering. We may therefore say that straight motion serves to transport materials for the construction of a work; but this, once constructed is to rest immovable— or, if movable, is to move only circularly.[72]

What is said here about circular motion would apply to any motion on a closed path, including, for example, an ellipse. If one or more bodies undergo motion on closed paths, they can continue in good working order indefinitely. This is how the solar system works. It is also how internal combustion engines, clocks, and other machines work. Straight line motion relative to a system, however, cannot continue indefinitely without causing disorder to the system. Straight line motion can bring a body that is out of place to its proper place, but if the motion continues the body

---

in *Galileo Studies*, 130. Weisheipl raises this as an objection to the Newtonian principle of inertia: *Nature and Motion in the Middle Ages*, 33 and 69.

70. Copernicus, *On the Revolutions of the Heavenly Spheres* I, 8.

71. Galileo, *Dialogue concerning the Two Chief World Systems*, second day, 233–46. He also makes comments suggestive of rectilinear inertia, but no clear statement is made: second day, 189–95.

72. Galileo, *Dialogue concerning the Two Chief World Systems*, first day, 19–20.

will move right through its proper place and then recede from it. If any part of a clock continued to move indefinitely in a straight line, for example, it would fly out of place and the clock would cease to function.

Unlike Salviati in this passage (Galileo's true view is difficult to parse out, given the dialectical character of the *Dialogue*), I accept the reality of rectilinear inertia. The fact, then, that it is natural for all bodies to move indefinitely in straight lines means that bodies are naturally orderable, but also naturally tend to fall out of order. This is just what I said about Aquinas's account of the elements in the previous chapter: the elements are naturally receptive of the forms of mixed and animate bodies, but such bodies also naturally tend toward corruption in virtue of the elements from which they are formed. That bodies can be set in inertial motion makes them responsive to our goals: one can play fetch with one's dog, one can utilize a flywheel to operate an engine, and so forth. But it also means that bodies tend to get out of control: a car skids off a road when it takes a turn too fast, a golf ball rolls past the hole, and so on.

Inertia must be understood in context, however. Gravitational motion is also natural to all bodies. (I reject, of course, Aquinas's view that some elements—fire at least—naturally levitate rather than gravitate, and accept Newton's law of *universal* gravitation instead.) In virtue of their weight (*gravitas*), the elements tend to coalesce so as to form stars and planets. In virtue of the combined principles of gravity and inertia, bodies tend naturally to undergo orbital motion around a massive body or center of gravity. These combined principles have produced and continue to maintain our solar system and other orbital systems. Orbital motion thus flows from the very nature of physical bodies, with their inertial and gravitational inclinations. (It is extraordinarily difficult, in fact, for a body to avoid orbiting something or other. As soon as a body launched from earth escapes earth orbit, it falls right into an orbit around the sun. Those few man-made objects that have escaped solar orbit—the Voyager, Pioneer, and New Horizons spacecraft—simply move into orbit around the center of the Milky Way galaxy.) Orbital motion is the fulfillment of an inanimate body's nature, and inertia and gravity are thus teleological, goal directed principles. The motion that flows from them is natural motion. Yet they are imperfect principles, and they imply also a tendency toward disorder and entropy. They embody a finite power of being (*virtus essendi*), so to speak, and produce stars and planets and orderly motion among them only for a finite—although huge—amount of time. As we will see later, the universe must eventually succumb, in virtue of these principles, either to gravitational collapse or to scattering and heat death.

On the understanding I am proposing, any motion that works against the goals of natural motion would be violent motion. This will be most obvious in the case of living beings, which move not only inertially and gravitationally, but grow, pursue food, and so on, and can suffer harm, pain, and death. At the level of the inanimate, however, violent motion includes the disruption of an orbital system, the breaking apart of planets and stars, the raising of bodies from the surfaces of their planets, as well as the breaking apart of chemical compounds (as discussed in chapter 5, any body tends toward its own preservation.)

Now the disruption of one orbital system may be the establishment of another, and the dissolution of one chemical compound may be the generation of another, so one might worry whether the differentiation between violent and natural motion is coherent.[73] Aquinas was already aware of this issue. In Thomistic philosophy, the words "natural" and "violent" are relative to specific natures. If a wolf preys on a deer, for example, the consumption of the deer is in accord with wolf-nature, but violent for deer-nature.[74] However, in addition to the specific natures of individual things, Aquinas utilizes the concept of nature as a whole, in the sense of "natural world" or "cosmos." For him it makes sense to ask whether a given occurrence—such as the wolf's consumption of the deer—is natural simply speaking, or in the big picture. In this case, the answer would be yes, because the wolf's consumption of the deer promotes the common good of the natural world, or in modern terms, the health of the ecosystem.[75] So too, the disruption of an orbital system, the separation of a body from its planet, or the dissolution of a chemical compound will generally involve the establishment of another orbital system or contact with another planet, or the forming of another chemical

---

73. This objection was suggested to me by Joe Zepeda.

74. See, for example, Aquinas, *ST* I, q. 49, a. 1, c. and ad 2; q. 48, a. 2, ad 3.

75. See, for example, Aquinas, *ST* I-II, q. 85, a. 6, c.: "We may speak of any corruptible thing in two ways: first, in respect of universal nature, second, as regards particular nature. A thing's particular nature is its own power of action and self-preservation. And in respect of this nature, every corruption and defect is contrary to nature, as stated in *De Caelo* II, since this power tends to the being and preservation of the thing to which it belongs. On the other hand, the universal nature is an active force in some universal principle of nature, for instance in some heavenly body, or again belonging to some superior substance, in which sense God is said by some to be *the Nature Who makes nature* (*natura naturans*). This force intends the good and the preservation of the universe, for which alternate generation and corruption in things are requisite. And in this respect corruption and defect in things are natural."

compound. Hence the process will be violent for the system disrupted, natural for the system formed. Whether it is natural or violent simply speaking will depend upon whether it promotes universal nature's higher goals for the inanimate: stars, galaxies, and above all stable solar systems with terrestrial planets and complex chemistry, that is, the necessary (but not sufficient) conditions for life. Some occurrences in nature will promote these goals, and some will counteract them. The later occurrences are cases of violent motion simply speaking.

In acting against nature's higher goals, however, violent motion will not be able finally to prevent the achievement of the most basic goal of all: thermal equilibrium. This corresponds to Aquinas's thesis that when the motions of the astronomical bodies cease, mixed and animate bodies will dissolve into their elements and the elements will return to their proper places and rest (see chapter 3). In both cases, when the universe is no longer moved toward its higher goals, it falls back toward its lowest goal, a state of relaxed tension and rest.

One might wonder, however, whether attributing final causes to inertial and gravitational motion, as I have done, is well-motivated. Is it not an empty attribution, simply pointing at a mere effect and arbitrarily labeling it an "end"? Does this *explain* anything?[76] Perhaps not immediately, but it certainly describes them more adequately, and in a way that calls for explanation. One must bear in mind that to attribute a natural purpose to something is not to attribute conscious desire to it. Rather, it is to say that a thing tends, by virtue of its nature, and not merely in virtue of accidental factors, toward an effect that is good. Modern astronomy has made it abundantly clear that matter tends *per se*, and not *per accidens*, to coalesce into stars, galaxies, and planets moving in orbital systems (recent years have witnessed the discovery of thousands of exo-planets, many of them terrestrial and in habitable zones around their stars). In such systems, where planets are warmed by their stars, atoms can engage in complex chemistry. These beautiful results are objectively good, as constituting a fuller realization of the potentialities latent in matter compared to the condition of particles scattered in cold space. Orbital systems also constitute the necessary but not sufficient conditions for living organisms. For St. Thomas, the three most basic goods for any being are existence, the full actualization of potential, and service to something greater.[77] Physi-

---

76. This objection was also suggested to me by Joe Zepeda.
77. See *ST* I, q. 6, a. 3 and q. 65, a. 2, c.

cal bodies tend toward these results *per se* in virtue of inertia and gravity, which must therefore be considered teleological principles.

It is time, then, to return to the first Thomistic objection to inertia: can natural philosophy accept the infinite character of inertial motion? Can a body really tend toward infinity? Can a finite force produce an infinite result, for example, an imaginary super-booster launching a satellite off into intergalactic space so as to move forever?[78] Well, why not? Aquinas himself says that in the infinite future time an infinite number of thoughts and affections will be produced by our finite, immortal souls.[79] This is a case of a finite power producing a quantitatively infinite result. But what is infinite quantitatively is still finite essentially; even if it does not have a quantitative limit, it is limited in its essence (it does not possess every aspect of being).[80] The same is the case with inertial motion: a finite force produces a quantitatively infinite result, namely unending motion. Yet this result is not infinite essentially, but quite limited in its mode of being. Moreover, the infinity of inertial motion is spread out over time and does not exist all at once. At no point will a body, moving inertially, occupy an infinite amount of space (just as, at no point, will a soul have an infinite number of thoughts). At any time, it will be in one place, not another, and it will be one kind of body and not another kind.

True, after infinite time the body moving inertially will be infinitely far away from the bodies it left behind (presuming it reached escape velocity). In a sense, though, this is just to say that inertial motion really tends toward a kind of rest after all. If there were a direction for a body to fly in which no matter lay,[81] by moving inertially it would become

---

78. This objection is raised in Feser, *Aristotle's Revenge: The Metaphysical Foundations of Physical and Biological Science* (Neunkirchen-Seelscheid, Germany: Editiones Scholasticae, 2019), 230–31; Wallace, "Newtonian Antinomies against the *Prima Via*," 184; and Garrigou-Lagrange, *God: His Existence and His Nature*, vol. I, 274.

79. Aquinas, *ST* I, q. 14, a. 12, c.

80. *ST* I, q. 7, a. 3, c.

81. If the universe contains an infinite amount of matter in an infinite space, then no body would ever be able to move inertially unto infinity, and the same would be true if space had a curved and closed geometry, such that inertial motion would eventually bring the body back to where it started. In these cases, the trajectory of the body would be deflected by gravitational forces, and it would eventually enter into orbit around or collide with another body. Even if one conceived of the projectile as threading a path between every one of the infinite bodies in the universe so as to continue in motion forever, it would necessarily be decelerated by the gravitational pull of some bodies (e.g., galaxies) and accelerated by others, and hence its motion would have an infinite number of partial causes. Hence the question of an infinite effect flowing from a finite cause would not arise. My point in the text is to consider what the *tendency* of inertia is toward, not whether a body can ever follow that tendency unimpeded. I thank Joe Zepeda for raising this issue.

less and less able to interact with anything else, and the ratio of the distance it covered in any finite time to the distance it already stood from all other bodies would approach zero ($\lim_{t\to\infty}((\Delta s/\Delta t)/s) = 0$, where s is displacement from the hypothetical center of gravity of the universe, and t is time). Thus continuing inertial motion eventually produces no noticeable effect. Inertial motion does tend toward a definite terminus, then, although it never *perfectly* achieves it: the terminus of inertial motion is complete isolation of a body from all others, which is just one form of thermal equilibrium. This terminus is not exactly a place, but rather a condition.

Having interpreted inertia teleologically, I should say a word or two about its ontological status. I am, in fact, inclined to meld together the concepts of modern inertia and scholastic impetus. Thomas McLaughlin, without in any way casting doubt on the real, physical validity of Newton's laws of motion, has pointed out that inertia ought to be interpreted as a natural *active* principle.[82] Newton states that the force of inertia is a *passive* principle, and that "a body exerts this force only during a change of its state, caused by another force impressed upon it."[83] But this way of looking at inertia leads to a puzzle, insofar as two inertially moving bodies, on colliding with each other, resist each other. If inertia were totally passive, neither would act on the other until the other acted on it, and thus neither could prompt the other to act. Each would be waiting for something that was waiting on it, and thus the process would never get started. One ought then to think of inertia rather as an active principle of perseverance, and that each of the colliding bodies resists the other insofar as it perseveres, rather than perseveres insofar as it resists.[84]

In virtue of corporeal nature, then, all bodies have an inclination to actively persevere in their state of rest or rectilinear, uniform motion. Yet this inclination is of itself indeterminate, being similarly related to rest and motion, to motion in this direction or that, and to this speed or that. Hence a body possessing inertia is also receptive, possessing the potentiality to receive any kind of motion that might be imparted to it. In addition to inertia then, which is a universal and unchanging accidental form that all bodies possess, momenta or impetuses can be impressed upon bodies

---

82. McLaughlin, "Nature and Inertia," *The Review of Metaphysics* 62, no. 2 (2008): 251–84.

83. Newton, *Principia*, Definition 3 in *Philosophical Writings*, 80. See also *Opticks*, Query 31, in *Philosophical Writings*, 182.

84. McLaughlin, "Nature and Inertia," 279–80.

as additional accidental forms, differing from body to body, and these impetuses are actively preserved by the more fundamental quality of inertia. These impetuses may be nothing more than the determination of direction and speed that inertial motion requires.[85] In this way, Aquinas's concern that merely moving a stone in one's hand seems incapable of imparting any new quality to it would be nullified, insofar as one must surely concede that one's hand can impart a direction and speed to a stone.[86]

Thomistic Gravity

Gravity, however, poses a further problem for the reconciliation of Thomism and classical mechanics. St. Thomas's understanding of gravity seems to conflict with the first law of motion. As I explained in detail in chapter 1, Aquinas's view of gravity is that heavy bodies tend downward in virtue of an intrinsic, active principle, with nothing impelling them. True, newly generated heavy bodies are set in motion by their generators, but they continue to accelerate without any new external force, and bodies that are already heavy, when lifted upward, will change direction and head downward without any new contact from their generators. Modern gravity can be interpreted in teleological terms, as I have explained in the previous section. But is not Aquinas's understanding of gravity incompatible with the modern understanding of gravity as an impressed force? And would not Thomistic gravity violate the principle of inertia insofar as the heavy body changes its "state" of motion without any impressed force?[87]

Gravity is, in fact, still not fully understood by scientists. Although Newton proved that gravitation is universal and provided a measure of its force (completed by the determination of the gravity constant by Cavendish in the eighteenth century), he professed ignorance of the cause of gravitation. Although he frequently speaks in terms of "attraction," he says that this word should be taken to refer only to the effect of gravitation, not its cause.[88] The one thing he says unequivocally is that gravity

---

85. Cp. McLaughlin, "Nature and Inertia," 278–79.

86. See this chapter above, section titled "Aristotle's Achilles Heel: Projectile Motion and Inertia," p. 190–191.

87. This form of objection was suggested to me by Thomas McLaughlin, "A Defense of Natural Place in a Contemporary Scientific Context." See also McLaughlin, "Nature and Inertia," 259–60.

88. For example, Newton, *Principia*, Definition 8 and bk. I, section XI, Scholium to Prop. LXIX, in Isaac Newton, *Philosophical Writings*, 83 and 106–07.

is not the instantaneous action at a distance of one body on another (the very thing often attributed to him, and the very thing for which he is often criticized).[89] The current theory of gravity is not Newton's, but Einstein's theory of general relativity. Yet it is difficult to render general relativity consistent with quantum mechanics. A theory of "quantum gravity" that would reconcile them is eagerly sought. The scientific theory of gravity is not in a final state, but we can give a Thomistic account of gravity in either the classical or the relativistic mode.

What is clear is that all bodies gravitate, but that not all bodies gravitate toward the same center. The moon gravitates toward the earth, but Jupiter's moons gravitate toward Jupiter; a hammer on earth gravitates toward the earth, but a hammer on the moon gravitates toward the moon. Since one cannot attribute cognitive powers to elemental bodies, there must be some kind of contact between gravitating bodies through some kind of medium, otherwise a body would not "know" which direction to tend. This granted, one possible explanation of gravitation is that a massive body such as the earth acts on a heavy body such as a rock through a medium (a gravitational field of some kind) and moves it toward itself, with downward motion remaining natural for the rock insofar as it fulfills a natural *passive* principle that the rock possesses in virtue of its form. (This is similar to Aquinas's view that the orbital motion of an astronomical body is natural for it insofar as it fulfills a natural passive principle in the body, even though such motion is caused by an external, immaterial mover.) This explanation would modify Thomas's understanding of *gravitas* but would preserve the natural/violent distinction and thus the basic principles of Thomistic natural philosophy.[90]

On the other hand, one could hold that the contact between massive bodies, through the gravitational field, merely triggers the release of a heavy body's natural *active* principle for motion, directing it a certain way and also determining the intensity of the acceleration. The planet or other massive body affects the strength and direction of the gravitational field, and the gravitating object naturally and spontaneously responds to the contours of this field, seeking the center of gravity as its natural place. While inertia is a real, natural, active inclination of all bodies, it is not the only such inclination. Gravity too is an active inclination naturally shared

<hr>

89. Newton, Letter to Bentley, in *Philosophical Writings*, 136.

90. This view is advocated by Thomas McLaughlin, "A Defense of Natural Place in a Contemporary Scientific Context."

by all bodies. On this view, which I favor, a heavy body would move spontaneously, by its own force, just as Aquinas said. The "impressed force" required for such an acceleration by the first and second laws of motion would be a composite of the action of both bodies, the one establishing the contour of the field, the other following it. This explanation stretches the usual understanding of "impressed force," but it is reflected in classical mechanics' mathematical formula for gravitational force: $F_G = m_1 m_2 G/r^2$, where the mass of both bodies jointly determines the quantity of force.[91]

Alternatively, according to general relativity gravitation is just inertia looked at from another frame of reference, and thus gravitational motion need involve no impressed force at all. In this framework, gravitation is a body's spontaneous, inertial motion along a geodesic of a curved space-time, with the curvature of space-time determined by both bodies jointly.[92] In either case, provided one is not rigidly attached to the details of Aquinas's view but only seeks to preserve his most fundamental principles, one can reconcile a modern understanding of gravity with Thomism.

Not only Thomas's motion proof, then, but Thomistic natural philosophy in general is consistent with classical mechanics. The first two laws of motion merely instantiate the principle of inertia, which I have argued is consistent with Thomism. The third law of motion—that for every action there is an equal and opposite reaction—is actually anticipated by St. Thomas. For Aquinas holds that when a body acts on another it is always by means of mutual contact, and that a body is always acted upon at the same time as it acts.[93] I have explained how gravity can be understood in Thomistic fashion, and electromagnetism should be analyzable in much the same terms as gravity (although the analysis will be complicated by the duality of positive and negative charge). Hence Thomism has nothing to fear from classical mechanics, and everything to gain by embracing it.

91. It has also been suggested to me by Michael Bolin that the third law of motion—that for every action there is an equal and opposite reaction—requires that both bodies be active in the phenomenon of gravitation. The force by which one body gravitates toward another is equal to that by which the other gravitates toward it.

92. A view such as this is suggested by William Wallace, OP, in "Is the Pull of Gravity Real?" in *From a Realist Point of View*, 1st ed. 163–85 (Lanham, MD: University Press of America, 1979), at 172, 178–79, and fn. 54. See also Wallace, "Newtonian Antinomies against the *Prima Via*," 166–73. But it is not clear to me whether Wallace sees gravitation as due to a natural active principle or a natural passive principle, and, even more importantly, Wallace believes that all motion requires a continuously active mover, and in this we disagree.

93. Aquinas, *In III Phys.*, l. 2, n. 288 [6] and l. 4, n. 301–02 [5–6]. He does not, however, specify that the reaction is *equal* to the action.

Chapter 7

Thermodynamics and
the Motion Proof

In the early nineteenth century the principle of the conservation of energy—the first law of thermodynamics—was established beyond a reasonable doubt, and this principle poses a new challenge to Aquinas's motion proof. To make this clear, I must first review some physics concepts.

In modern accounts, energy is explained as a body's or system's ability to perform work, and work, in its turn, is defined as what is accomplished by a force acting through a distance ($\int f ds$). For example, a ball of a given mass rolling with a certain speed has a definite amount of "kinetic energy" ($\frac{1}{2}mv^2$).[1] It can depress a spring a certain distance, depending on the stiffness of the spring and hence on the force required to overcome its resistance. Depressing the spring is a case of doing work; the more energy the ball has, the further it can depress the spring, or, alternatively, the stiffer the spring it can depress a given distance. According to the principle of

---

1. The integral expression for work accounts for the coefficient ½ being prefixed to the older expression for *vis viva*, mv^2. Since $f = ma$, and work equals $\int f ds$, therefore work equals $\int ma\,ds$. Furthermore, acceleration, a, is the rate of change of velocity, dv/dt and velocity, v, is the rate of change of distance, ds/dt. Hence, work equals $\int m(dv/dt)ds = \int m(ds/dt)dv = \int mv\,dv = \frac{1}{2}mv^2$. Work done on a body offering no resistance would produce exactly this much kinetic energy. Energy and work have the same units; a given amount of energy can perform that much work, and in doing so transfers energy from one body to another, or from one form to another. See Carolyn Iltis, "D'Alembert and the *Vis Viva* Controversy," *Studies in History and Philosophy of Science Part A* 1, no. 22 (1970): 135–44, at 139 and fn. 24.

the conservation of energy, energy can never diminish (nor increase) in the universe by means of any physical process; it merely changes its form. For example, the depressed spring has gained "potential energy" and can now do work itself by expanding against a force.

According to the Newtonian analysis, quantity of motion, in an absolute sense, diminishes in all collisions and in all movements across frictional surfaces or through resisting media. But this loss of motion is accompanied by the generation of heat (and also sometimes sound and light), and by the mid-nineteenth century it had been demonstrated that not only could heat produce motion in turn, but that there was an exact numerical equivalence between heat and work: a definite quantity of work could generate a definite quantity of heat, and the consumption of that same quantity of heat could generate the same quantity of work. Energy is never destroyed, it merely changes its form, from mechanical, to thermal, to electrical, to chemical, back to mechanical, and so on. Is there any need, then, for God to reform the world to keep it going forever, as Newton had said, or any need for an immaterial mover to sustain motion in the universe, as Aquinas held?

An historical analysis of the rise of thermodynamics will, it turns out, once again vindicate the motion proof by means of the second law of thermodynamics. According to that law, in any closed system the amount of energy *available* to do work constantly decreases, or, put in other terms, entropy or disorder inevitably increases. The energy that could theoretically do work still exists, as the first law requires, but it can no longer be concentrated and harnessed so as to act over any given distance. For this reason, no closed system can be self-sustaining, and if there is no God the universe is a closed system.[2]

Roadblocks to the Conservation Principle

From Leibniz's day on through the eighteenth century there was continual debate over whether the proper quantity to use in analysis of physical problems was momentum, *mv*, or *vis viva*, eventually equated to $\frac{1}{2}mv^2$.[3] In many situations, *vis viva* seems a better choice, but momentum, understood as *mv* and not as *m|v|*, is empirically conserved in every collision

---

2. For more on this, see this chapter below, section titled "Objections to the Entropic Argument: Universe-Entropy, Infinity, and Statistical Mechanics," p. 246–247.

3. See L. L. Laudan, "The *Vis Viva* Controversy, a Post-Mortem," *Isis* 59, no. 2 (1968): 130–43 and Carolyn Iltis, "D'Alembert and the *Vis Viva* Controversy."

while *vis viva* is not. Leibniz and others wanted *vis viva* to be a universally conserved factor, but there were many obstacles to this idea. *Vis viva* seemed to diminish through friction, through the viscosity of liquids, and through the resistance of air. It also seemed in some situations to *increase*, at least temporarily: when a body is let go at a height it starts with zero velocity, and hence with no *vis viva*. As the body descends it accelerates and acquires a greater and greater velocity, and hence a greater and greater *vis viva*. But when the body hits the ground, it comes to rest, perhaps after a few bounces, and loses all the *vis viva* it gained. Many new concepts had to be put in place and many things empirically determined before the conservation of *vis viva* could be more than an unsupported presumption.

Newton thought of gravity as an active force increasing the quantity of motion in bodies, without specifying what the cause of gravity is. (Although he was clear that in his opinion it was not a force acting instantaneously through a distance.[4]) Leibniz, like Descartes, thought of gravity as caused by swirling vortices of subtle matter, and hence not as a cause of increase of total *vis viva*.[5] The swirling medium simply transferred some of its *vis viva* to the accelerating falling body. But this idea also had no empirical support and was eventually abandoned. But this aspect of the problem of energy conservation was solved by the invention of the concept of "potential energy," by William Rankine.[6] Potential energy is the energy that a body possesses in virtue of its position, which gives it an ability to get into motion and acquire *vis viva*, or kinetic energy. For example, a stretched slingshot, if held in place, has no kinetic energy but a great deal of potential energy; a soon as the impediment is removed it will accelerate the stone, thus generating kinetic energy. Once it has gone slack, it no longer has any potential energy and can produce no more acceleration. In the case of falling bodies, the higher above the ground a body is, the greater its potential energy, for in falling it would accelerate over a greater distance and obtain a greater kinetic energy. We now say that the total energy, potential plus kinetic, is conserved throughout the

4. Newton, "Letter to Bentley, 25th February 1692/3," in *Philosophical Writings*, 136.

5. Leibniz, "Planetary Theory, from a Letter to Huygens," in Leibniz, *Philosophical Essays*, ed. and trans. Roger Ariew and Daniel Garber (Indianapolis: Hackett, 1989), 309–312.

6. William John Macquorn Rankine, "Outline of the Science of Energetics," *The Edinburgh New Philosophical Journal*, New Series, 2 (July–October 1855), 129–30. See also ibid., "On the General Law of the Transformation of Energy," *Philosophical Magazine*, series 4, vol. 5 (January–June, 1853) 106.

fall. The gravitational force does not increase the amount of energy in the free-falling, accelerating body; it simply converts more and more potential energy into kinetic energy.

Potential energy is commonly treated as a kind of hidden energy, or energy in virtue of position.[7] But its name suggests that it is not actually energy, just the potential to acquire energy. This is, in fact, just what as great a scientist as James Clerk Maxwell says of it: "Rankine introduced the term Potential Energy, a very felicitous name, since it … signifies the energy which the system has not in possession, but only has the power to acquire."[8] In reality, the level of energy actually possessed by a system increases and decreases as potential energy is actualized or kinetic energy reduced to potential. For example, a body standing at an immense distance from the sun, outside our solar system, does not actually have energy, but it is subject to a slight gravitational force. This force can generate kinetic energy in the body, which begins to move slowly toward the sun and then accelerates at an ever increasing rate, until the entire potential for energy has been actualized, and the body plunges into the sun at an immense speed. Philosophical clarity requires conceptualizing "potential energy" as the potential for energy, and not as actually being energy.[9]

Newton is basically correct: energy increases and decreases in the universe from many different causes. It is not a physically conserved quantity. However, potential energy is a disposition to acquire actual energy, and potential energy can be precisely quantified. Furthermore, the sum of potential and kinetic energy *is* conserved in the natural world. This conservation principle is sufficient to challenge the motion proof for

7. See, for example, the sources cited in Thomas McLaughlin, "Act, Potency, and Energy," *The Thomist* 75, no. 2 (2011): 207–43, at 219. A body is said to have energy in virtue of position because, by being a certain distance from another body that exerts a force, or by being at a certain position in a field, it is able to accelerate and acquire a certain amount of kinetic energy.

8. James Clerk Maxwell, *The Theory of Heat*, ed. Peter Pesic (Mineola, NY: Dover, 2001), 91. This is a reprint of the ninth edition published in 1888.

9. That potential energy is not actually energy is argued convincingly by Thomas McLaughlin, "Act, Potency, and Energy." One might object that since energy is defined as the ability to do work, all energy is potency and not actuality. But one may respond that a body with kinetic energy can do work because it is actually in motion, whereas a body with potential energy can do work because it is in potency to motion. Furthermore, as described in this chapter below (p. 230–236), kinetic energy in thermal form, once it reaches thermal equilibrium, cannot do work. The definition of energy as the ability to do work is not a proper definition, but a definition through a characteristic effect. As great a scientist as Richard Feynman claims that we don't really have a definition of energy, but only know how to calculate its various forms (*The Character of Physical Law* [Cambridge, MA: MIT Press, 2017], 69–71). Yet as a philosopher I would hazard to define energy as the lowest, physical and inanimate, form of actuality.

God's existence, and henceforth I will speak in conventional terms of the principle of the conservation of energy, treating potential energy as actual energy.

But introducing the concept of potential energy is not enough to justify the conservation principle, for what happens to all the energy, potential and kinetic, when a free-falling body comes to rest on the ground? It no longer possesses potential energy, since it is not raised to a height, and it no longer possesses kinetic energy since it has come to rest. The conservation principle depends on yet another factor, namely, the mechanical equivalent of heat.

The Mechanical Equivalent of Heat:
James Prescott Joule

A descendant of Leibniz's hypothesized principle of the conservation of *vis viva* was finally demonstrated, convincingly, in the nineteenth century. It has become known as the principle of the conservation of energy, or the first law of thermodynamics (but it is absolutely general and not restricted to any sub-domain of physics). It was obvious from many phenomena in which motion appeared to be lost that heat was generated at the same time. For example, friction makes things hot. Also, from the earliest period of the scientific revolution the idea that heat was a form of microscopic motion had been entertained. Bacon and Newton both accepted this idea, for example. However, there was no way to verify this theory at the time, and there was also a competing theory that heat was the manifestation of a certain type of material element, "caloric." Several developments had to occur before the conservation of energy could be demonstrated.

First, a way of quantifying and measuring heat (as opposed to temperature[10]) had to be developed. Chemists such as Lavoisier led the way in developing calorimetry. Secondly, ways to quantify work and efficiency had to be refined. The rise of the steam engine in the eighteenth and nineteenth centuries, and economic concerns about how to maximize the amount of work derived from each pound of coal helped drive this conceptual progress. Thirdly, a whole series of conversion processes had to be discovered. During the eighteenth and early nineteenth centuries,

---

10. The transfer of heat can raise the temperature of a body, but need not. Heat might, for example, melt a solid substance without raising its temperature, if it is already at the melting point.

various ways of converting one form of action into another were developed: mechanical, thermal, chemical, electrical, magnetic, and optical. Any one of these forms of activity could be converted into any one of the others. For example, Ørsted discovered that an electrical current could move a magnetic compass needle. Using this discovery, Faraday invented an electric motor, converting electrical activity into mechanical activity. A generator works in reverse, producing electricity out of mechanical action. Most importantly, all of these forms of energy (as we now say) can generate heat, and heat can generate the others. For example: a mere difference in heat between two parts of a piston can generate mechanical action—a fact exploited by machines called Stirling engines—and heat can generate electricity when applied to two different conductors joined together.[11]

What finally proved the principle of the conservation of energy, however, was the establishment of the quantity representing the "mechanical equivalent of heat." If a given quantity of work (performed by mechanical action, say) always produced a given quantity of heat, and if that same quantity of heat could produce the same quantity of work, then and only then could it be asserted that the quantity of energy never increases nor decreases through any physical interactions. Four different scientists worked out the mechanical equivalent of heat in the 1840s: Mayer, Colding, Joule, and Helmholtz. Mayer had the priority (1842), but in many ways Joule's work was the most important, for he was a superb experimentalist, and measured the mechanical equivalent of heat in many different ways.[12] He also demonstrated that when a gas expands into a vacuum without doing work, no heat is consumed (or rendered latent, as the caloric theory would have it) and the temperature remains constant, whereas when an expanding gas does work against an external force, heat

11. I draw here on Thomas Kuhn, "Energy Conservation as an Example of Simultaneous Discovery," in *Critical Problems in the History of Science*, ed. Marshall Clagett, 321–56 (Madison, WI: The University of Wisconsin Press, 1959), as well as the responses to his paper by Carl B. Boyer, "Commentary on the Papers of Thomas S. Kuhn and I. Bernard Cohen" (384–90) and Erwin Hiebert, "Commentary on the Papers of Thomas S. Kuhn and I. Bernard Cohen" (391–400.) Kuhn's paper was reprinted in Kuhn, *The Essential Tension: Selected Studies in Scientific Tradition and Change* (Chicago: University of Chicago Press, 1977). I leave out of account another factor identified by Kuhn: German *Naturphilosophie*.

12. See, for example, James Prescott Joule, "On the Existence of an Equivalent Relation between Heat and the ordinary Forms of Mechanical Power," (1845) in *The Scientific Papers of James Prescott Joule*, vol. 1 (London: Taylor and Francis, 1884), 202–205. For a fuller account of Joule's contribution, see D. S. L. Cardwell, *From Watt to Clausius: The Rise of Thermodynamics in the Early Industrial Age* (Ithaca, NY: Cornell University Press, 1971), 231–38.

is consumed and the temperature drops.[13] (His work also had the most influence on Kelvin and Clausius, who led the way in the next stage in the development of thermodynamics.)

In perhaps his most famous experiment, Joule agitated water in an enclosed vessel by means of paddles that were driven by falling weights external to the vessel. The resistance of the fluid hindered the falling of the weights and consumed mechanical work. At the same time, the temperature of the water was raised, as measured by a thermometer. In a series of experiments Joule measured the amount of work that raised the temperature of the water one degree and came up with a number in the same ballpark as he had arrived at by means of other types of experiments. Over the years Joule experimented again and again to refine his value for the mechanical equivalent of heat, and arrived at good results.

Joule conceived of heat as the *vis viva* or kinetic energy of the microscopic parts of bodies (this was the "mechanical" or "dynamical" theory of heat).[14] It had been known for a long time that heat is generated by collisions and friction. Now that it was known that heat could generate motion (e.g., in the steam engine) and that a given quantity of work could generate a given quantity of heat, the idea that *vis viva* or energy was universally conserved was finally on a firm footing. The energy that appeared to be lost in collisions, friction, and resisting media was not lost, it was simply transformed into heat energy. To return to the case of falling bodies, now it could be stated that not only is energy not generated during free fall (rather, potential energy is transformed into kinetic energy), but energy is not lost on collision with the earth either; rather, kinetic energy is simply transformed into thermal energy.

Yet the principle of conservation of energy, the first law of thermodynamics, did not spell victory for Leibniz and Descartes over Newton and Aquinas. The first law of thermodynamics is incomplete without the second law of thermodynamics, which sets limits on the conditions under which energy can be converted back into mechanical, electrical, or other usable forms, after it has found its way into thermal form. As we shall see, the second law vindicates Newton and Aquinas.

13. D. S. L. Cardwell, *From Watt to Clausius*, 233–34. To be precise, when a gas expands into a vacuum, a tiny bit of heat is consumed, since the gas does work against its own intermolecular attractive forces.

14. D. S. L. Cardwell, *From Watt to Clausius*, 236–37.

THE ENTROPY PRINCIPLE

The Second Law of Thermodynamics:
Carnot, Clausius, and Kelvin

The second law of thermodynamics was established jointly by Rudolf
Clausius (1850) and Lord Kelvin (1851, at the time he was known simply
as William Thomson). But it has its roots in the work of Sadi Carnot,
who published in 1824 a little book titled *Reflections on the Motive Power
of Fire*. The purpose of this book was to provide a theoretical account of
heat engines and determine whether there are theoretical limits to their
efficiency.[15] Carnot held, at the time, to the caloric theory that heat was
a conserved material substance.[16] He argued that heat/caloric can only
produce work by "falling" from a body at higher temperature to a body at
lower temperature, likening this to the way in which water can only power mills by falling from higher elevation to lower elevation.[17] In a steam
engine, this meant that heat had to flow from the furnace, through the
boiler, into the piston, and onwards to the cold water in the condenser.
The amount of work that heat can do depends jointly on its quantity and
the temperatures over which it falls.[18]

Nevertheless, heat does not always produce work in falling. Whenever bodies of different temperatures are in direct contact, some heat
flows from the hotter to the colder body without doing any work.[19] To
determine the maximum efficiency of a heat powered engine, Carnot described what has come to be called the Carnot cycle, a perfectly reversible
series of operations that a heat engine could ideally (but not really) perform.[20] In a Carnot cycle a certain amount of heat is transferred from a

15. Carnot also proposed to determine whether steam or air or any other substance might
provide an advantage over others when used in heat engines. Eric Mendoza, ed., *Reflections on the
Motive Power of Fire and other Papers on the Second Law of Thermodynamics by É. Clapeyron and
R. Clausius* (Mineola, NY: Dover, 1988), 5–6.

16. D. S. L. Cardwell, *From Watt to Clausius*, 191–92. But see also Stathis Psillos, "A Philosophical Study of the Transition from the Caloric Theory of Heat to Thermodynamics: Resisting the
Pessimistic Meta-Induction," *Studies in History and Philosophy of Science*, Part A, 25, no. 2 (1994):
159–90, at 173–78.

17. Carnot, *Reflections*, 15. See also Cardwell, *From Watt to Clausius*, 193.

18. Not only the temperature difference, but the temperature values themselves matter: Carnot,
Reflections, 36–37. Cf. Cardwell, *From Watt to Clausius*, 204–6. Cardwell compares Carnot's conclu-
sion to "the modern formula: $W=J(Q_1-Q_2)=J.Q_1(T_1-T_2)/T_1$." I wish to thank my father Laurence
Shields for rescuing me from an error on this point.

19. Carnot, *Reflections*, 12–13.

20. Carnot, *Reflections*, 17–19.

warmer body to a cooler one without direct contact at any point between bodies at different temperatures. The cycle produces a certain amount of work. That same amount of work, if applied to the engine, could run the cycle backward and transfer the same amount of heat from a colder body to a hotter one. Carnot reasons that no engine, no matter how constructed or what substance it employs, could ever produce more work from the same amount of heat and the same temperature difference than an engine operating in a Carnot cycle. Otherwise perpetual motion could be generated.[21]

The Carnot cycle is a thought experiment only, for it depends on the existence of perfect insulators and the complete absence of friction, both of which are impossible. Real engines can only approach, more or less, to the character of Carnot engines, which thus set the theoretical maximum of efficiency in producing work from heat.[22]

Carnot's work had a profound but delayed impact. It sank at first into obscurity, but finally made an impact in the 1840s and '50s. Both Kelvin and Clausius first came to know of Carnot's work through another author, Émile Clapeyron.[23] After searching in vain in French bookstores,[24] Kelvin finally acquired a copy of Carnot's own book in 1848.[25]

By the time Kelvin was beginning to publish work on heat, the dynamical theory that heat was microscopic motion was beginning to gain traction. Kelvin was interested in Joule's work, but could not fully accept his theory because he was taken by Carnot's argument in the *Reflections*, which utilized the caloric theory that heat was a conserved material fluid. In 1849 he published "An Account of Carnot's Theory of the Motive Power of Heat" in which he still adheres to Carnot's assumption that no

21. This is because, by employing a portion of the work generated by the supposedly more efficient engine one could run the Carnot engine backward and restore the heat transferred from the warmer body to the cooler one back to the warmer one, with the excess work performing any other task one likes. The restored heat could then continue to run the more efficient engine, which would power the Carnot engine *and* perform a task, and so on *ad infinitum*. See Carnot, *Reflections*, 11–12.

22. Cardwell, *From Watt to Clausius*, 193–95.

23. In 1834 Clapeyron published in French an account of Carnot's work in his "Memoir on the Motive Power of Heat." Clapeyron, also holding to the caloric theory of heat, developed Carnot's argument by illustrating it geometrically (plotting volume and pressure in a Cartesian coordinate system) and analyzing it with differential equations. (Ingo Müller, *A History of Thermodynamics: The Doctrine of Energy and Entropy* [Berlin: Springer, 2007], 56.) Clapeyron's work was translated into English in 1837 and republished in a German journal in 1843.

24. Kelvin, "On the Dissipation of Energy," in *Popular Lectures and Addresses* (London: Macmillan, 1894), 458, note.

25. Crosbie Smith and Matthew Norton Wise, *Energy and Empire: A Biographical Study of Lord Kelvin* (Cambridge: Cambridge University Press, 1989), 301.

heat is consumed by the heat engine, but merely transferred from a hotter body to a colder one, although he expresses some reservations given Joule's work.[26] This paper influenced Clausius, who, when he published his groundbreaking memoir in 1850, had still not yet gotten hold of a copy of Carnot's book and knew of it only through Clapeyron and Kelvin.[27] But Clausius had already accepted the dynamical theory of heat and found a way to reconcile Carnot's work with Joule's:[28]

> It is not at all necessary to discard Carnot's theory entirely…. A careful examination shows that the new method [of treating heat as consisting in "a motion of the least parts of bodies"] does not stand in contradiction to the essential principle of Carnot, but only to the subsidiary statement *that no heat is lost*, since in the production of work it may very well be the case that at the same time a certain quantity of heat is consumed and another quantity transferred from a hotter to a colder body, and both quantities of heat stand in a definite relation to the work that is done.[29]

Clausius argued that Carnot was correct that, in order to produce work, heat had to flow from a hotter body to a colder body. But while Carnot thought that the colder body received as much heat as the warmer body lost, according to Clausius when heat does work the colder body receives less heat than the warmer body loses; some of the heat is converted into mechanical energy (or some other kind of energy).[30] The proportion of heat converted to heat transferred, in ideal conditions, depends upon the temperature difference between the two bodies, as well as the absolute temperature of the body supplying the heat.[31] By 1851 Kelvin had come to the same conclusion. He accepted the dynamical theory of heat as well as the principle of the conservation of energy, and formulated the second law of thermodynamics in the following terms: "It is impossible, by means of inanimate material agency, to derive mechanical effect from any portion of matter by cooling it below the temperature of the coldest of the surrounding objects."[32]

26. In Sir William Thomson (Lord Kelvin), *Mathematical and Physical Papers*, vol. I (Cambridge: Cambridge University Press, 1882), 113–54, at 115–17 and 118–119, note. On this paper and its significance, see D. S. L. Cardwell, *From Watt to Clausius*, 240–43.

27. Rudolf Clausius, "On the Motive Power of Heat, and on the Laws Which Can Be Deduced from It for the Theory of Heat," in Mendoza, ed., *Reflections*, 107–52, at 109, note.

28. Clausius, "On the Motive Power of Heat," 109–12. Note the references to Joule.

29. Clausius, "On the Motive Power of Heat," 112.

30. On Clausius's analysis of Carnot, see Psillos, "A Philosophical Study of the Transition from the Caloric Theory of Heat to Thermodynamics," 183–85.

31. Clausius, "On the Motive Power of Heat," 134. See also Maxwell, *Theory of Heat*, 160.

32. William Thomson (Kelvin), "On the Dynamical Theory of Heat, with Numerical Results

Kelvin seems to have been the first to realize the profound consequences of this principle. Although the quantity of energy never increases nor diminishes according to the First Law of Thermodynamics, nevertheless energy tends to find its way into thermal form. Heat, however, always tends toward temperature equalization. For example, hot coffee cools to room temperature by transferring its heat to the air. Once energy is in thermal form, and once that thermal energy exists in a state of temperature equality—thermal equilibrium—that energy can no longer be used to do work. And even before temperature equality is reached, only a portion of the thermal energy can be converted into useful work, a portion that depends on the degree of temperature inequality. This means that energy, although constant, tends to "dissipate," to become locked away and unusable. In 1852 Kelvin published "On a Universal Tendency in Nature to the Dissipation of Energy," in which he states:

> II. When heat is created by any unreversible process (such as friction), there is a *dissipation* of mechanical energy, and a full *restoration* of it to its primitive condition is impossible.
> III. When heat is diffused by *conduction*, there is a *dissipation* of mechanical energy, and perfect *restoration* is impossible.
> IV. When radiant heat or light is absorbed, otherwise than in vegetation, or in chemical action, there is a *dissipation* of mechanical energy, and perfect *restoration* is impossible.[33]

He concludes the paper with the following powerful remark:

> 1) There is at present in the material world a universal tendency to the dissipation of mechanical energy. 2) Any *restoration* of mechanical energy, without more than an equivalent of dissipation, is impossible in inanimate material processes, and is probably never effected by means of organized matter, either endowed with vegetable life or subjected to the will of an animated creature. 3) Within a finite period of time past, the earth must have been, and within a finite period of time to come the earth must again be, unfit for the habitation of man as at present constituted, unless operations have been, or are to be performed, which are impossible under the laws to which the known operations going on at present in the material world are subject.[34]

Deduced from Mr. Joule's Equivalent of a Thermal Unit, and M. Regnault's Observations on Steam," in *Mathematical and Physical Papers*, vol. I, 174–332, at 179. On the significance of this paper, see D. S. L. Cardwell, *From Watt to Clausius*, 254–56.

33. William Thomson (Kelvin), "On a Universal Tendency in Nature to the Dissipation of Energy," in *Mathematical and Physical Papers*, vol. I, 511–14, at 512.

34. William Thomson (Kelvin), "On a Universal Tendency in Nature to the Dissipation of Energy," in *Mathematical and Physical Papers*, vol. I, 514. Emphasis in the original.

Despite the conservation of energy, the natural world cannot, on its own, continue forever just as it is. Kelvin, like Newton and Leibniz, considers questions of dynamics to be cosmological in their implications.

The second law of thermodynamics eventually came to be expressed in terms of what is called "entropy," a concept introduced by Clausius. To understand this concept, it is necessary to appreciate the progression of Clausius's work. In 1854 he published another memoir, "On a Modified Form of the Second Fundamental Theorem in the Mechanical Theory of Heat." Here he introduces the quantity Q/T which he refers to as the "equivalence-value of a transformation."[35] (Q represents the quantity of heat absorbed, released, consumed, or produced by a process, and T the absolute temperature.) When any physical system operates it goes through a number of transformations; in a steam engine, for example, the temperature of the steam, its volume, and its pressure change continuously. When work produces heat, or when heat flows from a higher temperature to a lower temperature, Clausius assigns a positive value to the system's transformation; the opposite processes are assigned a negative value.[36] In ideal, perfectly reversible, cyclical operations such as the Carnot cycle, the total equivalence-value of the transformations, positive and negative, ($\int dQ/T$) equals zero.[37] But in all real operations, the total equivalence-value is greater than zero, never less than zero.[38] Heat generated by friction, heat equalized by conduction, heat generated by resistance in electrical circuits, and many other phenomena are one-way, positive transformations that cannot be reversed.[39]

<hr>

35. Clausius, "On a Modified Form of the Second Fundamental Theorem in the Mechanical Theory of Heat," in *The Mechanical Theory of Heat with its Applications to the Steam-Engine and to the Physical Properties of Bodies*, ed. Thomas Archer Hirst (London: John van Voorst, 1867), 111–35, at 125–26. As Cardwell relates, Kelvin had already made use of the quantity Q/T to express the second law of thermodynamics in his 1854 paper "Thermo-electric Currents," part V of "On the Dynamical Theory of Heat" (see *Mathematical and Physical Papers*, vol. I, 236). Cardwell believes that Clausius was influenced by this paper of Kelvin's in his own 1854 paper (*From Watt to Clausius*, 258–60, 265). However, Clausius's paper was published in December 1854. Kelvin's paper was presented in May 1854, but not published until 1857 in the *Transactions of the Royal Society of Edinburgh* 21 (1857): 123–71. It seems unlikely that Clausius would have had a chance to read it before that, and he does not cite it. Clausius and Kelvin seem, then, to have arrived at this formulation independently (as recognized by Christopher J. T. Lewis, *Heat and Thermodynamics: A Historical Perspective* [Westport, Conn.: Greenwood Press, 2007], 113), although Kelvin preceded Clausius by a matter of months.

36. Clausius, "On a Modified Form of the Second Fundamental Theorem," 123.

37. Clausius, "On a Modified Form of the Second Fundamental Theorem," 129. See also "On the Application of the Theorem of the Equivalence of Transformations to Interior Work," (1862) in *The Mechanical Theory of Heat*, 215–66, at 218–19.

38. See D. S. L. Cardwell, *From Watt to Clausius*, 266–67.

39. Clausius, "On a Modified Form of the Second Fundamental Theorem," 133–34.

In 1862 Clausius expanded his analysis to include the internal constitution of a body and introduced the concept of "disgregation." Whenever a body, under the action of heat, expands, melts, or boils its disgregation increases.[40] When a gas expands into a vacuum, it does no work and the temperature remains constant, as Joule had demonstrated. Yet this transformation is irreversible. Since the pressure of the gas has decreased, its ability to do work has also decreased, and to recompress the gas work would have to be done by drawing without compensation on an external reservoir of energy.[41] Hence the mere disgregation of a body's parts is related to its ability to do work and must be treated as a transformation with an "equivalence value." Clausius assigns a positive "equivalence value" to an increase of disgregation.[42] When an increase in disgregation occurs reversibly, the body does work against an external pressure and the temperature decreases; heat is consumed at a continuously varying temperature. (But the work done by the expanding body decreases the external body's disgregation and increases its ability to do work, which is why the process is reversible.) Hence disgregation can be mathematically equated with, and measured by, the quantity $\int dQ/T$.[43]

In a further memoir, "On Several Convenient Forms of the Fundamental Equations of the Mechanical Theory of Heat," published in 1865, Clausius introduces the term "entropy" to take the place of "equivalence-value," and symbolizes it with the letter S ($\Delta S = \int dQ/T$).[44] Entropy, in fact, is a quantity representing the disorder present in a physical system. The greater the entropy, the more transformation a system has been through, and the less its capacity for further transformation. The more disordered a system is, the less it is capable of performing further work.

The mature results of the development of thermodynamics in the

40. Clausius, "On the Application of the Theorem of the Equivalence of Transformations to Interior Work," 219–20, 240. Yet at 222 Clausius points out that increase of "disgregation" does not *always* involve an expansion; when water ice is melted, it contracts, and continues to do so as it is heated from 0° to 4°C, only beginning to expand after that point. Disgregation indicates, most essentially, the degree to which internal forces have been overcome.

41. See D. S. L. Cardwell, *From Watt to Clausius*, 269–71.

42. Clausius, "On the Application of the Theorem of the Equivalence of Transformations to Interior Work," 227, 240, 242. See also Clausius, "On the Second Fundamental Theorem of the Mechanical Theory of Heat," *Philosophical Magazine*, 4th series, vol. 35, no. 239 (June 1868): 405–19, at 409.

43. Clausius, "On the Application of the Theorem of the Equivalence of Transformations to Interior Work," 242–43.

44. Clausius, "On Several Convenient Forms of the Fundamental Equations of the Mechanical Theory of Heat," in *The Mechanical Theory of Heat*, 327–74, at 357.

1840s through 1860s are the first and second laws of thermodynamics. According to the first law, energy never increases nor decreases, and it depends on the idea that heat is a form of energy. According to the second law, entropy constantly increases and never decreases overall (it can be decreased in one body by an over-compensating increase in some other body interacting with it). The second law depends on the facts that heat will only flow spontaneously from a hotter body to a colder one (i.e., that heat always tends toward equalization of temperature), and that heat cannot do work without flowing. The amount of energy never decreases, but less and less of it is available for useful purposes.

Entropy and Cosmology:
Helmholtz, Clausius, and Kelvin

Scientists of the first rank, pioneers of thermodynamics, themselves drew cosmological implications from the second law of thermodynamics.[45] We have already seen Kelvin's remarks in his 1852 paper. In 1854, Kelvin argued that nearly all the energy present on earth came from astronomical sources. Animals get their energy from food, and the food chain terminates in plants that derive their energy from the sun (photosynthesis). The fuels coal, gas, and wood are all plant-based material, and thus sources of energy deriving ultimately from the sun. Energy can be derived from wind (e.g., windmills), rain (e.g., water mills), or tides (tidal mills), but all of these phenomena derive from astronomical causes as well:

> We must look then to the sun as the source from which the mechanical energy of all the motions and heat of living creatures, and all the motion, heat, and light derived from fires and artificial flames is supplied. The natural motions of air and water derive their energy partly, no doubt, from the sun's heat, but partly also from the earth's rotary motion and the relative motions and mutual forces between the earth, moon, and sun. If we except the heat derivable from the combustion of native Sulphur, and of meteoric iron, every kind of motion (heat and light included) that takes place naturally, or that can be called into existence through man's directing powers on this earth, derives its mechanical energy either from the sun's heat or from motions and forces among bodies of the solar system.[46]

45. See Christopher J. T. Lewis, *Heat and Thermodynamics*, 111–17.
46. William Thomson (Kelvin), "On Mechanical Antecedents of Motion, Heat, and Light," in *Mathematical and Physical Papers*, vol. 2, 34–40, at 36–37.

This should remind us of Aquinas's view that the motion of the heavenly bodies is responsible for all motion here on earth. But Kelvin went on to reason, in regard to the planets, that "the potential energy of the mutual gravitation of those bodies is gradually expended … If we trace them forwards, we find that the end of this world as a habitation for man, or for any living creature or plant at present existing in it, is *mechanically inevitable*."[47] In another piece from the same year he considers the sun, and states that "the energy, that of light and radiant heat, thus emitted, is dissipated always more and more widely through endless space, and never has been, probably never can be, restored to the Sun, without acts as much beyond the scope of human intelligence as a creation or annihilation of energy, or of matter itself, would be."[48] The sun's supply of energy is finite, and it will eventually grow cold.

Throughout his career Kelvin returns to this again and again. He is especially concerned to refute the views of Hutton, Lyell, and other uniformitarian geologists,[49] who thought that the earth and living beings had been around for an indeterminably vast amount of time, with no discernible beginning, and that they could continue indefinitely into the future. Present processes could go on forever, and have gone on forever already, just as they are. Kelvin refutes this view as physically impossible on thermodynamical principles.[50]

Rarely does Kelvin extend his application of the second law of thermodynamics to the universe as a whole, usually restricting himself to the solar system. However, he does make the extension in at least two texts, both from 1862. In a piece co-authored with the physicist Peter Guthrie

47. William Thomson (Kelvin), "On Mechanical Antecedents of Motion, Heat, and Light," 37, emphasis in original.

48. William Thomson (Kelvin), "On the Mechanical Energies of the Solar System," in *Mathematical and Physical Papers*, vol. 2, 1–27, at 2.

49. They did not actually deny that there was a beginning, but argued that no matter how far back scientists would ever look in the geological record, no evidence for a beginning could ever emerge. See Lyell, *Principles of Geology*, ed. James A Secord (New York: Penguin, 1997), 436–38 (vol. III, Concluding Remarks, 1st edition, 1833). Hutton ended his work "Theory of the Earth; or an Investigation of the Laws Observable in the Composition, Dissolution, and Restoration of Land upon the Globe" (*Transactions of the Royal Society of Edinburgh* 1, no. 2 [1788]: 209–304), with the following statement: "The result, therefore, of our present enquiry is, that we find no vestige of a beginning,—no prospect of an end."

50. He underestimates the age of the sun, since he was unaware of the existence of nuclear reactions, which can generate heat and light for much longer than any of the mechanisms known to Kelvin; yet the sun's store of nuclear fuel is still finite, and limits are now set on the age of the earth and sun. Thus Kelvin was basically correct.

Tait, in the Presbyterian magazine *Good Words*,[51] a future "heat death" of the universe is declared inevitable, barring a supernatural act of God:

> Created simply as difference of position of attracting masses, the potential energy of gravitation was the original form of all the energy in the universe; and as we have seen that all energy tends ultimately to become heat, which cannot be transformed without a new creative act into any other modification, we must conclude that when all the chemical and gravitation energies of the universe have taken their final kinetic form, the result will be an arrangement of matter possessing no realizable potential energy, but uniformly hot—an undistinguishable mixture of all that is now definite and separate—chaos and darkness as "*in the beginning.*" But before this consummation can be attained, in the matter of our solar system, there must be tremendous throes and convulsions, destroying every now existing form. As surely as the weights of a clock run down to their lowest position, from which they can never rise again, unless fresh energy is communicated to them from some source not yet exhausted, so surely must planet after planet creep in, age by age, towards the sun....
>
> Thus we have the sober scientific certainty that heavens and earth shall "wax old as doth a garment;" [Ps 102:26] and that this slow progress must gradually, by natural agencies which we see going on under fixed laws, bring about circumstances in which "the elements shall melt with fervent heat." [2 Pt 3:12][52]

This view is qualified, however, in another, sole-authored piece of Kelvin's from the same year, one which he chose to include as an appendix in the textbook he co-authored with Tait, *Treatise on Natural Philosophy*:

> The second great law of Thermodynamics involves a certain principle of *irreversible action in nature*. It is thus shown that, although mechanical energy is *indestructible*, there is a universal tendency to its dissipation, which produces gradual augmentation and diffusion of heat, cessation of motion, and exhaustion of potential energy through the material universe. The result would inevitably be a state of universal rest and death, if the universe were finite and left to obey existing laws. But it is impossible to conceive a limit to the extent of matter in the universe; and therefore science points rather to an endless progress, through an endless space, of action involving the transformation of potential energy into palpable motion and thence into heat, than to a single finite mechanism, running down like a clock, and stopping for ever. It is also

---

51. Smith and Wise, *Energy and Empire*, 535.

52. Thomson (Kelvin) and Tait, "Energy," *Good Words* 3 (October 1862): 601–7, at 606–7. In 1879 Kelvin stood by this article in print, when his co-authorship was challenged by Clausius: *Mathematical and Physical Papers*, vol. 5, 6.

impossible to conceive either the beginning or the continuance of life, without an overruling creative power; and therefore, no conclusions of dynamical science regarding the future condition of the earth can be held to give dispiriting views as to the destiny of the race of intelligent beings by which it is at present inhabited.[53]

Kelvin thus shows some hesitance concerning the theory of a heat death of the universe. He is certain of the heat death of any finite system, such as our solar system. This is what he chooses to focus on throughout his career. That life on earth had a beginning is sufficient to prove that God exists. The universe, however, he thinks of as infinite, both in space and in matter. This suggests that there is an infinite amount of gravitational potential energy, which no definite finite time could exhaust. (Nevertheless, it still seems to follow, although Kelvin does not clearly say so, that time cannot be infinite *in the past* without God's intervention, although it can be potentially infinite in the future. For if the universe were infinite in the past, an infinite amount of time would have already elapsed. That infinite time would have been sufficient to consume the infinite amount of gravitational potential energy, converting it all into thermal energy in equilibrium by now, contrary to fact.[54] Thus, although no given finite amount of time would be sufficient to exhaust the useful energy in the universe, and there would be no definite upper limit to possible past time, nevertheless past time could not be positively infinite, but would need an arbitrary limit set to it somewhere. I will return to this below.)

Another pioneer of thermodynamics to predict a heat death of the universe is Hermann von Helmholtz, who was one of the first to argue for the conservation principle, in 1847.[55] He took up the issue of the sec-

---

53. Thomson (Kelvin), "On the Age of the Sun's Heat," in *Popular Lectures and Addresses*, vol. 1 (London: Macmillan, 1891), 356–75, at 356–57. Emphasis in original. First published in 1862.

54. Kelvin, working before the discoveries of Hubble, thought of the universe as contracting, rather than expanding. He conceives of the gravitational potential energy of a dispersed infinite system of bodies as generating, over time, an infinite number of solar systems, each capable of existing for only a finite time. He certainly believes that the universe had a beginning in time, but does not seem to believe that such is provable by science. In his early days Kelvin toys with the idea that Fourier's heat equation demonstrates an absolute beginning to temperature distributions, but he seems to have given up the idea later. See Silvanus P. Thompson, *The Life of William Thomson, Baron Kelvin of Largs* (London: Macmillan, 1910), 111–12, quoted in Helge S. Kragh, *Entropic Creation: Religious Contexts of Thermodynamics and Cosmology* (London: Routledge, 2008), 35. For an account of Kelvin's reasoning regarding Fourier's heat equation, see Maxwell, *Theory of Heat*, 264–65. For Kelvin's unwillingness to consider this as a proof that the universe had a beginning, see Thomson (Kelvin), "On Mechanical Antecedents of Motion, Heat, and Light" (1854), 37–38.

55. Hermann von Helmholtz, "On the Conservation of Force," in John Tyndall and William

ond law during a lecture delivered in 1854, "On the Interaction of Natural Forces." He, in fact, seems to be responsible for the language of a heat "death" of the universe. His account is worth quoting at length:

> If, however, all the bodies in Nature had the same temperature, it would be impossible to convert any portion of their heat into mechanical work. According to this we can divide the total force store of the universe into two parts, one of which is heat, and must continue to be such; the other, to which a portion of the heat of the warmer bodies, and the total supply of chemical, mechanical, electrical, and magnetical forces belong, is capable of the most varied changes of form, and constitutes the whole wealth of change which takes place in Nature.
>
> But the heat of the warmer bodies strives perpetually to pass to bodies less warm by radiation and conduction, and thus to establish an equilibrium of temperature. At each motion of a terrestrial body a portion of mechanical force passes by friction or collision into heat, of which only a part can be converted back again into mechanical force. This is also generally the case in every electrical and chemical process. From this it follows that the first portion of the store of force, the unchangeable heat, is augmented by every natural process, while the second portion, mechanical, electrical, and chemical force, must be diminished; so that if the universe be delivered over to the undisturbed action of its physical processes, all force will finally pass into the form of heat, and all heat come into a state of equilibrium. Then all possibility of a further change would be at an end, and the complete cessation of all natural processes must set in. The life of men, animals, and plants could not of course continue if the sun had lost his high temperature, and with it his light,—if all the components of the earth's surface had closed those combinations which their affinities demand. In short, the universe from that time forward would be condemned to a state of eternal rest....
>
> We must admire the sagacity of Thomson [Kelvin], who, in the letters of a long-known little mathematical formula which only speaks of the heat, volume, and pressure of bodies, was able to discern consequences which threatened the universe, though certainly after an infinite period of time (*aber freilich erst nach unendlich langer Zeit*), with eternal death.[56]

Francis, eds., *Scientific Memoirs, Selected from the Transactions of Foreign Academies of Science and from Foreign Journals: Natural Philosophy* (London: Taylor and Francis, 1853), 114–62.

56. Hermann von Helmholtz, "On the Interaction of Natural Forces," in *Popular Lectures on Scientific Subjects*, trans. E. Atkinson (London: Longmans, Green, and Co., 1912), 137–71, at 153–54. German text: Hermann von Helmholtz, *Ueber die Wechselwirkung der Naturkräfte und die darauf bezüglichen neuesten Ermittelungen der Physik: Ein popular-wissenschaftlicher Vortrag*, 2nd ed. (Königsberg: Verlag von Gräfe & Unzer, 1854), at 26.

Presumably, the reason Helmholtz added the phrase "though certainly after an infinite period of time" is that the process of heat equalization slows down as heat differences diminish. Fourier's equation of heat conduction, for example, has heat differences asymptotically approaching zero as a limit, only reached at infinity of time forward. Yet any given degree of temperature approximation, no matter how tiny, will be reached in a finite time.

Clausius draws the same conclusion of a heat death from the science of thermodynamics, famously ending his memoir "On Several Convenient Forms of the Fundamental Equations of the Mechanical Theory of Heat" (1865) simply as follows: "*1. The energy of the universe is constant. 2. The entropy of the universe tends to a maximum.*"[57] In a later lecture, he elaborates. His discussion is also worth quoting at length, because he summarizes much of what has been said in this chapter:

> One hears it often said that in this world everything is a circuit. While in one place and at one time changes take place in one particular direction, in another place and at another time changes go on in the opposite direction; so that the same conditions constantly recur, and in the long run the state of the world remains unchanged. Consequently, it is said, the world may go on in the same way for ever.
>
> When the first fundamental theorem of the mechanical theory of heat [the conservation of energy] was established, it may probably have been regarded as an important confirmation of this view....
>
> Notwithstanding that the truth of this theorem is beyond a doubt, and that it expresses the unchangeableness of the universe in a certain very important respect, we should yet be going too far were we to assume that it affords a confirmation of the view according to which the whole condition of the universe is represented as unchangeable, and all involved in never-ending cycles. The second fundamental theorem of the mechanical theory of heat [the entropy principle] contradicts this view most distinctly....
>
> The ergon [i.e., work] which the forces of nature are capable of performing, and which is contained in the existing motions of the bodies which make up the system of the universe, will be gradually converted more and more into heat. The heat, inasmuch as it always tends to pass from hotter to colder bodies, and so to equalize existing differences of temperature, will gradually acquire a more and more uniform distribution, and a certain equilibrium will be attained even between the radiant heat existing in the aether and the heat existing in material bodies. Lastly, in relation to their molecular

---

57. Clausius, "On Several Convenient Forms of the Fundamental Equations of the Mechanical Theory of Heat," in *The Mechanical Theory of Heat*, at 365. Emphasis in the original.

arrangement, material bodies will get nearer to a certain condition in which, regard being had to the existing temperature, the total disgregation is the greatest possible....

Hence we must conclude that in all the phenomena of nature the total entropy must be ever on the increase and can never decrease; and we thus get as a short expression for the process of transformation which is everywhere unceasingly going on the following theorem:

The entropy of the universe tends towards a maximum.

The more the universe approaches this limiting condition in which the entropy is a maximum, the more do the occasions of further changes diminish; and supposing this condition to be at last completely attained, no further change could evermore take place, and the universe would be in a state of unchanging death....

It yet remains an important result that a law of nature should have been discovered which allows us to conclude with certainty that everything in the universe does not occur in cycles, but that it changes its condition continually in a certain direction, and thus tends towards a limiting condition.[58]

Despite the conservation principle, the rise of thermodynamics did not, then, support the contentions of Descartes, Leibniz, Hume, and others who thought that the universe could go on as it is forever in virtue of the principles of physics alone. Rather, time has the character of an arrow. Unless an immaterial being routinely energizes the universe time is not, on the largest scale, cyclical—rather it is headed somewhere, with a *terminus a quo* and a *terminus ad quem*. If no immaterial being were acting on the universe, then time would have to have a beginning, for otherwise the universe would have already reached heat death by now, and it clearly has not.

AQUINAS'S MOTION PROOF TODAY

Corroboration from Thermodynamics

Aquinas's motion proof for God's existence is, as I have argued, fundamentally disjunctive. Clearly, the natural process of the universe either has an absolute beginning in time or it does not. If it has a beginning, then an immaterial mover must exist to get it started. If it does not, an immaterial mover must exist to keep it going forever. Behind this argument is a view

58. Clausius, "On the Second Fundamental Theorem of the Mechanical Theory of Heat" (1868), 417–19.

of material beings as naturally tending toward dissipation. Although naturally receptive of form and the higher influences that bestow it, material beings left to themselves naturally fall into relative formlessness. This view is a conclusion of philosophy, natural philosophy in particular, yet it is not opposed by modern science, in particular not by the law of inertia nor by the law of the conservation of energy. In fact, it is corroborated by the scientific laws of motion and thermodynamics, in particular by the law of entropy increase. Since the amount of free energy available to do macroscopic work is constantly decreasing in closed systems, if the universe is a closed system—if an immaterial mover is not at work on it—the amount of free energy in *it* is constantly decreasing. In that case, since the universe has not already reached a minimum of free energy, an infinite amount of time cannot have already elapsed. Hence the universe, or at least motion within it, must have had an absolute beginning, which no natural process could produce. Hence an immaterial mover would have had to set the universe in motion initially. Aquinas's disjunctive motion proof is as valid as ever. (Of course, it could also be the case *both* that the universe was set in motion by an immaterial being, *and* that it is sustained in motion by that being.)

According to contemporary cosmology, there are two possible fates for the universe: either matter is scattered so far apart that nothing can interact meaningfully with anything else anymore, and temperatures approach absolute zero—the heat death proper—or matter collapses gravitationally and gathers until it forms a black hole.[59] In either case, maximum entropy will be reached.[60] The evidence today favors the heat death scenario.[61] The universe appears to be expanding at an accelerated rate, and hence gravity will never be able to collapse it.

The laws of thermodynamics are in harmony with Thomistic natural philosophy. The first law, the conservation of energy, is a quantified and restricted version of Aquinas's principle of proportionate causality coupled with his principle that physical beings are always acted on when they

---

59. Some cosmologists favor a variant of the heat death scenario known as "the big rip." Evidence suggests that the universe is accelerating in its expansion. If this acceleration continues indefinitely, eventually space will expand so fast that all structures in the universe will be ripped apart, including even atoms.

60. John F. Hawley and Katherine A. Holcomb, *Foundations of Modern Cosmology*, 2nd ed. (Oxford: Oxford University Press, 2005), 370–75.

61. Delia Perlov and Alex Vilenkin, *Cosmology for the Curious* (Cham, Switzerland: Springer, 2017), 140.

act. The principle of proportionate causality states that something can be brought into act only by a being that already possesses that act formally or eminently. The scientific concept of energy should be compared to its Greek philosophical namesake, *energeia*, and its Latin counterpart *actus* or *actualitas*. What scientists call energy is, in philosophical terms, the lowest, inanimate form of actuality. And nothing can be brought into any given energy state except by causes possessing at least that much energy.[62] Furthermore, since, as Aquinas says, physical causes act by contact and through contrary qualities, they are simultaneously acted on by those material beings on which they act.[63] Hence in imparting energy/actuality they lose as much as they impart. (This is reflected in Newton's third law of motion, that for every action there is an equal and opposite reaction.) Hence the conservation of energy law corresponds to Aquinas's principle of proportionate causality. In fact, Mayer, who was the first to advance the conservation of energy law with a calculation of the mechanical equivalent of heat, actually appealed explicitly to a version of the principle: "Forces are causes: accordingly, we may in relation to them make full application of the principle—*causa aequat effectum* [the cause equals the effect]."[64]

For its part, the second law of thermodynamics, the principle of entropy increase, reflects the Thomistic view of elemental beings as tending toward dissolution and rest. I described this tendency in chapter 5 as the basic, lowest level of teleology in elemental beings. The tendency reflects the fact that to be a material being is to be an extended body. To be extended is to have spatially distinct parts, to have one's substance spread out and divided from itself. The tendency of a material being is, correspondingly, toward dissipation. (This is, at least in part, why human beings tend to be lazy and let themselves go, in appearance and psyche.)

62. One might object that the scientific account allows for potential energy to be converted into kinetic energy, and I have maintained above that potential energy is not actually energy. If that is the case, then sometimes there is less actuality in the cause than in the effect. I must, then, be more precise, and propose the following: kinetic energy is what Thomists call second actuality, whereas potential energy is second potentiality/first actuality. Second potentiality can proceed on its own to second actuality; it can act because it is in act (see above, chapter 1, p. 28–31, 39–42). Thus potential energy can count toward the actuality necessary in the cause to produce a given effect, saving the principle of proportionate causality.

63. Aquinas, *In III Phys.*, l. 2, n. 288 [6] and l. 4, n. 301–2 [5–6].

64. Mayer, "Remarks on the Forces of Inorganic Nature" (1842), trans. G. C. Foster, in George Sarton, "The Discovery of the Law of Conservation of Energy: With Facsimile Reproductions (nos. V and VI) of Mayer's and Joule's earliest Printed Contributions, and of a Manuscript Note by Sadi Carnot (no. VII)," *Isis* 13, no. 1 (1929): 18–44, at 27; see also 32.

But there is something minimally good about this tendency: all material beings, in virtue of their materiality, tend toward a relaxation of tension. This is the lowest level of good, a sort of lowest common denominator. Material beings also have teleological tendencies toward higher goods, representing states of excellence, arduous goods, but these tendencies can only be activated by the influence of higher, living, even intelligent principles. The second law of thermodynamics is, then, also a quantified and restricted version of a Thomistic principle. According to the second law, physical systems always tend toward equilibrium, in which potential energy is at a minimum and kinetic energy, in the form of heat, is evened out as much as possible. It too represents a state of relaxed tension.[65]

It seems then, that Thomistic natural philosophy in general, and the motion proof in particular, are fully consistent with classical mechanics, even corroborated by them. But before leaving this topic, some objections have to be considered.

Objections to the Entropic Argument:
Universe-Entropy, Infinity, and Statistical Mechanics

The relevance of the second law of thermodynamics for cosmology and natural theology has been recognized for quite awhile now,[66] and several strategies for avoiding its theistic implications have been developed. One way to avoid the conclusion that the universe must have had a beginning (without invoking an immaterial being to sustain it) is to deny that the second law of thermodynamics is valid in cosmological contexts.[67] Another way is to posit an infinity of matter, and thus an infinity of potential energy.[68] Another way is based on late nineteenth century developments in science, whereby the second law came to be interpreted as a merely statistical principle, for example, by Boltzmann. If entropy decrease is not strictly impossible, but only wildly improbable, then one could appeal to the idea that in infinite time any event with a nonzero probability will occur at some point. Thus a spontaneous, massive reduction of entropy

---

65. In St. Thomas's medieval physics, the terminus of the process of dissipation is the dissolution of all bodies into the four elements, each in its natural place. In contemporary physics the analogue seems to be the conversion of mass-energy into red-shifted photons.

66. See Helge S. Kragh, *Entropic Creation: Religious Contexts of Thermodynamics and Cosmology* (London: Routledge, 2008).

67. Kragh, *Entropic Creation*, 48, 80.

68. Kragh, *Entropic Creation*, 58–59.

in the universe could occur eventually, opening up the possibility of an eternal cyclical universe after all.[69] I will consider each of these objections in turn.

The first objection relies on the fact that the law of entropy increase has arisen from experience and experiments in terrestrial laboratories, all within a very limited region of space and time. We cannot experiment on the universe as a whole, and so it is presumptuous (so it is argued) to draw universal conclusions from limited experience. For all we know, entropy can decrease without compensation in other regions of the universe or during other epochs. Now a thorough analysis of this objection would take me too far afield into the territory of epistemology, but the following remarks should be sufficient to defuse it. Modern science arose in large part from an attempt to unify terrestrial and celestial physics. Galileo, for example, attacks at length Aristotle's (and Aquinas's) view that the heavenly realm is radically different from the terrestrial, that heavenly bodies are made out of a different kind of matter, undergo different kinds of motion, and are incorruptible and perfect unlike bodies here below. Newton's huge success was to show in detail how the bodies of the solar system obeyed precisely the same laws of motion that terrestrial bodies did. The whole contemporary disciplines of cosmology, astronomy, and astrophysics depend upon the assumption that the same fundamental laws that apply on earth apply to the rest of the universe. To deny that cosmological implications can be drawn from the laws of thermodynamics, including the second law, would be to give up the project of modern science altogether.

But one might push back on this.[70] Max Planck, for instance, reports that some people objected to Clausius's claim that the energy of the universe remains constant and its entropy increases to a maximum. They argued that "the energy and the entropy of the world have no meaning, because such quantities admit of no accurate definition." But Planck defends Clausius by pointing out that the first and second laws of thermodynamics only hold for closed systems, and that the concept of a closed system is an idealization. No system of bodies with which we can experiment is perfectly closed; external bodies and forces always affect the

---

69. Kragh, *Entropic Creation*, 56–57.

70. For some common objections to the applicability of entropy and the second law of thermodynamics to the universe, see https://en.wikipedia.org/wiki/Heat_death_of_the_universe, section titled "Opposing Views," accessed 5/11/2021.

system at least slightly, increasing or decreasing its energy and potentially decreasing its entropy. But as one expands one's defined system to include a greater and greater region, the deviation of the system from the ideal of a closed one decreases toward negligibility, so that the first and second laws hold most of all for the system of the universe as a whole (presuming no divine intervention takes place, I would add), rather than applying least of all to it.[71]

Nor does the lack of a precise formula for the entropy of the universe preclude its applicability. Some scientists (e.g., Roger Penrose[72]) are, in fact, able to give a rough calculation of the entropy of the universe as a whole. Furthermore, just because we do not yet have a universally accepted mathematical definition of the quantity does not mean that the concept of entropy has no application to the universe, but only that we have more progress to make in our understanding. In the meantime, the application of the concept of entropy to the universe as a whole is robust because it enables us to make predictions, such as that the average temperature of the universe has decreased over time.[73] This is what is in fact observed. At the time of the big bang the temperature throughout the universe was enormous, but the average temperature of the universe today can be estimated from the temperature of the cosmic microwave background, about 2.7 degrees Kelvin.

Another problem concerns the application of entropy to gravitational forces. In classic illustrations of entropic processes, such as the diffusion of a concentrated gas throughout an available space, clumped up arrangements of matter represent low entropy and spread out distributions represent high entropy. But the reverse seems to be the case with gravity: when matter clumps together gravitational entropy increases (black holes represent the maximum of entropy for gravity[74]). Low entropy for gravity would be represented by orbital systems, or diffuse material that can coalesce into orbital systems. (Matter that was so diffuse that gravity could no longer pull it together would also have a low available energy,

71. Max Planck, *Treatise on Thermodynamics*, 3rd ed., trans. Alexander Ogg (New York: Dover Publications, 1969, originally published 1917), 104–5.

72. Roger Penrose, *The Road to Reality: A Complete Guide to the Laws of the Universe* (New York: Alfred A. Knopf, 2004), 726–31.

73. $S = Q/T$, where S is entropy, Q is heat, and T is temperature. For the universe, Q should either increase as other forms of energy are converted to heat, or, eventually, stay constant (the energy of the universe is constant). Thus for entropy to increase, as the second law requires, T must drop.

74. However, the widely accepted but unobserved phenomenon of Hawking radiation would eventually evaporate black holes themselves, converting them into high-entropy photons.

at least effectively.) This is an area of ongoing research, but it is clear that the concept of entropy does apply to gravity, for it enables one to make predictions. In the early universe, when gravitational entropy was low, large-scale structure formation (of galaxies and galaxy clusters) would proceed throughout the universe. Later, when gravitational entropy is higher, large-scale structure formation would slow significantly and become rare. This is what is observed by astronomers.

It is sometimes also objected that one cannot define the entropy of a system not in equilibrium; if the universe is not now and never has been in equilibrium in the past, then its entropy could not be defined. But the inability to define the entropy of a system out of equilibrium has not stopped the science of thermodynamics from concluding that systems not in equilibrium proceed toward a state of equilibrium and then remain in it. (This is, in fact, what the second law of thermodynamics states.) There is no reason to believe that the same is not true of the universe as a whole (once again, barring divine intervention). We thus have every reason to accept the common view of cosmologists that the universe must evolve toward a condition of maximal entropy, the heat death.

The second main objection to the entropic argument has already been touched upon; it posits an infinity of matter in an infinite space. It is difficult (but not impossible, I would add) to conceive a boundary to space, and it seems unlikely to many people that all but a limited region would contain matter. But if there is an infinity of matter spread out within an infinite space, then the universe would contain infinite potential energy.[75] Hence, although potential energy is constantly being converted into kinetic energy, and thence into a thermal form—which in turn tends toward equilibrium—nevertheless the supply of potential energy never runs out, and hence the universe can go on forever, all by itself. (One can also think of this objection as denying that the universe would be a closed system even without God. Since it is infinitely large it is open to itself, so to speak.)

However, this does not establish what it is supposed to establish. At most it would suggest that no given finite time would be enough to

---

75. This can be illustrated using the case of gravity. Each particle of matter would only have a finite gravitational potential energy toward any other individual particle, since $\int_a^\infty F_G dr$ (the improper integral of gravitational force from a distance of a = surface contact to infinity) yields a finite quantity. However, each particle would gravitate toward an indefinite number of other particles, and hence there would be an indefinite sum of finite quantities of potential gravitational energy for each particle. Since there are an infinite number of such particles, the total potential energy is infinite.

exhaust the potential energy. An infinite time *would* exhaust the infinite potential energy. Consider the case of gravitational energy. An infinite number of gravitational processes, each carried on at a finite rate for an infinite time, would completely exhaust an infinite amount of energy. One way to think about this is that particles would only gravitate toward other particles that were a finite distance away. Particles standing at an infinite distance from each other would experience zero attractive force. In a truly infinite amount of time, every particle would have already clumped together with every other particle within a finite distance. No more clumping could occur. Hence all gravitational potential energy would have been converted into kinetic energy, and thence into heat, and thermal equilibrium would have been reached already. Hence the fact that the universe is not currently in thermal equilibrium proves that either the universe is not infinitely old or an immaterial power is at work within it, adding new energy or converting unusable energy back into usable energy. However, the second law cannot provide any definite upper boundary to the possible amount of past time; given any finite quantity of past time, a universe with an infinite amount of potential energy could have remained out of thermal equilibrium for a greater finite amount of time.

An important objection to my argument here, however, can be drawn from St. Thomas himself. In response to the claim that the universe must have a beginning, because otherwise the infinite number of past days could never have been traversed, Aquinas objects that "passage is always understood as being from term to term. Whatever by-gone day we choose, from it to the present day there is a finite number of days which can be passed through."[76] Now I am not arguing that an infinite past is impossible, but only that an infinite past without divine intervention is impossible. Nevertheless, Aquinas's reasoning would seem to apply here: whatever specific time one picks in the past, there is a finite duration from then to now. (On this understanding, saying that the past is infinite just means that whatever past time one picks, there is always more time further back.) If there was an infinite amount of potential energy at that time, it would not yet be exhausted. One can, of course, always pick another time further in the past, but at that time there was also infinite (and greater) potential energy, and from that earlier time till now there is still only a finite duration, insufficient to exhaust the infinite available energy.

76. Aquinas, *ST* I, q. 46, a. 2, ad 6.

In this way potential energy would not yet be exhausted even if the universe had no beginning.[77]

But recall that I demonstrated in chapter 2 that nonsimultaneous, successive causal series can be (but are not always) essentially ordered series of causes. Any identifiable process in which a closed system of bodies heads from a nonequilibrium condition to a state of equilibrium constitutes an essentially ordered causal series. When an agent places a system of bodies in a nonequilibrium condition (as the generator of a heavy body, when it generates in an upward region, does in St. Thomas's medieval physics), it causes the whole, predictable process by which that system heads toward its equilibrium condition (toward its natural place, quantity, and quality in St. Thomas's physics). Free energy is not self-explanatory; possessing free energy (being out of equilibrium) is not the natural condition of a body or system of bodies, and so requires a causal explanation. The free energy present at a given point in the process has to come from somewhere, either immediately from an external agent or from a prior state of the system in which *more* free energy was present. The series of physical interactions that constitute the steps of the process by which the system heads toward equilibrium thus constitutes an essentially ordered causal series.

In tracing the essentially ordered series of causes backward, we either come to a point where the free energy comes immediately from an external agent, or we continue backward in time from one state of the system to a previous one with more free energy, without ever coming to an external agent.

In the former case, the external agent could not be a body, for if it were it would have to possess free energy itself and then the regress would continue on, against the assumption. (And since the system in question is the universe as a whole, there is no body outside it anyways.) The external agent would have to be an immaterial being, which is what I set out to prove. But this would not show that there was a first moment in time, for there could have been prior states of the universe, before the immaterial being gave it its current supply of free energy. It would be irrelevant to what is going on now whether the unmoved mover had given the universe a supply of free energy for the first time, the second time, the billionth time, or the "infinitieth" time. If there were an infinity of previous cycles, they would constitute an accidentally ordered series.

77. I thank an anonymous reviewer for raising this objection.

In the latter case, on the other hand, in which we trace the system backward in time without ever coming to an external agent, there must have been an infinite supply of free energy, so that no finite amount of time—no finite series of physical interactions—would exhaust it. But in that case, the infinite series of past interactions would not be an accidentally ordered series, but an essentially ordered series of causes: at each moment in time, the energy condition of the system of bodies would depend essentially upon the physical interaction of the bodies in a previous condition in which they had more free energy. Hence, in virtue of Aquinas's arguments against infinite regress, the successive series of physical interactions among the bodies in the system must have had a first member. In that case, the universe would have had a beginning in time after all, and God would have to exist to get it started and give it its supply of free energy, contrary to the assumption (but this is what I set out to prove anyways).[78]

The fact remains, therefore, that unless God intervenes in it, the universe cannot have an infinite past, for otherwise all available energy would have been consumed by now, and the universe would already be in a condition of heat death.

The third main objection is the most important one. In the late nineteenth century, the concept of entropy came to be interpreted as a statistical concept, above all due to the work of Ludwig Boltzmann. Maxwell, Boltzmann, and others helped to develop the kinetic theory of gases, according to which pressure, temperature, volume, and other macroscopic, measurable quantities are functions of the number, positions, and momentums of the microscopic atoms bouncing around in a gas, which cannot be directly observed or measured. According to the new discipline of statistical mechanics, not every macroscopic state of a body is to be regarded as equally probable because not every "macrostate" represents the same number of possible "microstates," while every microscopic state is regarded as equally probable. For example, the same gas could occupy a volume of 1 cm^3 or 2 cm^3; in the latter macrostate there are many, many more different microscopic configurations that the molecules of the gas

---

78. Furthermore, if one unreasonably tried to deny that the series had a beginning, then one would have to posit the infinite amount of past time in the universe as given *as a whole*, for only as a whole could it even implausibly be claimed to provide any kind of explanation for the current state of the universe (an infinite series of boxcars pulling a caboose, rather than a finite series of them). But in that case, in infinite time the infinite universe would have consumed even an infinite supply of free energy by now, contrary to observed fact.

could occupy than in the former macrostate, and so the latter macrostate is the more probable one. Over time, it is probable that any isolated system will find its way into more and more probable states, that is, into the macrostates that can be instantiated by the largest number of microstates. Entropy is conceived as a measure of this probability, higher entropy corresponding to more probable macrostates.[79] Heat, understood as chaotic microscopic motion, is a highly probable and hence highly entropic condition. Entropy, formerly understood as a function of heat and temperature ($\Delta S = \int dQ/T$), was now interpreted as a function of the number of possible microstates: $S = k \log W$, where W is the number of microstates compatible with a given macrostate and k is Boltzmann's constant.[80]

On the statistical view it is not impossible for entropy to spontaneously decrease—that is, for a system to spontaneously bounce out of thermal equilibrium—just very highly improbable. Hence, the argument goes, given an infinite amount of time, one should expect the universe to wind down into a condition of heat death, and then, after unimaginably vast amounts of time, to randomly fluctuate so far out of equilibrium that an orderly universe with stars, planets, galaxies and organisms will evolve again, as the universe slowly winds back down to thermal equilibrium. This would go on all by itself in endless cycles, so that there could be an infinity of time past, and an infinity of time future without the influence of any immaterial being. This is a refrain of Hume's view.[81]

According to classical statistical mechanics, tiny fluctuations away from perfect equilibrium occur all the time (e.g., Brownian motion), and bigger fluctuations are possible but correspondingly less frequent.[82] Yet

79. An accessible account of these historical developments in science can be found in Christopher J. T. Lewis, *Heat and Thermodynamics*, ch. 6. A penetrating philosophical discussion of thermodynamics, entropy, and statistical mechanics is found in David Z. Albert, *Time and Chance* (Cambridge, MA: Harvard University Press, 2000), esp. ch. 2–4.

80. Although this is commonly referred to as Boltzmann's entropy formula, and does indeed derive from Boltzmann's seminal work, it was actually first given in this form by Max Planck, as is often acknowledged. The earliest publication that I have been able to find it in is Planck's *The Theory of Heat Radiation*, 2nd ed., trans. Morton Masius (Philadelphia: P. Blakiston's Son & Co., 1914, German text 1913), 119. Planck's formulation is supported by Nernst's theorem (the third law of thermodynamics), which states that the entropy of a crystalline substance at absolute zero temperature is precisely zero. This allowed for an absolute measure of entropy, rather than mere entropy differences between states. If there is only one microstate possible for a crystalline substance at absolute zero, then $S = k \log 1 = 0$.

81. See chapter 6 above, p. 199–200.

82. Thomists should hesitate about statistical mechanics insofar as it reduces qualities such as temperature and their changes entirely to quantities and to local motion. Another potential worry is that Aquinas himself rejected the existence of atoms. But the atomic assumptions of statistical

this will not block the inference from entropy to an immaterial mover. As Leo Szilard states, "if we want to use the fluctuation phenomena in order to gain energy at the expense of heat, we are in the same position as playing a game of chance, in which we may win certain amounts now and then, although the expectation value of the winnings is zero or negative."[83] The house always wins in the long run. The gambling analogy can be extended: although there is a nonzero chance that a gambler will win, say, thirty-six times his money in a given play, the amount the gambler actually wins is based on how much money he bet. If he plays long enough, he is almost guaranteed to make some big wins; however, he is also guaranteed to lose everything eventually. He loses far more often than he wins, and has less and less money to play with. Hence his big wins get smaller and smaller in absolute value. The house always wins.

In the same way, in statistical mechanics there is a nonzero though wildly tiny chance that particles interact in such a way that they become more organized and reduce entropy. However, the amount of macroscopically available energy that is gained for the universe depends in part on how much microscopic kinetic energy was involved in this spontaneous concourse. When the universe enters a heat death, the finite amount of thermal energy present is spread ever thinner in infinite space. Thus any given region has less and less energy to gamble with, and the payoffs of the rare wins gets smaller and smaller. Barring divine intervention, entropy always wins.

---

mechanics do not actually constitute a serious difficulty. One must preserve the substantial unity of natural bodies revealed in experience, but Aquinas himself allowed for distinct and differentiated integral parts—moving with respect to one another—in the case of living bodies (e.g., the heart and limbs). While he believed inanimate bodies were homogenous, there is no philosophical reason why an inanimate, substantially unified body cannot possess distinct integral parts, in motion relative to one another. Thus the atomic structure of matter can be accepted by a Thomist without sacrificing the hylemorphic unity of natural bodies. (I thank John Goyette for making this point to me in conversation.) Furthermore, even though the quality of heat cannot be entirely reduced to the local motion of atoms, atomic motion is the necessary material substrate for the quality of heat, and so statistical mechanics can legitimately treat this quantitative aspect of heat in abstraction from its irreducibly qualitative aspects. However, given that there is more to heat than microscopic motion, I have my reservations about statistical mechanics' claim that bodies can fluctuate far out of equilibrium on their own, with a tiny but definable probability. Experience does not demonstrate this, and it may be an artifact of theory. Nevertheless, since statistical mechanics is widely accepted, I will proceed in this book as if its claims are simply true.

83. Leo Szilard, "On the Decrease of Entropy in a Thermodynamic System by the Intervention of Intelligent Beings," trans. Anatol Rapoport and Mechthilde Knoller, in *Maxwell's Demon 2: Entropy, Classical and Quantum Information, Computing*, ed. Harvey S. Leff and Andrew F. Rex (Philadelphia: Institute of Physics Publishing, 2003), 110–19, at 111.

My claim is not that the amount of energy in the universe decreases (that would violate the conservation of energy[84]) but that the energy *density* of the universe approaches zero as a limit at infinite time. Recall the ground that has been covered in this chapter and the last: observable, macroscopic collisions are not perfectly elastic. Some of the energy is dissipated into heat. On the dynamical theory, however, heat itself is simply uncoordinated microscopic motion. It is often assumed that microscopic collisions are perfectly elastic so that none of the energy involved is ever lost. But this is not actually the case. Microscopic collisions constantly redistribute the kinetic energy represented by heat. In doing so, they emit electromagnetic waves, that is, radiant heat, which carries away part of the energy the bodies possessed. In fact, all bodies possessing a nonzero temperature constantly emit thermal radiation across a range of frequencies, approaching more or less to an ideal "blackbody" spectrum, with an intensity and peak frequency that rises with the temperature.[85]

Radiant heat is composed of photons. Many of the emitted photons are reabsorbed by other particles. But many of them escape into intergalactic space. Each photon carries away an amount of energy that depends on its frequency: $E = hf$, where E is energy, h Planck's constant, and f is the photon's frequency.[86] Now contemporary observation has revealed that the universe is expanding (almost all galaxies are receding from ours), and on the prevailing General Theory of Relativity, this expansion is conceived of as the expansion of space itself. Photons travelling through an expanding space undergo a "cosmological redshift"[87] that is usually distinguished from (although compared with) "Doppler redshifts" and

84. Some cosmologists in fact claim that energy conservation does *not* hold, but others claim that it does. I don't want to take a position on this, but will make my case assuming the situation most favorable to the atheist's position, namely, that energy conservation *does* hold.

85. Andrew M. Steane, *Thermodynamics: A Complete Undergraduate Course* (Oxford: Oxford University Press, 2017), ch. 19, 268. The precise mechanisms producing such radiation are complicated and involve quantum mechanics. Some explanation is the following: When charged particles or ions change speed or direction, as they must in collisions, they radiate energy away in the form of electromagnetic waves. If a molecule is electrically polarized, it too can emit photons when accelerated. Furthermore, even electrically neutral molecules can rotate and vibrate internally (at discrete energy levels), and the electrons in molecules and atoms can orbit at different energy levels. As collisions constantly redistribute thermal energy, atoms and molecules jump between different quantum states. If an atomic collision involves enough translational kinetic energy, it can kick an electron up to a higher energy level, which then emits a photon when it drops back down. This effectively converts some of the translational kinetic energy into the form of a photon. See Richard Feynman, *The Feynman Lectures on Physics*, vol. 1, sections 41-2, 41-3, and 40-5, 40-6.

86. Hawley and Holcomb, *Foundations of Modern Cosmology*, 106.

87. Perlov and Vilenkin, *Cosmology for the Curious*, 116–117.

"gravitational redshifts."[88] The cosmological redshift lowers each photon's frequency, thus reducing the amount of energy it can deliver upon impacting with a particle. If the universe is flat and infinite (careful observations have indicated that the geometry of the universe is flat to within experimental error)[89] then these photons will dissipate energy off into space and perhaps never deliver it anywhere. If the universe is closed and finite and has a spherical geometry (as it may well), then perhaps these photons could come back around and return the energy they carry away. But by that point they would have been redshifted so significantly as to be unable to return as much energy as they carried away. In fact, even if the universe does have a spherical geometry, the current understanding is that the accelerating expansion of the universe will eventually cause space to expand faster than the speed of light,[90] and thus the energy dissipated into photons will never arrive anywhere and will be lost forever.[91]

It is thus clear that the energy density of the universe approaches zero as a limit, and hence the entropy-gambler has less and less to bet with over time. The probability of winning any given amount falls so fast that it is never even remotely likely that a significant win will be made no matter how much time elapses. To put this in technical terms: if the probability function of a cosmologically significant entropy reduction approaches zero as a limit as time approaches infinity, then the total probability obtained by integrating the function from time zero to infinity can still equal much less than 1. To illustrate what I mean, suppose there were a chance equal to 1 in 10^{100} for a fluctuation that was big enough to generate our visible universe to occur in the course of a year. One might say that, given 10^{100} years it would become likely for such an event to happen. Yet if the chances fell significantly each passing year, so that after 10^{10} years they had become 1 in $10^{100,000}$, then it would be incredibly unlikely for such a massive fluctuation to *ever* occur. These are just hypothetical numbers of course; the key point is that in infinite time the chance drops to zero as the energy density drops to zero.[92]

88. Hawley and Holcomb, *Foundations of Modern Cosmology*, 279–80, 305–7.
89. Perlov and Vilenkin, *Cosmology for the Curious*, 139.
90. Perlov and Vilenkin, *Cosmology for the Curious*, 140.
91. Cp. Hawley and Holcomb, *Foundations of Modern Cosmology*, 414–15.
92. This can be put in more precise, but still abstract mathematical terms. Let C_f be a cosmologically significant fluctuation in entropy, and $p(t)$ be the probability density of such a fluctuation occurring at any given time ($t=0$ can represent now). Because the probability decreases asymptotically toward zero at a rapid enough rate, the following inequality holds: $P(C_f) = \int_{t=0}^{t=\infty} p(t)\,dt \ll 1$.

However, some might appeal to quantum mechanics and say that energetic particles can pop into existence out of even a "vacuum" with the lowest possible energy density, and that any given result always has a definite, tiny, but nonzero probability of occurring. Given an infinite amount of time, then, it *would* become probable that a random fluctuation on a cosmological scale would occur. I do not propose to deal definitively with quantum mechanical versions of the statistical objection; doing so would require giving a natural philosophical account of quantum mechanics as a whole, something I am not prepared to do. The following remarks should be sufficient for the present context.

The proposal that the whole universe is a bare, massively improbable quantum fluctuation is not very convincing. It amounts to answering the question of why the universe exists and is so orderly by saying that it just does; it is more of a refusal to see any need for an explanation than an explanation. Many materialists, however, invoke the so-called "weak anthropic principle" in an attempt to provide a kind of explanation for such a highly improbable fluctuation. (Appeal to this principle is often connected with the hypothesis of a "multiverse"; I will address this version of the objection in the next chapter, when I consider the fine-tuning of the universe for life.) They say that it should not surprise us to be living in improbable conditions, because all the probable conditions would not be able to support human life. Hence we could not possibly observe any kind of world other than a highly improbable one.

But this argument fails for two reasons. First, it does not succeed at providing an explanation of what it seeks to explain. The "anthropic principle" does explain the *connection* "if we exist, then necessarily the universe was in a special condition." But while the whole "if … then" clause (the consequence) is necessary, neither the antecedent (protasis) nor the consequent (apodosis) are necessary in themselves. What we seek is an explanation of the consequent, namely, that the universe is in a very special condition. The fact that the connection between the antecedent and the consequent is necessary does not make either proposition in itself probable, nor explain either.[93] On the atheist's view our existence certainly does not explain, in the sense of identify any kind of cause of, the universe's special life-supporting condition. According to the atheist we neither produce the universe nor are its purpose. Hence the atheist who proposes

---

93. This response was first suggested to me by Michael Bolin.

an anthropic explanation of our universe's special conditions does not *succeed* at providing an explanation of a fact that clearly calls for one.

Secondly, as Vilenkin and Perlov point out, it does not fit well with what we actually observe in the universe. The bigger the fluctuation the less probable it is. Hence if we were living in a random fluctuation, then even granting the anthropic principle we should expect to see a universe that is only sufficiently far from equilibrium to allow for intelligent life. Yet we observe innumerable galaxies in every direction. If we were living in a bare quantum fluctuation, it would be highly probable that our visible universe were much smaller than it is.[94] Richard Feynman makes a similar point: if the anthropic explanation were correct, we should expect to see a lack of order when we look toward new regions of the universe, but we don't.[95] In fact, on statistical mechanical principles, it would be far more likely that our nervous system in its current state emerged randomly out of chaos, full of vivid memories of things that never happened and sense perceptions of things that don't exist—these hypothetical nervous systems are called "Boltzmann Brains"—than that a whole universe with an orderly history of many billion years would have been generated by a random fluctuation. This "Boltzmann Brain" paradox shows that our universe is not a mere random fluctuation, since we are clearly not Boltzmann Brains.

Objections to the Entropic Argument:
Contemporary Cosmology

The currently standard, more robust option for defending an eternal universe is to couple quantum fluctuations with a process called "cosmic inflation." According to this view, the universe underwent extremely rapid exponential expansion shortly after the big bang, doubling its size in less than every nanosecond. By means of such an expansion, even quite

---

94. Perlov and Vilenkin, *Cosmology for the Curious*, 87–88. One might argue that given the nature of our visible universe life is so improbable that millions of galaxies would be needed to make the development of life on even one planet probable. Even if this were true the Boltzmann Brains described in the text would be more probable than the universe that actually exists. It should be noted that Perlov and Vilenkin support reasoning based on the weak anthropic principle if it is coupled with the multiverse hypothesis. See chapter 8 below, section titled "Confirmation of Aquinas's Teleological Argument for God's Unity," p. 282.

95. Richard Feynman, *The Character of Physical Law* (Cambrdidge, Mass.: The MIT Press, 2017), 114–16. Feynman's hope is that scientists will one day discover a new law of physics that requires the earlier conditions of the universe to be more ordered than they are today.

modest quantum fluctuations could produce effects on a cosmological scale. This theory is often extended into a theory of "eternal inflation," positing that there are an infinity of universes continually inflating within the "multiverse" at large. The gambler can thus start with a clean slate, and with an infinity of dice rolls is bound to hit the jackpot with a universe like ours eventually.

There are some pieces of evidence, observational and theoretical, for cosmic inflation,[96] and it is currently popular with cosmologists, but it is a recent theory and has not yet stood the test of time. Scientific realism does not involve giving the same weight to new theories as to well-established ones. The history of science indicates that the theory of inflation could end up being discarded, going the way of phlogiston, caloric, and the luminiferous ether. But neither can one afford to ignore more recent developments, especially when they have widespread support.

One piece of evidence for the theory was the discovery of "dark energy" in the late 1990s.[97] The universe appears to be accelerating in its expansion—contrary to what one would expect given the gravitational attraction between galaxies—and whatever is causing this acceleration is termed "dark energy." The explanation often proposed for "dark energy" is that it is "vacuum energy," the uniform energy contained in empty space that is held to explain phenomena such as the Casimir effect. In the framework of general relativity, such vacuum energy creates a *repulsive* gravitational force,[98] and it is postulated that the vacuum energy was much higher during a brief period in the early universe, driving inflation.

The theory of inflation also correctly predicts the observed density fluctuations in the early universe as observed in the Cosmic Microwave Background.[99] So far, however, another of its observational predictions has not been verified. In 2014 it was announced to great fanfare that the theory's prediction of gravity waves with "B-mode polarization" had been verified, but this announcement was retracted a year later when it became clear that galactic dust was skewing the results.[100]

A serious and well-known problem with theories such as inflation that depend on vacuum energy is the "vacuum catastrophe" or "cosmological

96. See Perlov and Vilenkin, *Cosmology for the Curious*, ch. 17.
97. See Perlov and Vilenkin, *Cosmology for the Curious*, 136–39.
98. Perlov and Vilenkin, *Cosmology for the Curious*, 84–85, 88–89.
99. Perlov and Vilenkin, *Cosmology for the Curious*, 256–60.
100. Perlov and Vilenkin, *Cosmology for the Curious*, 262–63.

constant problem."[101] The theoretical prediction of the energy density of a vacuum based on quantum mechanics yields a value that is wildly divergent from the observed value of the "dark energy" density, "by a factor of about 10^{123}." There are speculative models that might reduce this discrepancy, but no accepted way to get the vacuum energy density to come out nonzero yet quite small, as dark energy has been measured to be. [102] There is something amiss in our current understanding. Furthermore, significant discrepancies in the calculation of the rate of the universe's expansion (the Hubble constant) have emerged in the last few years, depending on what method is used to determine it.[103] This problem is referred to as the "Hubble tension," and many are suggesting that fundamental revisions in the scientific community's understanding of the physics of the universe, including dark energy, are necessary.[104] This illustrates how fluid the field is; one cannot take the latest theoretical developments in cosmology over the past forty years or so as established fact, although more well time-tested theories can be confidently relied upon, such as the Hot Big Bang cosmological framework.

But let it be granted that there was a period of inflation in the early universe, caused by a much higher level of vacuum energy that then decayed into present values. Still, *eternal* inflation has no direct evidence supporting it. Theoretical models of inflation predict that it will be eternal, but none of those models is settled science. Everything that we know about the universe indicates that explosive processes such as inflation cannot sustain themselves forever. If inflation is not an eternal process, then the conclusion that the universe must have had a beginning (if not sustained in disequilibrium by an immaterial power) is inevitable.

Moreover, even the theory of eternal inflation has a cost for the atheist. If eternal inflation were occurring, the Borde-Guth-Vilenkin (BGV) theorem proves that the process can only be everlasting in future

---

101. Dark energy is often regarded as setting the value of the cosmological constant Λ, a constant that Einstein originally added to his equations for gravity in a failed attempt to model a steady-state universe. But dark energy is not unanimously considered to be constant throughout the universe's history.

102. Perlov and Vilenkin, *Cosmology for the Curious*, 304–6. See also Hawley and Holcomb, *Foundations of Modern Cosmology*, 472–73.

103. NASA, "Mystery of the Universe's Expansion Rate Widens With New Hubble Data," accessed August 23rd, 2019, https://www.nasa.gov/feature/goddard/2019/mystery-of-the-universe-s-expansion-rate-widens-with-new-hubble-data.

104. A quick internet search for "Hubble tension" will reveal several recent suggestions for dealing with this problem.

time, not in past time. According to that theorem, if the universe is on average expanding over the course of its history (which is necessarily the case in eternal inflation theories), then its past cannot extend backward infinitely.[105] (Guth was one of the key architects of the theory of inflation to begin with.) Only if an immaterial being existed who could reverse the process of inflation repeatedly (an infinite number of times) could the universe exist with no beginning. Opponents may hope that a theory of quantum gravity is developed that avoids the BGV theorem (which depends on the reigning general relativistic theory of gravity, as does the theory of inflation itself), but no well-developed and testable theory of quantum gravity currently exists.

Finally, there is reason to think that inflation will not actually reduce the improbability of the random fluctuation required to generate our universe. Many physicists think that inflation could only occur in very precise, improbable situations, and that in order for inflation to produce a universe with entropy as low as ours, an even lower entropy, more improbable state had to precede inflation. Inflation expands the universe exponentially. If the region that inflation expands is not exquisitely smooth to begin with, inflation could not leave it relatively smooth after it is finished. But in order to explain our observed universe, it has to do this. Hence the theory of inflation, without God, leaves us in the same place as we started: the universe would have to be a massively improbable, random fluctuation, and we would have no explanation for the world we live in.[106] On the other hand, if inflation were an instrument in the hand of God, one could understand the precision exhibited in its action.

CONCLUSION

Natural philosophical reflection on general observation of nature reveals that inanimate motion tends to continue on its own after it leaves contact with the mover, but also that it constantly diminishes and cannot sustain itself forever. The history of science confirms this view. Repeatedly, developments have occurred that seemed to suggest that motion was perpetually self-sustaining, but the finitude of motion reasserted itself each time.

---

105. Perlov and Vilenkin, *Cosmology for the Curious*, ch. 22.

106. Robin Collins, "The Teleological Argument: An Exploration of the Fine-Tuning of the Universe," in *The Blackwell Companion to Natural Theology*, ed. William Lane Craig and J. P. Moreland, 202–81 (Malden, MA: Wiley-Blackwell, 2009), at 265.

This happened when the newly arisen principle of inertia was balanced with the observation that the absolute quantity of motion diminishes whenever one body comes into contact with another. It happened again when the first law of thermodynamics was followed immediately by the second law. It happened yet again when, the kinetic theory of gases and statistical mechanics seeming to guarantee that energy would always remain available in the long run, quantum mechanics and general relativity came on the scene and entailed that when particles collide, they dissipate energy by releasing photons that are then red-shifted into oblivion. One should expect that the same thing will happen with the latest developments in cosmology: if inflation proves true, it will turn out that it cannot be an eternally self-sustaining process.

The material world is dependent upon the immaterial. The material world is dead and lifeless unless energized by an immaterial being that is not subject to the laws of physics. The universe is not a closed system. Aquinas is right: either God sets the universe in motion, or sustains it in motion, or both, and in any case God must exist. Aquinas's unmoved mover argument is as valid as ever, except that now the empirical evidence at least *suggests* that the universe actually had a beginning in time, as Christians believe.

Chapter 8

Entropy, Information, and Fine-Tuning

One Living God

In this final chapter I wish briefly to explore the connections that empirical science has studied between entropy, information, life, and intelligence, indicating ways in which science confirms and corroborates Aquinas's claim that the first mover of the universe must be intelligent and alive. I will also consider the "anthropic coincidences" unearthed by contemporary physics and cosmology, which support Aquinas's teleological argument for God's unity. My presentation will be necessarily schematic; I cannot give an in-depth account of the large topics explored in this chapter, including statistical mechanics, information theory, and biology as well as fine-tuning. But it should be remembered that my goal is not to use science to prove God's existence, intelligence, life, or unity. My goal is to show that science not only does not contradict Aquinas's natural philosophical proof for God, but even lends some support to it. My account will be sufficient for such a purpose.

What are some of the ways in which science has confirmed Aquinas's position? In the first place, contemporary scientists have themselves found the thermodynamic behavior of living organisms to be quite remarkable. It is a characteristic property of living beings—one might say a defining characteristic—that unlike other physical and chemical systems they do not progress toward an equilibrium condition and then come to rest. Rather, they operate continuously in a thermodynamically unstable condition.[1] Establishing and maintaining a low-entropy condition is a property of life; all organisms maintain their own bodies in a low-entropy condition, but higher forms of life order the external environment (e.g., birds build nests and humans build houses). The unmoved mover of the universe must have this property of life; it does not have a body nor is it subject to entropy, but it does bring order to the universe, and it remains eternally capable of doing so.

Secondly, the long history of scientific reflection on the so-called "Maxwell's Demon" thought experiment has revealed that reducing entropy and avoiding equilibrium depends upon the ability to process information. Living beings, in fact, have been compared to Maxwell's Demons insofar as they can manipulate and set in order individual molecules. They contain information in their DNA and are able to discriminate between healthy and unhealthy environmental factors and react appropriately. Even unconscious, merely vegetative life thus possesses an analog of intelligence, namely, the capacity to detect things and process information. This is what enables them to avoid the decay into equilibrium. Higher levels of life participate less remotely in intelligence through the possession of conscious perception. Truly intelligent, human life possesses the capacity to organize not only its own body but external beings as well, for example, by building machines. Humans do not only act on the information contained within their own DNA, but gather and synthesize new information and autonomously construct new kinds of ordered systems.

But living organisms, since they are physical beings, cannot in the end violate the second law of thermodynamics. Individual organisms die, species go extinct, and, once the sun burns out and the energy it supplies dries up, all biological life will cease. Since the universe either had an

---

1. Erwin Schrödinger, *What is Life?*, 69: "What is the characteristic feature of life? When is a piece of matter said to be alive? When it goes on 'doing something,' moving, exchanging material with its environment, and so forth, and that for a much longer period than we would expect an inanimate piece of matter to 'keep going' under similar circumstances. When a system that is not alive is isolated or placed in a uniform environment, all motion usually comes to a standstill very soon as a result of various kinds of friction; differences of electric or chemical potential are equalized, substances which tend to form a chemical compound do so, temperature becomes uniform by heat conduction. After that the whole system fades away into a dead, inert lump of matter. A permanent state is reached, in which no observable events occur. The physicist calls this the state of thermodynamical equilibrium, or of 'maximum entropy.'" Cp. Aquinas, *ST* I, q. 18, a. 1, obj. 2 and ad 2.

absolute beginning or continues forever in motion, its low-entropy condition must be effected by a different kind of living being, one without the limitations of physicality/materiality and thus not subject to the laws of thermodynamics. This living being must have the highest kind of life, not an analog of intelligence but true intelligence. Human intelligence, with all of its limitations, is itself intelligent merely analogously when compared to the divine intelligence.

Finally, contemporary cosmology has uncovered many so-called anthropic coincidences, ways in which the universe is fine-tuned to support living organisms. The basic laws of physics, the universal constants, and the initial conditions of the universe are precisely coordinated with each other to make life possible, harmonizing in ways that they do not logically have to. Since this contingent coordination concerns the most fundamental physical characteristics of the world, and extends over the whole universe, the universe itself must be governed by a single intelligent being who can embrace in His mind all its various components and coordinate them so as to achieve His purposes. In other words, there is a single first mover for the universe, who is living and intelligent, as well as immaterial, everlasting, and immovable.

TWO PUZZLES

Although my goal is to break new ground, I start with a couple of objections to my conclusion from the previous chapter, namely that without an immaterial mover the universe would have already wound down to equilibrium by now and would remain forever thereafter in a condition of heat death. The first objection concerns what is called in the literature the "Maxwell's Demon" thought experiment. Briefly put, the nineteenth century giant of physics James Clerk Maxwell imagined a microscopic, living, physical being that could perceive the individual molecules of a gas in equilibrium and open and close a door in response to what he sees. If, for example, he opened the door only when faster than average molecules approached from the left, or slower than average ones approached from the right, and closed it at all other times, he could sort out the random molecules and produce a temperature difference (or, in some versions of the thought experiment, a pressure difference) that could later be utilized to perform work. The demon would lower the entropy of the collection of molecules without expending work or generating more entropy (one is supposed to imagine that the demon moves an idealized, frictionless door[2]). Maxwell's point was that the second law of thermodynamics, in his opinion, was of merely statistical validity; in other words, it is not physically impossible for the second law to be violated, but only extremely unlikely. Even without the demon, it is not impossible for the right molecules to bounce through an open door on their own and create a temperature difference, although this is wildly unlikely.[3]

This thought experiment gave rise to speculations about the possibility of some kind of mechanical device that might be able to extract work from a gas or other body in equilibrium. According to statistical mechanics, a gas or other body in equilibrium is not perfectly inert, but rather undergoes microscopic fluctuations away from the mean value of any of its parameters due to its thermal energy. Temperature, for example, represents the *average* translational kinetic energy of the body's molecules, but not all molecules have exactly the same energy, and as they collide with each other they redistribute their energy. This is the source of the phenomenon called "Brownian motion," that is, the wandering, chaotic motion of motes in a liquid that can be observed in ordinary microscopes. Might a properly designed machine be able to detect and harness the microscopic fluctuations and in this way to extract work at the expense of heat *without* a preexisting temperature difference? This would constitute a kind of perpetual motion machine. If such were possible, then perhaps the second law of thermodynamics is not strictly true, and the universe might have a way of staying out of—or getting out of—heat death without God's activity.

The second objection is that material bodies that can avoid equilibrium indefinitely seem in fact actually to exist. Living organisms do this. As an embryonic organism develops itself and matures, it brings a high degree of order to the raw materials that it takes in from its environment, spontaneously constructing and expanding a region of very low entropy, namely, its own body. Although the organism eventually dies and returns to equilibrium, it reproduces and multiplies itself before it does so, thus

---

2. Alternatively, one can imagine the door to be of arbitrarily small friction. In other words, the friction is imagined to be reduced to such a small amount that the entropy it generates is considerably less than the entropy reduction gained by operating the door and sorting the molecules. Such idealizations are commonly accepted in the literature, but their impractical and even unrealistic character casts doubt on the significance of many of the thought experiments.

3. James Clerk Maxwell, *The Theory of Heat*, 328–29. The first edition of this work was published in 1871.

perpetuating and extending the low-entropy condition. If a material, physical entity can do this on a small scale, then how do we know that a larger scale physical entity can't do this for the universe, or rather, how do we know that the universe can't do this perpetually for itself?

On the one hand, this second objection has an immediate and widely accepted answer: living organisms do not violate the second law of thermodynamics, for they depend on a low-entropy energy source, namely, light streaming from the sun. Living organisms receive this low-entropy energy (plants receive it directly in the process of photosynthesis, animals and fungi by eating plant matter), utilize it to do work, and then release it to the environment in the form of high-entropy heat. Biological processes thus increase entropy more than they decrease it and obey the second law. The second law says only that the entropy of a closed system cannot decrease, but an organism is an open system; to specify a closed system one must include the sun and the environment together with the organism. The sun, however, possesses a finite supply of nuclear fuel and cannot supply energy to organisms forever. Once the sun burns out, organisms must succumb to equilibrium rather quickly.

On a closer look, however, the puzzle remains. In a seminal work, *What is Life?*, one of the founders of quantum mechanics, Erwin Schrödinger, draws attention to living organisms' unique and mysterious ability to export all of their entropy outside themselves and to focus on themselves a stream of "negative entropy":

> It is by avoiding the rapid decay into the inert state of "equilibrium" that an organism appears so enigmatic.... How would we express in terms of the statistical theory the marvelous faculty of a living organism, by which it delays the decay into thermodynamical equilibrium (death)? We said before: "It feeds upon negative entropy," attracting, as it were, a stream of negative entropy upon itself, to compensate the entropy increase it produces by living and thus to maintain itself on a stationary and fairly low entropy level.[4]

As Schrödinger points out, animals find their negative entropy source in the food they eat, and plants in the sunlight they use to photosynthesize. But inanimate things are unable to find energy sources for themselves, or to utilize them "intelligently" so as to maintain their low-entropy condition.

If living organisms are physical beings that are able to bring order to

---

4. Schrödinger, *What is Life?*, 70, 73.

their own bodies by focusing low-entropy energy sources, why couldn't a more exquisite physical organism organize itself, or even its environment, by utilizing mere energy fluctuations in an energy source in equilibrium? Could an organism have such an improved ability to extract available energy from its environment that it could "feed" on these fluctuations, rather than on rich sources like sunlight? In this way the organism would constitute a true "Maxwell's Demon" capable of acting as a perpetual motion machine. One thus sees that the two objections—the one about Maxwell's Demon, the other about living organisms—are closely interrelated.

INFORMATION THEORY AND THE RESOLUTION
OF THE MAXWELL'S DEMON PUZZLE

The possibility of a purely mechanical Maxwell's Demon was disproved by the Polish scientist Marian Smoluchowski in 1912.[5] Smoluchowski's reasoning is reflected in physicist Richard Feynman's more well-known discussion.[6] In brief, in order to profit from microscopic thermal fluctuations, any mechanical device would have to be exquisitely sensitive. But that would make the operation of the device itself very susceptible to random fluctuations. Its own thermal energy would cause it to backfire just as often as it operated successfully. For example, if a gas in equilibrium were spread over two chambers separated by a trap door, one might think one could equip the door with a spring of just the right tension to yield only one way and only to molecules travelling at faster than the average speed. Over time this would decrease the average speed of the gas in one chamber and raise it in the other, thus creating a temperature difference that could be exploited to do work. However, the trapdoor and spring would itself be subject to Brownian motion and open randomly, letting the wrong molecules through and in the wrong direction. Thermal equilibrium would be maintained.

5. Marian Smoluchowski, "Experimentell nachweisbare der üblichen Thermodynamik widersprechende Molekularphänomene" ("Experimentally Demonstrable Molecular Phenomena that Contradict Ordinary Thermodynamics"), *Physikalische Zeitschrift* 13 (1912), 1069–80, and "Gültigkeitsgrenzen des zweiten Hauptsatzes der Wärmetheorie," ("Limits of the Validity of the Second Principle of Thermodynamics") in *Vorträge über die kinetische Theorie der Materie und der Elektrizität* (Leipzig: Teubner, 1914). These papers are discussed in Earman and Norton, "Exorcist XIV: The Wrath of Maxwell's Demon. Part I. From Maxwell to Szilard," *Studies in the History and Philosophy of Modern Physics* 29, no. 4 (1998): 435–471, at 444–51.

6. Richard Feynman, *The Character of Physical Law*, 116–21. See also Feynman, Leighton, and Sands, *The Feynman Lectures on Physics* (Reading, MA: Addison Wesley, 1964–66), vol. 1, ch. 46.

Smoluchowski, however, explicitly left open the possibility that a living, *intelligent* being might be able to utilize fluctuation phenomena to extract work from a system in thermal equilibrium (although he thought that even this was probably not possible).[7] In a seminal 1929 paper that helped to inspire the field of information theory, the physicist Leo Szilard explored this question.[8] In order to treat the issue as a physicist, instead of an actual living organism he considered as an analogue an inanimate device that could measure some microscopic property of a system, record the result, and then utilize the information to determine which procedure to execute so as to extract work from the system. In order to utilize the energy of the fluctuations of a system in equilibrium, any Maxwell's Demon would have to detect what kind of microscopic fluctuation was occurring, when, and where, and would then have to perform the appropriate intervention—opening the door or closing it, for example. The key to reducing entropy, therefore, is the ability to gather and process information.

Szilard calculated how great the average entropy production of making a measurement would have to be if the second law were not to be violated by the utilization of the recorded information. Then he used Fermi statistics to calculate how much entropy would be generated on average by an idealized measuring device that worked by heat conduction, and found that it was just enough to prevent the second law from being violated.[9] This means that a Maxwell's Demon is impossible. Whether it is an inanimate device or a living organism, it will inevitably generate more entropy that it disposes of. (If one does not grant all of the unrealistic idealizations found in any suggested Maxwell's Demon, e.g., frictionless doors and pistons, then it is all the more clear that no Maxwell's Demon is possible.)

A generation later information theory was born out of the study of new communication devices such as radios and telephones. The mathematical formulae for calculating the information capacity of communication channels were directly connected with the thermodynamic expressions for entropy. In the light of these studies, Leon Brillouin, a physicist

---

7. Earman and Norton, "The Wrath of Maxwell's Demon. Part I," 450–51.

8. Leo Szilard, "On the Decrease of Entropy in a Thermodynamic System by the Intervention of Intelligent Beings," in *Maxwell's Demon 2: Entropy, Classical and Quantum Information, Computing*, ed. Harvey S. Leff and Andrew F Rex, 2nd ed. (Philadelphia: Institute of Physics Publishing, 2003, 1st ed. Princeton University Press, 1990), 110–19.

9. Szilard, "On the Decrease of Entropy," 116–118.

and leading information theorist, proposed the "negentropy principle of information." According to this principle, information gathered equals an increase in negentropy (Brillouin shortens the term "negative entropy" to "negentropy"; as entropy increases, negentropy decreases, and vice versa).[10] Information about a system implies a reduction in the number of possible microstates it might be in, and since entropy is the logarithm of the number of these states ($S = k \log W$), information reduces entropy. A decrease in entropy means that the energy present is more available to do work. Information does in fact enable one to take advantage of the energy in a system, but one cannot get information for nothing. One needs to do work, utilizing preexisting negative entropy (available energy), to make an observation in the first place. Thus "negentropy → information → negentropy."[11]

Brillouin and another scientist, Dennis Gabor, considered the most obvious method by which a hypothetical Maxwell's Demon might gather information about molecules so as to "intelligently" operate, namely, by utilizing light to "see" them. They calculated how much entropy would have to be generated on average to detect a molecule with photons, as well as the entropy reduction achieved by sorting the molecules on the basis of that information. They found that more entropy was generated detecting the molecules than eliminated by utilizing the information. Once again, no real Maxwell's Demon could violate the second law.[12]

Since the late twentieth century, however, it is no longer widely accepted that making a measurement *inevitably* generates enough entropy to save the second law. As Leff and Rex write:

> The prevailing modern view is that one must not prejudice the demon's operation by assuming the use of light signals, for that is too restrictive. The fundamental question is whether measurement in general is necessarily irreversible. The clever mechanical detector (Bennett, 1987) proposed in the context of Szilard's 1929 model suggests that, in principle, the presence of a molecule can be detected with arbitrarily little work and dissipation. Bennett's scheme is compelling, but is limited to a one-molecule gas. The general

10. Leon Brillouin, *Science and Information Theory* (Mineola, NY: Dover, 2013, reprint of 2nd edition, 1962), 153, 116. When entropy increases from 5 to 6, for example, negentropy would decrease from −5 to −6.

11. Brillouin, *Science and Information Theory*, 164.

12. Brillouin, *Science and Information Theory*, ch. 13, and Gabor, "Light and Information," in Leff and Rex ed., *Maxwell's Demon: Entropy, Information, Computing*, 1st ed. (Princeton: Princeton University Press, 1990), 148–59.

question of whether measurement in a many-particle gas must be irreversible lacks a correspondingly compelling answer.… The possibility of measurement without entropy generation in a macroscopic system is not universally accepted.… Yet it is also true that there is no reason to believe that work and entropy thresholds exist for such measurements.[13]

However, even though it is not universally accepted that making a measurement inevitably generates sufficient entropy to counterbalance the gain, it is widely accepted that *erasing* information does inevitably generate a certain minimum entropy. This was proposed by Rolf Landauer in 1961.[14] "Landauer's Principle," as it has come to be known, states that an amount of entropy equal on average to at least $k\ln2$ must be added to the environment when a bit of information is erased.[15] As Charles Bennett argued in 1982, this is sufficient to preserve the second law and prevent a Maxwell's Demon from successfully operating. For no information processing device can have infinite data storage capacity and must eventually erase information and generate entropy if it is to continue to make measurements and operate.[16]

The conclusion that information erasure requires a certain minimum generation of entropy, and that this renders a Maxwell's Demon fundamentally impossible, is widely but not universally accepted. John Earman and John Norton are two of the most well-known critics. However, "the criticisms alluded to have not convinced the bulk of the scientific community that the LPB [Landauer-Penrose-Bennett] framework should be rejected."[17] Although there are ongoing debates, some recent work has in fact provided experimental support to Landauer's Principle: as the speed of the erasure operation approaches zero, the energy dissipated/entropy

13. Leff and Rex, "Overview," in *Maxwell's Demon 2*," 1–39, at 8–9.

14. Rolf Landauer, "Irreversibility and Heat Generation in the Computing Process," in Leff and Rex, ed., *Maxwell's Demon 2*, 148–56.

15. Recall that Boltzmann's entropy formula is $S=k\log W$, where S is entropy, k is Boltzmann's constant, and W is the number of microstates available for a given macrostate. The constant k is used when the base of the logarithm is e, in other words, when using the natural logarithm ($\log_e$, log, or ln, depending on the convention one wishes to use). Erasing one bit of information means taking a digit that can be either 0 or 1, and writing them all to 0. The available states are reduced from 2 to 1, and hence the entropy of the bits is reduced. The former entropy was $S=k\ln2$, and the new entropy is $S=k\ln1=0$. Hence the reduction in entropy is $k\ln2$. According to Landauer's principle, this entropy reduction must be compensated for by the generation of heat, increasing the entropy of the environment by at least $k\ln2$. Landauer, "Irreversibility and Heat Generation in the Computing Process," 162.

16. Charles Bennett, "The Thermodynamics of Computation—A Review," in Leff and Rex, ed., *Maxwell's Demon 2*, 283–318.

17. Leff & Rex, "Overview," 35.

generated decreases toward the value specified by Landauer as a limit.[18]

The scientific community has tended to support the idea that the key to using fluctuations to reduce entropy or do work is the ability to gather and utilize information about the particular fluctuations within a system. It has further supported the idea that gathering information and/or the eventual need to erase information (to open up space for new information) prevents any physical system from violating the second law in the long run. A perpetual motion machine is impossible, but a well-designed information processing machine can approximate to a perpetual motion machine. As we will see in the next section, scientists have also drawn connections between information theory and biology, and these connections shed new light on some of Aquinas's positions explored in chapter 5 above.

LIFE AND INFORMATION

When Aquinas discusses the lowest level of life, vegetative life, he says that unlike percipient life it only performs purely physical actions and only by means of physical qualities. Yet even vegetative life differs in its operation from inanimate bodies in two ways: it moves *itself* in its operation and it coordinates and moderates its operation so as to produce an orderly outcome;[19] it displays *ratio* in its structure and activity without actually being rational.[20] This idea is borne out by modern science. A multicellular organism develops itself from a relatively undifferentiated

---

18. Philip Ball, "The Unavoidable Cost of Computation Revealed," *Nature* (2012), News, https://www.nature.com/news/the-unavoidable-cost-of-computation-revealed-1.10186, accessed June 8th, 2020, and Zeeya Merali, "Demonic Device Converts Information to Energy," *Nature* (2010), News https://www.nature.com/news/2010/101114/full/news.2010.606.html, accessed June 8th, 2020. See also Massimiliano Esposito, "Landauer Principle Stands up to Quantum Test," *Physics* 11, no. 49 (2018), https://physics.aps.org/articles/v11/49, accessed June 8th, 2020.

19. *QDA*, a. 13, ad 14: "The powers of the vegetative soul are called natural powers because they do not perform any actions except those that nature performs in bodies. But they are called powers of the soul because they do this in a higher way." Translation mine. *ST* I, q. 78, a. 1, c.: "The lowest of the operations of the soul is that which is performed by a corporeal organ, and by virtue of a corporeal quality. Yet this surpasses the operation of the corporeal nature, because the movements of bodies are caused by an extrinsic principle, while these operations are from an intrinsic principle; for this is common to all the operations of the soul, since every animate thing, in some way, moves itself. Such is the operation of the vegetative soul; for digestion, and what follows, is caused instrumentally by the action of heat, as the Philosopher says." *QDP* q. 3, a. 11, c.: "The vegetative soul, however, although it does not act except by means of the aforesaid qualities [e.g., hot and cold], nevertheless its operation attains to something to which the aforesaid qualities do not extend themselves, namely to producing flesh and bone, and to fixing an end to growth, and to such like things." Translation mine.

20. See chapter 5 above, p. 156–158.

single-celled zygote into a mature adult organized out of many cells and then maintains that organization in spite of its highly unstable, non-equilibrium condition. And even single-celled organisms are highly organized, respond autonomously to their environment, reproduce themselves, and maintain their own organization. In doing these things, all organisms, utilizing only physical and chemical processes, sort the atoms and molecules found randomly in their environment and place them within their bodies in a highly intelligent way, much as a Maxwell's Demon is imagined to do to a system previously in equilibrium.

In this respect, automated, computer controlled systems can be similar to living organisms, although much less adept in their operation. A robot could be designed to sort out recyclable material and make something useful out of it, for example. (Of course the robot does not violate the second law, since as long as it operates it consumes energy provided by the local power plant. But the same thing is true of living beings, which depend on energy from the sun.) As Aquinas often says, the highest of a lower genus—in this case computers in the genus of inanimate things—approaches the condition of the lowest in a higher genus—plants and microbes in the genus of animate things.[21] Yet in *moving itself* vegetative life exceeds the condition of any computer or robot. Computer systems are set in motion by their designers, operate for a finite time, and then break down. Automated systems are in frequent need of repair and maintenance by living human beings, and they do not reproduce. Living beings, by contrast, reproduce and perpetuate their motion. As long as the energy supply from the sun remains in place, life will keep itself going.

In order to perform its vegetative functions, an organism utilizes protein-enzymes that bind to highly specific individual molecules and cause them to react in predetermined ways suited to the organism's needs.[22] Scientists have likened these enzymes to Maxwell's Demons:

> These [biological] phenomena, prodigious in their complexity and their efficiency in carrying out a preset program, clearly invite the hypothesis that they are guided by the exercise of somehow "cognitive" functions.... The enzymes function exactly in the manner of Maxwell's demon corrected by

---

21. E.g., Aquinas, *ST* I, q. 78, a. 2, c.: "That which is highest in an inferior nature approaches to that which is lowest in the higher nature."

22. Jacques Monod, *Chance and Necessity: An Essay on the Natural Philosophy of Modern Biology*, trans. Austryn Wainhouse (New York: Alfred A. Knopf, 1971), ch. 3.

Szilard and Brillouin, draining chemical potential into the processes chosen by the program of which they are the executors.[23]

These proteins are encoded for in the organism's information bearing molecule, DNA.[24] This predetermined information helps to set the organism on a certain life path. Yet the organism also responds—in predetermined ways—to information coming from outside, for it detects environmental factors on the molecular level (without conscious perception) and then utilizes the proper gene to respond appropriately to its environment.[25]

Vegetative life illustrates the intrinsic connection between self-motion—the defining characteristic of life—and intelligence—the highest form of life. Vegetative life is a distant analog of self-conscious intelligence. Higher forms of life participate in intelligence in higher ways. Animals possess conscious perception and organize not only their own bodies, but sometimes their environment as well, for example, spiders build webs, birds build nests, and beavers build dams. Nevertheless they are still bound by their instincts and the information encoded in their DNA. Humans possess true intelligence and a correspondingly higher form of life. They are self-conscious and can recognize ends, means, and the relationship between them. In so doing they can find radically new means to achieve their ends and can even set their own ends. This enables humans to understand the world, to build robust machines, and to organize their environment on a large scale.

Yet even humans are limited in the information they have, and fallible in their use of that information. We have to struggle to maintain order, and often fail and have to abandon things and projects, for example, old cars, writing projects, landscaping projects, and so on. And all living things increase entropy and dissipate energy as they operate. According to Charles Bennett, "the molecular apparatus of DNA replication, transcription, and protein synthesis, whose components are truly

23. Monod, *Chance and Necessity*, 59, 61.

24. Monod, *Chance and Necessity*, 193–196, 92–94.

25. For example: a certain gene in the E. coli bacteria codes for enzymes that enable the bacteria to metabolize lactose. To save energy, this segment of DNA is usually inactive because a repressor protein binds to it and blocks its transcription. But that same repressor protein binds to a lactose molecule when present and lets go of the DNA strand, thus initiating the synthesis of large amounts of lactose metabolizing enzymes. When the lactose is gone, the repressor protein binds again to the DNA segment and stops the synthesis of lactose metabolizing enzymes. See Monod, *Chance and Necessity*, 72–76. This is an example of the way in which vegetative life gathers and processes information. In fact, Monod discovered this process by following up on a suggestion made to him by Szilard.

microscopic, has a relatively high energy efficiency, dissipating 20–100 kT per nucleotide or amino acid inserted under physiological conditions." On the other hand, the neurons required for sense-perceptive life "dissipate about $10^{11}kT$ per discharge."[26] Hence no living thing can violate the second law of thermodynamics. It increases entropy even as it processes information, and this increase is greater than the decrease it succeeds in achieving.

It is not information *as such*, nor its acquisition, processing, or utilization that requires an increase in entropy. Information as such represents order, a reduction in the degree of uncertainty regarding a system's microstates, and is thus the opposite of entropy. It is the fact that information can only be acquired *by physical means* and can only be processed in and utilized by physical organs that are subject to friction, resistance, and other dissipative factors, that constrains an organism to increase the total balance of entropy. A being that could possess and use information without physical means would be capable of bringing order to the world and reducing the overall balance of entropy. Aquinas's unmoved mover, who either starts the universe, sustains it, or both, and is responsible for its low entropy condition, possesses the characteristic of life in an entirely immaterial way. Life is self-motion and the highest degree of self-motion is intelligent self-determination. God has this kind of life, otherwise He would not be capable of giving the universe a radical beginning and establishing its order, nor capable of setting it back in order always and in all circumstances, thus sustaining it forever. (Physical living beings are limited in terms of what sorts of disorder they can withstand and overcome. Their DNA does not possess the information to deal with any and every blow, toxin, or virus.) Science thus helps to flesh out and give concreteness to Aquinas's analogical account of life, comprising both vegetative and intelligent forms, an account according to which God is the prime analogate, alive in the truest sense.

---

26. Bennett, "The Thermodynamics of Computation," 285. Boltzmann's constant k has units of Joules per Kelvin, that is, energy divided by absolute temperature, which corresponds to Clausius's original formula for entropy, Q/T, heat (a form of energy) divided by temperature. The expression kT is frequently used in statistical mechanics and is an energy unit dependent on temperature, a unit suitable for microscopic applications. The average translational kinetic energy ($\frac{1}{2}mv^2$) of a single molecule in a gas is $3/2kT$, for example: the higher the temperature, the greater the average energy per molecule.

FINE-TUNING AND GOD'S UNITY

In chapter 5 I explained Aquinas's teleological arguments for God's existence and unity. A transcendent intelligence must be at work in the universe because natural causes are moderated and coordinated in such a way as to attain beneficial ends beyond anything that such causes could produce if left to themselves, the way that a saw and hammer can only make a table out of wood and nails if guided by the hand of a craftsman. Furthermore, since the universe as a whole demonstrates a teleological *unity*, it must fall under the providence of a single transcendent intelligence.

But this latter claim seemed much more obvious in Aquinas's day than in our own. In medieval cosmology, the universe was constituted by a series of concentric spheres, with the earth at its center. According to medieval physics, the sun, moon, planets, and stars all had important physical effects here on earth that were coordinated to make life possible and to serve human needs. But modern cosmology has transitioned from a closed world to an open universe. Is a natural philosophical argument for God's unity such as Aquinas's even plausible today?

I believe that it is. Advances in cosmology in the twentieth and twenty-first centuries have revealed an astonishing number of apparent "anthropic coincidences," ways in which the universe is "fine-tuned" to permit the existence of living organisms with complex central nervous systems. Even mainstream and atheistic scientists have supported the existence of such anthropic coincidences. Contemporary scientists and philosophers of science fall into three main camps in this regard. Some claim that these anthropic coincidences are real but point to a natural explanation, such as the existence of a "multiverse" and an observer selection effect (e.g., Stephen Hawking and Martin Rees).[27] Others deny that there really are impressive anthropic coincidences (e.g., Victor Stenger).[28] Others claim that they are real and point to God's existence (e.g., Stephen Barr, John Polkinghorne, and Robin Collins).[29] Given the

27. Stephen Hawking and Leonard Mlodinow, *The Grand Design*, (New York: Bantam Books, 2010) and Martin Rees, *Just Six Numbers: The Deep Forces that Shape the Universe* (New York: Basic Books, 2000).

28. Victor Stenger, *The Fallacy of Fine-Tuning: Why the Universe is Not Designed for Us* (Amherst, NY: Prometheus Books, 2011).

29. Stephen Barr, *Modern Physics and Ancient Faith* (Notre Dame, Ind.: University of Notre Dame Press, 2003), John Polkinghorne, "A Potent Universe," in *Evidence of Purpose: Scientists Discover the Creator*, ed. John Marks Templeton (New York: Continuum, 1994), 105–15; Robin Collins, "The Teleological Argument: An Exploration of the Fine-Tuning of the Universe," in *The Blackwell*

widespread acknowledgement of anthropic coincidences by even atheist scientists, Stenger's position is not particularly plausible, but a look at some of the evidence will help.

Evidence for Fine-Tuning

Contemporary science has discovered a number of facts that ultimately show that there is a teleological unity to our universe. The goal—whether ultimate or subordinate—toward which all things are ordered is the existence of living organisms. Organisms require a complex chemistry and are composed of about 25 different elements,[30] of which the most important are carbon (atomic number 6), hydrogen (1), oxygen (8), nitrogen (7), phosphorus (15), and sulfur (16), but even heavier elements such as iron (atomic number 26) or even iodine (53) can be important. These same elements are combined into an enormous variety of different biomolecules to fulfill different purposes, each enzyme, for example, having a very specific, unique function. These biomolecules are in turn organized into different types of cells, which in turn compose different types of tissues and organs, which in turn compose different types of organisms. The different biomolecules, despite having different immediate purposes, all serve the same ultimate goal: enabling the organism to live and thrive. The different elements out of which the biomolecules are formed are themselves composed of different combinations of the same subatomic particles: protons, neutrons, and electrons.

Living organisms depend upon the existence of a habitable planet stocked with the above mentioned elements, with a suitable temperature, and containing liquid water. It must also orbit a star that can provide a source of low-entropy energy. This has come about in our universe in the following manner: the nuclei of elements heavier than hydrogen (atomic number 1) and helium (2) are forged out of protons and neutrons in the nuclear furnaces of stars and made available to planets when supernova explosions eject these elements into the interstellar medium. The stars must coalesce into galaxies so that this material is not lost to empty space. It is only the second generation of stars, formed out of material that has

---

Companion to Natural Theology, ed. William Lane Craig and J. P. Moreland, 202–81 (Malden, Mass.: Wiley-Blackwell, 2009) and "Evidence for Fine-Tuning," in *God and Design: The Teleological Argument and Modern Science*, ed. Neil A. Manson, 178–99 (New York: Routledge, 2003).

30. Barr, *Modern Physics and Ancient Faith,* 119, referring to human bodies in specific.

been ejected from a prior generation of stars, that can form solar systems with rocky planets orbiting about them, suitable for life.

Our own planet is kept warm by the sun but also deep inside by the decay of heavy, radioactive elements. This keeps the metal core partly liquid, and since the earth rotates relatively rapidly, this metal core generates a magnetic field that protects our earth from highly energetic particles streaming from the sun, which could destroy sensitive chemical compounds. This magnetic field, which Mars lacks, is necessary for the existence of life on the surface of our planet.[31]

For all of this to come into place in orderly sequence and provide the necessary environment for life, a process spanning billions of years and utilizing at least a whole galaxy worth of material is required. In fact, it requires much more than that, since to last long enough, the universe must be vastly bigger than a single galaxy.[32]

For all of this to happen, the initial conditions of the universe as well as the strength of its four fundamental forces (gravity, electromagnetism, the strong nuclear force, and the weak nuclear force) must be coordinated with each other into a complex, teleological unity. The following examples will illustrate what I mean. First, the strength of gravity—reflected in the value of the gravitational constant G—must be coordinated with the initial mass density and expansion velocity of the Big Bang. Otherwise the universe would have collapsed into a big crunch early in its history, or each bit of material would have been carried so far away from all the others that no structures would have had time to form.[33] Since the observable universe is roughly homogenous and isotropic overall, this coordination of gravity with mass density must have covered at least every part of the initial universe that later expanded into a part of the observable region of our present universe.

Furthermore, it has been argued that the strength of gravity has to be within a narrow range and properly adjusted to the strength of electromagnetism in order for stars of the right sort to stably exist. Stars have to produce the right sort of elements, especially a sufficient amount of carbon and oxygen, and must expel those elements into the interstellar medium. And they must also emit light in the right frequency so as to

<hr>

31. Geraint F. Lewis and Luke A. Barnes, *A Fortunate Universe* (Cambridge: Cambridge University Press, 2016), 83–85.

32. Polkinghorne, "A Potent Universe," 111.

33. Lewis and Barnes, *A Fortunate Universe*, 166–167.

be useful for powering complex chemical reactions. If their light is too energetic (e.g., primarily ultraviolet) it will blast most molecules apart, and if it is too weak (e.g., primarily infrared) it will not be able to activate the necessary chemical reactions on the habitable planet. If gravity were weaker or stronger, and were not coordinated with the strength of electromagnetism, the right sort of stars would not exist, or would not exist long enough for complex life to evolve.[34] The relative strengths of gravity and electromagnetism also determine the effective strengths of ordinary materials, since electromagnetic forces determine their intrinsic strength and gravity determines the amount of weight/pressure they are subject to.[35]

The strength of the electromagnetic force must also be coordinated with the strength of the strong nuclear force. The nuclei of all elements are made out of protons and neutrons. The neutrons are electrically neutral, but all the protons are positively charged. They thus repel each other, and would not stick together unless the strong nuclear force—which only acts over very minute distances—held them together. The heavier the element, the more protons there are in its nucleus, and the stronger the electromagnetic repulsion experienced within the nucleus. Hence the relative strengths of these two forces determine which elements can and cannot exist. Their ratio is such as to permit the existence of elements up to uranium, thus allowing for the elements needed to compose living organisms and to heat the interior of the earth radioactively.[36]

Moreover, the relative strengths of these two forces determines the energy level at which carbon resonates, and this is very precisely positioned to make the synthesis within stars of nuclei heavier than helium (atomic number 2) possible, and in particular to produce good quantities of carbon and oxygen, so essential to living organisms.[37] This is one of the more well-known anthropic coincidences, first indicated by the atheist astronomer Fred Hoyle in the middle of the twentieth century. In his time there was a serious puzzle as to how the nuclear synthesis of elements could possibly get past the initial stage (the stage at which helium is produced). Hoyle realized that *if* carbon resonated at a precise energy

---

34. Lewis and Barnes, *A Fortunate Universe*, 106–111. Although it does not affect the argument here, I should be clear that, on metaphysical and religious grounds, I believe that human beings can only come to exist by a direct, new, creative act of God. Their bodies are prepared for by a natural process of evolution, but their immaterial souls cannot arise through a natural process.

35. Collins, "Evidence for Fine-Tuning," 189–90.

36. Barr, *Modern Physics and Ancient Faith*, 125–26.

37. Collins, "Evidence for Fine-Tuning," 183–86.

level, *then* there would be a clear pathway to synthesize all the heavier elements within stars, and in the precise, relative abundances in which they are observed to exist in the universe today. Experimental research was then done and the proper resonance level was found to exist. This was an astounding and fortuitous coincidence.[38]

The strength of the weak nuclear force is also important. As cosmologists Delia Perlov and Alex Vilenkin state:

> When a massive star runs out of nuclear fuel, its core collapses in a supernova explosion. The strength of the weak interaction is perfectly suited to allow neutrinos to stream out of the core and drag along the outer layers of the star. This is a critical part of the cycle that enriches the interstellar medium with heavy elements. If weak interactions were much stronger, neutrinos would remain stuck in the core. If they were much weaker, neutrinos would stream out without dragging along other particles.[39]

Furthermore, the weak force is responsible for radioactive β decay. The electromagnetic and strong forces are responsible for α decay. (Radioactive decay transforms one element into another while releasing energy.) These are adjusted in such a way as to leave many elements stable—either indefinitely or for very large periods of time—while also leaving pathways, nuclear decay series, for certain heavy elements to decay radioactively over huge periods of time, eventually stopping at the element lead. Having more radioactivity could be hazardous to the health of living organisms, but without the radioactive heating of the Earth's interior, it would not remain hospitable to life.[40]

One final fine-tuning fact concerns entropy and the initial condition of the universe. The second law of thermodynamics, as I have explained before, requires entropy to increase from the past to the future. The standard statistical mechanical explanation of this fact is that any system will tend to occupy more and more probable states over time, higher entropy representing more probable states. But the argument is widely acknowledged to work in reverse: it is overwhelmingly more likely that the current state came *from* a higher entropy condition than from a lower one. If the current state is a low entropy, unlikely one, then a lower entropy state in the past is even more unlikely. Hence statistical mechanics would lead one to expect that entropy does not decrease toward the past, unless the

---

38. Barr, *Modern Physics and Ancient Faith*, 121–23.
39. Perlov and Vilenkin, *Cosmology for the Curious*, 303.
40. Lewis and Barnes, *A Fortunate Universe*, 82–91.

universe just happened to *start* in a very improbable, very low entropy condition. How improbable would the initial condition of our universe have been? The atheist astronomer Roger Penrose has calculated that the probability of the universe being in the initial condition it had to be in, for the universe to have the kind of life-permitting history it has in fact had, is roughly 1 in $10^{10^{123}}$.[41]

Confirmation of Aquinas's Teleological Argument for God's Unity

There are other important cases of fine-tuning in the literature, including the fine-tuning of the masses of particles via the Higgs field,[42] and the possible fine-tuning of the cosmological constant.[43] But what all this amounts to is that the fundamental forces (gravity, electromagnetism, the strong nuclear force, and the weak nuclear force), the most important particles (proton, neutron, electron, photon, and neutrino), and the initial conditions of our universe seem to be teleologically unified so as to promote complex living organisms with a long evolutionary history. Aquinas's argument holds that such teleological unity requires unity in its intelligent cause. This argument is not undercut by the conclusions of modern science, but can reasonably claim confirmation. God coordinated the basic features of the universe so as to set the stage for the creation of life.

God fine-tunes the universe in several very different ways. As Creator He establishes the natures of things. As mover He sets in motion and/or sustains in motion, at times even redirecting motion (whenever miracles occur). The fine-tuned initial conditions of the universe are determined in part by God as mover. The most fundamental laws of nature are determined by God as Creator. The constants/strengths of the forces are an ambiguous case. If these are physically unchangeable, as they were long held to be, then they would be determined by God as Creator. However, if they are set by "symmetry breaking" processes and the energy

41. Collins, "The Teleological Argument," 220; Roger Penrose, *The Road to Reality: A Complete Guide to the Laws of the Universe* (New York: Alfred A. Knopf, 2005), 726–32; Lewis and Barnes, *A Fortunate Universe*, 124–28, 318–19.

42. Barr, *Modern Physics and Ancient Faith*, 126–29.

43. Barr, *Modern Physics and Ancient Faith*, 129–30; Collins, "Evidence for Fine-Tuning," 180–82 and "The Teleological Argument," 215–20. So little is understood about dark energy, the proposed inflaton field, and other factors that relate to the cosmological constant that I find this case of fine-tuning very uncertain and speculative.

landscapes of various fields, as many modern theorists hold, then they may be determined by God as a mover.

Before I conclude, however, I should briefly address the possibility that anthropic coincidences could be explained by a multiverse and an observer selection effect, rather than by God. According to this view, only a tiny fraction of universes can support life, but we can only encounter life-permitting universes, not any of the vastly greater number of other universes—because we could not possibly exist in them so as to observe them. There is, of course, a vibrant debate in the literature about this idea, and I cannot give it an adequate treatment here. However, there are several problems with the atheist position. First, John Leslie proposed a good analogy for the view that observer selection effect makes our universe unsurprising and not in need of explanation. Suppose someone is condemned to execution and placed before a large firing squad. After the guns have fired, he finds himself alive and unhurt, every member of the squad having shot wide. According to the reasoning of atheists like Rees and Hawking, he should not be surprised at his continued life, because he could not have been alive to observe any other result! This is clearly wrong; the survivor is right to look for an explanation for what happened to him (or rather, what didn't happen), and in the same way observer selection effect (the "weak anthropic principle") cannot render the fine-tuning of our universe unsurprising and not in need of an explanation.[44] Of course, *if* we are alive, *then* necessarily the conditions for life obtain. But even if the connection between two propositions is not a cause of wonder, that does not mean that the truth of the propositions themselves is not a cause of wonder. What it means is that the two connected propositions are either together a cause for wonder, or together not a cause for wonder. In this case, they clearly are a cause of wonder, and call for an explanation.

Secondly, even if a multiverse did exist, it would still have to have just the right sort of laws to generate myriads of universes *each with different parameters and conditions*, and with the ability to give them life-permitting characteristics.[45] Hence the need for divine fine-tuning would only be pushed up a level, not eliminated.

Third, unless the different "universes" interacted with each other, the

---

44. John Leslie, "Anthropic Principle, World Ensemble, Design," *American Philosophical Quarterly* 19, no. 2 (1982): 141–51, at 150.

45. Barr, *Modern Physics and Ancient Faith*, 153–54; Collins, "The Teleological Argument," 263–65.

other universes would be unobservable in principle, and hence not within the domain of scientific investigation. The existence of a multiverse would be a philosophical theory (which is not always a bad thing!) and an extravagant one at that. If the different universes do interact with each other, there must be testable predictions about their effects on one another. But it is difficult to identify any (although some cosmologists suggest some possibilities[46]) and certainly none have been verified.[47]

A final problem with the nontheistic view is the "Boltzmann Brain" issue.[48] On a purely chancy, statistical mechanical account, it is far less improbable that observers with human brain states like ours would have spontaneously congealed out of pure chaos, with false memories and future expectations that will not be realized, than that a whole universe with innumerable galaxies *and* our brains inside it would have arisen out of a chaos and gone through such a complex, orderly history of billions of years, leaving us with true memories and future expectations that would largely be fulfilled. Of course, we cannot take seriously the possibility that we are "Boltzmann Brains." Hence, if one is to hold that we came to exist merely by chance, one has to have good reason to believe that it is less improbable that a universe-generating multiverse exists—and one of such a kind that it would produce orderly, life-permitting universes more frequently than Boltzmann Brains—than that Boltzmann Brains would congeal out of pure chaos. This is true even if observer selection effect did carry significant weight, for the weak anthropic principle would only lead us to expect that we inhabit the most likely universe for an observer to inhabit. (The long history of the universe described above is only necessary for the presence of life *if* life is to come about by an intelligible, natural process rather than by a purely random fluctuation. If God exists and is an intelligent being, the former is much more likely than the latter.)

---

46. Perlov and Vilenkin, *Cosmology for the Curious*, 284–86,

47. Perlov and Vilenkin, in *Cosmology for the Curious*, 316–19, do suggest one type of empirical support that they say may be "indirect evidence" (286) for the multiverse, but it consists only in that the observed value of dark energy is within a range that permits the formation of very many galaxies, and thus potentially many observers. They argue that, across all the universes in a multiverse, most observers would find themselves within a universe with a value of dark energy like ours. More finely-tuned universes with higher numbers of observers would be rarer and thus contribute less to the total number of possible observers, and less finely-tuned universes would have too few observers to contribute much to the total number. We find ourselves within one standard deviation of the value of dark energy that most observers would see, so they argue. But this is not really observational evidence of another universe or of its effects on ours, and furthermore the evidence fits the hypothesis that the universe is divinely fine-tuned for life equally well.

48. See Collins, "The Teleological Argument," 266–71.

It is safe to say, then, that contemporary cosmology has unearthed some important evidence for the teleological unity of our world, confirming Aquinas's natural philosophical argument for God's unity. And I have shown above that there is plenty of reason to think that contemporary science can provide confirming evidence for Aquinas's claim that God is intelligent and living. Aquinas's First and Fifth Ways are robust and persuasive, and they demand the serious consideration of contemporary philosophers. Thomists should not avoid philosophical engagement with contemporary science, but rather embrace it.

A Perennially Relevant Proof

Aquinas's proof for an unmoved mover is a philosophical proof, not a scientific one. As such it depends upon conceptual analysis and reflection upon human experience, rather than detailed mathematical work based upon precise data gathered from artificially controlled experiments. On a certain level, therefore, the second part of this book is in itself unnecessary; Aquinas's proof can stand on its own and does not need authorization from science. Truth cannot conflict with truth, however, and so Aquinas's proof and valid science must be shown to be consistent with one another. As a scientific realist I cannot take the easy way out by claiming that science cannot possibly affect or cast doubt on Aquinas's philosophy because science is merely a mental construction with predictive capacity and instrumental value, and it does not uncover the way the world actually is. I don't accept this picture of science, and at any rate, such an approach would lead most of our contemporaries to dismiss Thomism as reactionary. Hence there is a need to integrate Thomistic philosophy with science, especially when one of its central arguments—the motion proof—seems to run counter to basic physics. And so I have had to delve into modern physics and undertake the task of detailed reconciliation.

The historical approach to physics I have used has been strategic. In general, an historical approach to science enables a deeper understanding of its conceptual framework. The work of a philosopher always requires deep conceptual analysis, and for my particular task, gesturing toward the second law would have been thoroughly unconvincing. To rejuvenate Thomistic natural philosophy on the contemporary stage requires thorough engagement with the basic structures of physics, rather than superficial appeal to laws and facts as presented in introductory textbooks.

My historical work, moreover, has uncovered a pattern: more than once a new development in physics has appeared to sanction perpetual motion, but each time further developments proved this impossible, although the dialectical process sharpened our understanding of the precise sense in which perpetual motion is impossible. In Aquinas's physics, all motion must come to an end when it reaches a defined terminus. The development of inertia opened the door to perpetual motion, but Newton showed that friction, resistance, and other factors would diminish motion, and that the only motion that could be perpetual would be straight-line motion off into endless empty space. Orbital motion and ordinary motion here on earth cannot continue forever on its own. Then the development of the mechanical theory of heat and the principle of the conservation of energy once again seemed to open prospects for perpetual motion, but along came the second law of thermodynamics and the door was closed. Then statistical mechanics arose, suggesting that there was a tiny but nonzero chance for entropy to reduce all on its own, so that the universe could go on forever, without beginning or end. But then quantum mechanics and general relativity arose, implying that energy would be radiated away as photons that would undergo cosmological redshift, and contemporary cosmology indicated that the universe began in a big bang and would end in a heat death. In the history of science, it has *never* been a universally accepted, uncontroversial claim that the universe could go on as it is without beginning or end.

The takeaway from this is that normal sense experience speaks the truth, and natural philosophy can be confident in its analysis: natural bodies do not have the power to continue in motion forever. They are destined toward some condition, and when they reach it they stop. The episodes in the history of science that I have recounted in fact provide inductive confirmation of this philosophical fact. Thinkers will continue to come up with scientific theories to avoid the conclusion, but they will always be defeated by the truth in the end, although their theories may deepen our understanding of the truth along the way. The same thing will be true of the unsettled contemporary theories of cosmic inflation. Whether inflation turns out to be true or not, it will not show the universe to be capable of continuing forever, without beginning or end, all on its own, for that would contradict the basic nature of bodily being.

What has this book accomplished? The first part has provided a more accurate historical analysis of Aquinas's motion and teleological proofs for God's existence than any heretofore, and that alone is worthwhile. The First Way does not claim that things would freeze in place instantly without a mover moving them. Rather, they would proceed toward their natural places and conditions and then rest. The motion proof works by a disjunction: either the universe has a beginning or it does not. If it has a beginning, God exists so as to start it. If it does not have a beginning, God exists to sustain it in motion, otherwise it would have come to rest by now.

In the second part of the book, I have further shown the robustness and enduring relevance of Aquinas's argument. It is not debunked by inertia but supported by thermodynamics and cosmology. Science does not conflict with the proof, but in fact provides additional confirmation of its claims. Furthermore, the picture of the universe and its history that modern science has given us supports Aquinas's teleological argument for God's existence, intelligence, and unity, and it supports Aquinas's understanding of life as self-motion, participating in various degrees in the paradigm of life, namely intelligence.

I have also given a Thomistic, natural philosophical analysis of inertia, gravity, and the two laws of thermodynamics, and indicated in many places how various scientific concepts can be integrated into Thomistic philosophy. This has the potential to breathe new life into Thomistic philosophy of nature and opens avenues for an attractive integration of Thomism with contemporary science. This has to happen in order for Thomistic philosophy to be competitive in the contemporary debate, in other words, in order for Thomists to lead God's people to the truth. We have a duty not to hide our light under a bushel basket but to let it shine. We have to wade into the forum, where people are at, although discerningly, seeing the opportunities where they really exist.

Bibliography

Albert, David Z. *Time and Chance*. Cambridge, MA: Harvard University Press, 2000.

Aquinas, St. Thomas. *Commentary on Aristotle's* De Anima. Translated by Kenelm Foster, OP, and Silvester Humphries, OP. Notre Dame, IN: Dumb Ox Books, 1994.

———. *Commentary on Aristotle's* Metaphysics. Translated by John P. Rowan. Notre Dame, Ind.: Dumb Ox Books, 1995.

———. *Commentary on Aristotle's* Physics. Translated by Richard J. Blackwell, Richard J. Spath, and W. Edmund Thirlkel. South Bend, Ind.: Dumb Ox Books, 1995.

———. *Commentary on the Book of Causes*. Translated by Vinent A. Guagliardo, OP, Charles R. Hess, OP, and Richard Taylor. Washington, DC: The Catholic University of America Press, 1996.

———. *Commentary on the Gospel of John*. 3 volumes. Translated by Fabian Larcher, OP, and James A. Weisheipl, OP. Washington, DC: The Catholic University of America Press, 2010.

———. *In Duodecim Libros Metaphysicorum Aristotelis Expositio*. Edited by M. R. Cathala and R. M. Spiazzi. Turin: Marietti, 1971.

———. *In Octo Libros Physicorum Aristotelis Expositio*. Edited by P. M. Maggiolo, OP. Turin: Marietti, 1954.

———. *In Aristotelis Libros De Caelo et Mundo, De Generatione, Meteorologicorum Expositio*. Edited by Raymund Spiazzi. Turin: Marietti, 1950.

———. *Liber de Veritate Catholicae Fidei contra errores Infidelium seu Summa Contra Gentiles*, ed. Ceslai Pera, OP, Peter Marc, OSB, and Peter Caramello. Turin: Marietti, 1961.

———. *Light of Faith: The Compendium of Theology*. Translated by Cyril Vollert, SJ. Manchester, NH: Sophia Institute Press, 1993.

———. *On Being and Essence*. Translated by Armand Maurer. Toronto: Pontifical Institute of Mediaeval Studies, 1968.

———. *On the Power of God*. Translated by English Dominican Fathers. Eugene, Oreg.: Wipf and Stock, 2004.

———. *On Truth*. 3 volumes. Translated by Robert W. Mulligan, James V. McGlynn, and Robert W. Schmidt. Indianapolis: Hackett, 1994.

———. *Quaestiones Disputatae*. Volume II. Edited by P. Bazzi, Mannes Calcaterra, Tito S. Centi, E. Odetto, and P. M. Pession. 10th edition. Turin: Marietti, 1965.

———. *Opera omnia iussu impensaque Leonis XIII P.M. edita*. Rome: Commisio Leonina, 1882–.

———. *Scriptum super libros Sententiarum magistri Petri Lombardi episcopi Parisiensis.* Edited by P. Mandonnet and M. F. Moos. Paris: P. Lethielleux, 1929–56.

———. *Summa Contra Gentiles.* 5 volumes. Translated by Anton C. Pegis, James Anderson, Vernon J. Bourke, and Charles O'Neil. Notre Dame, IN: University of Notre Dame Press, 1975.

———. *Summa Theologiae.* Translated by Fr. Laurence Shapcote, OP. Edited by John Mortensen and Enrique Alarcón. Lander, WY: The Aquinas Institute for the Study of Sacred Doctrine, 2012.

———. *Super Evangelium Sancti Ioannis Lectura.* Edited by Raphaelis Cai. 6th edition. Turin: Marietti, 1972.

———. *Super Librum De Causis Expositio.* Edited by H. D. Saffrey. Louvain: Société Philosophique-Nauwelaerts, 1954.

———. *The Division and Methods of the Sciences: Questions V and VI of the Commentary on the* De Trinitate *of Boethius Translated with Introduction and Notes.* 4th edition. Translated by Armand Mauer. Toronto: Pontifical Institute of Mediaeval Studies, 1986.

———. *Treatise on Separate Substances: A Latin-English Edition of a Newly Established Text Based on 12 Mediaeval Manuscripts.* Edited and translated by Francis J. Lescoe. West Hartford, CT: Saint Joseph College, 1963.

Aristotle. *The Basic Works of Aristotle.* Edited by Richard McKeon. New York: Random House, 2001.

———. *Physica.* Edited by W. D. Ross. Oxford: Clarendon Press, 1973.

Ashley, Benedict, OP. *The Way toward Wisdom: An Interdisciplinary and Intercultural Introduction to Metaphysics.* Notre Dame, Ind.: University of Notre Dame Press, 2006.

Avicenna. *The Metaphysics of* The Healing. Edited and translated by Michael E. Marmura. Provo, UT: Brigham Young University Press, 2005.

Augros, Michael. "Ten Objections to the *Prima Via.*" *Peripatetikos* 6 (2007): 59–101.

———. *Aquinas on Theology and God's Existence: The First Two Questions of the* Summa Theologiae *Newly Translated and Carefully Explained.* Neunkirchen-Seelscheid: Editiones Scholasticae, 2019.

Bailey, Andrew M. "Thomas' Lesser Way: A Critique." *Ars Disputandi* 6, no. 1 (2006): 6–16.

Baldner, Steven. "Thomas Aquinas and Natural Inclination in Non-Living Nature." *Proceedings of the American Catholic Philosophical Association* 92 (2018): 211–22.

Barnett, Martin K. "Sadi Carnot and the Second Law of Thermodynamics." *Osiris* 13, no. 1 (1958): 327–57.

Barr, Stephen M. *Modern Physics and Ancient Faith.* Notre Dame, IN: University of Notre Dame Press, 2003.

Bennett, Charles H. "Demons, Engines and the Second Law." *Scientific American* 257, no. 5 (1987): 108–16.

Blackwell, Richard J. "Descartes' Laws of Motion." *Isis* 57, no. 2 (1966): 220–34.

Boyer, Carl B. "Commentary on the Papers of Thomas S. Kuhn and I. Bernard Cohen." In *Critical Problems in the History of Science,* edited by Marshall Clagett, 384–90. Madison, WI: The University of Wisconsin Press, 1959.

Brillouin, Léon. "Life, Thermodynamics, and Cybernetics." In *Maxwell's Demon:*

Entropy, Information, Computing, edited by Harvey S. Leff and Andrew F. Rex, 89–103. Princeton, NJ: Princeton University Press, 1990.

———. *Science and Information Theory*. Mineola, NY: Dover, 2013.

Brock, Stephen L. "The Causality of the Unmoved Mover in Thomas Aquinas's *Commentary on Metaphysics* XII." *Nova et Vetera* 10, no. 3, English edition (2012): 805–32.

Brown, Patterson. "Infinite Causal Regression." *The Philosophical Review* 75, no. 4 (1966): 510–25.

Buridan, John. *Super Octo Libros Physicorum Aristotelis*. Paris: 1509.

Callender, Craig. "Measures, Explanations and the Past: Should 'Special' Initial Conditions be Explained?" *The British Journal for the Philosophy of Science* 55, no. 2 (2004): 195–217.

Cardwell, D. S. L. *From Watt to Clausius: The Rise of Thermodynamics in the Early Industrial Age*. Ithaca, NY: Cornell University Press, 1971.

Carnot, Sadi, Emile Clapeyron, and Rudolf Clausius. *Reflections on the Motive Power of Fire and other Papers on the Second Law of Thermodynamics by É. Clapeyron and R. Clausius*. Edited by Eric Mendoza. Mineola, NY: Dover, 1988.

Clarke, Samuel. *A Demonstration of the Being and Attributes of God and Other Writings*. Edited by Ezio Vailati. Cambridge: Cambridge University Press, 1998.

Clausius, Rudolf. "On the Second Fundamental Theorem of the Mechanical Theory of Heat." *Philosophical Magazine*, 4th series, vol. 35, no. 239 (June 1868): 405–19.

———. *The Mechanical Theory of Heat with its Applications to the Steam-Engine and to the Physical Properties of Bodies*. Edited by T. Archer Hirst. London: John van Voorst, 1867.

Cohoe, Caleb. "There Must Be a First: Why Thomas Aquinas Rejects Infinite, Essentially Ordered Causal Series." *British Journal for the History of Philosophy* 21, no. 5 (2013): 838–56.

Collins, Robin. "Evidence for Fine-Tuning." In *God and Design: The Teleological Argument and Modern Science*, edited by Neil A. Manson, 178–99. New York: Routledge, 2003.

———. "The Teleological Argument: An Exploration of the Fine-Tuning of the Universe." In *The Blackwell Companion to Natural Theology*, edited by William Lane Craig and J. P. Moreland, 202–81. Malden, MA: Wiley-Blackwell, 2009.

Copernicus, Nicholas. *On the Revolutions of Heavenly Spheres*. Translated by Charles Glenn Wallis. Amherst, NY: Prometheus Books, 1995.

Côté, Antoine. "The Five Ways and the Argument from Composition: A Reply to John Lamont." *The Thomist* 61, no. 1 (1997): 123–31.

Craig, William Lane. *The Kalām Cosmological Argument*. New York: Barnes & Noble, 1979.

———. "The Teleological Argument and the Anthropic Principle." In *The Logic of Rational Theism: Explanatory Essays*, ed. William Lane Craig and Mark S. McLeod, 127–53. Lewiston, NY: The Edwin Mellen Press, 1990.

Decaen, Christopher A. "The Impossibility of Action at a Distance." In *Wisdom's Apprentice: Thomistic Essays in Honor of Lawrence Dewan, O.P.*, edited by Peter A. Kwasniewski, 173–200. Washington, DC: The Catholic University of America Press, 2007.

Descartes, Rene. *Principia Philosophiae*. Amsterdam: Elsevier, 1644.

———. *The Philosophical Writings of Descartes*. 3 volumes. Translated by John Cottingham, Robert Stoothoof, and Dugald Murdoch. Cambridge: Cambridge University Press, 1984–91.

———. *The World and Other Writings*. Translated by Stephen Gaukroger. Cambridge: Cambridge University Press, 1998.

Dewan, Lawrence, OP. "St. Thomas and Infinite Causal Regress." In *Idealism, Metaphysics and Community*, edited by William Sweet, 119–30. Aldershot: Ashgate, 2001.

Dodds, Michael J., OP. "From the Action of Creatures to the Existence of God: The First Way, Science, and the Philosophy of Nature." *Nova et Vetera* 19, no. 3, English edition (2021): 739–68.

Drake, Stillman. "The Case against 'Circular Inertia.'" In *Galileo Studies: Personality, Tradition, and Revolution*, 257–78. Ann Arbor, MI: The University of Michigan Press, 1970.

———. "Galileo Gleanings – XVII: The Question of Circular Inertia." In *Essays on Galileo and the History and Philosophy of Science*, selected and introduced by N. M. Swerdlow and T. H. Levere, vol. 2, 69–85. Toronto: University of Toronto Press, 1999.

Druart, Thérèse-Anne. "Al-Ghazali." In *A Companion to Philosophy in the Middle Ages*. Edited by Jorge J. E. Gracia and Timothy B. Noone, 118–26. Malden, MA: Blackwell Publishing, 2003.

Duhem, Pierre. "History of Physics." In *Essays in the History and Philosophy of Science*, translated and edited by Roger Ariew and Peter Barker, 163–221. Indianapolis, IN: Hackett, 1996.

———. "Physics of a Believer." In *The Aim and Structure of Physical Theory*, translated by Philip P. Wiener, 273–311. Princeton: Princeton University Press, 1991.

Earman, John and Norton, John D. "Exorcist XIV: The Wrath of Maxwell's Demon. Part I. From Maxwell to Szilard." *Studies in History and Philosophy of Modern Physics* 29, no. 4 (1998): 435–71.

———. "Exorcist XIV: The Wrath of Maxwell's Demon. Part II. From Szilard to Landauer and Beyond." *Studies in History and Philosophy of Modern Physics* 30, no. 1 (1999): 1–40.

Ebbing, Darrell D. *General Chemistry*. 5th edition. Boston: Houghton Mifflin, 1996.

Eberl, Jason. *The Routledge Guidebook to Aquinas' Summa Theologiae*. New York: Routledge, 2016.

Edwards, Paul. "The Cosmological Argument." In *The Cosmological Arguments: A Spectrum of Opinion*, edited by Donald R. Burrill, 101–23. Garden City, NY: Anchor Books, 1967.

Effler, Roy R. *John Duns Scotus and the Principle "Omne quod movetur ab alio movetur."* St. Bonaventure, N.Y.: Franciscan Institute, 1962.

Einstein, Albert. *Essays in Science*. Translated by Alan Harris. New York: Philosophical Library, 1934.

Esposito, Massimiliano. "Landauer Principle Stands up to Quantum Test." *Physics* 11, no. 49 (2018)

Feser, Edward. *Aquinas: A Beginner's Guide*. Oxford: Oneworld Publications, 2009.

———. "Existential Inertia and the Five Ways." *American Catholic Philosophical Quarterly* 85, no. 2 (2011): 237–67.

———. "On Aristotle, Aquinas, and Paley: A Reply to Marie George." Evangelical Philosophical Society, 2011, accessed October 12th, 2021. http://www.epsociety.org/library/articles.asp?pid=83&mode=detail.

———. "Reply to Michael Rota." *Proceedings of the Society for Medieval Logic and Metaphysics* 10 (2012): 20–21.

———. "The Medieval Principle of Motion and the Modern Principle of Inertia." *Proceedings of the Society for Medieval Logic and Metaphysics* 10 (2012): 4–16.

———. "Between Aristotle and William Paley: Aquinas's Fifth Way." *Nova et Vetera* 11, no. 3, English edition (2013): 707–49.

———. *Scholastic Metaphysics: A Contemporary Introduction*. Heusenstamm: Editiones Scholasticae, 2014.

———. "Motion in Aristotle, Newton, and Einstein." In *Neo-Scholastic Essays*, 3–27. South Bend, IN: St. Augustine's Press, 2015.

———. "Teleology: A Shopper's Guide." In *Neo-Scholastic Essays*, 28–48. South Bend, IN: St. Augustine's Press, 2015.

———. *Five Proofs of the Existence of God: Aristotle, Plotinus, Augustine, Aquinas, Leibniz*. San Francisco: Ignatius Press, 2017.

———. "The God of a Philosopher." In *Faith and Reason: Philosophers Explain Their Turn to Catholicism*, edited by Brian Besong and Jonathan Fuqua, 27–52. San Francisco, Ignatius Press, 2019.

Feynman, Richard. *The Character of Physical Law*. Cambridge, Mass.: The MIT Press, 2017.

Feynman, Richard, Robert Leighton, and Matthew Sands. *The Feynman Lectures on Physics*. 3 volumes. Reading, MA: Addison Wesley, 1964–66.

Flew, Antony. *God and Philosophy*. New York: Harcourt, Brace & World, 1966.

Galileo Galilei. *Dialogue concerning the Two Chief World Systems—Ptolemaic and Copernican*. Translated by Stillman Drake. Berkeley: University of California Press, 1967.

———. *Selected Writings*. Translated by Willam R. Shea and Mark Davie. Introduction by William R. Shea. Oxford: Oxford University Press, 2012.

Garrigou-Lagrange, Réginald, OP. *God: His Existence and His Nature*. 2 volumes. Translated by Dom Bede Rose, OSB. St. Louis: Herder, 1949.

Geach, P. T. "Aquinas." In G. E. M. Anscombe and P. T. Geach, *Three Philosophers*, 65–125. Ithaca, NY: Cornell University Press, 1961.

George, Marie. "On the Occasion of Darwin's Bicentennial: Finally Time to Retire the Fifth Way?" *Proceedings of the American Catholic Philosophical Association* 83 (2009): 209–25.

———. "An Aristotelian-Thomist Responds to Edward Feser's 'Teleology.'" *Philosophia Christi* 12, no. 2 (2010): 441–49.

———. "What Would Thomas Aquinas Say about Intelligent Design?" *New Blackfriars* 94, no. 1054 (2013): 676–700.

———. "On the Meaning of 'Immanent Activity' according to Aquinas." *The Thomist* 78, no. 4 (2014): 537–55.

———. "'Intrinsic' and 'Extrinsic' Teleology: Their Irrelevance to Aquinas's Fifth

Way and to Paley's Argument from Design." *Evangelical Philosophical Society*, 2015, accessed October 12th, 2021. http://www.epsociety.org/library/articles. asp?pid=285&mode=detail.

———. "Thomistic Rebuttal of Some Common Objections to Paley's Argument from Design." *New Blackfriars* 97, no. 1069 (2016): 266–88.

Godfrey of Fontaines. *Les Quodlibet Cinq, Six, et Sept*. Edited by M. De Wulf and J. Hoffmans. Louvain: Institut Supérieur de Philosophie de l'Université, 1914.

Hall, Alfred Rupert and Hall, Marie Boas. "Clarke and Newton." *Isis* 52, no. 4 (1961): 583–85.

Hanson, Norwood Russell. "The Law of Inertia: A Philosopher's Touchstone." *Philosophy of Science* 30, no. 2 (1963): 107–21.

Hawking, Stephen and Leonard Mlodinow. *The Grand Design*. New York: Bantam Books, 2010.

Hawley, John F. and Katherine A. Holcomb. *Foundations of Modern Cosmology*. 2nd edition. Oxford: Oxford University Press, 2005.

Hassing, Richard F. "Thomas Aquinas on *Phys.* VII.1 and the Aristotelian Science of the Physical Continuum." In *Nature and Scientific Method*, edited by Daniel O. Dahlstrom, 109–56. Washington, DC: The Catholic University of America Press, 1991.

Heimann, P. M. and McGuire, J. E. "Cavendish and the *Vis Viva* Controversy: A Leibnizian Postscript." *Isis* 62, no. 2 (1971): 225–27.

Henry of Ghent. *Quodlibet IX*. Edited by Raymond Macken. Leuven: Leuven University Press, 1983.

———. *Quodlibetal Questions on Free Will*. Translated by Roland J. Teske, SJ. Milwaukee, WI: Marquette University Press, 1993.

Hiebert, Erwin. "Commentary on the Papers of Thomas S. Kuhn and I. Bernard Cohen." In *Critical Problems in the History of Science*, edited by Marshall Clagett, 391–400. Madison, WI: The University of Wisconsin Press, 1959.

———. *The Historical Roots of the Principle of Conservation of Energy*. Madison, WI: The State Historical Society of Wisconsin, 1962.

Helmholtz, Hermann von. "On the Conservation of Force." In *Scientific Memoirs, Selected from the Transactions of Foreign Academies of Science and from Foreign Journals: Natural Philosophy*, edited by John Tyndall and William Francis, 114–62. London: Taylor and Francis, 1853.

———. "On the Interaction of Natural Forces." In *Popular Lectures on Scientific Subjects*, translated by Edmund Atkinson, 137–71. London: Longmans, Green, and Co., 1912.

———. *Ueber die Wechselwirkung der Naturkräfte und die darauf bezüglichen neuesten Ermittelungen der Physik: Ein popular-wissenschaftlicher Vortrag*. 2nd edition. Königsberg: Verlag von Gräfe & Unzer, 1854.

Hume, David. *Dialogues concerning Natural Religion*. Edited by Richard H. Popkin. 2nd edition. Indianapolis: Hackett, 1998.

Hunter, J. F. M. "Note on Father Owens' Comment on Williams' Criticism of Aquinas on Infinite Regress." *Mind*, New Series, 73, no. 291 (1964): 439–40.

Hutton, James. "Theory of the Earth; or an Investigation of the Laws Observable in the Composition, Dissolution, and Restoration of Land upon the Globe." *Transactions of the Royal Society of Edinburgh* 1, no. 2 (1788): 209–304.

Huygens, Christian. *The Motion of Colliding Bodies.* Translated by Richard J. Blackwell. *Isis* 68, no. 4 (1977): 574–97.

Hyman, Arthur, James J. Walsh, and Thomas Williams, eds. *Philosophy in the Middle Ages: The Christian, Islamic, and Jewish Traditions.* 3rd edition. Indianapolis, Hackett: 2010.

Iltis, Carolyn. "D'Alembert and the *Vis Viva* Controversy." *Studies in History and Philosophy of Science Part A* 1, no. 22 (1970): 135–44.

———. "Leibniz and the Vis Viva Controversy." *Isis* 62, no. 1 (1971): 21–35.

Jaki, Stanley. *The Road of Science and the Ways to God.* Chicago: The University of Chicago Press, 1978.

Johnson, Mark F. "St. Thomas's De Trinitate, q. 5, a. 2, ad 3: A Reply to John Knasas." *The New Scholasticism* 63, no. 1 (1989): 58–65.

———. "Immateriality and the Domain of Thomistic Natural Philosophy." *The Modern Schoolman* 67, no. 4 (1990): 285–304.

———. "Does Natural Philosophy Prove the Immaterial? A Rejoinder." *American Catholic Philosophical Quarterly* 65, no. 1 (1991): 97–105.

Joule, James Prescott. *The Scientific Papers of James Prescott Joule.* Volume 1. London: Taylor and Francis, 1884.

Kant, Immanuel. *Critique of Judgment.* Translated by Werner S. Pluhar. Indianapolis: Hackett, 1987.

———. *Critique of Pure Reason.* Translated by Paul Guyer and Allen W. Wood. Cambridge: Cambridge University Press, 1998.

Kass, Leon R. *Toward a More Natural Science: Biology and Human Affairs.* New York: The Free Press, 1985.

Kelvin, Lord, Sir William Thomson. *Mathematical and Physical Papers.* 6 volumes. Cambridge: Cambridge University Press, 1882–1911.

———. *Popular Lectures and Addresses.* London: Macmillan, 1894.

Kelvin, Lord, Sir William Thomson and Peter Guthrie Tait. "Energy." *Good Words* 3 (October 1862): 601–7.

Kenny, Anthony. *The Five Ways: St. Thomas Aquinas' Proofs of God's Existence.* New York: Schocken Books, 1969.

Kerr, Gaven. "Essentially Ordered Series Reconsidered." *American Catholic Philosophical Quarterly* 86, no. 4 (2012): 541–55.

———. *Aquinas's Way to God: The Proof in* De Ente et Essentia. Oxford: Oxford University Press, 2015.

———. "Design Arguments and Aquinas's Fifth Way." *The Thomist* 82, no. 3 (2018): 447–71.

———. "A Deeper Look at Aquinas's First Way." *Nova et Vetera* 20, no. 2, English edition (2022): 461–84.

King-Farlow, John. "The First Way in Physical and Moral Space." *The Thomist* 39, no. 2 (1975): 349–74.

Klein, Martin J. "Order, Organisation and Entropy." *The British Journal for the Philosophy of Science* 4, no. 14 (1953): 158–60.

Koyré, Alexandre. *Galileo Studies.* Translated by John Mepham. Atlantic Highlands, NJ: Humanities Press, 1978.

Knasas, John F. X. "Thomistic Existentialism and the Silence of the *Quinque Viae*." *The Modern Schoolman* 63, no. 3 (1986): 157–71.

———. "*Ad Mentem Thomae*: Does Natural Philosophy Prove God?" *Proceedings of the American Catholic Philosophical Association* 61 (1987): 209–220.

———. "'Does Natural Philosophy Prove the Immaterial?': An Answer to Mark Johnson." *American Catholic Philosophical Quarterly* 64, no. 2 (1990): 265–69.

———. "Materiality and Aquinas' Natural Philosophy: A Reply to Johnson." *The Modern Schoolman* 68, no. 3 (1991): 245–57.

———. "Thomistic Existentialism and the Proofs *ex Motu* at *contra Gentiles* I, C. 13." *The Thomist* 59, no. 4 (1995): 591–615.

———. "The 'Suppositio' of Motion's Eternity and the Interpretation of Aquinas' Motion Proofs for God." In *God: Reason and Reality*, edited by Anselm Ramelow, 147–78. Munich: Philosophia, 2014.

———. *Thomistic Existentialism and Cosmological Reasoning*. Washington, DC: The Catholic University of America Press, 2019.

Kondoleon, Theodore J. "The Start of Metaphysics." *The Thomist* 58, no. 1 (1994): 121–30.

———. "The Argument from Motion and the Argument for Angels: A Reply to John F. X. Knasas." *The Thomist* 62, no. 2 (1998): 269–90.

Koons, Robert C. and Logan Paul Gage. "St. Thomas Aquinas on Intelligent Design." *Proceedings of the American Catholic Philosophical Association* 85 (2011): 79–97.

Kragh, Helge S. *Entropic Creation: Religious Contexts of Thermodynamics and Cosmology*. London: Routledge, 2008.

Kretzmann, Norman. *The Metaphysics of Theism: Aquinas's Natural Theology in* Summa contra gentiles *I*. Oxford: Clarendon Press, 1997.

Kronen, John and Sandra Menssen. "Hylomorphism and Design: A Reconsideration of Aquinas's Fifth Way." *The Modern Schoolman* 89, no. 3/4 (2012): 155–80.

Kubrin, David. "Newton and the Cyclical Cosmos: Providence and the Mechanical Philosophy." *Journal of the History of Ideas* 28, no. 3 (1967): 325–46

Kuhn, Thomas S. "The Caloric Theory of Adiabatic Compression." *Isis* 49, no. 2 (1958): 132–40.

———. "Energy Conservation as an Example of Simultaneous Discovery." In *Critical Problems in the History of Science*, edited by Marshall Clagett, 321–56. Madison, Wis.: The University of Wisconsin Press, 1959.

———. *The Structure of Scientific Revolutions*. 2nd edition. Chicago: University of Chicago Press, 1970.

Kutrovátz, Gábor. "Heat Death in Ancient and Modern Thermodynamics." In *The Kalām Cosmological Argument: Volume Two: Scientific Evidence for the Beginning of the Universe*, edited by Paul Copan with William Lane Craig, 232–42. New York: Bloomsbury, 2018.

Lamont, John R. T. "An Argument for an Uncaused Cause." *The Thomist* 59, no. 2 (1995): 261–77.

Lang, Helen S. "Aristotle's First Movers and the Relation of Physics to Theology." *The New Scholasticism* 52, no. 4 (1978): 500–17.

———. *Aristotle's* Physics *and Its Medieval Varieties*. Albany: State University of New York Press, 1992.

Laudan, Larry. "The *Vis Viva* Controversy, a Post-Mortem." *Isis* 59, no. 2 (1968): 130–43.

Leff, Harvey S. and Andrew F. Rex, eds. *Maxwell's Demon: Entropy, Information, Computing*. Princeton: Princeton University Press, 1990.

———. *Maxwell's Demon 2: Entropy, Classical and Quantum Information, Computing*. Philadelphia: Institute of Physics Publishing, 2003.

Leibniz, G. W. *New Essays concerning Human Understanding*. Translated by Alfred Gideon Langley. New York: Macmillan, 1896.

———. *Philosophical Essays*. Translated by Roger Ariew and Daniel Garber. Indianapolis: Hackett, 1989.

———. *Philosophical Papers and Letters*. Edited by Leroy E. Loemker. 2nd edition. Dordrecht: D. Reidel, 1969.

Leslie, John. "Anthropic Principle, World Ensemble, Design." *American Philosophical Quarterly* 19, no. 2 (1982): 141–51.

Lewis, Christopher J. T. *Heat and Thermodynamics: A Historical Perspective*. Westport, Conn.: Greenwood Press, 2007.

Lewis, Geraint F. and Luke A. Barnes. *A Fortunate Universe*. Cambridge: Cambridge University Press, 2016.

Lobkowicz, Nikolaus. "Quidquid Movetur ab Alio Movetur." *The New Scholasticism* 42, no. 3 (1968): 401–21.

Lyell, Sir Charles. *Principles of Geology*. Edited and abridged by James A Secord. New York: Penguin, 1997.

MacDonald, Scott. "Aquinas's Parasitic Cosmological Argument." *Medieval Philosophy and Theology* 1, no. 1 (1991): 119–55.

MacIntyre, Alasdair. *Dependent Rational Animals: Why Human Beings Need the Virtues*. Chicago: Open Court, 1999.

Mackie, J. L. *The Miracle of Theism*. New York: Oxford University Press, 1982.

Maier, Anneliese. "Galileo and the Scholastic Theory of Impetus." In *On the Threshold of Exact Science: Selected Writings of Anneliese Maier on Late Medieval Natural Philosophy*, edited and translated by Steven D. Sargent, 103–123. Philadelphia: University of Pennsylvania Press, 1982.

———. "The Significance of the Theory of Impetus for Scholastic Natural Philosophy." In *On the Threshold of Exact Science: Selected Writings of Anneliese Maier on Late Medieval Natural Philosophy*, edited and translated by Steven D. Sargent, 76–102. Philadelphia: University of Pennsylvania Press, 1982.

Maimonides, Moses. *The Guide of the Perplexed*. Translated by Shlomo Pines. 2 volumes. Chicago: The University of Chicago Press, 1963.

Martin, C. F. J. *Thomas Aquinas: God and Explanations*. Edinburgh: Edinburg University Press, 1997.

Maxwell, James Clerk. *The Theory of Heat*. Edited by Peter Pesic. Mineola, NY: Dover, 2001.

McGinnis, Jon. "Avicennan Infinity: A Select History of the Infinite through Avicenna." In *Documenti e Studi sulla Tradizione Filosofica Medievale* 21 (2010): 199–222.

McLaughlin, Thomas. "Aristotelian Mover-Causality and the Principle of Inertia." *International Philosophical Quarterly* 38, no. 2 (1998): 137–51.

———. "Local Motion and the Principle of Inertia: Aquinas, Newtonian Physics, and Relativity." *International Philosophical Quarterly* 44, no. 2 (2004): 239–64.

———. "Nature and Inertia." *The Review of Metaphysics* 62, no. 2 (2008): 251–84.

———. "Act, Potency, and Energy." *The Thomist* 75, no. 2 (2011): 207–43.

———. "A Defense of Natural Place in a Contemporary Scientific Context." *Proceedings of the American Catholic Philosophical Association* 93 (2019): 101–15.

Meli, Domenico Bertoloni. "Newton and the Leibniz-Clarke Correspondence." In *The Cambridge Companion to Newton*, edited by I. Bernard Cohen and George E. Smith, 455–64. 1st edition. Cambridge: Cambridge University Press, 2002.

Monod, Jacques. *Chance and Necessity*. Translated by Austryn Wainhouse. New York: Alfred A. Knopf, 1971.

Moreno, Antonio, OP. "The Law of Inertia and the Principle *Quidquid Movetur ab Alio Movetur*." *The Thomist* 38, no. 2 (1974): 306–31.

Mulcahey, M. Michèle and Timothy B. Noone. "Religious Orders." In *A Companion to Philosophy in the Middle Ages*, edited by Jorge J. E. Gracia and Timothy B. Noone, 45–54. Malden, MA: Blackwell Publishing, 2003.

Müller, Ingo. *A History of Thermodynamics: The Doctrine of Energy and Entropy*. Berlin: Springer, 2007.

Murray, Gemma, William Harper, and Curtis Wilson. "Huygens, Wren, Wallis, and Newton on Rules of Impact and Reflection." In *Vanishing Matter and the Laws of Motion: Descartes and Beyond*, edited by Dana Jalobeanu and Peter R. Anstey, 153–91. New York: Routledge, 2011.

Nagel, Thomas. *Mind and Cosmos: Why the Materialist Neo-Darwinian Conception of Nature Is Almost Certainly False*. New York: Oxford University Press: 2012.

Newton, Sir Isaac. *Philosophical Writings*. Edited by Andrew Janiak. 2nd edition. Cambridge: Cambridge University Press, 2014.

———. *Principia Mathematica Philosophiae Naturalis*. Translated by Andrew Motte. Revised by Florian Cajori. Berkeley: University of California Press, 1934.

Newton, William. "A Case of Mistaken Identity: Aquinas's Fifth Way and Arguments of Intelligent Design." *New Blackfriars* 95, no. 1059 (2014): 569–78.

Noone, Timothy B. "Scholasticism." In *A Companion to Philosophy in the Middle Ages*, edited by Jorge J. E. Gracia and Timothy B. Noone, 55–64. Malden, MA: Blackwell Publishing, 2003.

Ockham, William. *Philosophical Writings*. Edited and translated by Philotheus Boehner, OFM. Revised by Stephen F. Brown. Indianapolis: Hackett, 1990.

Oderberg, David S. "Teleology: Inorganic and Organic." In *Contemporary Perspectives on Natural Law: Natural Law as a Limiting Concept*, edited by Ana Marta González, 259–79. Burlington, VT: Ashgate, 2008.

———. "'Whatever is Changing is Being Changed by Something Else': A Reappraisal of Premise One of the First Way." In *Mind, Method, and Morality: Essays in Honour of Anthony Kenny*, edited by Peter Hacker and John Cottingham, 140–64. Oxford: Oxford University Press, 2010.

———. "Synthetic Life and the Bruteness of Immanent Causation." In *Aristotle on Metaphysics and Method*, edited by Edward Feser, 206–35. New York: Palgrave Macmillan, 2013.

Oppy, Graham. *Arguing about Gods*. Cambridge: Cambridge University Press, 2006.

Owens, Joseph, CSsR. "Aquinas and the Proof from the 'Physics.'" *Mediaeval Studies* 28 (1966): 119–50.

———. "Aquinas and the Five Ways." In *St. Thomas Aquinas on the Existence of God: Collected Papers of Joseph Owens, C.Ss.R.*, edited by John R. Catan, 132–41. Albany: State University of New York Press, 1980.

———. "Aquinas on Infinite Regress." In *St. Thomas Aquinas on the Existence of God: Collected Papers of Joseph Owens, C.Ss.R.*, edited by John R. Catan, 228–30. Albany: State University of New York Press, 1980.

———. "The Conclusion of the *Prima Via*." In *St. Thomas Aquinas on the Existence of God: Collected Papers of Joseph Owens, C.Ss.R.*, edited by John R. Catan, 142–68. Albany: State University of New York Press, 1980.

———. "The Starting Point of the *Prima Via*." In *St. Thomas Aquinas on the Existence of God: Collected Papers of Joseph Owens, C.Ss.R.*, edited by John R. Catan, 169–91. Albany: State University of New York Press, 1980.

Pawl, Timothy. "The Five Ways." In *The Oxford Handbook of Aquinas*, edited by Brian Davies and Eleonore Stump, 115–31. Oxford: Oxford University Press, 2012.

Pegis, Anton C. "St. Thomas and the Coherence of the Aristotelian Theology." *Mediaeval Studies* 35 (1973): 67–117.

Penrose, Roger. *The Road to Reality: A Complete Guide to the Laws of the Universe.* New York: Alfred A. Knopf, 2004.

Perlov, Delia and Alex Vilenkin. *Cosmology for the Curious.* Cham, Switzerland: Springer, 2017.

Planck, Max. *The Theory of Heat Radiation.* 2nd edition. Translated by Morton Masius. Philadelphia: P. Blakiston's Son & Co., 1914.

———. *Treatise on Thermodynamics.* 3rd edition. Translated by Alexander Ogg. New York: Dover Publications, 1969.

Plato. *Complete Works.* Edited by John M. Cooper and D. S. Hutchison. Indianapolis: Hackett, 1997.

Polkinghorne, John. "A Potent Universe." In *Evidence of Purpose*, edited by John Marks Templeton, 105–15. New York: Continuum, 1994.

Price, Huw. "Boltzmann's Time Bomb." *The British Journal for the Philosophy of Science* 53, no. 1 (2002): 83–119.

Pross, Addy. *What is Life?* 2nd edition. Oxford: Oxford University Press, 2016.

Pruss, Alexander R. "The Hume-Edwards Principle and the Cosmological Argument." *International Journal for Philosophy of Religion* 43, no. 3 (1998): 149–65.

Pseudo-Al-Ghazali. *Algazel's Metaphysics: A Medieval Translation.* Edited by J. T. Muckle, CSB. Toronto: Pontifical Institute of Mediaeval Studies, 1967.

Psillos, Stathis. "A Philosophical Study of the Transition from the Caloric Theory of Heat to Thermodynamics: Resisting the Pessimistic Meta-Induction." *Studies in History and Philosophy of Science*, Part A, 25, no. 2 (1994): 159–90.

Ptolemy. *Almagest.* Translated and Annotated by G. J. Toomer. Princeton: Princeton University Press, 1998.

Rankine, William John Macquorn. "Outline of the Science of Energetics." *The Edinburgh New Philosophical Journal*, New Series, 2 (July–October 1855).

———. "On the General Law of the Transformation of Energy," *Philosophical Magazine*, series 4, vol. 5 (January–June, 1853).

Reitan, Eric A., OP. "Aquinas and Weisheipl: Aristotle's *Physics* and the Existence of God." In *Philosophy and the God of Abraham: Essays in Memory of James A.*

Weisheipl, OP, edited by Raymond James Long, 179–90. Toronto: Pontifical Institute of Mediaeval Studies, 1991.

Rees, Martin. *Just Six Numbers: The Deep Forces that Shape the Universe*. New York: Basic Books, 2000.

Rota, Michael. "Infinite Causal Chains and Explanation." *Proceedings of the American Catholic Philosophical Association* 81 (2007): 109–22.

———. "Comments on Feser's 'The Medieval Principle of Motion and the Modern Principle of Inertia.'" *Proceedings of the Society for Medieval Logic and Metaphysics* 10 (2012): 17–19.

Rowe, William L. *The Cosmological Argument*. Princeton: Princeton University Press, 1975.

Sarton, George. "The Discovery of the Law of Conservation of Energy." *Isis* 13, no. 1 (1929): 18–44.

Scotus, John Duns. *A Treatise on Potency and Act: Questions on the* Metaphysics *of Aristotle, Book IX*. Translated by Allan B. Wolter, OFM. St. Bonaventure, NY: Franciscan Institute Press, 2000.

———. *Opera Omnia*. Edited by C. Balic et al. Vatican City: Typis Polyglottis Vaticanis, 1950–

———. *Opera Philosophica*. Edited by G. Etzkorn et al. St. Bonaventure, NY: Franciscan Institute, 1997–2006.

———. *A Treatise on God as First Principle: A Revised Latin Text of the* De Primo Principio *Translated into English along with Two Related Questions from an Early Commentary on the* Sentences. Translated and edited by Allan B. Wolter, OFM. Chicago: Franciscan Herald Press, 1966.

———. *Philosophical Writings: A Selection*. Translated by Allan Wolter, OFM. Indianapolis: Hackett, 1987.

Schrödinger, Erwin. *What is Life? With Mind and Matter and Autobiographical Sketches*. Cambridge: Cambridge University Press, 1992.

Shapiro, James. *Evolution: A View from the 21st Century*. Upper Saddle River, NJ: FT Press Science, 2011.

Shenker, Orly and Meir Hemmo. "Introduction to the Philosophy of Statistical Mechanics: Can Probability Explain the Arrow of Time in the Second Law of Thermodynamics?" *Philosophy Compass* 6, no. 9 (2011): 640–51.

Shields, Christopher and Robert Pasnau. *The Philosophy of Aquinas*. 2nd edition. New York: Oxford University Press, 2016.

Shields, Daniel. "Aquinas on Will, Happiness, and God: The Problem of Love and Aristotle's Liber de Bona Fortuna." *American Catholic Philosophical Quarterly* 91, no. 1 (2017): 113–42.

———. "Everything in Motion is Put in Motion by Another: A Principle in Aquinas' First Way." *American Catholic Philosophical Quarterly* 92, no. 4 (2018): 535–61.

Smith, Crosbie and Matthew Norton Wise. *Energy and Empire: A Biographical Study of Lord Kelvin*. Cambridge: Cambridge University Press, 1989.

Spitzer, Robert J., SJ. *New Proofs for the Existence of God: Contributions of Contemporary Physics and Philosophy*. Grand Rapids, MI: Eerdmans, 2010.

Steane, Andrew M. *Thermodynamics: A Complete Undergraduate Course*. Oxford: Oxford University Press, 2017.

Stenger, Victor. *The Fallacy of Fine-Tuning: Why the Universe is not Designed for Us.* Amherst, NY: Prometheus Books, 2011.

Suarez, Francisco, SJ. *On Efficient Causality.* Translated by Alfred J. Freddoso. New Haven, CT: Yale University Press, 1994.

———. *On the Essence of Finite Being as Such and on the Existence of that Essence and their Distinction.* Translated be Norman J. Wells. Milwaukee: Marquette University Press, 1983.

———. *The Metaphysical Demonstration of the Existence of God: Metaphysical Disputations 28–29.* Translated by John P. Doyle. South Bend, Ind.: St. Augustine's Press, 2004.

Swinburne, Richard. "Argument from the Fine-Tuning of the Universe." In *Modern Cosmology & Philosophy*, edited by John Leslie, 160–79. Amherst, N.Y.: Prometheus Books, 1998.

———. *The Existence of God.* 2nd edition. New York: Oxford University Press, 2004.

Szilard, Leo. "On the Decrease of Entropy in a Thermodynamic System by the Intervention of Intelligent Beings." Translated by Anatol Rapoport and Mechthilde Knoller. In *Maxwell's Demon 2: Entropy, Classical and Quantum Information, Computing*, edited by Harvey S. Leff and Andrew F. Rex, 110–19. Philadelphia: Institute of Physics Publishing, 2003.

Thompson, Silvanus P. *The Life of William Thomson, Baron Kelvin of Largs.* London: Macmillan, 1910.

Torrell, Jean-Pierre OP. *Saint Thomas Aquinas: Volume 1: The Person and His Work.* Translated by Robert Royal. Washington, DC: The Catholic University of America Press, 1996.

Twetten, David B. "Back to Nature in Aquinas." *Medieval Philosophy and Theology* 5, no. 2 (1996): 205–43.

———. "Clearing a 'Way' for Aquinas: How the Proof from Motion Concludes to God." *Proceedings of the American Catholic Philosophical Association* 70 (1996): 259–78.

———. "Why Motion Requires a Cause: The Foundation for a Prime Mover in Aristotle and Aquinas." In *Philosophy and the God of Abraham: Essays in Memory of James A. Weisheipl, OP*, edited by Raymond James Long, 235–54. Toronto: Pontifical Institute of Medieval Studies, 1991.

Wallace, William A., OP. "Newtonian Antinomies against the *Prima Via.*" *The Thomist* 19, no. 2 (1956): 151–192.

———. "The Cosmological Argument: A Reappraisal." *Proceedings of the American Catholic Philosophical Association* 46 (1972): 43–57.

———. "Aquinas on the Temporal Relation between Cause and Effect." *Review of Metaphysics* 27, no. 3 (1974): 569–84.

———. "Is the Pull of Gravity Real?" In *From a Realist Point of View: Essays on the Philosophy of Science*, 163–85, 1st edition. Lanham, MD: University Press of America: 1979.

———. "Aquinas, Galileo, and Aristotle." *Proceedings of the American Catholic Philosophical Association* 57 (1983): 17–24.

———. "A Second Look at the 'First Way.'" In *From a Realist Point of View: Essays on the Philosophy of Science*, 325–32, 2nd edition. Lanham, MD: University Press of America: 1983.

―――. "Cause and Effect: Temporal Relationships." In *From a Realist Point of View: Essays on the Philosophy of Science*, 99–114, 2nd edition. Lanham, MD: University Press of America: 1983.

―――. "Immateriality and Its Surrogates in Modern Science." In *From a Realist Point of View: Essays on the Philosophy of Science*, 297–307, 2nd edition. Lanham, MD: University Press of America: 1983.

―――. "Aquinas and Newton on the Causality of Nature and of God: The Medieval and Modern Problematic." In *Philosophy and the God of Abraham: Essays in Memory of James A. Weisheipl, OP*, edited by Raymond James Long, 255–79. Toronto: Pontifical Institute of Mediaeval Studies, 1991.

―――. *The Modeling of Nature: Philosophy of Science and Philosophy of Nature in Synthesis*. Washington, DC: The Catholic University of America Press, 1996.

Weisheipl, James A., OP. "Space and Gravitation." *The New Scholasticism* 29, no. 2 (1955): 175–223.

―――. "Quidquid Movetur ab Alio Movetur: A Reply." *The New Scholasticism* 42, no. 3 (1968): 422–31.

―――. "Thomas' Evaluation of Plato and Aristotle." *The New Scholasticism* 48, no. 1 (1974): 100–24.

―――. "The Axiom '*Opus naturae est opus intelligentiae*' and Its Origins." In *Albertus Magnus Doctor Universalis: 1280/1980*, edited by Gerbert Meyer, OP, and Albert Zimmermann, 441–63. Mainz: Matthias Grünewald Verlag, 1980.

―――. *Nature and Motion in the Middle Ages*. Edited by William C. Carroll. Washington, DC: The Catholic University of America Press, 1985.

Williams, C. J. F. "Hic autem non est Procedere in Infinitum." *Mind*, New Series, 69, no. 275 (1960): 403–5.

Wippel, John F. *The Metaphysical Thought of Thomas Aquinas: From Finite Being to Uncreated Being*. Washington, DC: The Catholic University of America Press, 2000.

Index

*Nature and Nature's God: A Philosophical and Scientific
Defense of Aquinas's Unmoved Mover Argument* was designed
in Garamond and Mr Eaves Sans and composed by
Reflective Book Design of Durham, North Carolina.